Bible Contradictions

The Attack Of Christian Scholarship & The Faith Of Men—Its Failure & Result

By Lee Allen Williams

Copyright © 2023 Lee A. Williams

All Rights Reserved

ISBN: 979-8-851-47715-7

All Scripture quotations are from the Authorized King James Bible unless otherwise noted. Any deviations thereof are not intentional. The italics and/or capital letters in Bible quotations are from the author. Any deviation thereof was not intentional and do not represent an alteration of the text. The author is not responsible for dead website links or any other inaccessible media links found in the footnotes.

All rights reserved. This work may not be reproduced in any form or by any means electronic or otherwise without written permission from the author.

For questions or concerns the author can be reached at: williamslee0000@yahoo.com

To The Lord Jesus Christ

Table of Contents

Table of Contents v

Preface vi

Introduction 1

The Book 15

Chapter 1: A Bucketful Of … "Contradictions" 17

Chapter 2: The Actors 36

Chapter 3: More "Contradictions" 85

Intermission 137

Chapter 4: The Witnessed 154

Chapter 5: Oranges & Vitamin C 209

Chapter 6: The Archaic Arcade 244

Chapter 7: Two Bibles 271

Chapter 8: Saving Private Ehrman 339

Chapter 9: The Righteous Atheist 398

Chapter 10: Conclusion 445

Appendix A 462

Appendix B 463

Appendix C 468

Appendix D 469

Faith & Works 470

Preface

Within the realm of religious scholarship, a seismic shift has occurred in the way we look at *the* Bible. In this work, titled *"Bible Contradictions: The Attack Of Christian Scholarship & The Faith Of Men—Its Failure & Result,"* we look at that shift. In the pages that follow, we delve into the core essence of modern Christian scholarship and its profound impact on the faith of believers and nonbelievers.

What does it truly mean to be a modern-day Pharisee? *Has* Christianity, under the weight of societal transformations, succumbed to a process of modernization? What does it mean to have a final authority? These pivotal questions, lay the groundwork for our exploratory endeavor.

In this work, we dare to challenge the assertions of renowned figures such as James White, Daniel B. Wallace, Bart Ehrman, Bruce Metzger, and an array of "influential personalities."

We scrutinize the evidentiary foundations they present, casting light upon the hidden fallacies and distorted narratives present in their work, ultimately leaving believers in a state of spiritual disarray and *causing thousands to leave the faith altogether.*

Throughout the annals of history, a timeless query has persisted: Who possesses the ultimate authority? Who wields the crown, who sits upon the throne and proclaims the final verdict? For devout Christians, the resounding answer resides within the sacred pages of *the* Bible. However, in an era boasting an excess of 300 newly minted translations, the perplexity arises—which translation assumes the mantle of *Final Authority?* Is it a "translation," or "the original Greek," or something else? As we venture forth, we interrogate the very essence of "biblical scholarship" and ponder its relevance amidst an array of competing doctrines.

This work dissects the alleged "contradictions" and "discrepancies" presented by a diverse cast of dissenting voices, including Atheists such as Sam Harris and Bart Ehrman, Rabbis such as Tovia Singer, Western and Eastern Muslim scholars, and most notable, those teaching in Christian seminaries.

The Bible will illuminate these perceived contradictions, recognizing their potential to erode the bedrock of faith. The examination of these contentions by *"The Actors"* reveals a depressing and concerning reality

—a vacuum of intellectual integrity camouflaged behind authority, status, and "theological prowess."

In the grand tapestry of *Final Authority*, Bible translations, and the tactics employed by "The Actors," this work stands as an essential companion. As we navigate the vast expanse of contradictory claims and textual puzzles, the following pages beckons the reader *to question, to ponder, and to reflect upon the implications of "modern Christian scholarship"* in the community as a whole.

"Thy word is a lamp unto my feet, and a light unto my path" —Psalm 119:105

Introduction

"But without faith it is impossible to please him: for he that cometh to God must believe that he is, and that he is a rewarder of them that diligently seek him."
— Hebrews 11:6

THERE are many a reason why you are to believe the Bible has mistakes in it. When I say Bible, I mean a King James Authorized Version of the Protestant Reformation, not a "modern," "more clear," "updating of language in order to shed more light on the text" type of a bible version. The light you get is from The Holy Spirit, not from a new edition of a book being touted as a bible. I realize that this may be a put-off for some, but as you'll see throughout this work, there is something to it. One of the most common reasons for *not* believing you have the Scriptures that are *inspired, infallible, without error, and a resolution in all matters of a Christian's life*, is the simple fact that at some point you were *told* you don't have them. Someone told you the Bible was written by men and therefore it *must* contain "mistakes" and "scribal errors." Hook, line, and sinker you bought it and then integrated it into your beliefs.

The same people that buy *that* are the same types that think that politicians are "genuine people" and that the news media has your "best interest at heart." Who in 2023 believes that? Did you consider that Facebook would be selling your data back in 2008; maybe you did maybe you didn't. How about Google rigging search results back in 2013? Perhaps you have been led to believe that oranges possess the highest vitamin C content among fruits and vegetables, a notion perpetuated by marketing companies (which, incidentally, we will explore in greater detail later on). It is an odd consideration, yes, but like marketing companies, most modern Christian "scholars" talk out of both sides of their mouths. They publicly profess one set of beliefs while harboring a different set in their hearts. In some cases, they brazenly engage in outright deception. I understand that it may be challenging to entertain the notion that individuals deemed "good," "godly," "scholarly," and "honorable" could stoop to falsehoods. The reality is that they are susceptible to the same flaws as any other human being on this earth. When you factor in the pressures of maintaining prestige and establishing a personal legacy, you'll have fertile soil for self-preservation.

Amidst the many issues at hand, this work will explore a particular predicament: the abysmal failure of Christian seminaries in the realm of "biblical scholarship"—a pandemic. These "contradictions" presented may be found in any version of a bible and some have been around for more than 3,500 years (Old Testament), while others have been around for at least 1,900 years (New Testament). Did ancient scribes attempt to "smooth out" these apparent discrepancies, or do the Scriptures we possess today accurately reflect their "original form"? Is what we have genuine? Can new bibles be trusted? How does God work throughout history? What does any of this have to do with my relationship with Jesus Christ?

No Greek will be used unless to *enhance* the English, or for purposes of *manuscript evidence* concerning decisions on the English (see Chapters 5-7). Hebrew will be looked at in like fashion. There will be many versions of bibles considered (NKJV, NIV, ESV, NRSV, NASV, etc.) but the only Book I will be referring to throughout this work *to reconcile* the issues before me is an English Reformation Bible. I am well aware that some of you may be saying, *"this isn't scholarly!"*...or, *"that isn't proper scholarly rigor!"* However, that is exactly what this book is about: what is scholarship? Is what you have been taught the truth, or were you spoon-fed something else? Who taught you? Who taught them? Why did you fall away from Christ (if you did)?

There will be various references of a wide variety on the work of others made at times; some agnostic, some atheist, Catholic, Protestant, etc., but in the main, the core foundation of this book rests on a single Book—a Book that many have failed to *properly* employ while relying on multiple versions of a bible or resorting to Greek language analysis to resolve these so-called "discrepancies"—the proper employment being that of *belief.* Those who employ the former method are such as the likes of Ken Ham, Kittel, Robertson, Ehrman, Price, White, Taylor, Wuest, Smyth, Hort, Bruce, Lightfoot, Phillips, Souter, Haley, McDowell, etc. None of that will be happening here. There will be no "easy way out."

This work is also a Bible *study*. When verses are mentioned, it is best to check them. For all you know I could just be blowing smoke. Don't believe *me*, just read it for yourself—*read it and check it.*

Most modern Christian seminary students have been "re-educated." They have been turned into cloned stormtroopers parroting what they heard a Greek professor say in seminary class. Most ideas start in higher levels of academia and then trickle down to the public before the public even knows what hit 'em. Before long, most Christians believe the same things, and have the same opinions as those of the "most renown" scholars of our day, usually received through soundbites in commentaries, sermons, literature, or any other such source that's plugged into the electric socket of modern Christianity. Some will get their information from

YouTube videos and some of those channels are the very ones that follow these types of "scholars," and the cycle goes on.

In Christian academia the question is, "do we have the scriptures? How can we get *back to the originals?*" The "status quo" is that translations contain mistakes of men. Let me ask a question: Moses and his people made the Tabernacle and the Ark which was inside (Exod. 25-30). Now read Exodus 31:1-10. Did the Tabernacle contain mistakes of men? Here is a case where some kids were killed for an "error" in the Tabernacle (Levi. 10:1-2) over some incense. So, you have to ask yourself, did Moses make the Tabernacle **"as the LORD commanded"** or **"which he commanded them not."**

The question comes up, *"what is Scripture?"* What Scripture is *used for* and what *is defined as Scripture* is given in 2 Timothy 3:16, **"All scripture is given by inspiration of God, and is profitable for doctrine, for reproof, for correction, for instruction in righteousness."** Since Scripture is **"given by inspiration"** we next have to find out what exactly *is* **"inspiration."** It literally means, *"God Breathed"* in Hebrew (רוּחַ). In Greek it retains the same meaning of "God breathed" or "breath of God." The word Spirit "pnuma" (πνεῦμά) in Greek means "breath," hence where we get our words for *pneumonia* and *pneumatic* from—as in *wind* or *breath*.

In the English, inspired means "in-spirit" which has its roots in Latin also meaning "breath." To just look at the English here, when someone or something is *inspired* or "in-spirit," what does that mean? It means aliveness, creative, motivated, or energetically charged. *Breath* is the movement of this energy. For something to be inspired means God has to breathe on it like He did with Adam in Genesis 2:7 and Job 33:4, **"The SPIRIT of God hath made me, and the BREATH of the Almighty hath given me life."** Job also says that *understanding is given by the breath of God* in Job 32:8, **"But there is a spirit in man: and the INSPIRATION of the**

Almighty giveth them understanding." God's breath is also seen bringing *life to the dead* (Ezek. 37:4-10), hence turning a *dead* lifeless book into *living* Scripture, making that Book the closest material thing you have to Jesus Christ on this earth. Does God's "breathing" of inspiration make mistakes? When a person is inspired, as in God's breath is moving through them, is God making a mistake?

One crowd says, *"God does not make mistakes, but men do,"* which is very true, even though it is a bit of a play on words. When God makes a *promise* about his *words*, is He not able to keep his promise to man? Is God a promise breaker? Is God unable to give and preserve his words the way He wants them and therefore without error? In 2 Timothy 3:16 it says **"all Scripture."** Do we have it **"all**," or just about 70-80% of it like most modern scholars would have you believe. Maybe 99%? It says **"all**," do we have it? Since Scripture is God breathed, do we have the infallible Scriptures today, the *living Book?* Were they lost sometime in antiquity? Most scholars would have you believe that because they are referring to *"the originals*," as in the original autographs that the writers first wrote such as John, Mark, Luke, the letters of Paul, etc., that we do not have the scriptures today. Of course we don't have the original autographs today. They are long gone. So, why is it that in the Bible when it says **"scripture"** it's in reference to *non-original autographical writings?* Where might these "biblical scholars" be getting the idea that only the original autographs are inspired given what the Bible says about Scripture?

According to 2 Timothy 3:15, *Timothy* had Scripture as a child. According to Acts 8:32 the copy of Isaiah the *Ethiopian* had could not have been the "original" since *Jesus* just read it in Luke 4:17-21. They cannot be reading the same *original* scroll, no *original* of Isaiah existed at the time and the one Jesus read was in a completely different area. Yet, *they are Scripture, according to the Book.* Not one reference is to an "original autograph"; *not one time.*

In Acts 8:30 when Philip asks the Ethiopian, **"Understandest thou what thou readest?,"** the Ethiopian responded with **"How can I, except some man should guide me"**? Now, did Philip respond with, *"A better translation would be,"* or did he say, *"Our translations read...but in the original it probably said..."* or maybe he said, *"Is that the version you prefer? Let me get you a less archaic version that you can understand."* He did *not* say anything of the kind. He expounded on the Scriptures right there, and *preached* Jesus Christ.

Another reason to believe there are mistakes is simply that you'd rather not believe anything else to challenge your viewpoint. You aren't a Christian and you don't know anything about it (agnostic) so you think it's just an old book written by patriarchal men a long time ago that has no value today other than symbolism and allegorical playgrounds for the more "spiritually minded" individual, or maybe just an ancient attempt to "control people" and answer basic questions in which humans have posed such as the origin of life, what happens after we die, and so forth. Maybe you think the writings are just a set of heuristics for early human societies.

This next reason goes in hand with the one above, but for the atheist, who at one point possibly was a church goer but was then exposed to Dawkins and performed a 180 because he thinks he's found the sad ultimate truth of reality that Christians just don't want to face (evolutionary reductionism). He has looked on atheists.org and seen the "mistakes" and "contradictions" which are so *thoroughly* (sarcasm is mine) examined and well thought out that he is convinced there is no other way. The Bible is a farce.

The unsaved man has *a hatred for absolute truth* (John 3:18-20; Eph. 2:1-4). Without the Spirit of understanding, how does this man make it through the Bible *without* finding problems (1 Cor. 2:14). It helps to know the Author. A genuine skeptic, for instance, would humbly seek the guidance of the Holy Spirit in their quest for truth, yet this particular group often remains oblivious to the Spirit's work and displays no interest in discovering it. The true skeptic would *"try it out,"* but true skepticism is dead. They just parrot off things that other atheists say from their own "bible studies." This group is a dime a dozen in 2023. If you threw a penny outside a window on a busy street, you'd hit 5 before it hit the ground.

We now have the group who says there are no errors or mistakes in "God's *Word"* (emphasis on the capital "W"). Which means that this "Word" is the very thing that guides you in truth even if what you are viewing is an *actual mistake,* such as 2 Samuel 21:19 in an ESV or Hebrews 3:16 in an NIV (but wait, it isn't a mistake according to this group). The *"Word"* to a Bible-believing Christian who *has* the Scriptures is pre-incarnate Jesus Christ and incarnate Jesus Christ (John 1:1, 1:14; Rev. 19:13). It's another *name* for Jesus Christ while bringing attention to the importance of *"words."* For instance "Jesus" means "Jehovah saves," "Emanuel" means "God is with us." The man has a lot of names.

Many churches today have taken the *Neo-Orthodox* position on the "Word" (Barth and Brunner[1]). Neo-Orthodox, literally meaning, "new teaching" or "new tradition." So even if you have a bible riddled with errors that are *actual* errors, thus causing *real* contradictions, as seen in the NIV, ESV, CSB NASV, NRSB, etc., the *"Word"* is true

---

[1] Karl Barth (1886-1968) and Emil Brunner (1889-1966) were two theologians who popularized this view. Almost everyone growing up now or born after 1980 has willingly or unwillingly accepted their view on Scripture. In Barth's opus titled, *"Church Dogmatics"* he discusses the stance in detail. It was not the "liberal" stance, which tried to discount the Bible as a mere product of fallible men, but it wasn't the "orthodox" stance either, which held that the Bible contained the very *words* of God and was inerrant hence, the term given to their view—"Neo-orthodox." Their middle position was that the Bible was written by men therefore, it *did* contain errors, but since you could *"encounter"* God through that book, it was then inerrant. Their view was indeed radically different from that of the orthodox position held since the 1700's, and it caught on; one preacher at a time until today, as it is the "normal" view held by the majority of Christians, even though the view is not Biblical but produced by two "theologians" who had beef with each other just before they died.

and infallible. Well, of course Jesus Christ is true and infallible, but we are talking about *"words"* (as in: Psa. 12:6-7; Prov 30:5-6; John 12:48; Heb. 4:12-13; Deut. 4:36; Prov. 22:21; Jer. 23:22, and so on). Where do you find what God said *today*? In a Book with **"WORDS"** who's author is the **"Word,"** or more specifically: The Holy Spirit (1 John 5:7; 2 Peter 1:21).

According to this perspective, the notion of the *"Word"* is portrayed as an elusive concept, detached from tangible sources, floating in some intangible realm. Those who adhere to this viewpoint argue that in order to truly discern what God said, one must possess all versions of the Bible and meticulously identify what is true and what is false in each one (ask John R. Rice) and maybe, *just maybe*, eventually, sometime, we will get back to the *"originals"* and see what God said. Then we can really say, **"thus saith the LORD."** So, until then, the entirety of Christendom is just flat out of luck—absolute and unadulterated truth doesn't exist.

This group will present you with two volumes titled, *"Demolishing Supposed Bible Contradictions" (Ken Ham, 2010)*, all while using a NKJV, NASV, Latin, Greek, Septuagint, KJB, NIV, Tyndale's, ASV, Hebrew Masoretic, and over ten different authors "solving" these contradictions. Half the time they just used whatever translation was *most convenient* in attempting to solve the problem at hand. None of them had a *final authority* in which to rest, so they "wrested to their own destruction." If you want to read something humorous, I suggest picking up a copy of the first volume of their work. Below is an example:

On page 46, volume 1, the reader will see:
> *"The difficulty with Genesis 2:19 lies with the use of the word "formed." The same style is read in the KJB. The NIV has a subtly different rendition."*

This is *their answer* to "solving" the differences in the "creation account" of Genesis chapter 1 and 2. (You will find this solved in the chapter, *"Saving Private Ehrman"* in this work by using one Book: *the* Bible.) Another example can be found on page 115 of their book in which the Catholic myth of "Good Friday" is propagated. The idea is that Jesus must have been crucified on Thursday, died on Friday, and rose again on "Easter Sunday." That is *only 36 hours*. The problem lies with the prophet Jonah and what Jesus said about his death in Matthew 12:39-41. Jesus was to die and not rise until *three days and three nights* had passed, giving a full *72 hours* of time that had elapsed. So, is it 36 hours or 72? Ken Ham's book has it laid out so that Jesus died on Good Friday and was resurrected on Sunday morning, all while *admitting* it's only "part of Friday," but still counts it as a full day and night. What in the world, man? We are talking 24 hour periods here. *He has a chart laid out and everything.* So, what really happened?

As usual, the "bible scholars" who can speak ten languages can't seem to read English. Jesus' death was prophesied in Exodus 12:1-10, with relation to the Passover, where *the blood of the lamb* will allow the wrath of God to pass over. The lamb is also *not* given water, like Jesus, the lamb is also roasted with *fire*, as Jesus when He went to hell and back (Acts 2:27-31; Jonah 2:6; Eph. 4:9; 1 Peter 4:6, 3:18-20), the lamb is *"a* lamb," *"the* lamb" and *"your* lamb" (Exod. 12:3-5). Jesus is the "**Lamb of God**" (John 1:29). The Jewish month mentioned in Exodus 12 is Abib, which is our March-April. The day of the Passover is the 14th of Abib so Jesus too must be crucified on the 14th of Abib, *which He was* according to the Gospel accounts, a Wednesday more specifically according to the Gospel of Mark and by figuring where the *High Sabbath* and *regular Sabbath* land. According to Jewish time, a new day begins at our 6pm, a Jewish day is from 6pm to 6pm, that is their twenty-four hour period as opposed to our 12am to 12am. It can be strange to think about since it isn't familiar to the Gentile/Western mind. So, example being, *it's Wednesday on Jewish time while it is still Tuesday evening for Gentiles.*

To get three nights we have:
- Wednesday night, Thursday night, Friday night

For three whole days we have:
- Thursday day, Friday day, Saturday day

Like Jesus' death at 3-6pm in the *evening* (John 19:30-42; Matt. 27:50-61; Mark 15:37-47; Luke 23:46-56), Christ's resurrection is between *3-6pm on Saturday*. He appeared to Mary on "the first day of the week" which is *Sunday very early in the morning*. Sunday started 6pm on our Gentile Saturday. He was resurrected *before* Sunday but people like to think that just because Mary witnessed the empty tomb *at that moment*, then that meant Jesus Christ was resurrected right at that time. According to Scripture, this is not so and just a myth that had been propagated by the Catholic Church. How do you know it was a Wednesday and the 14th of Abib (a.k.a. Nisan) that Christ was crucified? Mark details it: Mark 11:1-11 is *Sunday*, Mark 11:12-19 is *Monday*, Mark 11:20-14:1 is *Tuesday*. The passover lamb was killed on *Wednesday*, Mark 14:12, 17, as Jesus was crucified and killed. Jesus was **"our passover"** (1 Cor. 5:7). The passover feast began afterword (John 19:31). The entire feast matches His crucifixion with the Passover down to the day, hour, and not getting any water to drink. *(See Appendix A, Figure 1.)*

This next type is the devout religious person who lives on works such as baptismal regeneration, mass, sabbath observance, sacraments, the Golden Rule, meditation, Yoga practices, Kundalini, etc. When this person goes through the book *(if they do)* they will be at odds with *"tradition"* and what the Bible *says*. They will often side with a leading spiritual *figure* such as a "priest" or lean on the "great interpreter of the scriptures" (Roman Catholic Church), or rely on works and comments from Don Miguel Ruiz, Eckhart Tolle, or Deepak Chopra. This person has possibly had years of prejudices build up and slanted renderings of the text read to them such as John 3:5 to prove that water baptism saves a person when the interpretation is in *the very next verse*. A lot of the Book is just like that. This group may also believe the Bible supports ideas such as reincarnation, and that hell is metaphorical. This is often the most diverse group and uses phrases like, *"it's my truth"* and *"I write my own truth," "we value tradition, reason, and the Bible* [see the chapter titled "Intermission" and pages 419, 427]." Black and white is scary and they would rather live in a big gray mush-pit of self-absorption and *relativism* than heed to any such notion that the Bible may be a source of absolute truth.

There are actual cases in the Bible that present themselves as real conundrums and a person with preconceived notions will er in that direction. Such as the book of Judges not being chronological for example. If you have the idea that the entire Bible should be chronological then you've already set yourself up. The Bible dictates its own terms, not you. Some of these terms are listed below.

1. Grandsons can be counted as sons as well as even older generations

2. Son-in-laws can be counted as sons

3. Sons who are kings can reign with an older father who could be sick or actively engaged in a military campaign

4. Mothers (Queens) can reign alongside their sons

5. Lapses of time can occur such as in Judges, Jeremiah, Chronicles, and Kings

6. A book does not need to be in chronological order from start to finish (Judges, Jeremiah)

7. Adopted sons can be called and counted as "begotten"

8. Two different periods accounted of six months counts as a year in a kings reign

9. Multiple people can go by the same name or one person can have three different names

10. The same place can have more than one name just like today (ex. "The Windy City" = Chicago)

With these simple rules of thumb you will be far ahead of many a Ph.D. In the same vein, many of the Gospels give contrary accounts in certain details and problems arise when the person or scholar has predetermined in his mind on how things *should* be read or how it *should* be written. For instance: how can Christ be in two places at once (John 3:13)? So, modern versions change it because it doesn't make sense. Well, did you know that you are in two places at once, right now, *as a saved Christian*? (See Eph. 2:5-6.)

How might these conundrums be solved? By method of "sola Scriptura" which simply means, "Scripture alone." Since the words of Scripture are **"spirit"** (John 6:63) then they are spirit—ual (spiritual). By **"comparing spiritual things with spiritual"** (1 Cor. 2:13) we are actually *comparing what God said with what God said* in relation to various topics or themes, not what a commentator said *about* the words of Scripture but what is said *within* Scripture about *itself*.

An example in brief would be the **"leaven"** in Scripture. According to Philip Schaff who was on the committee of the 1901 ASV, the "leaven" is *the Gospel* which will fill the entire world eventually like bread rising. Is this true about leaven? What does Scripture say leaven is? In Mark 8:15 we find a warning against leaven, **"And he charged them, saying, Take heed, beware of the leaven of the Pharisees, and of the leaven of Herod."** The disciples of Jesus have a hard time with this saying (Mark 8:16) because they take it literally, sort of like how the Catholic Church takes the wafer at the Lord's supper to be the literal Body of Jesus Christ. In Matthew 16:12 the leaven is the **"doctrine of the Pharisees,"** In Luke 12:2 we are told that the leaven is **"hypocrisy,"** and in 1 Corinthians 5:8 we read **"Therefore let us keep the feast, not with old leaven, neither with the leaven of malice and wickedness; but with the unleavened bread of sincerity and truth."** The "leaven" by no means is the Gospel, in fact it's just the opposite. It's lies, hypocrisy, and deception. **"A little leaven leaveneth the whole lump"** (Gal. 5:9).

Having noted this tragedy of Philip Schaff, he believes he can tell you what should and should not belong in your Bible, or any version of a bible. What on God's green earth is a man doing making bibles *"more clear"* and *"easier to understand"* when he himself gets something so fundamentally *wrong* in relation to the bread and butter of a Christians faith; *The Gospel?* He mistook *hypocrisy* for *the Gospel*. Think about that.

This is written for the Christian soldier to **"war a good warfare"** (1 Tim. 1:18), to **"endure hardness, as a good soldier of Jesus Christ"** (2 Tim. 2:3), and to **"Fight the good fight"** (1 Tim. 6:12). There are many a soldier who are MIA, shot down by infantry fire, heavy artillery, or even the friendly fire within Christian seminaries. This is mostly on the subject of friendly fire coming straight from the Christian frontlines shooting at their own troops with powdered rounds of *doubt, fear, unbelief, and lies* all while the soldiers are trusting in their higher ranking officers. Even though my writing at times can be blunt, I am not putting doubt in the minds of men called to the ministry or of the faith, **"God forbid"** but rather building them up and putting a foot down and a Bible on the table when professors and teachers at seminaries are *too scared* to take a stand. It is also written as a reference for those who are true skeptics and seek truth rather than fame, light rather than limelight, humility rather than the acceptance of their peers, and honor from *God* rather than honor from *men*.

Christians no longer identify with Christ unless it suits them. Let me remind you that Jesus *was not* just a warm and fuzzy type who would never hurt a fly, but in fact he called the leading political and religious leaders of his day **"that fox"** (Luke 13:32), **"serpents"** and **"vipers"** (Matt. 23:33), **"fools and blind"** (Matt. 23:19), that would *"fall into a ditch"* (Matt. 15:14), **"blind guides"** (Matt. 23:16), who **"outwardly appear righteous unto men, but within… full of hypocrisy and iniquity"** (Matt. 23:28), they **"hold the tradition of the elders"** (Mark 7:3), **"making the word of God of NONE effect"** (Mark 7:13).

They do not blow their **"trumpet"** (Isa. 58:1) for Him unless they are *comfortable* around the camp. **"Let us go forth therefore unto him without the camp, bearing his reproach"** (Heb. 13:13). **"Without the camp"** of societal norms, political norms, religious norms, and academic norms. It is a **"burden"** (Haba. 1:1; Mal. 1:1) to sound the **"trumpet"** (Jer. 4:19, 6:17, 51:27; Ezek. 33:3-6). Every Christian has a "trumpet" to sound. God blew His so hard that no one wanted to hear it again (Exod. 19:16, 20:19; Deut. 18:16). His voice shook the very souls of the people. Do you suffer for Christ **"without the camp"**? Do you **"consider him"** (Heb. 12:3)? Did you ever *"consider"* what He would say to the "biblical scholars" of our day (Matt. 23; John 3)? He was betrayed, tempted, out of money, He took the bitter cup, and was weary…**"consider him."**

> *"Have not I commanded thee? Be strong and of a good courage; be not afraid, neither be thou dismayed: for the LORD thy God is with thee whithersoever thou goest."– Joshua 1:9*

The Book

THE LORD brings a scholar a book and the scholar said, "I must learn more about the time period and archeological finds in that area. I need to know what the authors original intent was for his social/cultural norms will determine as to what the writer was really expressing...Oh, yes, and I must know the theories of my associates and peers. I can't read it."

The LORD then brings the same book to a redneck, base, cracker of a man in the deep south. The LORD asks him to read it like He asked the scholar. So, the redneck responds, "Well, see hear Mr., I donhav much learnin'. Ima be reel blunt'wit'cha, I caint read dat."

A learned man and a non-learned man can't read the Book.

What's all the trouble?
It's a matter of the heart.
The LORD then turns everything upside down and brings to nothing the wisdom of the world and *makes things seemingly foolish wise*. The LORD will rejoice.
(Isa. 29:11-14; Luke 10:21; 1 Cor. 1:19-28)

Chapter 1: A Bucketful Of ... "Contradictions"

"Thy word is true from the beginning" — Psalm 119:160

In the following list, you will find a compilation of supposed "discrepancies" gathered from prominent seminaries across the country. These discrepancies are presented in a straightforward manner, allowing you to observe the verses in question along with the perceived problems, followed by an explanation addressing the issue. When it comes to reading the Scriptures, one of the significant challenges for Christians, particularly scholars, lies in *"considering"* Christ. Although it may seem audacious or unfair to suggest, the truth is that they often fail to extend the Lord the benefit of the doubt and thereby, do not **"consider him."**

Genesis 22:1 **"God did temp Abraham"**
vs
James 1:13-14 **"Let no man say when he is tempted, I am tempted of God: for God cannot be tempted with evil, neither tempteth he any man: But every man is tempted, when he is drawn away of his own lust, and enticed."**

Problem: God tempted Abraham, but God can't temp anyone, right? Only the devil can tempt.

Answer: The temptation of James 1:2-3 is not the same as James 1:14-15. There are a diversity of temptations so *what kind* did Abraham have?

According to Hebrews 11:17 it was a *"trial."* The Scriptures interpret themselves.

"By faith Abraham, when he was TRIED, offered up Isaac: and he that had received the promises offered up his only begotten son" (Heb 11:17).

As a Christian you will have trials, tribulations, and temptations, **"Wherein ye greatly rejoice, though now for a season, if need be, ye are in heaviness through manifold temptations: That the TRIAL of your faith being much more precious than of gold that perisheth, though it be TRIED"** (1 Peter 1:6-7), note the **"tried"** in the passage.

"My brethern, count it all joy when ye fall into divers temptations; knowing this, that the trying of your faith worketh patience" (James 1:2-3). **"Blessed is the man that endureth temptation: for when he is tried...** (James 1:12).

Genesis 11:5 **"And the LORD came down to see the city and the tower, which the children of men builded."**

vs

Proverbs 15:3 **"The eyes of the LORD are in every place, beholding the evil and the good."**

Problem: Why would God come **"down to see"** if His "eyes are in every place?"

Answer: Every time God comes **"down"** to a place geographically He does it in the shape of a being...with ears, legs, nose, arms, and eyes. Genesis 19:1-22; Judges 13:3-20.

He wanted to mingle with the people "unawares" (Heb. 13:2) in a particular way (also see Gen. 18:1-18: Judg. 6:11-21). He can appear as the angel of the LORD. **"And the angel of the LORD appeared unto the woman,"** (Judg. 13:3). Look at what the woman told her husband, **"A man of God came unto me."** (Judg. 13:6). His reaction is unbelief, as seen in verses 7-20, and his final admission that it was indeed not just "a man," but an angel in verse 21 **"Then Manoah knew that he was an angel,"** as in, he *didn't* know before.

What convinced him? Same thing it takes modern Christian scholars today; a flaming altar in which an angel ascends into Heaven from (verse 20).

Joshua knew there was something up with **"a man."** Joshua sees **"a man"** standing with his sword drawn (Josh. 5:13). Unlike Balaam, who is scared to death of him (Num. 22:31) and fell flat on his face, Joshua walks over to the angel of the LORD and asks him if the **"man"** is for him or for his adversaries. Why would Joshua ask this? What an odd thing to ask a single **"man"** standing out in the open. Joshua is a man that has gone through 40 years wondering the wilderness, seen many people die, and fought in many battles, but he asks *a single man* that question. Joshua asked because **"the man"** *looked* human but different, like a "man" but more than a man. Just like the angels that were about to get raped in Genesis 19, there is *something different* about these men. Unless it's revealed to you, you just don't know if it's **"a man"** or an **"angel."**

I'll give you another example of the Lord wanting a different perspective on things. In Luke 24:13-15 Jesus comes to two disciples but **"their eyes were holden that they should know him"** (verse 16), meaning that the Lord had a veil over their eyes to keep his identity from them. The two go on talking, and Jesus asks them why they are sad and what they were reasoning about. In a sarcastic manner, they dismiss Jesus as an ignorant outsider, as if he had no knowledge of the preceding events described in the earlier chapters of Luke.— those **"things."** Jesus responds with, **"what things"** in verse 19. You ever stop to think about that? That is the Lord, the Creator of the Universe (Col. 1:15-17) asking **"what things."** Doesn't He know **"what things"**? Yes, He does. He wants to hear *what you have to say about it.* He wants fellowship. Just like in Romans 14:12, **"every one of us shall give account of himself to God."** Well *why*, if He **"sees"** and knows everything? Again, Just how the stone was rolled back at His tomb, it wasn't for Jesus to get out, *it was for them to go in.*

Deuteronomy 7:22 **"And the LORD thy God will put out those nations before thee by little and little: thou mayest not consume them at once, lest the beasts of the field increase upon thee."**

vs

Deuteronomy 9:3 **"Understand therefore this day, that the LORD thy God is he which goeth over before thee; as a consuming fire he shall destroy them, and he shall bring them down before thy face: so shalt thou drive them out, and destroy them quickly, as the LORD hath said unto thee."**

Problem: Is it **"quickly"** or "little by little?"

Answer: The verses aren't even related. The nations in Deuteronomy 7:22 are the Canaanites, Hittites, Amorites, Perizzites, Hivites, and Jebusites (vs. 1). In Deuteronomy 9:3 we are dealing with the giants (the Anakims) which would be driven out **"quickly."** Remember these "problems" aren't brought to you by atheists, but Christian "scholars." Let that sink in.

2 Chronicles 36:9 **"Jehoiachin was eight years old when he began to reign, and he reigned three months and ten days in Jerusalem: and he did that which was evil in the sight of the LORD."**

vs

2 Kings 24:8 **"Jehoiachin was eighteen years old when he began to reign, and he reigned in Jerusalem three months. And his mother's name was Nehushta, the daughter of Elnathan of Jerusalem."**

Problem: Was Jehoiachin eight or eighteen when he started his reign?

Answer: Jehoiachin is deported (2 Chron. 36:9-10) and his mother goes with him (2 Kings 24:12) because she is the Queen (Jer. 13:18, 22:26, 29:2). Joint reigns happen in the Bible (1 Kings 22; 2 Kings 1; 2 Kings 3). He had a joint reign with *his mother the Queen* for 10 years, making his total reign 18 years, 3 months, and 10 days. He turned 18, sat on the throne and ruled for a few months, but at eight years old the throne was *rightfully* his; his mother ruled in his stead during this time.

Sound familiar? How about David being the king of Israel but didn't sit on the throne to rule until *10-15 years later* after his anointing (1 Sam. 16:13). What about Jesus Christ who is King but hasn't taken the Throne of David yet (Mark 11:10; Luke 19:38)? Like David, He has yet to take the Throne that is rightfully His (Rev. 19:16; Matt. 25:31, 19:28; Luke 1:30-33; Gen. 49:10). Here is a nugget for you, Jehoiachin **"did that which was evil,"** he reigned *three and a half months* (2 Chron. 36:9),...sort of like the antichrist who reigns for three and a half years. (Here are the references: Rev. 13:5; Matt. 24:15; Dan. 8:13, 11:31; 2 Thess. 2:3-9.)

There is always an advanced revelation tucked away in something God makes you look at more than a few times.

No Greek professor saw it. Just an English Reformation Bible and as a wise man once said, *"a believing heart, and a humble mind."*

Ecclesiastes 1:4 "One generation passeth away, and another generation cometh: but the earth abideth for ever."
vs
2 Peter 3:10 "But the day of the Lord will come as a thief in the night; in the which the heavens shall pass away with a great noise, and the elements shall melt with fervent heat, the earth also and the works that are therein shall be burned up."

Problem: Is the earth forever or not?

Answer: It is truly astonishing to witness the elaborate measures people often take to evade the truth. Let's keep reading 2 Peter 3 and read verses 11-13. I will quote verse 13 here, read the rest yourself. **"Nevertheless we, according to his promise, look for new heavens and a new earth, wherein dwelleth righteousness."** We have earth *one* being burned up and now an earth *two* which is a *renovation of earth number one*. This "contradiction" is brought to you by *atheists.org*, which I will be going through their list in another chapter.

Another crucial aspect, often overlooked by atheists who fail to grasp it (the feeble minded), is the significance of considering *the context* of the text. What is the writer, Solomon trying to say in Ecclesiastes 1:4, certainly not what it literally sounds like since in Ecclesiastes 3:11 there *is* an end. This end has a beginning as well (see Rev. 21-22). We may be way over these guys heads here, I'll tone it down. Solomon is stating that *man is small and lowly* in the large scope of things, just like *half* of the book of Ecclesiastes.

Proverbs 31:6 **"Give strong drink unto him that is ready to perish, and wine unto those that be of heavy hearts."**
vs
1 Timothy 5:23 **"Drink no longer water, but use a little wine for thy stomach's sake and thine often infirmities."**

Problem: The Bible says to drink alcohol and condones alcohol use.

Answer: Here we have yet another reading problem. 1 Timothy 5:23 says **"and thine often infirmities,"**... **"for thy stomach's sake,"** which means as *medicine*. Alcohol is used and has been used for medicine for thousands of years. In Proverbs 31:6 you have a person who is condemned to death, a criminal. (The Bible does not condone alcohol use, see Haba. 2:15 and Levi. 10:9-10; Prov. 23:29-35, etc.) Yes, Jesus turned water to wine, but if it was the wine we drink today then those people would have been hospitalized for alcohol poisoning. John 2:6 reads **"two or three firkins apiece"** in *6 water pots*. Thats *72-162 gallons*. Face it, if Jesus did turn the water to the *same* wine we drink, then he would have *broken* the law (Haba. 215). Are we separating the men from the boys yet?

What did they drink in John 2? It was certainly unlike any wine they had, **"And saith unto him, Every man at the beginning doth set forth good wine; and when men have well drunk, then that which is worse: but thou hast kept the good wine until now"** (John 2:10). Maybe it was "the good stuff" that those "uppidy ups" keep under lock and key? When it says **"when men have well drunk"** it is not saying that the men were "drunk." See how the word is used in the Bible in Ruth 3:7 and 1 Samuel 1:13-15. **"Drunk"** is past tense of "to drink," the matter is *what are you drunken with*—**"I have drunk neither wine nor strong drink."**

Matthew 8:17 **"That it might be fulfilled which was spoken by Esaias the prophet, saying, Himself took our infirmities, and bare our sicknesses."**
vs
Isaiah 53:4 **"Surely he hath borne our griefs, and carried our sorrows: yet we did esteem him stricken, smitten of God, and afflicted."**

Problem: The prophecy don't match.

Answer: This reminds me of a conversation I had with someone about a final authority. For them it came to *"preference."* "I prefer..." What is true? That's the question, who cares what your or my own *"preferences"* are. You can hear the average Sunday school class teacher now, ."..now children everyone is on their own journey." **"Prove all things"** (I Thess. 5:21).

This passage *does* match in the LXX Septuagint (and many other passages *written to match* the New Testament on purpose). The Septuagint is a complete Old Testament manuscript with *the Apocrypha as part of the manuscript* (red flag #1) written in 200-300 B.C. by 72 Jews commissioned in Egypt (red flag #2). It is written in Greek instead of Hebrew. New Testament writers used it to quote from (red flag #3), Mark, Matthew, Luke, and Paul and favored this Greek text over the Hebrew ones passed down for generations (red flag #4). Now, *behold the red flags*:

- There is *no evidence* for it ever being written in or around 200 B.C. , ask your professor or your pastor. He will lead you to a *shady* letter which you can examine

A Bucketful of ...

online called the "Letter to Aristeas." There *is* evidence for it being written around A.D. 200-300 by a guy named Origen, his Hexapla.

• It was written by 72 Jews but it goes by the name LXX, which is the number 70 (L=50, X=10, X=10; 50+10+10=70).

• All Orthodox Jews *reject it.* Jews are the **"oracles of God"** (Rom. 3:2). This is the reason why many Jews don't accept modern Christian versions of the bible, because they *use and incorporate the LXX.* They believe it is a mythological creature, which it is. The LXX contains the Apocrypha *as part of* the O.T. which *no* Jew accepts as canonical.

• *No* New Testament author would have given it the time of day after they saw the deliberate and fallacious changes done to their own texts.

• The Hebrew scriptures have an unbelievable amount of *consistency* and evidence behind them, which is what's in the Old Testament of a King James Bible, except the *order* of the books is different. The "Septuagints" we have today are: Sinaiticus א A.D. 330-350 , Vaticanus B A.D. 330-350, a few other Alexandrian Codices, and Origen's Hexapla A.D. 140-250.

• The Jews who wrote it were *in Egypt*, the place that they were *called out of* and told *not to go back* (Jer. 44:25-26, 42:13-22; Gen. 49:29, 50:25; Ezek. 32:2, 31-32; Isa. 19-20:4). Why would you consider anything written in Egypt by an apostate group worth anything more than tissue paper when it comes to its reliability and genuineness?

- To *advance* in Christian academia you must *accept the myth* of this creature. As we have seen so far, Christian academia is failing, **"they shall be turned unto fables"** (2 Tim. 4:1-4).

- Origen wrote it with a New Testament *on his desk* and intentionally changed verses to match the N.T. in order to convert Jews or thinking he was doing a favor for the Body of Christ. (Obvious places of manipulation are: Prov. 11:31; Psa. 14:3; Amos 5:26; Prov. 3:11-12; Amos 4:13; Haba. 3:13; Isa. 61:1, etc... in order to match the N.T. writings written *after* A.D. 90-95.)

- Proof often cited for the existence of a pre-Jesus Christ Septuagint is within the Dead Sea Scrolls. The earliest Septuagint fragments are the Ryland Papyri No. 458 with portions of Deuteronomy 23:24, 26–24:3; 25:1–3; 26:12; 26:17–19; 28:31–33; 27:15; 28:2, dated 150 B.C. and called *"the oldest Septuagint"* which was *not* even found in the caves of The Dead Sea Scrolls. Papyri Fouad No. 266 with Deuteronomy 31:28-32:7 and dated 50 B.C. . A Greek Exodus 28:4-7 dated 140-37 B.C.. Every other Greek O.T. or *"Septuagint"* book found was dated from A.D. 100 to A.D. 1400, with the vast majority of O.T. texts written in *Hebrew, not Greek...no Septuagint*. Many of the texts found are unidentified, or were O.T./N.T. *Apocryphal* books and commentaries. Is this enough to say that Matthew, Mark, Luke, John, Paul, etc... *quoted from a Greek O.T.?* It doesn't look like it. It must have been in a some what of wide circulation *if* the Gospel writers *all* quoted from it, given that the Gospels were written at different times. *There had to have been enough B.C. Septuagint's around for the N.T. writers to quote from.* Based on the findings of the Dead Sea Scrolls, most people would come to the conclusion that it was a very

A Bucketful of ...

eclectic group of people living together collecting/reviewing manuscripts, and most likely had a group of manuscripts that they deemed *"sketchy."*

- Then there is also the given date *ranges* for the above mentioned Greek O.T. papyri, which is actually between *300 B.C. and A.D. 100* by Carbon-14 dating, *that's 400 years of wiggle room* according to the University of Groningen who does research on the topic. In 1950 the inventor of the dating method himself (Willard Libby) was there to test a piece of linen from Qumran Cave 1 which was the site of *"The Great Isaiah Scroll,"* one of the most notable discoveries. The date ranges for the linen cloth was *between 167 B.C. and A.D. 233*. This is a sizable 400 year gap to *guesstimate*. Libby also tested wood in the area, with dates between 70 B.C. and A.D. 90 leaving 160 years of wiggle room to cast a feasible date in the waters of history. About twenty years later, Libby returned and tested "The Great Isaiah Scroll." The date came out to be a range of 200 B.C. to A.D. 1. *Zurich Institute of Technology* did the Carbon-14 testing in 1991 and again another dating was done by the *University of Arizona* in 1995. The dates we have today are by no means conclusive, as much as some will want to demand upon you. We have dates from Libby, Zurich, and University of Arizona. "The Great Isaiah Scroll" was dated between 351-295 B.C. or 230-53 B.C. by the University of Arizona and similar findings from Zurich. There was another piece of linen tested in a different cave (Qumran 4) by University of Arizona with the dates between 197 B.C. to A.D. 46. Naturally, scholars will try and push back the dates to fit whatever theory they are trying to prove, or push it forward in some cases. A test on a non-biblical scroll found (that was a "community guidelines" of sorts) tested from A.D. 129-255 and A.D. 303 to 318 *for the first test* by Arizona,

Chapter 1

and *for the second test* 50 B.C. to A.D. 130. Not very reliable.

• No one has been able to find one piece of a *Greek* O.T. written *before* the time of Christ that any N.T. writer ever quoted. Just scraps of paper with small portions of Deuteronomy and a few verses of Exodus in Greek with *a variable dating of about 400 years.* Every other *Greek* O.T. writing found was dated 100+ years *after* the death of Jesus Christ. Before I get misquoted or misunderstood, I would like to state that *I do* believe there was a pre-Jesus Christ Greek OT, most likely around 200-50 B.C., but *I do not believe any NT writer ever quoted one a single time.* Philo probably translated the Hebrew into Greek but it didn't go very far. Was the OT written in Greek before Christ by some scribes? Yes. Was it widely used? Probably not/highly doubtful. *Come to your own conclusions.*

• The "scholar" accepts *on faith* the idea of a pre-birth of Christ LXX but *does not show the same exercise of faith when it comes to the text of the King James Bible, or any bible, or any set of manuscripts, anywhere on earth when it comes to calling it Scripture or having a final authority.*

Back to the answer of the text. Any author *can quote his work freely* so as to not cause a contradiction, this is called a *"free quotation."* The author of the Book is The Holy Spirit. For an example of how the author does this aside from what we have just discovered, see Isaiah 61:1-2 and its quotation in Luke 4:18-19. Read it. You will notice two very distinct things after "a careful read" in a King James.

1.) In Luke 4, Jesus stops right at the comma in Isaiah 61:2 and then closes the Book. *Why?* There are two comings of Christ: one when He *came* as an offering for sin and to set us free, give spiritual sight through the New Birth, and to be

A Bucketful of ... 29

delivered from this condition (as seen in the text). Now, look after the comma in Isaiah 61:2, and keep reading past the comma after He stopped. At his Second Coming, He brings *vengeance, judgment, and a restoration of Israels kingdom with Himself on the Throne.* Jesus Christ was reading *what he came to do* out loud to the Jews and then stopped because the rest is *not* what he had come to do, yet. What a strange Book.

2.) Notice in Isaiah 61:1 the words **"Spirit," "Lord"** and **"GOD."** In Luke 4:18 we have **"Spirit"** and **"Lord."** *Where is the other person of the Trinity?* Why bless my soul, he's *right there in the temple reading the passage to the Jews.* That's **"GOD"** in the flesh. The lovely LXX goes back to Isaiah and changes 61:1 *to match* Luke 4:18. Attacking a God given revelation to His people and attacking a fundamental of the faith, the manifestation of God in the flesh.

John 19:14-16 **"And it was the preparation of the passover, and about the sixth hour: and he saith unto the Jews, Behold your King!...Then delivered he him therefore unto them to be crucified. And they took Jesus, and led him away."**

vs

Mark 15:25 **"And it was the third hour, and they crucified him."**

Problem: John says Jesus was crucified at the *sixth hour* and Mark says the *third hour*; they can't both be right.

Answer: John is the only writer to write *after* the destruction of Jerusalem in A.D. 70. His writings are from around A.D. 90-96, including his Gospel account. With this in mind John *does not* hold to Jewish time like Mark, Matthew, and Luke do in every case. The **"sixth hour"** is

Gentile time; 6 AM. This makes complete sense given the chronology of the crucifixion.
- *6 AM* or the **"sixth hour"** Gentile time, Jesus is in front of Pilate for the last time but has not taken the road to Calvary yet bearing his cross (John 19:14-16)
- *9 AM* or the **"third hour"** in Jewish time, Jesus is crucified (Mark 15:25; John 19:18; Luke 23:33)
- *12 PM - 3 PM* or in Jewish time the **"sixth hour"** to the **"ninth hour"** there was **"darkness over the whole land"** (Mark 15:33; Matt. 27:45; Luke 23:44)
- *3 PM - 6 PM* Jesus dies (Luke 12:46; Matt. 27:46-50; Mark 15:34-37; John 19:29-30)

It could not fit together any more perfectly than that. The Book is a critic (Heb. 4:12). It was written in a way to mess someone up and sometimes they get messed up *bad*. You also have to **"study"** it. You have to spend some time in it instead of being in front of the TV.

Matthew 5:22 "But I say unto you, That whosoever is angry with his brother without a cause shall be in danger of the judgment: and whosoever shall say to his brother, Raca, shall be in danger of the council: but whosoever shall say, Thou fool, shall be in danger of hell fire."

vs

Matthew 23:17 "Ye fools and blind: for whether is greater, the gold, or the temple that sanctifieth the gold?"

Problem: Jesus contradicts himself; he calls people **"fools"** after saying not to do that.

Answer: If you notice the *punctuation* of Matthew 5:22 it will become clear. The pretext given is **"without a cause"**; in Matthew 23:17 *Jesus had* **"cause"** *to call the Pharisees* **"fools."** *Ironically, Matthew 23:17 is directly aimed at the destructive* *critic*. They are always looking for **"gold"** instead of the one who sanctifies it. You could't just call someone a **"fool"** for no reason *before Jesus Christ was glorified*.

In the Church age, you can. Paul *calls himself* a fool in 2 Corinthians 11:16, **"I say again, Let no man think me a fool; if otherwise, yet as a fool receive me, that I may boast myself a little."**

In 1 Corinthians 4:10 Paul says *all saved Christians* are fools, **"We are fools for Christ's sake, but ye are wise in Christ; we are weak, but ye are strong; ye are honourable, but we are despised."**

In 1 Corinthians 3:18 Paul is saying, **"let him become a fool, that he may be wise."** Why? Because Calvary turned everything upside down, **"But God hath chosen the foolish things of the world to confound the wise; and God hath chosen the weak things of the world to confound the things which are mighty"** (1 Cor. 1:27).

In 1 Corinthians 15:36 Paul *calls ignorant people* fools, **"Thou fool, that which thou sowest is not quickened, except it die."**

2 Samuel 8:4 **"And David took from him a thousand chariots, and seven hundred horsemen, and twenty thousand footmen: and David houghed all the chariot horses, but reserved of them for an hundred chariots."**

vs

1 Chronicles 18:4 **"And David took from him a thousand chariots, and seven thousand horsemen, and twenty thousand footmen: David also houghed all the chariot horses, but reserved of them an hundred chariots."**

Problem: Was it 700 or 7000 horsemen?

Chapter 1

Answer: Most will chalk this up as a *"scribal error"* or an *"error of the pen,"* but that would mean for thousands of years the Hebrews had, *over and over*, added a zero to the text or subtracted a zero from it. Can Hebrews count? For the Targum Jonathan, an Aramaic translation of the Hebrew bible reads 700 and 7000, the Talmud Bavli (a commentary of sorts), the Dead Sea Scrolls having a Hebrew copy of Samuel, Kennicott Bible, and the Complutensian Polyglot, *all read 700 and 7000*. The vast majority of Hebrew manuscripts read 700 and 7000. Essentially you are calling them dumb and stupid by them repeatedly not "fixing" it or not noticing it.

There is something more going on here than a *"bad stroke of the pen."* There are currently a number of possible solutions to the text by various individuals but before I delve into one of them, I am reminded of a conversation I had a while back.

I was talking to a Christian about bible versions one day, and he ended the conversation by saying, *"well how do you resolve the 700 or 7000 horsemen? What does knowing whether it was 700 or 7000 have anything to do with my relationship with God?"*

A very salient question to say the least, which only shows the *mentality* of modern Christianity. How does one get to know God? That is the question at hand. It reminds me of Samuel; **"Now Samuel did not yet know the LORD, neither was the word of the LORD yet revealed unto him."** (1 Sam. 3:7). *How* did that young Samuel get to know God? **"For the LORD revealed himself to Samuel in Shiloh by the word of the LORD"** (1 Sam. 3:21); *by His word*. Where do you find what God said to Samuel today? As w-o-r-d-s (1 Sam. 3:19) written *in a Book*. By trying to see about this 700 or 7000 conundrum, *you are spending time in the Book; where God reveals Himself*. What this man was really saying was, *"how does studying the Bible get me closer to the one who wrote it?"* That is your average 2023 Christian.

Now, was it 700 or 7000? First let's look at another place that is *similar*:

"And the Syrians fled before Israel; and David slew the men of seven hundred chariots of the Syrians, and forty thousand horsemen, and smote Shobach the captain of their host, who died there." (2 Sam. 10:18)

"But the Syrians fled before Israel; and David slew of the Syrians seven thousand men which fought in chariots, and forty thousand footmen, and killed Shophach the captain of the host." (1 Chron. 19:18)

Again, we have a similar phenomena happening. What could be going on? The answer is in the verse itself. One says **"David slew the men of seven hundred chariots"** and the other says **"David slew of the Syrians seven thousand men which fought in chariots."** The men *of* seven hundred chariots is actually 7000. There are 10 men trained to operate one chariot if one goes down. With 10 men for every chariot, 700 chariots would equal out to 7000 men total.

The difference is a two letter word **"of"** and **"in."** Also, notice that in one passage a **"footman"** is also called a **"horsemen"** in the other. These soldiers, while in reserve, would be fighting on foot until a chariot needed assistance with either a man or a horse. It's all standard military training and procedures.

The same thing is going on with those horses/riders first mentioned. There are 10 horses/riders trained and ready to go if a chariot horse/rider dies or goes down. A good captain always has reserves and knows that heavy weaponry on the field of battle is a plus. Solomon, for example, kept stables big enough to hold his reserves.

"And Solomon had forty thousand stalls of horses for his chariots, and twelve thousand horsemen." (1 Kings 4:26)

"And Solomon had four thousand stalls for horses and chariots, and twelve thousand horsemen; whom he

bestowed in the chariot cities, and with the king at Jerusalem." (2 Chron. 9:25)

See there? He had **"forty thousand stalls of horses for his chariots"** means he had 40,000 horses, hence the word **"of"** and **"for."** Then you are told he has **"four thousand stalls for horses and chariots,"** note the word **"for."** Solomon had 10 horses per stall and chariot. These horses were trained *chariot horses.* You will see this pattern throughout the books of Chronicles and Kings because the writers of each book are giving you different information to paint a better picture with; *like the Gospel accounts.*

The last part of the verse in each account of 2 Samuel and 1 Chronicles is, **"but reserved of them an hundred chariots"** simply means that David held back 1000 horses instead of injuring them so the enemy couldn't use them. What he took were the horse*men*.

Now to the doctoring of the Scriptures. *"The"* LXX (Vaticanus, A.D. 4th Century) reads, *"seven thousand horsemen"* in 1 Samuel 8:4 instead of **"seven hundred"** and in 1 Chronicles 18:4 it reads again, *"seven thousand horsemen."* What the writer of Vaticanus did was fix up 1 Samuel 8:4 *to make it read like* 1 Chronicles 18:4, thereby *"solving"* the discrepancy. What they did was ruin the continuity of the Old Testament, for they *did not touch* 2 Samuel 10:18 and 1 Chronicles 19:18. Someones "scholarship" and "academic training" got in the way.

1 Samuel 16:10 **"Again, Jesse made seven of his sons to pass before Samuel."**
vs
1 Chronicles 2:13-15 **"And Jesse begat his firstborn Eliab, and Abinadab the second, and Shimma the third, Nethaneel the fourth, Raddai the fifth, Ozem the sixth, David the seventh"**

Problem: Are there *eight* sons of Jesse or *seven*? David would be the eighth in 1 Samuel 16:10.

Answer: One of the brothers could have been adopted or a relative. It is not uncommon practice in the Bible to do so (see 1 Chron. 6:10 Cf. 1 Kings 4:2; 1 Chron. 18:16. Also see Exod. 4:22; Gen. 45:8; 2 Kings 2:12; Ruth 1:11-13). This would explain his exclusion in the other passage.

This wraps up the first round of "contradictions." Most of the trouble comes from either *not believing* what you are reading, having someone *teach you out of believing it* by not giving you the solutions to the passage at hand, or not spending *time in the Book*. In the next chapter I will go more in depth on the subject in front of us, but pertaining to the types of people who will teach you out of your faith in the Book and the mentality that a standard seminary education produces from 1940-present. These are not isolated occurrences that only happen in "liberal" seminaries or "liberal" churches. People are taught out of believing in a final authority in fundamental, militant, conservative seminaries and churches around the nation.

Chapter 2: The Actors

"How are the mighty fallen in the midst of the battle!"
— 2 Samuel 1:25

MANY "scholars" that emerge from the factories (seminaries) are as the very people who've been to a "reeducation camp" of World War II Nazi Germany or the Gulags of Soviet Russia. They then impart their "reeducation" to the public starting in the local churches and other local assemblies. One of these "re-educated" fellows is a man named James White, who falls in line with Semler, Hort, John MacArthur, Rick Norris, D. A. Carson, Custer, Fred Butler, Wallace, Metzger, Price, Ehrman, etc. All of the above are *destructive* critics of the word of God, all while *proclaiming* to believe in the preserved *"Word"* of God or the *"original autographs"* which no one has or has seen.

Ask any one of these men or the teachers that taught them and they will give you the *party line: "We believe in the infallible Word of God and its preservation. It is the final authority in all matters of faith and practice in a Christians life."* Press them a little more and ask if they can *give you* or lead you to *a copy of* the infallible, preserved word of God, to use in faith and your walk with God. They will lead you to any translation while giving you some nonsense about how each translation is different and used for different purposes. That would make *your own preferences your final authority.* Picking out a bible version has become like picking out a new pair of shoes; does it look nice, is it comfortable, do you like it? They will tell you that some are "paraphrases," some are "thought for thought," and some are "literal translations" and "word for word" and "formal correspondence," on and on it goes; but *not once will they hand you a copy of the God breathed Scriptures that you can hold in your hands and read.* They will give you a *"reliable translation."* Its reliability is based on comparing it with the original texts...*that don't exist.* Imagine bringing any of this to a courtroom.

They don't have them. They are *liars* if you ask them "is this Scripture" and they say *"Yes,"* while holding to the previous belief (John 8:44; Gen. 3). They will lie directly to your face, because the men that taught them showed them how to do it—and people wonder why all of a-sudden we have "gay theologians." It starts with the leaders and they are trained in seminaries. They are scared to tell you what they *really learned in seminary* because it will hurt *their image,* or that it may *"shake your faith,"* as it did to countless others who left. These people believe we don't have God's *word* because it *was* in the *"originals."*...but we are *close* to finding out what He said. Upward and onward! (Gen. 11.) *"Things are getting better all the time..."—The Beatles 1967* (They did not get better for John Lennon or for Paul McCartney. They got worse).

I had a conversation with the assistant of a pastor for a very large church the other day. It summed up the mentality of this bunch pretty well. I was looking around for a church to attend in my area and was e-mailing some of them to see what they believed at the time. These e-mails are between an assistant of the pastor and myself. Names have been changed in the responses (mainly to protect the assistant), Dr. Pufferfish is the pastor of a fundamental, Evangelical Baptist church and Ms. LovelyGal is one of his assistants. Here it is:

Me:

"Hello, I am currently looking around for a church but I had a question for *Dr. Pufferfish*: What is the churches position on the final authority for all matters on faith and the Christian life? Is the word of God inspired, infallible, and inerrant? What is the word of God?"

Response:

"Good evening! Pastor responded with the following: I love this question! We do believe that God's Word is the final authority on faith and the Christian life. We also believe with conviction that God's Word is inerrant, infallible, and authoritative.

Thank you for your question! Blessings!"

Notice the capital "W" there and the *claim and professing* that God's Word is inerrant? He also *avoided* my question: "What is the word of God?" This is the classic shuck-and-jive maneuver you will see from someone who *professes* one thing but *believes* something different entirely.

My response:

"Thank you for your response! Yes but what do you mean by "Word" Do you mean every word from the oracles of God, as in the "words," all of them? If so, which bible do you use, since they differ in some major places and are not all the same. Thank you for your assistance and for answering my questions"

Response:

"We believe *every bit* of God's Word from Genesis to Revelation. Pastor [Pufferfish] *uses* the ESV translation. "

This will be the response of just about every pastor, dean, head of a Bible Department, Biblical Studies Department, et al. It is also *a lie*, in other words, "We believe every bit of the

The Actors 39

ESV, NIV, NASV, NRSV, NEB, NLT...." *No they don't*. Take note of the word he used—"*uses* the ESV," does he not *believe* it? Why am I saying this? Let's see.

My response:
"Okay, thank you. Why did he decide on the ESV?"

Response:
"The ESV is an accurate translation from the original Hebrew and Greek texts. It reads well, too. Pastor's desire is to use a translation that's faithful to the original languages."

Notice the phrase *"original Hebrew and Greek texts"* there? Notice the word *"use"* again? What does he *believe*? Notice the dodging of my questions by a Phd; he's the one telling her what to say. Note the phrases *"Original Greek Text,"* *"Original Tongues,"* *"THE Greek Text,"* *"The Originals"* or anything to make you *think* that they have the "originals," which they don't, *no one does*. Did Timothy when he was a child in 2 Timothy 3:15? Did the Ethiopian have it in Acts 8:30-32? How about the same prophet read by Jesus in Luke 4:17-21? Moses broke the "original" Ten Commandments (Exod. 32:19) and Jeremiah had a roll *burned and rewritten with some new additions* made by The Holy Ghost (Jer. 36:2-4, 17-18, 23, 28-32). Anytime the word **"scripture"** shows up in your Bible, it is never in reference to an *"original"* anything. It's a copy of a copy *faithfully preserved*. Watch the hypocrisy unfold.

My response:
"Again, I appreciate you answering my questions. What does he mean by an "accurate translation of the originals." Would the RSV or NRSV be accurate? Thanks "

Response:

"The NRSV is at an 11th grade reading level. It is a word-for-word translation, but not as literal as the ESV, yet has some formal wording that isn't commonly used in modern English. The NRSV is used in many academic settings. The NRSV is going to use more gender-neutral language. The ESV is second to the New American Standard as being the most literal translation."

He essentially just said nothing at all: the ESV also has *"some formal wording that isn't commonly used in modern English."* Notice the tricks of the trade my friend: neither the ESV or NASV are *"literal"* translations. If you had a "literal" translation you wouldn't be able to make heads from tails in your reading. The proper lingo would be, *"formal correspondence (formal equivalence)."* By using this method you translate words according to a Greek lexicon so that it's *almost* a "word for word" (literal) translation. *No translation solely uses this method.* It also depends on *what* Greek text the "word for word" translation is coming from. In the introduction to the ESV you will read under, "Translation Philosophy" that *"the ESV is an essentially literal translation,"* which "essentially" means... *nothing.* It is no different than the NRSV when you get right down to brass tax.

My response:
"Okay, so back to the "words" and the "Word." If the ESV and the NRSV being gender neutral are different, which one is infallible and inspired?"

There we have it, the knife to the jugular. The asinine thought process of the cloned and re-educated is shaken with a simple question. This poor girl. Are you ready for their response? Here it is....

Response:

"The Word of God is inerrant and infallible. The ESV and NRSV *are translations*. The chapter divisions were added during the translation process. As I said earlier, the Word of God is inspired...*the original texts.*"

Remember this: Let this be a lesson in the logic of this kind of group-think. He said he believed in *"every bit"* of God's Word earlier—*"every* bit." He also said that it was the *"final authority"* for a Christian. How can the NRSV, NASV, or ESV be the final authority when they differ amongst themselves, and differ from the King James in over 5,000 places in the New Testament alone? He said he believes in final authority of the Scriptures, but gave multiple *conflicting* authorities. He then said the *original texts* are inspired and what we have are *reliable "translations."* HE BELIEVES IN THE ORIGINAL TEXTS THAT DON'T EXIST. The ESV, NRSV and EVERYTHING ELSE are just *"translations"* i.e., NOT inspired. You're reading a *dead book* according to this pastor, but it's "reliable," and he reads a dead book every Sunday at the pulpit to his church while SAYING, *"let us turn to the word of God."* The whole time he is *letting you believe* that what he is reading IS THE INSPIRED WORD OF GOD, WHEN HE DOESN'T BELIEVE IT HIMSELF. That is called a Hypocrite and a liar. From the beginning of this e-mail chain he *lead you on* to believe that *he* believed in the inspired Scriptures, which *he has* in his possession. Later you find out that he *doesn't* have them, and that he *doesn't* believe that what he reads to his congregation *are* the inspired words of God; he is reading a *"reliable translation"*—it's the "originals" that are inspired and inerrant. Learn from this. This will be a theme throughout this book. He then digs the ditch.

My response:
"The pastor believes the "original texts" are Infallible and inspired? Could you define as to what you mean by original texts? Do you mean The original autographs or the many

Hebrew and Greek manuscripts we have today that are copies of copies? Thanks"

Response:
"The *original Hebrew and Greek manuscripts*. We have *reliable translations* from the *original manuscripts*."

"*Reliable translations*" is code for *not* inspired, just a book. See these little tricks they pull, because they think you are *stupid* and just want to *save face* and *keep attendance up*. They want to *pretend* to be like you but in reality the belief that God did what He said He would do is *"identified with the arrogant superstition of Bible-belt fundamentalism."*[1] Biggest bunch of Pharisees if I ever saw 'em. After my next response, he's just trying to save face at this point, he gots fount out. I ask him (from the available manuscripts) what he believes would be God's inspired word.

My response:
"Yes, the Hebrew manuscripts (in Hebrew) are very reliable but which Greek manuscripts does the pastor consider infallible, since there are many Greek manuscripts and the majority agree with each other except for a few. Which Greek manuscripts out of the many would he say is Gods preserved word and inspired, without error. Just to make sure I understand the pastor, he believes that translations are not inspired and have errors since they are translations of the Hebrew and Greek. Is that correct? I appreciate your courtesy and kindness."

---

[1] Book review from Brill Journals on Sturz's, *"The Byzantine Text-Type."* Sturz was very cautious to present both sides and explain how he claimed neutrality and objectivity of the *research*. He did, but it is sad that an earned scholar has to be cautious on the subject for appearing as *"one of those types"*—you know—*those* people that actually *believe Scripture. Those people are a* bunch of rednecks who don't know Greek. Note: Some of the greatest Greek professors are some of the *worst* expositors of the Bible. They can't make heads or tails of things that any eight year old had learned in VBS.

Response:
"Pastor's response: In no way do I believe the translations have errors. We have the Word of God! Pastor would be happy to meet with you in-person in you have more questions! If you are interested in that let me know or you can email his assistant *Ms. LovelyGal* at _____.org and we can schedule a time."

You don't believe they have errors? What about Hebrews 3:16 in your ESV? He can't tell you what the "Word of God" is because he's a liar and doesn't what to be found out. He wants to stay in the dark. Before you start accusing me of "semantics" or anything else you may be thinking, just listen to the numerous other examples given in this book. At this point he backtracks, he has *been found out* and his assistant has many questions, I'm sure of it. Keep in mind how Dr. Pufferfish said the *"originals"* were inspired, then claims that the translations are *"reliable"* but not inspired, then claims all translations are error free, but not inspired.

A few days later as I was reading and came to John 14:23, the phone rang by an unknown caller. It was the pastor. He needed to save face, so we talked.

I asked him the same questions as I did in the e-mails and I called him out on the term *"reliable translations."* I asked what that meant. He said that the *"original languages"* were inspired *but* we have *"reliable translations."*

I asked if the *"reliable translations"* have errors in them and *which* Greek text he considered inspired since there are *many* Greek texts (in case he was going to say, "I mean the Greek and Hebrew manuscripts we have *now*," Erasmus, Colinaeus, Stephanus, Beza, Elzevir, Nestle, Hort, Tregelles, Metzger, Merk, Vogles, and there are 28 editions of Nestles for instance, with *changes in each one,* and several editions of Erasmus, etc). The King James is from a *different* Greek text than the ESV so they can't both be right.

He backtracked while ending the conversation with *"I believe all translations are inspired and without error"* while *claiming* in the e-mails that the *"originals"* were, but the English translations are *"reliable."* He lied. The question is, why? Why couldn't he just admit what he believed? The answer to that question is a sad one, but it is exactly what will be shown throughout this book. He believed his teachers over the Book. He knew the two were at odds so he lied. He *professes* to believe that the word of God is the final authority on all matters, but at the end of the day, *he is his own final authority*, just like his teachers, and just like the teachers who taught his teachers. He *uses* the ESV but doesn't *believe* for a second that it's **"scripture."**

He resorted to the party line when faced with his hypocrisy and stupidity. The man in the trenches dug the trench deeper and settled in.

I threw a well known error at him in the *"infallible"* book he uses (ESV). I showed him 2 Samuel 21:19; 1 Chronicles 20:5; and 1 Samuel 17:51 through text-message, since we were off the phone call. There is no way to fix that blasphemous error done by a *"literal"* translation.

He ended the conversation in text *without* an answer and said, *"have a blessed day."* Pius.

What a raging lunatic man. This man has an earned Ph.D. You have to go to school for 6-8 years to have all that common sense *taught out of you*. No one is born that dumb. I mean, what in the world, man. I may sound harsh, but I have no remorse for *wolves* and those who lie to their congregations *weekly*.

"Therefore have I also made you contemptible and base before all the people, according as ye have not kept my ways" (Mal. 2:9).

Back to James White and his book *"The King James Only Controversy,"* I will select at random an "error" of the King James Bible as presented in his book, which is written in order to justify that *all translations have errors* and therefore we do *not* have an inspired, infallible word of God, but the *"Word"* of God, *we do have* (bonkers). Same group of clones, different players.

Page 290 White claims Acts 12:4 to be in error (as every other destructive critic does). He claims the NASB *correctly* translates the Greek word "pascha" or "πάσχα" to "passover" instead of what the King James translates it, which is **"Easter."** If you translated every passage "literally" (which no translation ever does) you would have Saul's *"wing"* cut off in 1 Samuel 24:4, instead of his **"skirt."** The Hebrew word (כָּנָף) "literally" means *"wing."*

This is the *only time* the English word **"Easter"** occurs in a King James. The word **"Easter"** was both used by Luther and Tyndale some 90 or so years before the Authorized Version appeared. Luther actually changes many of the verses with "passover" in them to **"Easter"** throughout his bible. This occurrence is called a *"dynamic equivalence": substituting one word for a similar word or phrase,* such as the Greek word for love (ἀγάπη) being used as **"charity"** many times in a King James.

All translations use these "dynamic equivalences" but when the King James does it, *it's in "error."* Hypocrisy. The use of **"charity"** in 1 Corinthians 13 was an amazing *foresight* on the part of the translators of the King James and The Holy Ghost since "love" means *many things* to different people in our day. Just search *"what love means to people"* on YouTube and you'll understand what I mean. Charity means *one* thing: *giving without expecting anything in return, like Jesus did for you if you accept his FREE GIFT* (Rom. 5:14-18). When in doubt, just read your Bible.

The "error" in Acts 12:4 actually says a lot, all of which White *couldn't see.* If you look at Acts 12:1-2 you see Herod (there are many Herod's), which this one is a half-Roman-Edomite who murdered James the brother of John. Verse 3 states, **"then were the days of unleavened bread"** since we are talking about "Jews" in the verse, Passover is the *Jewish* designation. Now in verse 4 where the famous "mistake" is we read, **"And when he had apprehended him, he put him in prison, and delivered him to four quaternions of soldiers to keep him; intending after Easter to bring him forth to the people."** Herod is planning on killing Peter in the passage. Normally it would be translated as *"after the passover"* but you are already told in verse 3 that *it was* **"the days of unleavened bread"** *which is part of the passover*. Now verse 4 is *the Roman* designation of the Passover, **"Easter"** or *Ishtar, or Eostre*. The Romans had a feast around the same time celebrating the remnants of *Ashtaroth* (Judg. 2:13, 10:6: 1 Sam. 7:3; 1 Kings 11:5; 2 Kings 23:13).

Eostre was the Saxon version of a Germanic goddess called *Ostara*, a spring equinox celebration roughly around the time of Christ's Resurrection. *Ashtaroth* is the queen of heaven (Jer. 44:18), a female deity, worshipped over the course of centuries under different names. The Roman feast which corresponds to the Passover would *probably* be Vinalia. This feast is a wine harvest in celebration of Jupiter (Zeus) and Venus (Aphrodite) held in late April. Today the name of this female deity is *Mary*. Today the Roman holiday "Christ*mas*" is on December 25th, a *Roman* day of worship that corresponds with the Festival of Dies Natalis Solis Invicti celebrating Helios, the sun god. This date was adopted by the Roman Catholic Church[2] for the birth of Christ because the Empire was trying to convert its population. What a better day than one of the biggest festivals of the year and then just slap the name of Jesus on it, right? Beats paying people to get baptized (which they did). Christ's actual birthday is sometime in September (September 23rd+/-).

If you don't like the work of Hislop, or if that sounds too "out-there" for you, there happens to be a side explanation to the insertion of **"Easter"**; *it was intentional*. The translators used the word due to the adoption of early Christians and its

---

[2] Philip Schaff, *"History of the Christian Church. Vol. 3,"* 1910, page 396, see also *Vol. 4*

The Actors 47

celebration; separating it from the Jewish Passover. Early Christians celebrated the Jewish Passover because it was the same time as our Savior's Resurrection. If it was translated to "passover," then the word **"Easter"** would occur no where in your Bible. The **"days of unleavened bread"** means that it was sometime *after* the day Jesus Christ was crucified (after the 14th of Abib/Nisan), which would be closer to the time of his Resurrection, hence **"Easter"** instead of "passover."

On the same page, on footnote 21 White goes on to tell you that the Holy Spirit should not be referred to as an **"it"** as in Romans 8:26, while trying to convince you that it's a double standard that "KJ Only" people have since it's *"denying the Holy Spirit's personality."* The Greek word for **"Spirit"** is a neuter (not feminine or masculine) which White admits but he believes *all* these cases referring to the Holy Spirit should say "Him" or some variant.

Let's see, shall we?

When the Holy Spirit's *work* is referred to, it is usually translated in the King James as **"it,"** as in 1 Peter 1:11 or Romans 8:26. When it is referring to the *personality* of the Holy Ghost, it is then referred to as **"him,"** as in John 14 where the *personality of the Holy Spirit is revealed*. In the Old Testament you are only seeing the Holy Spirt's *work and influence, not as a person* (Gen. 1:2, 6:3: Exod. 31:3, 35:21; Num. 11:29; Isa. 11:2, 61:1, etc). The personality of The Holy Ghost was a *revelation* in the New Testament so **"it"** or **"he"** is suitable and revealing to the reader, but a hinderance to the destructive critic. To be sound in White's logic, he would then need to go back through the entire Hebrew Old Testament and change every case. He won't do it.

In Luke 1:35 *Jesus Himself* is referred to as **"that holy thing."** If you take out the neuter you lose the cross reference to Genesis 3:15, where Christ is called an **"it,"** as the **"seed."** Sounds like White just doesn't understand the difference between the two aspects of The Holy Spirit given in *both* Testaments. He, like many others only *"go to the Greek"* when it is convent for them, and usually as a result, then destroys a God given revelation based on *"preference."*

A great example is found in John 3:8 after Jesus talks about the new birth to Nicodemus. **"The wind bloweth where it listeth, and thou hearest the sound thereof, but canst not tell whence it cometh, and whither it goeth: so is every one that is born of the Spirit."** The Greek word for **"wind"** here is "πνεῦμα" (pneuma), and the word for **"Spirit"** here is "πνεύματος" (pneuma-tos). Both are *neuter*. Jesus is describing the **"Spirit"** as an **"it."** That is *Jesus Christ himself, saying* **"it."**

Jesus Christ calling the **"Spirit"** an **"it"** also occurs in the NASB and NIV, two of White's *favorite* translations. He didn't seem to mention John 3:8 *because he never even saw it*. This man wants to school *you* on what should and should not be in your Bible; what in the world man. He doesn't even know what's in the Book!

Translators of new versions are perfectly fine with making non-neuter words such as masculine words into neuters i.e. "he" and "his" into *"it"* or *"they"* to appeal to more people by being *"gender neutral/friendly."* You can thank the NCCC for that decision to change God's words *in order to fit what culture wants,* which is exactly the opposite of what the bible tells you (1 Cor. 6:14-17). Hypocrites (Matt. 23). You will find in the NIV's *Guidelines for Gender-Neutral Translation*, item "e" reads:

> *"Gender-inclusive language must be made in light of exegetical and linguistic attention to individual texts in their contexts; e.g., the legal and wisdom literature. In narratives, parables, exemplary stories, metaphors and the like, the gender-specific elements are usually not to be*

The Actors

replaced or added to in order to achieve gender balance."[3]

"It was recognized that it was often appropriate to mute the patriarchalism of the culture of the biblical writers through gender-inclusive language when this could be done without compromising the message of the Spirit."[4]

These men such as White, Origen, and Hort all claim to have an inner light that helps them determine what is correct and what isn't in translation. A guiding *intuition* and *judgment* for what should and shouldn't be in the Bible. Don't let them fool you. This sounds oddly close to the guiding of truth by The Holy Spirit that Jesus talks about in John 14-16.

Satan has an equal an opposing counterfeit; he always does. He is called god (2 Cor. 4:4) like Jesus Christ (1Tim. 3:16). He cites scripture (Luke 4:10-11) like Jesus Christ (Luke 4:1-12), he is called an angel (2 Cor. 11:11-14) as Jesus Christ is (Gal. 4:14), has a bride (Rev. 17) as Jesus Christ does (Eph. 5:23-32), called a lion (1 Peter 5:8) as Jesus Christ is (Rev. 5:5), he is called a serpent (Gen. 3:1; Rev. 12:9) as Jesus Christ is (John 3:14), he is anointed (Ezek. 28:14) as Jesus Christ is (Acts 4:26 — Christ means "messiah/anointed"), called a king (Job 41:34) just as Jesus is (Rev. 19:16), etc. Lucifer wants to be **"like the most high"** (Isa. 14:12-14), so he has to *copy* everything God does.

Would the Holy Spirit *deify* Jesus Christ or *subtract from* His deity? (See the chapter *"Oranges & Vitamin C"* and *"Two Bibles."*) If you didn't have a Bible, you wouldn't be able to tell the difference in the world.

---

[3] Preface from *"The Holy Bible: New International Version, Inclusive Language Edition,"* 1996.

[4] Ibid

To give you some insight as to the King James translators and what they thought *about themselves*, the "Epistle Dedicatorie" of the AV states:

> *"We are poore instruments to make GODS holy trueth to be yet more and more knowen unto the people."*

In the "Translators to the Reader":

> *"There were many chosen, that were greater in other mens eyes then in their owne, and that sought the truth rather than their own praise"*

My, my, what modesty by the group of men that changed human history and helped spread literacy throughout the world by their work; not to mention *the greatest revivals in history*. For further contrast read *any* translators introduction to the readers in *any* new version. You will see credential after credential in trying to convince *themselves* and *you* that they were worthy enough to be involved in a translation.

Furthermore, in White's book *(King James Only Controversy, 1995)* there are many articles of *false information*, such as his statements on page 243 about the preservation of God's words. He asks the question, *"where does Psalm 12 say the the 'words of the Lord' refer to the King James Version of the Bible?"* and therefore *misrepresenting* the entire "King James Only" crowd. White doesn't even know the other side of the "debate."

The issue is: did God *preserve* His words, as in *all* of them, as in **"all scripture"** (2 Tim. 3:16), *or* did He not? White sidesteps *the entire question* throughout his *entire* book. He holds to the *"liberal view"* of preservation instead of the *"conservative view,"* which he *claims to be*.[5]

---

[5] James R. White, *"The King James Only Controversy,"* 1995, page VII of the introduction

The *"liberal view"* is the view that the Bible's *canon* (66 books) and *general gist* (message) has been preserved. This view is increasingly being adopted by *conservative* Christians. On pages 6, 118, 119, 55, 56, etc, White routinely *makes fun* of those who *do* uphold the belief that God followed through *on His promise of preservation*. He even implies that people who believe that God would have a Book, containing Scripture, lack *"wisdom"* (page VII). He *fails to realize* that those who believe the King James, believe it because of its *track record, history,* and *400 plus years of having no proven error, and its attitude towards Jesus Christ*. Whether this book bears the title "The King Thomas Bible" or any other name is inconsequential. Even if it happened to be the NIV, which it unequivocally is *not*, there would inevitably emerge a faction known as the "NIV only" group, many would be determined to criticize and ostracize them. The fact of the matter is that the Holy Spirit *did not* bear witness to the NIV through any historical manifestations and there aren't large groups consisting of members in the Body of Christ defending the NIV's contents. It is the contents of the pages in which people believe, and that it has been **"given by inspiration"** (2 Tim. 3:16). The w-o-r-d-s.

White claims that manuscripts 𝔓66, 𝔓75, ℵ, B all carry *"great weight"*[6] due to the *"antiquity"* of these manuscripts instead of their content and influence of the scribe when trying to *justify* the Jehovah Witness reading of John 1:18 where there are *two gods* ("no man hath seen God [*god #1*] at any time: the only begotten God [*god #2*]." The manuscripts mentioned contain "only begotten God." This passage, or a similar rendition touting two gods, can be found in the NIV and NASV, etc. Many modern translations have gone back on their duel-god readings in recent updates.

Can readings be attested for based solely on *antiquity*? The corruption of the N.T. text started at its beginnings as

---

[6] Ibid, page 259

attested by many early writings of the Church Fathers,[7] and by Scrivener (a *"true scholar"*, see pages 54-55), who states:

> *"The worst corruptions to which the New Testament has ever been subjected, originated within one hundred years after it was composed."*[8]

This puts the date of vast corruptions between A.D. 90 and A.D. 190, just as Paul was warning in 2 Corinthians 2:17. Older does *not* mean better. Colwell states:

> *"the nearly 200 nonsense readings and 400 Itastic spellings in ℘66 are evidence of something less than disciplined attention to the basic text."*[9]

Bart Ehrman dedicated an entire thesis[10] to the topic of manuscript corruption, particularly the scribes' tendency to "clarify doctrine" in relation to what is now considered "orthodox." Alongside Walter Bauer, Ehrman highlighted that the establishment of "orthodoxy" occurred primarily as scribes modified manuscripts in the 4th century to align with contemporary "theological reasons," subsequent to the Catholic Council of Nicea in A.D. 325 (see the chapter *"Two Bibles"*). People still do this today in fact: Mormons, Catholics, and Jehovah Witnesses for example.

Ehrman forgets that *there was a church* in the early period that *did* keep the words—the church in Philadelphia (Rev. 3), and that early church Fathers were getting their "orthodox" opinions *from Scripture that they had and read*. Those Scriptures were then corrupted by people *just like* Ehrman,

---

[7] Wilbur N. Pickering, *"The Identity of the New Testament Text, IV,"* 2014, page 111

[8] F. H. A. Scrivener, *"A Plain Introduction to the Criticism of the New Testament, fourth edition, Vol. II,"* 1894, page 264

[9] Ernest Colwell, *"What Is The Best New Testament Text,"* 1969, page 121

[10] Bart D. Ehrman, *"The Orthodox Corruption of Scripture,"* 2011

The Actors

Metzger, Wallace, and White. He also forgets that from A.D. 33-300, Christians were more concerned about not being murdered by Roman dictators than refining doctrine. This places the *"two oldest and best"* manuscripts *after* a period of corruption from the official line and just *after* this period of "refined" orthodoxy set by the Catholic Church via Origen and Jerome. Remind me again how ℵ and B are the two "oldest and best"?

Later on I will get deeper into manuscripts ℵ and B and the *"weight"* that they *really* have. Besides that, like most people who have the same attitude towards the Bible and the same schooling as White (just as his teachers did), he didn't give you *all the evidence*. He just gives you what he wants you to know and *what his teachers* taught him. He left off the testimony of Arius and Athanasius, where Arius' (A.D. 250-336) reading was *rejected as heresy*. Arius believed that Jesus was a *created* being or god and *not* equal with the Father (Arianism) just as Jehovah Witnesses and Mormons do today. White believes *"only begotten God"* should be in your Bible on the basis of the "oldest and best manuscripts" —*"antiquity."*

> *"P66 seems to reflect a scribe working with the intention of making a good copy, falling into careless errors..."*[11]

> *"Superstitious reverence has been claimed for ℵ and B..."*[12]

What is the further evidence? Igantius (A.D. 110) and many other Church Fathers such as Tertullian (around A.D. 212) has **"only begotten Son."** In the later part of the Second

---

[11] Ernest Colwell, *"Method in Evaluating Scribal Habits: A Study of P45, P66, P75," in Studies in Methodology in Textual Criticism of the New Testament, New Testament Tools and Studies 9,"* 1969, page 118

[12] Dean Burgon, *"The Revision Revised,"* 1883, page 319

Century there is Archelaus, in his *Disputation with the Heresiarch Manicheus* which still has **"only begotten Son."** Hippolytus (A.D. 170-235) has **"only begotten Son."** Athanasius writes against Arius and the Arian heresy and always refers to **"only begotten Son."** The ante-Nicene mss which have *"only begotten God"* seem to be from *one* place; *Alexandria*, where Platonism and Gnosticism flourished, thus being incorporated into the New Testament text.[13] Ehrman himself even concedes to the reading of the KJB in John 1:18[14] based on the majority of *evidence*, the *style* of the writer, and *a clear line of representation* through many centuries and geographic locations.

White will use John 1:18 when debating Muslims on the topic of God in the flesh and if Jesus Christ was or was not God in the flesh. You couldn't pick *a more confusing verse for a Muslim*. He appeals to this verse, one with many holes according to how he believes it should be translated, instead of appealing to 1 Timothy 3:16 which *is the definitive verse on the incarnation in the N.T.* Why doesn't White appeal to 1 Timothy 3:16 when debating Muslims? He does admit (reluctantly) that 1 Timothy 3:16 should read **"God"** as the KJB does in his book but then goes on supporting the NASV, NIV, NRSV, and other new translations. Where is his final authority? There is *zero evidence* for the reading "He."

Mr. White also calls Dean Burgon and Scrivener *"true scholars of the first rank."*[15] Now this is a prime example of the split-tongue, two-faced, side-winding, slithering mind of someone with White's mental caliber. After trying to convince you that the Jehovah Witness reading in John 1:18 is *totally fine* and acceptable, that you should *replace* your King James reading *for his preference*, that the very manuscripts he recommends to use for evidence are the very

---

[13] Jay P. Green, "The Gnostics, the New Versions, and the Deity of Christ," 1994, page vi

[14] Ehrman, "The Orthodox Corruption of Scripture," pages 92-93

[15] James R. White, "King James Only Controversy," 1995, page 91

pieces of *trash* the *"true scholars"* Burgon and Scrivener *dismissed* as *corruptions* back in the late 1800's.

How does one man call another man a *"true scholar"* while *disagreeing with the very nature of the scholars work*? You could call them "hard working," but a "true scholar?" I wouldn't call White a "true scholar." That is layin' it on a-bit thick don't ya think? James White does *not* believe in the scholarly work of Burgon any more than he believes he has the preserved words of God called Scripture. He just wants you to think he is *"spiritual"* by calling his opponents *"true scholars."* Are they *"true"* Mr. White?

Here are a few things that Burgon had to say on the matter, from a *"true scholar"*:

- "Without a particle of hesitation ℵ, B, and D are the most scandalously corrupt copies extant"[16]
- "Lastly, we suspect that these two manuscripts (ℵ and B) are indebted to their preservation, *solely to their ascertained evil character*; which has occasioned that the one eventually found its way, four centuries ago, to *a forgotten shelf in the Vatican library*: while the other, after exercising the ingenuity of several generations of critical Correctors [10+ according to Scrivener who collated it], eventually got *deposited in a waste-paper basket* of the Convent at the foot of Mt. Sinai."[17]
- "That they exhibit fabricated texts is *demonstrable*."[18]
- Also see over *900 pages* on the subject in *"The Revision Revised," "The last Twelve Verses of Mark," "Traditional Text,"* and *"Causes of Corruption"* by Burgon.

To really hit it home, see numerous other works by Pickering, Hills, Fuller, Sturz, Ellicott, Wilkinson, and doctors of the Trinitarian Society. The contents of Burgon's books are still widely *undisputed* to this day (2023). The

---

[16] Dean Burgon, *"The Revision Revised,"* 1883, page 16

[17] Ibid, page 319

[18] Ibid, page 318

evidence I will discuss in the chapter called *"Two Bibles"* (in true Wilkinson form) is *entirely ignored* by the modern scholar. Christian academia seems to have created an echo-chamber where obvious and significant facts are overlooked. One is either inside this chamber or outside of it, almost as if it were a form of cognitive impairment—a mental derangement.

White continues further on, arguing that belief in God's promise is *based on a "theological argument."*[19] This is the *same* shade that was thrown on Dean Burgon by Metzger.[20] Somehow, Burgon is a *"true scholar."* This is *the* argument presented by all those who cherish manuscripts א, B, 𝔓66, 𝔓75, C, D, A, and other *Alexandrian* type manuscripts. Why is it *the* argument? *Why bash an opponent for believing in the Scriptures and believing what they say, and giving an enormous amount of evidence to back up his claim?*

Theology doesn't seem to be worthy of consideration for White or Metzger when revising bibles or consulting for those that do. Mind you that *"theology"* is the *study of God*.

Heretical readings in manuscript א alone are: John 1:19, 34, 3:13, 35, 6:69, 9:38-39; and Mark 1:1. These readings either *deny* or *subtract* from the deity of Jesus Christ *(see pages 328)*. Seems that one would need to *"study God"* in order to have a good nose for the matter.

White is simply arguing the way his teachers and the majority of Greek professors do; *"the oldest are the best."* Meanwhile, they aren't even giving you the "oldest" manuscripts and in this case, *disregard* Church Father quotations when it suits them. This is hardly *scholarship* but rather *subjective nonsense based on a false pretense*. If the foundation in which the house it built upon is faulty, it's just a matter of time before it topples *down*. You can objectively

---

[19] *"King James Only Controversy,"* page 258

[20] Bruce M. Metzger, *"The Text of The New Testament: It's Transmission, Corruption, and Restoration,"* 2005, page 181

see that, in the past 100 years with the adoption of Textus Receptus readings back into Nestles Greek text after some odd 80 years, someone spotted a rotten foundation. They could have just listened to a *"true scholar"* or someone *"arguing from a theological stance"* who said all of this over 100 years ago. It only took them 80 years to do it, but even now the leaven is still there.

We just dealt with a few of the issues in his book, it is 271 pages long and full of *false assumptions, bad evidence, accusations, a false sense of what being "spiritual" means, a practically boastful type of religiosity towards Sinaiticus ℵ and Vaticanus B, twists, turns, and slithering logic* that only someone who was re-educated at *"the best of seminaries"* could come up with.

This group thinks that if you just *talk nice* (Rom. 16:18) and *sound smart* (Rom. 16:18) *that people will believe you*, and many do. Many also fell for the communist musings of Soviet Russia. Many also fell for the Nazi party. Many also fall for Mormonism, Catholicism, et al. It is actually impressive how he has become the very type of person he writes *against* in his own book. If someone really wants the truth, they'll take it any way it comes.

Here is a summary:
- Not based on evidence
- A *religious* argument (instead of theological)
- A cult-like approach to evidence
- Hypocritical/Conspiratorial
- Poor scholarship, leaving out facts and evidence so the reader can't accurately judge for themselves
- One sided
- Superstitious favor of "ancient authorities" (see the following pages)
- Not able to think for himself (re-educated)
- Word of God = whatever scholarship says (tradition of man instead of the Bible)

What did White *accomplish* with his work? His entire work is telling you that the "Word of God" is the *majority of agreed upon readings in manuscripts* and that it could not be a King James or actually *any* version of a bible. It's the *majority* of readings that agree...unless it's John 7:53-8:11; Mark 16:9-20; 1 John 5:7-8; John 1:18; Philippians 1:14; Colossians 2:9, 11; 1 Timothy 3:16, 6:10; 2 Timothy 2:15; 2 Corinthians 2:17; Matthew 1:22, 6:13, 5:22, etc. Many are only supported by 1-5% of Greek manuscript evidence and have the support from the Jesuit Douay Rheims bible. Is it majority or minority?—He can't decide. In *those* cases he bases his *opinion* on the *"weight"* of the evidence, meaning that his *preferred* reading has the support from a few shady manuscripts touted as supreme by those he looks up to (א, A, B, C, D, 𝔓66, 𝔓75, 𝔓45).

You are *not* to believe that God has *any* book, *anywhere* in its entirety that has also been *preserved* in its entirety.

That statement above isn't possible according to White. Now contrast that with someone telling you *there is a Book*, it is complete, it has been preserved (100% of it), and we don't have to debate over the other some-odd 5-30% of verses that scholars have been debating on adding/subtracting *new* words to and subtracting/adding to an old Book since before 1881.

Trying to convince you to rid your Bible of **"Jesus"** in Matthew 8:29, **"firstborn"** in Matthew 1:25, **"Study"** in 2 Timothy 2:15, change **"corrupt"** to "peddle" in 2 Corinthians 2:17 to cover up for the corruption of the text, remove **"take up the cross"** in Mark 10:21, remove entire verses such as Matthew 17:21, 18:11, 23:14; Mark 7:16, etc. John 7:53-8:11 should be removed from everyones Bible, **"blood"** should be removed from Colossians 1:14, **"God"** knocked out of 1 Timothy 3:16, **"every word of God"** removed in Luke 4:4, the **"Red Sea"** should be the "Sea of Reeds" since Israel did not actually pass through the Red Sea, **"Son of God"**

The Actors

removed from Daniel 3:25, change **"them"** to "us" in Psalm 12:7 to *rid the Bible of a pungent verse on the preservation of Scripture,* and take **"Lord"** out of a dying mans mouth who is about to get saved in Luke 23:42. *This is modern Christian Scholarship.* These are *"the actors."* Lucifer will be handing out the Oscars this year to *"good, godly, dedicated men, who hold to the fundamentals of the faith."*

"The actors" are also the ones that get up on a stage and preach while holding a bible in hand and saying, *"This is the word of God"* when they don't believe it for a minute. They are the ones that will pass out an offering plate after saying, *"Turn in the Scriptures today to…"* and *"now, God said…."* They don't believe it. They believe that the words of God are still yet to be found, *but what we do know are the fundamentals and the message*: the Virgin Birth, the Trinity, Jesus was the Son of God, the death and Resurrection of Jesus Christ, etc. Catholics believe the same fundamentals of the faith. According to them, this is all that was said in a 1,200 page book with 1,189 chapters, 31,102 verses, 783,137 words, and 3,116,480 letters. *"The message."*

Another actor I must mention is Daniel Wallace of Dallas Theological Seminary. He believes[21] that the *"majority text argument"* isn't even biblical. The majority text argument consists of choosing verses in which the majority of manuscripts agree upon. Most of the time they are King James readings but not always. Something White says he agrees with, but then often chooses *minority* readings based on the *"weight"* of evidence. Who's weight? The Majority Text is usually from the Byzantine text family/tradition. In his "opinion" the majority text isn't biblical due to God using the *minority* instead of the *majority* (a.k.a. the remnant).

Before I dive into the typical asinine thinking of a mentally unstable individual, let's see what he means. God saved

---

[21] Daniel Wallace, bible.org *"Inspiration, Preservation, and New Testament Textural Criticism,"* June 26th, 2004

Noah and his family over the world at large for example (Genesis 7:7, also see Isaiah 10:21; 1 Kings 19:18; Isaiah 1:9) and God will save the remnant of Israel, Israel itself is a small group compared to the rest of the world i.e. God always chooses the minority. Get it? Sounds good doesn't it? I'll get back to this in a minute.

Wallace also misrepresents Jasper James Ray by a statement Ray made on "being saved" *only* from a KJB. Here is the direct quote from Ray, *"If the Word is corrupt, then the resulting faith which comes from it will also be corrupt and without life giving essentials."*[22]

It's absurd to think Ray was saying that a person can *only* be *saved* by reading a KJB. What Ray is doing is likening a bible to the human circulatory system. If there is *poison* (modern updated bible versions) in *the blood* then *it will affect the entire organism on some level or another*. Which it *has!* Aside from that, it has been well known that reading practically anything will cause changes in a persons brain[23] and thus behavior.[24] This has been well known in the *marketing* scene for many-a-day, as well as the concentration camps in Nazi Germany, the Gulag's, and reeducation centers in China that are active today. Further, Burgon said something similar as to what Ray said over 50 years *before* him when talking about Hort's Greek text; *"It is, however, the systematic depravation of the underlying Greek which does so grievously offend me: for this is nothing else but a poisoning of the River of Life at its sacred source."*[25] Guess that means anyone who doesn't read the

---

[22] Jasper James Ray, *"God Wrote Only One Bible,"* 1976, page 10

[23] Human Brain Mapping, Issue 36 Volume 5, *"Reading in the brain of children and adults: A meta-analysis of 40 functional magnetic resonance imaging studies,"* 2015

[24] Djikic, M., & Oatley, K., *"The art in fiction: From indirect communication to changes of the self,"* Psychology Of Aesthetics, 2014

[25] Dean Burgon, *"Revision Revised,"* pages vi-vii

Greek Textus Receptus is damned to hell—only someone like Wallace would come to that conclusion.

Wallace goes further on and says, *"there is not one solid shred of evidence to show that the Byzantine text even existed in the first three centuries of the Christian era,"* well I've given you several "shreds" already, I'll give more here and more later. This guy is *off his rocker, and he is a Greek professor*. The Byzantine readings go back to the Second Century AD, two hundred years *before* the Alexandrian family (א and B) and Wallace knows this; he's just playing word-games. Byzantine readings can be found *within Alexandrian texts-types*,[26] such as:

𝔓45 (A.D. 250)

𝔓46 (A.D. 175-225)

𝔓66 (A.D. 200)

𝔓75 (A.D. 175-225)[27]

One of the oldest known manuscripts that exists today, dated around A.D. 200[28] *contains Byzantine type readings* such as what is found in John 1:32; 3:24; 4:14, 51; 5:8; 6:10, 57; 7:3, 39; 8:41, 51, 55; 9:23; 10:38; 12:36; 14:17.[29] In other words, it

---

[26] Harry A. Sturz, *"The Byzantine Text-Type & New Testament Textual Criticism,"* 2022, page 55-61

[27] Author's Note: Martin and Kasser give it this date. Orsini dates it late third to early fourth century, and Nongbri dates it fourth century.

[28] Author's Note: There are three conflicting date ranges for 𝔓66, one by Martin A.D. 200 and one by Hunger A.D. 100-150, another by Nongbri at A.D. 300-350.

[29] Bruce M. Metzger, *"Chapters in the History of New Testament Textual Criticism,"* 1963, page 38. Author's Note: The reader may have noticed that Metzger agrees with Sturz but Metzger outright denied and threw the work of Sturz in the garbage can on page 221-222 of *"The Text of The New Testament"* by Metzger and Ehrman. Metzger tries to dismiss Sturz on the grounds that 𝔓66, 𝔓45, etc, are not of a "Byzantine text-type." He is throwing the baby out with the bathwater. Christian academia at its best. Metzger could ruin a persons career with a stroke of his pen, and he knows it. Metzger also accepts the idea of "text-type" readings being found within other families i.e. the Gothic versions being primarily Byzantine while having some Western type readings within them (see *"Chapters in The History of New Testament Textual Criticism,"* page 28). So, why the shade on Sturz? There is a hatred for the Book, see *"The Text of the New Testament,"* 2005, pages 142-145 and note the tone.

contains *King James readings*. This old manuscript is 𝔓66, which also contains *corruptions and deviations*. The Manuscript in all contains John 1:1–6:11, 6:35–14:26, 29–30, 15:2–26, 16:2–4, 6–7, 16:10–20:20, 22–23, 20:25–21:9, 12, 17. (These text-types such as Alexandrian and Byzantine, their character, what is a family or "text-type," and other manuscripts will be discussed more in detail in the chapter titled, *"Two Bibles."*)

Now, to get back to his claim on majority readings. This logic is somewhat faulty. He doesn't apply this idea of "the remnant" and minority/majority readings (see above) to *himself* and *within the realm of scholarship*. The vast "majority" of those who have gone to Liberty, Princeton, Dallas, and every other major seminary in the country (U.S.) agree that Alexandrian manuscripts should be given *precedence*, but a *"small but vocal group"*[30] holds to *other views*. Could this be *"the remnant"* inside the scholarly community? It was a good shot, but like White, Wallace *fails to use logic and facts*. Not only can he not see himself in his statement but *he is calling the Body of Christ, which is in the minority, wrong for believing and accepting the KJB as Scripture for the past 400 years.*

There are roughly 2.4 billion Christians in the world out of a total of 7.8 billion humans on earth. That is a *minority* in and of itself.

Out of those 2.4 billion *self-proclaimed* (this number includes Mormons, Seventh Day Adventists, Jehovah Witnesses, etc.) "Christians," about half (1.3 billion) are Catholic which believe that the Roman Catholic Church is the interpreter of Scripture. Out of that remaining 1.1 billion of *self-proclaimed* "Christians," do you know how *few* people actually believe that God preserved His words *in one Book* for the English speaking people? It isn't a lot. Who's in the majority/minority now? The Body of Christ *has always been*

---

[30] Bruce M. Metzger, Bart D. Ehrman, *"The Text of The New Testament: Its Transmission, Corruption, and Restoration,"* 2005, page 218.

in the minority and Wallace just said that whatever the Body accepts *is wrong*. Ponder that for a few months.

Wallace thinks *"A theological a priori has no place in textual criticism."* What pride, man. Look at that blowing fart. Well, he's in the wrong business because those who are reading the Book he is critiquing would beg to differ. That is the same attitude by Metzger (a practical atheist), Ehrman (who is a proclaiming atheist) who both called Burgon's work a *"theological argument,"* and likewise many proponents of modern textural criticism, which have had since 1611 to create a "perfect bible" and have not succeeded as yet. Something must be wrong with their "theories." Oh, for Hort sake, no! No! It can't be!

What Wallace meant by *"a theological a priori"* was that, if a person *does* believe in Scripture as a Book one can hold and read, then that person reached that conclusion via an already held superstition that there would actually be such a Book out there. In other words, the person believes it because he is a close-minded bigot that somehow got this idea that God would actually have a Book and it just so happened to be a King James just because someone told him that it was. Now, where might a person get the idea that there would be a Book of Scriptures? Oh my, I wonder where that idea might have come from (see pages 449-456)!?!?

I have come across many people who came to the view of Scripture in such a way, which Wallace views as false, by examination, experience, study, and discovery. It was shown to those people by the means of The Holy Spirit and by means of what Scripture said about *itself*—not what some dumb-thump taught them—and/or by means of examining *evidence*. It bears witness to itself for it testifies Christ (John 16:14) more than the NIV, NET, NASV, NASB, NRSV, ESV, etc.

Wallace would rather convince you that such a view is false *without* showing you that "textual criticism" as it exists today is *conjectural* and by no means "theological," nor is it "scientific" as he so claims (see pages 278-81). He wants you to think that he sets aside all of his biases and preconceived notions about the text in order to work on the text from a "neutral" stance.

The King James has been accepted by the Body of Christ for over 400 years and is one collective Organism or Body (1 Cor. 12:13). To this day, the King James Bible is the number *one* selling book *of all time*. As a whole, this Body has chosen this Book *over all others*. This Organism is *still* in the *minority* of the world and the believers of the King James are in the *minority* of academia. It would only make logical sense that the living Organism would all agree *providentially* on certain things since the guiding force of the collective itself *is Jesus Christ.*

In Wallace's twisted mind he believes that the agreements made by the Body are *non-biblical.* The *priests* of the O.T. were the Levites who took care of the Scriptures and guarded them and the *priests* of the N.T. are the *individuals that make up the Body of Christ* (1 Peter 2:5, 9; 1 Cor. 12:13). There is no special Levitical class of priests in the N.T., instead it's made up of believing Christians. All of the agreements made by such groups, in Wallace's case, would be nonsensical and non-biblical.

Are the Hebrew Scriptures of the O.T. also wrong because they have majority readings? I beg your pardon! Some of these Christian's may not *know Greek or Hebrew*, but they *believe* that Book is what God *said* down to the letter, and modern scholars have been *trying* to "re-educate" them on the matter by telling them that it's *not* what God said (Gen 3:1). "Let us highly educated intellectuals tell you what should and should not be in your bible." In other words, you're a *dumb redneck if you believe in the Scriptures how the Scriptures say to believe in them.* If they met the Apostle John on the street, they would probably think he was just a dumb fisherman for believing what he believed and correct him on his grammar.

The Actors

If they actually had the "original autographs" they would "polish" them up in just the same way as they did the ESV.

Ever since the Monarch showed up in a black-backed suit there has been the likes of Theophilus Lindsey (A.D. 1723-1820), Joseph Priestly (1733-1804), William Hazlitt (1737-1820), and Hosea Ballou (1771-1852) who taught hell *wasn't eternal, everyone gets saved,* and Jesus Christ was more of a *legend* than anything else. There is De Bette (1780-1849) who thought all 12 Apostles were *liars*[31] and *made up* Jesus' Death, Burial, and Resurrection. You can't forget Semler (1725-1791), Eichhorn (1752-1826), and Paulus (1761-1851) who taught that the 12 Apostles were having *hallucinations.* This is just a tiny fraction of the "highly esteemed scholars" who invaded Christian college campuses around the world.

Do you have any idea what sort of mental-break these men had to achieve in order to teach what they did about the Bible? They would have to deny almost everything in it and then profess to believe in it. That sort of life creates a two faced, fork tongued liar. That is the same type of person you are dealing with when Metzger and White have to view ℵ and B manuscripts as the "best" and the "closest to the original." The mind just splits. It can't reconcile it. You are being taught one thing while common sense and the Bible teaches you another. They favored **"the tradition of men."** When they sought the help of God, they never saw:

"I the LORD will answer him that cometh according to the multitude of his idols" (Ezek. 14:4)

There are still those within the Body who read another book and this *does not* exclude them from being in the Body by any means whatsoever. Over time more and more Christian's will leave behind the belief of preservation and pick up *any* book touted as the *"newest"* and *"most clear"* rendering of *"The Greek text."* This is part of the **"falling away"** (2 Thess. 2:3) that is to come.

---

[31] H. S. Miller, *"General Biblical Introduction From God to Us,"* 1937, pages 74-76

In Genesis 3, the *first thing* Lucifer did *before the fall of man* was question what God *said.* According to Revelation the church of Philadelphia "**kept my word**" (Rev. 3:7-8), but the church that followed them could not make a stand for anything, they were "**neither cold nor hot**." See how God reacted to that in Revelation 3:15-16. Isn't it interesting how Philadelphia was written in sequence right *before* Laodicea in Revelation? The Lord has a funny way about things. Philadelphia also had **"not denied"** (Rev. 3:8) God's name, **"for thou hast magnified thy word above all thy name"** (Psa. 138:2). To deny God's word *is to deny his name.* The passage said **"above all thy name"** including the name in this passage:

"Wherefore God also hath highly exalted him, and given him a name which is above every name: That at the name of Jesus every knee should bow" (Phil. 2:9-10). Think about that for 2 years.

To further on in our exploration of *"the actors,"* next is an exchange between Fuller Theological Seminary and myself. Just as the e-mail chain you read towards the beginning of this chapter, nothing has been altered and is presented "as is."

"Thanks for reaching out to us. You might want to check here to see our Statement of Faith. We believe Scripture is an essential part and trustworthy record of this divine self-disclosure. All the books of the Old and New Testaments, given by divine inspiration, are the written word of God, the only infallible rule of faith and practice. They are to be interpreted according to their context and purpose and in reverent obedience to the Lord who speaks through them in living power.

We hope this helps, and let us know if you have any other questions."

This is the standard mess you get into, it means nothing really at all. It is no different than a politician taking the oath of office saying *"I do solemnly swear...,"* it means nothing. The question asked to Fuller was, *"what is the final authority at Fuller and its bible department?"* and *"what would you consider inspired and called scripture?"* Notice how they *did not answer either question*. Instead, saying that the O.T. and N.T. are given by inspiration and are to be *"interpreted according to their context and purpose and in reverent obedience to the Lord who speaks through them."* Nothing about a final authority and *no* Scripture citations given for their belief. Also note that the "infallibility" has changed from Scripture to the "rule of faith."

The question was presented again, *"What does fuller consider the inerrant and inspired scriptures to which they rely on for a final authority?"*

Response:
"We apologize as we are struggling to comprehend your question. We would like to direct you to our 'what we believe and teach' page as we have an excerpt titles 'THE LANGUAGE OF "INERRANCY" AND ITS DANGERS':

We recognize the importance that the word 'inerrancy' has attained in the thinking of many of our scholarly colleagues and the institutions which they serve. We appreciate the way in which most of them use the term to underscore the fact that Scripture is indeed God's trustworthy Word in all it affirms [but you don't have the 'Scripture', do you?]. *Where inerrancy refers to what the Holy Spirit is saying to the churches through the biblical writers* [ah, the redefining of the term 'inerrancy'], *we support its use* [that makes the local 'church' the final authority, just like Rome. They don't mean the Body, notice the plural on 'churches'. That is the exact position of all Roman Catholic priests, Bishops, and Popes]. *Where the focus switches to an undue emphasis on matters like chronological details, precise sequence of events, and numerical allusions, we would consider the term misleading and inappropriate* [so, in other words, the entire Bible]."

What you have there is Fuller (this is where White graduated) *admitting to errors in bibles* and *redefining positions.* They also *avoid* the questions, for a second time. They agree to the idea of the Book being a "general gist" of a story but *in no way literal or historical* when it comes to *"events," "sequence of events,"* and *"details"* about those events. Well, they just denied practically the entire Bible. Oh wait, no it's okay since they are guided by the Holy Ghost and what He's saying to *churches,* because the entire Bible was written for the sole purpose of speaking to churches—lunatics. *How do you know what He is saying if you don't believe in the "details" and "events" in the Book?* You rely on the "churches" as a second authority instead of the Book.

There is more than one spirit (1 John 4:1-3; John 4:24) and one of them is coming from an enemy who has been trying to undermine the Godhead since *day one.* What is a better way to do that than by *redefining* the term "inerrancy" and taking the authority *away* from the Book and *giving it to the local churches.* Who decides in the local churches? Who will be the third party to slip in and determine *the meaning of the text* given to the churches?

Enter Fuller seminary: their school will be able to tell you what is and what isn't instead of the Book itself. They answer *the same way a politician* would when presented with social issues on a stage.

Here is what Fuller believes on their *"what we believe and teach"* page concerning Scripture:

> *"At times, some Christians have become unduly attached* [!] *to the precise wordings of doctrine– whether of events in the last days, the meaning of baptism, or the use of a catch phrase* [!] *like 'the inerrancy of Scripture.' But it is well to remember that all our formulations of Christian truth* [!] *must ultimately conform not to some*

preset statement [like the present statement you are making now] *but to the Scriptures* [what Scripture, you don't have a page of it], *all parts of which are divinely inspired* [all parts of what?]. *Thus, sloganeering* [!] *can never be a substitute for the careful, patient analysis of what God's Word teaches, including what it teaches about itself."*

They have reduced the *doctrine* of Inspiration given in the *Scriptures* by the Holy Spirit down to a *"catchphrase"* and *"sloganeering!"*

Now, to just lightly touch on the complete insanity of what you just read, note the last sentence in the quote. They obviously don't read *any* version of the bible in *any* language because it teaches, by *"sloganeering,"* exactly what they are opposed to. I suppose one would need to take *"careful, patient analysis of what"* the Book teaches. (See the *"Conclusion"* to this work.)

Oh, how dangerous! Yeah, the Bible *is* a dangerous book—it's banned in about 50 counties including Somalia, Iran, and Libya. Fuller, like most institutions *claim* to be *"evangelical and conservative"* when it comes to Scripture, but in fact they have *the same position as the Catholic Church* in that their final authority is *scholarship* and *tradition*. They are no more conservative than White or Metzger.

They will ask you to have a *"patient analysis of what God's Word teaches"* without actually telling you what that actually is. The *"doctrines"* they mention in the passage *come from a Book*. By not telling you what that Book is or even what Scripture is, they have created an *out* for themselves. They want to be in bed with the *liberal view* of Scripture just as much as the *conservative view*, that way they can keep the attendance up ($$$) and a constant flow of students. Hence, they don't take a *stand* and have the loss of funds by means of *offending* anyone; they can change with the tide if need be to keep their *institution alive*.

"But let him ask in faith, nothing wavering. For he that wavereth is like a wave of the sea driven with the wind and tossed" (James 1:6).

The next e-mail chain is an interaction with Liberty University and their Divinity Department:[32]

"We believe the Bible is the word of God, and the Holy Scriptures consist of 66 books (39 in the OT and 27 in the NT). We believe that God has clearly spoken through His word, and His word is the final authority which should govern our lives."

They were asked the question, *"what the word of God was"* in response to their e-mail above, and to this they replied:

"The word of God is the Bible, the Old Testament and the New Testament. Obviously we believe the Bible teaches that Jesus is the incarnate Word."

Ah, there it is; *"the incarnate Word."* The Neo-orthodox, liberal view of Scripture. What *is* that *"final authority"* Liberty's Divinity department mentioned in their first e-mail? The *"final authority which should govern our lives"* was it?

What if one version "governs" differently than another version? There is a difference in how a Christian should *behave* in 1 Timothy 6:5-6 in most new bibles compared with a King James. There are also doctrinal passages concerning the the Virgin Birth, the Deity of Christ, and entire verses omitted. It is a valid question then to ask those at an

---

[32] divinity@liberty.edu

institution who teach "the Bible" what exactly they view Scripture to be.

The response is typical from those who have *nowhere to stand* and *no final authority to "govern"*:

> *"We believe that all of the Bible's words are authoritative as it is all the word of God. Even in places where the Bible seems to contradict itself, a careful reading of the entirety of Scripture helps to clear up any confusion.*
> *Do you have any specific examples?"*

Are you noticing a pious sort of attitude coming from the professors to those asking valid questions? How about, *"a careful reading of the entirety of Scripture..."* Man, you haven't stated what Scripture is and where I could get a copy yet.[33] If all 66 books are considered Scripture then I could just use The Living Bible or The Message version or Good News; they are all "bibles" according to the standards of Liberty University. You will also note the same attitude marked by the statements from Fuller: *"careful, patient analysis of what God's Word teaches."* This is the standard put-down by those who believe they are smarter than you by having knowledge in Greek and Hebrew, as if having knowledge of a dead language (biblical Greek) makes one smarter in matters of what is in the Bible. It is a plus, but if you take the words for what they are, there isn't anything a Greek "scholar" can find in the New Testament that a Born again Child of God can't find in an AV.

My response to Liberty concerning "specific examples" was:

---

[33] Write any seminary yourself and see. For a series of letters written to seminaries around the nation asking similar questions, see Peter S. Ruckman's *"Errors in the King James Bible,"* the Appendices. You'll find some-odd 20 letters written on official correspondence stationary to schools and their responses.

"Yes, Aleph and B disagree many times and neither contains Mark 16:9-20; John 7:53-8:11, one has the spear going into Jesus' side before he dies in John 19:34; Matt 27 amongst other incidents. They also contain apocryphal books which are part of the manuscripts. These two mss have great weight in textual criticism yet they are refused in translation for the mentioned passages above and others not mentioned [they don't translate the Apocryphal books even though they are part of the manuscripts ℵ and B cherished by modern scholarship].

Nestles 28th edition:
Matt 17:21, 18:11, 23:14; Mark 7:16, 9:44, 46, 11:26; Mark 15:28 and so on …vs the Textus Receptus for example.

As far as bibles, verses which seem to indicate differences of a wide variety would be:
John 1:18 ESV, NASB, NWT
1 Tim 2:15 ESV, NIV, NKJB et al
Heb 3:16 NIV ESV et al
2 Sam 21:19 ESV
1 Tim 6:5 ESV, NIV, NKJB
Col 1:14 ESV
And so on …Would you call the Jesuit Rheims bible scripture for instance? "

There was *no response* back from Liberty University. The Jesuit Rheims bible contains the Apocrypha, hence it has *more* than 66 books. If The Divinity department denies the Jesuit bible based on, simply, that it contains the Apocrypha, then it shows they do *not really* care about the *words* in the Jesuit Rheims version or *any* version for that matter (see appendix C).

You see, it is all just shuckin' and jivin' from *"the actors"* until they are finally faced with *facts* and are faced with their own *hypocrisy*. They do *not* have the Scriptures anymore than the Road Runner will get killed by Coyote in the next

The Actors

episode on the Saturday morning cartoon program. They will direct you towards *anything with 66 books* in it that has *"Holy Bible"* written on the cover and profess to believe that it's Scripture when they don't believe it themselves. The head of the Divinity department *knows very well* that *words and entire verses are different in a wide range of "bibles" and the differences in Greek manuscripts.* If he doesn't, then what is he doing as the head of a Divinity department?

His silence speaks volumes. Was Israel silent when they heard fellow tribes building an alter when God *said* not to (Deut. 12:14)? **"And when the children of Israel heard of it, the whole congregation of the children of Israel gathered themselves together at Shiloh, to go up to war against them"** (Josh. 22:12). God said it and it was written in a **"book"** (Exod. 17:14; Deut. 17:18) that you can now *read*.

You will also note that he said *"Obviously we believe the Bible teaches that Jesus is the incarnate Word."* This is the apostate position adopted by almost all fundamentalist, conservative, *and* liberal scholars today. It is the Neo-orthodox position. They say Jesus Christ is the incarnate *"Word"* because Jesus is inerrant, but what they are doing is *calling a book Jesus Christ.* I don't think you can highlight and write on Jesus Christ, and I don't see anyone praying *to* the Book. This is a very *sly* way of getting around the issue and not standing for anything except an ether-like statement.[34] This is the position that most are moving towards instead of the previously widely held position stating, *"we believe in the plenary inspired original autographs."* It's their pivot and it's their compromise.

The fact of the matter is they do not believe *any book on this earth* is God's preserved word. They tell themselves that Jesus Christ will *guide them* in *any* version of a bible, so it all comes down to *preference*. Do you *prefer* the Catholic NRSV or the atrocity that was "The Living Bible"? It doesn't matter,

---

[34] See footnote 1 in the *"Introduction"*

because the *"Word"* will speak to you through it no matter what you are reading. Well in that case, just pick up Harry Potter and read that.

What becomes evidently clear in this scenario is the tendency for scholarship and human opinions to supplant the ultimate authority of Scripture. By sidelining the Book itself, interpretation becomes reliant on the erudite scholars who endeavor to unravel the *"true meaning of the text"* and present you with supposedly clearer versions that seem to undergo frequent revisions every few months. A man of intelligence is always tempted to change what the text says. **"Professing themselves to be wise, they became fools"** (Rom. 1:22).

Next up is Dallas Theological Seminary with *no* response to the question whatsoever. They are *scared* to answer because maybe, someone has asked them before? No, that's silly. They didn't answer because they *don't stand for anything* even though they *profess* to. It would take a few seconds to answer the question.

I'll answer it below.

"What is the word of God?"

Answer: I believe the King James Bible is the word of God for the English speaking people and has been given by inspiration from God (2 Tim. 3:16). It's His Book and it has a track record, and long history without proven error for 400+ years. It is the most widely believed Bible in the world decided on by the Body of Christ, as a priestly class (1 Peter 2:5, 9). The *words* have been faithfully *preserved* throughout history, thus God has given us what He intended for us to have (Psa. 12:6-7; Jer. 36:17-18, 23, 28, 32; Prov. 30:5-6, and so on).

For those who may be bigoted and pretentious enough to say, *"why would God just pick one language to preserve His word?...what makes English so special?"*

My response is simple:

God chose *one* nation, Israel to be his chosen people *out of all nations of the earth* (Deut. 7:6). They spoke *Hebrew*. Before the New Testament, if you wanted to read the Scriptures, you had to read them in *Hebrew*; less than ~2% of the world spoke *Hebrew* (today it's less than 0.2%). Why would God choose English? It is the most *widely spoken language in the world* and suits the needs of the Gospel being spread throughout.

Now, I do not wish to be misrepresented here. *Let me make it clear that I believe the King James we have today*, is Scripture for the English speaking people, but I *cannot* speak for the French or the Hindi as pertaining to their own languages and translations. Hebrew was a *unique* language for a *peculiar* people (Deut. 14:2). After A.D. 33, Greek was the most commonly spoken language. This coincided with the spreading of the Gospel from Asia Minor. Today that language is English, a globally spoken language, making the Gospel accessible through the world at large, and the *words*.

The doctrinal statement of Dallas seminary is stated below as found on their website:

> *"We believe that 'all Scripture is given by inspiration of God,' by which we understand the whole Bible is inspired in the sense that holy men of God 'were moved by the Holy Spirit' to write the very words of Scripture* [which you do not have]. *We believe that this divine inspiration extends equally and fully to all parts of the writings—historical, poetical, doctrinal, and prophetical—as appeared in the original manuscripts* [there it is, the Scriptures, as in the ghost from Christmas past; the illusive Santa Clause]. *We believe that the whole Bible in*

the originals is therefore without error [note this well]."

How do you know *"the originals"* were without error? Talk about a *"theological a priori!"*—Have you seen them? Have you held them? What a stance to take given that *no reference to Scripture in the Bible is ever in connection with an original anything* (see *"Introduction"*). Just to hit home on this point, a *"Theological seminary"* has a *non-Biblical* stance on *the Bible*. Mark Yarbrough is the president of Dallas seminary currently (2023) who gives a sermon[35] on 2 Timothy 3:16-17 where he *professes* to have "Scripture" over and over *on the podium*, but he professes that "the originals" are Scripture according to his institution. Which Mark Yarbrough is right? There appears to be two of him—he's schizophrenic.

He states, "we believe Scripture is God's word" and tells the congregation to "trust the text" while quoting from an NIV. What is beyond the intellect of the speaker is that half the audience doesn't *use* an NIV, so when asked to read aloud 2 Timothy 3:16 from his NIV, there seems to be some trouble there, but "trust the text." Luckily the members see the Jumbotron. Yarbrough couldn't give you the Scriptures if his life depended on it, he'll avoid it in the same fashion that he avoids the term "inspired." This sermon is a prime example of the apostate, pious, outlook from *"the actors."*

To give you an idea of the text he reads from that you are to "trust," the NIV has knocked out **"infallible proofs"** from Acts 1:3, Christ is not **"the form of God,"** but only His "nature" in Philippians 2:6, has incorporated the Roman Catholic view of the Perpetual Virginity of Mary in Matthew 1:25, entirely omitted Matthew 23:14; Mark 7:16, 15:28; Matthew 17:21; Acts 15:34, 28:29; Romans 16:24; Acts 8:37, etc. In all, the NIV omits 64,098 words and the promise of

---

[35] *"Trust the Text"* by Mark Yarbrough. Author's Note: comments are conveniently turned off in the YouTube video https://www.YouTube.com/watch?v=dF6B1LVhn0Y

preservation has been *altered* in Psalm 12:6-7, which *disagrees* with just about *every* Hebrew Tanakh and Hebrew manuscript. This is what you are dealing with.

How can one tell that a person is a **"wolf"** aside from the obvious holes in logic and professions of someone like Yarbrough? **"Beware of false prophets, which come to you in sheep's clothing, but inwardly they are ravening wolves"** (Matt. 7:15). These wolves *appear as sheep*. How is one supposed to know, aside from pulling back the curtain? What does the next verse say in Matthew 7? **"Ye shall know them by their fruits"** (Matt. 7:16). What does someone like Yarbrough, Metzger, Ehrman, Fuller, Tennessee Temple, Moody, Liberty, et al., produce? What is their product, so to speak, *what are they producing*?

1. They cause distrust in the New Testament Text and cause disbelief (Rom. 14:1)
2. They remove the second most powerful being aside from the Godhead in relation to the Scriptures (Gen. 3:1)
3. They cause apostasy from Biblical doctrines, such as Preservation and Inspiration (2 Tim. 4:3)
4. They cause mass confusion surrounding the Scriptures and their origin (1 Cor. 2:13-14)
5. They believe and cause others to believe that a Roman Catholic bible is the best representation of the "original text"
6. These students then graduate and perpetuate the lie in your community under the guise of **"sheep"** and reproduce **"after his kind"** (Gen. 1:24; 2 Tim. 3:5)
7. They and their students hold scholarship and the minds of men above the words of Scripture (Prov. 18:1-2)
8. They hold admiration higher than Scripture (Jude 1:16)
9. They teach no final authority but themselves and the institutions they went to (2 Tim. 4:3)
10. They create likeminded students who then continue the cycle and split the Body of Christ in the process

11. They hold to **"fair speeches"** (Rom. 16:18) rather than **"great plainness of speech"** (2 Cor. 3:12)
12. They cause duplicity in the minds of believers and dissension amongst believers (1 Cor. 1:10)
13. They profess one thing, while believing another (Matt. 23:14)

The list could go on, but the remaining of this work delves deeper into the subject. Is any number mentioned above serving Jesus Christ our Lord or is each number serving someone *else*? Who would love to corrupt the Body from inside out? Who hates you? What spirit was working behind the Pharisees in the Gospel accounts? You get one guess.

There is a publication called *"The Sword of the Lord"* that inadvertently documents the original position on the Scriptures as given by Baptists and conservatives, then a falling away from it occurred, and then a return. The new editor is Dr. Shelton Smith and in the December 27th, 2019 issue of *"Sword of the Lord"* he says that the KJB is inspired and inerrant. The title of his article is *"Can You Tell Me about the King James Bible?"* Under the heading, *"Is the King James Bible Inspired, Inerrant, and Infallible?"* he answers, *"Yes! Yes! And yes!,"* on page 11. The originator of the publication is John R. Rice and his brother, which began in 1934 and reached a high state of apostasy after Rice began to believe his teachers at Baylor and other seminaries. It reached an all time high in the 60's-90's under the tail end of Rice and into the next editor, Curtis Hutson. Hutson died in 1995 which is when Smith took over. It has now come full circle in declaring the original position that *"The* Bible" and "the Scriptures" refer to the KJB. Reviewing these old publications will show the trail of apostasy.

It wasn't *all* Hutson's influence in the publication, Rice succumbed to the **"old man"** too—**"knowledge puffeth up."** Rice is noted for saying many things which line up with *"the best"* of modern Christian scholarship: "many think acts 8:37

was a gloss, added by copyists. The *truth* is, I think so too...I think the *ASV* of 1901, in *some details*, is *more accurate* than the King James...I *prefer* the King James Version, but still my life is based on what *the Bible* says."

What exactly is *"the Bible"* Rice is mentioning here? Where is it? Is it the ASV or the KJB or something else? If you care about *truth*, then how do your *preferences* enter into the discussion unless you are giving an *opinion*. According to Rice, God preserves His *"Word...not altogether, perhaps, in one copy or in one translation, but in them all collectively... Translators are not inspired"*—John R. Rice.[36] Well, I guess when a man is called to preach he can use the Jehovah Witness version or the Catholic Jesuit Rheims, or maybe "The Living Bible," and *tell his congregation that each one is true in SOME places*.

He then has the gumption to say, *"Translators are not inspired"*—By the way, Moses translated for Pharaoh (Exod. 5-11). Do you think all of those conversations Moses (who was raised Egyptian) had with Pharaoh were in the slave-tongue of the Hebrews? He spoke in Egyptian. **"And Moses was learned in all the wisdom of the Egyptians, and was mighty in words and in deeds"** (Acts 7:22). The decrees of Artaxerxes and Darius were translations (Dan. 3:29, 6:25-27; Est. 8:8-13). Furthermore, every single time the Hebrew O.T. was quoted in the New Testament it had to be *translated into Greek*. So if we go by Rice's logic, no N.T. book is inspired along with many places of the Old Testament and that the Holy Spirit never spoke through any of the writers in such cases.

What a mess! All you are doing in instilling a false sense of security through *prestige, doubt,* and *confusion* by teaching that the words of God aren't found in *any* book at all and then shielding yourself with the notion that they are in all of

---

[36] John R. Rice, *"Our God-Breathed Book: The Bible,"* 1969. Author's Note: The book is full of these sorts of examples and there are far too many to list here.

them. It isn't in a book—it's *the message found in 300+ corrupted bible versions where you have to rely on the "traditions of men" to tell you what is true and what isn't.* The authority of The Holy Spirit has been usurped. If you do happen to believe that the *words* of God are preserved in a *Book* somewhere, that you can *hold* and *read*, you are a *heretic* and a member of a *cult*—that's how far the apple has fallen from the tree—*those who believe the words of God are now members of a cult*.

Everyone has been reeducated with this one,

> *"Well, there are many, many translations. The differences in the translations are so minor, so insignificant, that we can be sure not a single doctrine, not a single statement of fact, not a single command or exhortation, has been missed in our translations."*[37]

See chapters 5 and 6 for a full discussion on the complete fallacy of, *"minor…insignificant…differences…not a single doctrine"* has been altered or *"missed."* Just because you can find *all the fundamentals* of the faith in *a* book doesn't make it *a Bible*. There are, in fact, many verses surrounding doctrines which *are* altered and thus, *"missed."* For instance, John 3:16 in an NIV confuses the idea of God having, or not having multiple sons, by leaving out the word **"begotten"**; Matthew 5:22 questions the sinless nature of Jesus Christ by removing **"without a cause"**; the prophecy of the New Birth was erased in Psalm 22:30 by altering **"a seed"** to *"Posterity"* and **"a generation"** to *"future generations"*; in Hebrews 1:3 Jesus is no longer the **"image"** of God but a *"representation"* of Him; in 1 Timothy 6:20 the valuable revelation of false **"science"** has been changed to only *"knowledge"*; the list goes on.

---

[37] Ibid

The Actors

To sum up the attitude by Price, Wallace, White, Metzger, Ehrman, Fuller, Dallas, Liberty, et al., I quote James D. Price talking about the following verse, **"Ye blind guides, which strain at a gnat, and swallow a camel"** (Matthew 23:24). Price states:

> *"To strain at something is not the correct English idiom for to remove or free by filtration. Instead, a new idiom has developed from a misunderstanding of strain at a gnat which means to hesitate or be unwilling; balk (at). Therefore, the word at must be a misprint for out."*

There you have it, that's it in a nutshell. Price is doing *exactly* what Jesus Christ is accusing the Pharisees of doing in Matthew 23:24.

In case you are wondering how so many *"smart"* Ph.D's could be bamboozled, I present you with the story of Ancel Keys (1904-2004). He was a researcher in the 1940-80's who hypothesized that heart attacks in the U.S. were caused by diet. In 1958 he embarked on a worldwide expedition to test his hypothesis. Many viewed the possible outcome of the study to be of great importance, because of that, he was well funded.

Keys went to seven countries, which is where the famous study gets its name: *"The Seven Countries Study."*[38] They include the United States, Finland, Japan, Italy, Greece, Yugoslavia, and the Netherlands. What he found was that people who have less cardiovascular disease ate less saturated fat (i.e. butter, coconut oil, ghee, lard, etc.). These people ate polyunsaturated (vegetable oils) and monounsaturated fat (olive oil, avocado oil) instead of the

---

[38] Angel Keys, *"Seven Countries: A multivariate analysis of death and coronary heart disease,"* 1980, Harvard.

"evil" saturated fat, ergo, saturated fat became enemy number one for the next four decades.

Doctors and physicians learned of his work in classrooms and then applied it *in practice*. His research did have some validity to it in that obesity and smoking were all of negative consequence to a persons health. Other researchers began to "discover" similar findings as Keys had. What they did not see was that there were negative cardiovascular events occurring when a persons cholesterol was *low* and when it was *high*. It was also discovered that the "size" of the LDL and what sort of LDL it actually was mattered. LDL had been deemed a *villain* for decades but as it turns out it's not as previously thought by Keys and other researchers.

There are also correlations between higher cholesterol and better cognitive function.[39] Cholesterol is also used to make certain hormones in the body, such as Vitamin D, testosterone, and estrogen. It turns out that it's more complex than just good or bad types of cholesterol.

You will still find many physicians prescribing vegetable oils for patients today who have high LDL cholesterol. *Keys changed the entire diet and nutrition scene* and he is the father of the "low fat" movement in the 80's and 90's.

So, what happened? How did they get from point A to point B? Turns out that Keys faked his research, that's what happened. Instead of using data from 22 countries, he cherry picked *seven*. With the full 22 countries added into the pool of data, his research began to look as if there was little correlation between cholesterol and heart attack; there were other variables at play as well.

The True Health Initiative[40] pointed out many of Ancel's inaccuracies: (1) the counties selected were to fit the expected

---

[39] Muldoon, Matthew F. MD, MPH; Ryan, Christopher M. PhD; Matthews, Karen A. PhD; Manuck, Stephen B. PhD, Psychosomatic Medicine, *"Serum Cholesterol and Intellectual Performance,"* July/Aug, 1997.

[40] Pett, Khan, Willett, Katz, *"Angel Keys and the Seven Countries Study: An Evidence-based Response to Revisionist Histories,"* 2017

outcome; (2) France was intently excluded as to avoid the "French paradox"; (3) data from Greece was taken during Lent; (4) sugar/carbohydrates were not considered as possible contributors to cardiovascular events.

Since we are delving into the history of "science," there was a man from the 19th Century who observed that cleanliness *may* have something to do with infections. He was ironically killed by an infection later on. His name is Semmelweis.

Semmelweis proposed that hand-washing with a chlorinated lime solution *before* examining patients could reduce the spread of disease. His ideas were met with *resistance and ridicule* from the medical *community*. He was eventually dismissed from his position and was later committed to a mental asylum, where he died from sepsis at the age of 47 in Vienna. Beware of **"science falsely so called"** (1 Tim. 6:20).

Some of the most vocal opponents of Semmelweis's ideas were Catholic priests, who believed (Catholic priests/bishops/cardinals do not hold to this idea anymore) that disease was solely a punishment from God and/or devil possession. They believed that it was *not possible* to prevent or cure it through scientific means. This is *not* Biblical because even-though disease *can be* a punishment, sometimes it's *not*; sometimes it's in the *permissive* will instead of the *directive* will of God. Paul is beaten and sick for not following the directive will, and so are some of his friends (1 Tim. 5:23, 4:14; 2 Tim. 4:20; Col. 4:14; 2 Tim. 4:11; 2 Cor. 12:7-12)—"you reap what you sow" (Gal. 6:8). *However* a saved Christian *can* lose his good health if he doesn't *judge his own sins,* as in, to examine yourself (1 Cor. 11:30), but this is *not always* the case. Sometimes a person gets sick for other reasons as seen in Matthew 4:24, **"and they brought unto him all sick people that were taken with divers diseases and torments, and those which were possessed with devils, and those which were lunatick, and those that had the**

palsy; and he healed them." There is a clear *distinction* made between devil possession and sickness made here. Sometimes it is due to possession, as seen in Matthew 12:22. As with Keys' falsifications and the opponents of Semmelweis, there's science and then there is *"science"* (1 Tim. 6:20).

In the next chapter I will be discussing the list of "bible contradictions" as listed on an atheist website. There are many today who do not believe in what the Bible has to say, as you've seen. There are many more who turn all into allegory. This pandemic extends beyond atheists and into Christian seminaries taught by professors who admire Nestle, Hort, Wallace, Metzger, et al. This group in target would be called *"practical atheists."* We have dealt with some in this chapter now past such as Wallace, White, and Metzger. These individuals *claim* belief but *demonstrate* a misalignment between their professed faith and their words and actions regarding the Book. In all *practical* purposes, they are atheists when it comes to the Book. They have the same view as the modern humanists that put together the website I'm about to quote from in the next chapter. You'll likely see that it isn't much of a shift away from the first chapter, *"A Bucketful of Contradictions."* Had I not disclosed the origin of these purported contradictions beforehand, you might not have discerned any difference at all. Subsequently, in the chapter titled *"Saving Private Ehrman,"* there will be many seminary "freshman classics" presented from Ehrman (a professing atheist) but are also commonly taught at esteemed seminaries such as Fuller, Dallas, Moody, Liberty, Princeton, Yale, Harvard, and others.

Chapter 3: More "Contradictions"

"The fool hath said in his heart, There is no God" —
Psalm 53:1

ALL of the following "contradictions" come from atheists.org. I will go through them in order, starting at the top of the website page under, "bible contradictions."

Exod. 20:8 **"Remember the Sabbath day, to keep it holy"**

vs

Rom. 14:5 **"One man esteemeth one day above another: another esteemeth every day alike. Let every man be fully persuaded in his own mind."**

Problem: Do we keep the Sabbath day or not?

Answer: Unfortunately, we have to point out an obvious fact first; each quote is in *a different Testament*. Another name for *"testament"* is *covenant* hence—"New Testament," or in other words, "new covenant." It's *"new"* because it involves the death of Jesus Christ, **"the testator"** (Heb. 9:16-17). I'm sure most have heard of a **"last will and *testament"*** as used in the passage, **"For where a testament is, there must also of necessity be the death of the testator."** The "Old Testament" or old covenant, is called *"old"* because Jeremiah 31:31 says

God will make a *"new"* one, **"Behold, the days come, saith the LORD, that I will make a new covenant with the house of Israel, and with the house of Judah."** You *also* have the previous one called **"old"** in Hebrews 8:13, **"In that he saith, A new covenant, he hath made the first old."** That is initially where the *division* comes from between the New and Old Testaments in the Bible.

What *is* "new" about it?—Jesus Christ. What did he do? He, **"redeemed us from the curse of the law"** (Gal. 3:13). What's part of the **"law"**? The first five books of Moses. What's in them? The Ten Commandments for instance, and many other commandments, judgments, and statutes. *What happens to be one of those Ten Commandments?* Observing the Sabbath (Exod. 20:8-11). **"For Christ is the end of the law for righteousness to every one that believeth"** (Rom. 10:4).

Now what does this mean for those in the Body of Christ? First, let's look at the Book of Romans. The context of Romans 14:5 is Paul talking about **"weak"** Christians (14:1). Some think they must only eat certain kinds of foods because their *religion* tells them to do so or possibly some sort of conviction. An example would be previous Jews continuing to abstain from pork (14:2), or another eating a vegetarian diet based on a religious or an otherwise presumptuous notion. Hence, at verse 5, where Paul is talking about the Sabbath but ends the verse, as he did in verses 1, 3, and 4, by basically saying, *"hey, if someone wants to observe the Sabbath and not eat pork, then go for it; but you aren't really understanding what Christ did for you. Nevertheless, God is the final judge."* As a Christian, as long as you **"giveth God thanks"** (Rom. 14:6) for, **"whatsoever ye do, do it heartily, as to the Lord, and not unto men"** (Col. 3:23), **"For every creature of God is good, and nothing to be refused, if it be received with thanksgiving"** (1 Tim. 4:4).

Also, *the Sabbath is not for the Church nor was it changed to Friday* (see page 167). It is a **"sign"** to Israel. **"It is a sign**

More "Contradictions"

between me and the **CHILDREN OF ISRAEL for ever**" (Exod. 31:17).

"**For it is a sign between me and YOU**" (Exod. 31:13).

"**Moreover also I gave them my sabbaths, to be a sign between me and THEM, that they might know that I am the LORD that sanctify them**" (Ezek. 20:12).

"**And hallow my sabbaths; and they shall be a sign between me and YOU, that ye may know that I am the LORD your God.**" (Ezek. 20:20).

"**The JEWS require a SIGN**" (1 Cor. 1:22).

The story of the nation of Israel began with **"signs"** (Exod. 4:8, 28, 8:23, 13:9, etc.). When they were being called out of Egypt there were **"signs"** (Exod. 7-14). Even before that with Abraham (Gen. 17:10), and even before that with Abel and his sacrifice (Gen. 4:4; Levi. 9:24). Physical **"signs"** accompany Israel and their ancestors. Spiritual things accompany the Church more than physical signs (Rom. 14:17; 1 Peter 2:5; Heb. 13:15), **"The just shall live by faith"** (Rom. 1:17).

The real kicker is that the Sabbath, which is a **"sign"** to Israel, will be reinstated and be reestablished in the future. Right now, in our current age, it means *nothing*. That probably upsets a lot of Seventh Day Adventists and those who believe that we are still in bondage to the Law of Moses. There is nothing wrong with setting a day aside for devotion to God, in case you miss the other six, but it *isn't a Sabbath* unless you practice it as it is presented in Levitical Law; otherwise you would be *breaking* the Sabbath.

You have Hosea 2:11 telling you, "**I will also cause all her mirth to cease, her feast days, her new moons, and her sabbaths, and all her solemn feasts.**" The "her" in the passage *is Israel*. The Sabbaths start up again in the 1,000 year reign of Jesus Christ (Rev. 20:1-6) at that time Israel is restored (Ezek. 37-48). This time period is also known as the Millennium, a heresy according to the Catholic Church. "**For as the new heavens and the new earth, which I will make,** shall remain before me, saith the LORD, so shall your seed and your name remain. And it shall come to pass, that from one new moon to another, and from one sabbath to another, shall all flesh come to worship before me, saith the LORD" (Isa. 66:22-23). *Notice* the **"all flesh come to worship before me,"** the passage is in a setting where God is on a throne before **"all"** *physically* like Jeremiah 31:34 and Isaiah 2:3. Did Jesus Christ appear to **"all"** at His First Coming?—No. He was actually telling people to keep His presence secret as in Luke 8:56 and Mark 8:30. God is there physically, in a bodily shape. Paul alludes to this reinstatement of the Sabbath in Colossians 2:16-17, **"Let no man therefore judge you in meat, or in drink, or in respect of an holyday, or of the new moon, or of the sabbath days: Which are a shadow of things to come."**

So, the Sabbath is forever for the Jew, and it is forever for the Christian, for both will be in eternity (Rev. 21-22). What about the Christian today? The Sabbath is a day of rest. Rest from what? Labor, as mentioned in Exodus 20:10 and Genesis 2:2. It is a rest from *work*. The Christian is in *a constant rest* from *his own work, if he* is *relying on the finished work of Jesus Christ* (John 19:30), **"There remaineth therefore a rest to the people of God. For he that is entered into his rest, he also hath ceased from his own works, as God did from his."** (Heb. 4:9-10, also see Heb. 9:14). Hebrews is directed at *Hebrews* hence a lot but not all of it is future and deals with the Tribulation, but there is Church doctrine spread throughout the epistle such as Hebrews 10:10-12, 13:1-25, 12:1-4, 9:11-23, etc. The reader must *"rightly divide"* (2 Tim. 2:15) to discern the applications of what he is reading.

The Sabbath for the Jew is on temporary probation just as God did nationally with the Gentiles as a whole by Genesis 11; but *reinstated* them on an individual basis by Acts 15, by opening the doors of faith (Acts 15:8-11, 22, 28; Rom. 1:21-32, 10:8-13; 2 Cor. 3:13-16; Rom. 11:1-11). Israel, on the other hand, will be restored *nationally* in the future, since God

More "Contradictions"

deals with them *as a nation* but *individually* anyone may believe the Gospel today; Jew or Gentile may believe on Jesus Christ (Rom. 10). That Book is tricky.

The short answer to the "contradiction" is that the Law was done away with due to the death of Jesus Christ (Gal. 3:13), but if a Christian wants to practice the Sabbath, they can. The Sabbath for the Christian is continual since he is in a rest from his own works with God currently, and will join the nation of Israel when they become nationally restored in the Millennium; where the Sabbath will be reinstated via the Levitical order for all.

Ecclesiastes 1:4 **"the earth abideth for ever."**
vs
2 Peter 3:10 **"the elements shall melt with fervent heat, the earth also and the works that are therein shall be burned up."**

Problem: Does it last forever or not?

Answer: This was already discussed in the chapter titled, *"A Bucketful of Contradictions."*

Genesis 32:30 **"I have seen God face to face, and my life is preserved."**
vs
John 1:18 **"No man hath seen God at any time"**

Problem: Has anyone seen God's face or not?

Answer: This is a common one, and is brought up often in Christian seminaries. First, what is Genesis 32:30 talking about? In Genesis 32:24 we read that Jacob is wrestling with "a man." A man that can **"bless"** with authority, which Jacob happened to really want from him (Gen. 32:26), he is **"a man"** that somehow, after seeing him, Jacob thinks he has **"seen God… face to face"** (Gen. 32:30).

Who is this **"man"**? If you recall earlier in this work, that angels are creatures that look like a "man" without having the typical, picturesque image of wings on their backs. Consider what Hosea 12:4 has to say about this same account dealing with Jacob from Genesis 32, **"Yea, he had power over the angel, and prevailed: he wept, and made supplication unto him: he found him in Bethel, and there he spake with us."** We now know that this **"man,"** is an **"angel."**

Up to the second colon the reference is to Jacob with "the man" in Genesis 32 and the later part is in reference to Genesis 28:11-19. The Bible has a particular way of dividing things and events in a single verse. Also, notice the word **"similitude"** in Hosea 12:10, keep that word in mind. Now that we have established that Jacob *did not* in fact see God, but **"a man"** who was an **"angel."**

Secondly, we have more things to consider. To complicate things further, we have verses that the website *missed*, which is the usual when dealing with amateurs *pretending* to know what their talking about. The verses state, **"And there arose not a prophet since in Israel like unto Moses, whom the LORD knew face to face"** (Deut. 34:10).

"And they saw the God of Israel: and there was under his feet as it were a paved work of a sapphire stone, and as it were the body of heaven in his clearness" (Exod. 24:10).

"Then said I, Woe is me! for I am undone; because I am a man of unclean lips, and I dwell in the midst of a people of unclean lips: for mine eyes have seen the King, the LORD of hosts" (Isa. 6:5).

It really does seem like people *saw* **"God face to face"** at some point or another.

What did they see? If Moses and all of Israel really saw the Lord (Exod. 24:10, 19:21), then why would Moses be requesting it *again* in Exodus 33:18 as if he had not, **"And he said, I beseech thee, shew me thy glory,"** with God *claiming that Moses could not see his face in verse 20*? What were they seeing if not God's face or God Himself?

Guess who shows up in place of the face of God? The angel of the LORD, or as stated in Numbers, a **"similitude,"** **"With him will I speak mouth to mouth, even apparently, and not in dark speeches; and the similitude of the LORD shall he behold"** (Num 12:8). A "similitude" is the quality or state of being similar to something. It is also used in the sense of comparing two things. This is how God constantly communicates to us in His Book; *"this is like this, well it's also like this over here, you still don't get it?... Well it's also like this here in case you didn't understand that over there."*

You will also *note* that Ezekiel says something similar to what is in Exodus 24:10. *Note the similitude* in Ezekiel 1:26-28, **"...likeness of a throne, as the appearance of a sapphire stone: and upon the likeness of the throne was the likeness as the appearance of a man above upon it...brightness round about...This was the appearance of the likeness of glory of the LORD.**

A horrendous blunder on the atheists part is that they have *left out* that *God is a Trinity* (Father, Son, Spirit), *like* man. Adam was made in the **"image"** of God (Gen. 1:27, 2:7), and *fallen man* still has His triune nature (1 Thess. 5:23) even though we are fallen. Therefore, if Adam was made in God's **"image,"** God would then have a soul, a spirit, and a body *like* Adam. The bigger issue at hand is actually all proof of a Trinitarian God in the O.T. Notice **"us"** in Hosea 12:4 and in Hosea 12:5 *three* names of God. Notice in Exodus 34:6, **"The LORD, The LORD God."** *The reason no one saw God* **"face to face"** was because *no one has ever seen God the Father, the soul.* They have only seen God the Son (the body) as mentioned in John 1:18, since **"the Word was made flesh"** (John 1:14), and

"the Word was God" (John 1:1) and Proverbs 30:4, **"what is his name, and what is his son's name, if thou canst tell?"** (Read the next verse to see what His Son's name is.)

The real question *is*: what *form of God* did they see? A **"similitude,"** or God the Father *(soul)*, God the Son *(body)*, or God the Sprit *(Spirit)*? It is pretty difficult to see God when he is everywhere. We already know that no one saw God the Father in the Bible. In the Old Testament, He must appear locally *somehow,* such as a pillar of smoke and fire guiding Israel (Exod. 13:21-22), or **"the angel of the LORD,"** who is Jesus Christ (Acts 27:23) in a different form. That angel is equated with God in Acts 7:35; Exodus 3:2; Acts 7:38, Acts 7:30. These are all in reference to Exodus 6:3; Gen. 32:24, 29-30. **"The angel of the LORD"** in Exodus 3:2 *is referred to as God* as verses 4, 6, 13, and 14 of Exodus 3, as well as Deuteronomy 33:16.

What they saw in the Old Testament was *a similitude* at times and at *other times* **"the likeness of the Glory of the LORD"** and on occasion, **"a man"** who is the angel of the LORD. All that will take some time to settle in. The short answer is: no one has seen God the Father (soul).

Leviticus 18:21 **"Thou shalt not let any of thy seed pass through the fire to Molech, neither shalt thou profane the name of thy God..."**

vs

Judges 11:30-31 ([*These are statements made by the website*] In Judges, though, the tale of Jephthah, who led the Israelites against the Ammonoites, is being told. Being fearful of defeat, this good religious man sought to guarantee victory by getting god firmly on his side. So he prayed to god)

."**.. If thou shalt without fail deliver the children of Ammon into mine hands, Then it shall be, that whatsoever cometh forth of the doors of my house to meet me, when I**

More "Contradictions"

return in peace from the children of Ammon, shall surely be the LORD's, and I will offer it up for a burnt offering"

([*further statements made by the website*] The terms were acceptable to god — remember, he is supposed to be omniscient and know the future — so he gave victory to Jephthah, and the first whatsoever that greeted him upon his glorious return was his daughter, as god surely knew would happen, if god is god. True to his vow, the general made a human sacrifice of his only child to god! - Judges 11:29-34)

Problem: God allowed human sacrifice of a child!

Answer: First off, they misspelled "Ammonoites," it's Ammonites. This is actually one of my favorites, because it says a lot about humanity, and about God, as do all of these issues being addressed. *There are a few things to note*:

> **1.** There were *not* a lot of Scriptures around at this time, **"every man did that which was right in his own eyes"** (Judg. 21:25). This is never a good sign in history. There is a time period characterized as "The Dark Ages" (recently re-dubbed "The Middle Ages" to distract from the ruler of the day and thus responsibility). The Roman Catholic Church was at the height of its power during that time and the Scriptures were being withheld to the common man and instead given to authorities such as priests, bishops, cardinals, et al. The period is characterized by human cruelty, war, bloodshed, political power struggles, and little to no technological advances—essentially people were *in the Dark* from roughly A.D. 500-1500.
>
> **2.** Note the hateful attitude towards God from an average unsaved man, *"remember… he is supposed to be omniscient"* (see John 3:19-20). The author of the article

here (atheists.org) is shining through. His "cultural and economic circumstances" are being "exemplified and characterized in his writing." Apparently, he believes that every time people do something dumb or hurtful that *God must intervene* or *that He approves of it*. This shows how Biblically illiterate the critic really is. *If you are going to critique something at least know what you are talking about, or at least read the Book.*

3. The writer also says, *"the terms were acceptable to God."* *Where* does it say that? It doesn't say anything of the kind. The author just out right lied to get a point across. This is to be expected by a person who's morals are based on "societal constructs." What the author to the article is actually doing, is making an *assumption* about the text. He thinks, *"since God allowed him to win the battle, then whatever happens in the future, must then be acceptable and approved of by God."*

4. You can just as well assume that God gave Jephthah the victory in order to give him an *opportunity* to change the course of his daughters fate, which we will get into shortly. If his case was presented in a courtroom, it would be thrown out. *There is evidence to the contrary, and much more of it.* God will always give someone chances. He gave Adam and Eve a chance. He gave Nineveh a chance (Jonah 3:4). Nineveh reacted, **"Who can tell if God will turn and repent, and turn away from his fierce anger, that we perish not? And God saw their works, that they turned from their evil way; and God repented of the evil, that he had said that he would do unto them; and he did it not"** (Jonah 3:9-10). He gave the servants of the Pharaoh in Exodus 9:20-21 a chance, **"He that feared the word of the LORD among the servants of Pharaoh made his servants and his cattle flee into the houses: And he that regarded not the**

word of the LORD left his servants and his cattle in the field." Which sounds oddly familiar to another chance that God gave: **"And some believed the things which were spoken, and some believed not"** (Acts 28:24), and sounds very close to, **"Verily, verily, I say unto you, He that heareth my word, and believeth on him that sent me, hath everlasting life, and shall not come into condemnation; but is passed from death unto life"** (John 5:24). There appears to be *a variable* in the system, a monkey wrench in the machinery, if you will. The *"decrees"* of God seem to be conditioned on...*free will*. No, no, that is silly—how can you have an omniscient God *and* free will together...yeah, that's just silly. (For more on this topic see the chapter titled, *"The Righteous Atheist"*).

5. Yes, he did indeed make a human sacrifice to God, *not* Molech, but why?

Now that I have noted a few issues let us get to the **"meat."** Judges is a time of great distress for Israel, and no one seems to know what in the world is going on. *Joshua has died* (Judg. 1:1, 2:8). The generation that fought with Joshua *had died* and another generation, right after them *fell into apostasy* (Judg. 2:10-11). The Lord raised up Judges to judge the people in the land of Israel but they usually *went deeper and deeper into apostasy* after a Judge died, or even while there was a Judge present (Judg. 2:17, 19, 8:24-27, 9:23, 10:6, 17:1-13, 18:19-24, 30-31, etc.). You even have a Levitical priest *chopping up a dead whore's* (Judg. 19:2) body and *sending the pieces abroad* (Judg. 19:29-30).

That was what the world was like *without Scriptures* available freely. This is also in line with Societal Collapse Theory: *"the fall of a complex human society characterized by the loss of cultural identity and of social complexity as an adaptive system, the downfall of government, and the rise of violence."*

Things tend to decay, not improve over time. If Israel can apostatize that *quickly*, why not modern Christianity? Especially with the advent of 300+ different versions in one language of what God *may* or *may not* have said.

Back to the text. Most of the commentators will take you to Numbers 30:2 and say the passage *"is about the depravity of what humans are capable of"* but that doesn't quite jive, even though it is partly true, sort of like our Levitical priest mentioned above who was *partially* right in doing what he did (Levi. 21:7; Deut. 22:21). Numbers 30:2 reads, **"If a man vow a vow unto the LORD, or swear an oath to bind his soul with a bond; he shall not break his word, he shall do according to all that proceedeth out of his mouth."** The lovely bunch there at atheist central have given us the reference of Leviticus 18:21. The reference given from the website of child sacrifice is to *other gods*, such as the Canaanite god Baal or Molech. The passage in Leviticus 18:21 goes with Leviticus 17:7, since it's dealing with sacrifices *to other gods* and not to the Lord. This is how badly these people have trouble with reading English and even following plot development in literature. Their scalding *hate* and need to *hide* from God, like Adam putting on fig leaves (Gen. 3:7-9), and running for the bushes, is getting in the way of their ability to comprehend English. **"Where art thou,"** Adam?

No one in Judges 11 sacrificed any child to any another god. *If Jephthah had a Bible he would have read Leviticus 5:4-10*. The passage states that *you can go back on an oath with certain conditions*, one of them being *ignorance*, such as trying to win a battle by making an oath to sacrifice whatever comes to the door of your home, then having *your child* come to the door instead of a chicken, or some other animal (Judg. 11:30-39) that you had in mind when you made the oath.

"Or if a soul swear, pronouncing with his lips to do evil, or to do good, whatsoever it be that a man shall pronounce with an oath, and it be hid from him; when he knoweth of

it, then he shall be guilty in one of these. And it shall be, when he shall be guilty in one of these things, that he shall confess that he hath sinned in that thing: And he shall bring his trespass offering unto the LORD for his sin which he hath sinned, a female from the flock, a lamb or a kid of the goats, for a sin offering; and the priest shall make an atonement for him concerning his sin—and—it—shall—be—FORGIVEN—HIM.** It's almost as if the Lord wrote that *for* Jephthah. He had *a choice* to look for the Book —**"Seek ye out of the book of the LORD, and read"** (Isa. 34:16), or any of the Law available at the time. *He did not.* He listened to the commentators and the seminary professors and stuck with Numbers 30:2.

Matthew 19:26 **"with God all things are possible."**
vs
Judges 1:19 **"The LORD was with Judah; and he drave out the inhabitants of the mountain; but could not drive out the inhabitants of the valley, because they had chariots of iron."**

Problem: God Couldn't drive them out! If God was with Judah and all things are possible, then why couldn't God drive out those inhabitants in Judges 1:19?

Answer: This is briefly talked about in the chapter later titled, *"The Righteous Atheist."* The problem is as old as Voltaire's prose; who claimed this verse states, *"God could not drive out the inhabitants."* Voltaire, like T. Jefferson, B. Franklin, and J. Adams, were *deists*. They believed there was *a* God, but that He most likely wanted nothing to do with humans, a very prominent idea during the Enlightenment. They also did *not* believe, at least later in life, that salvation was in a Person—the person of Jesus Christ.

Based on Voltaire's statement concerning Judges 1:19 you can see that he had trouble with English. He also tried to rewrite an Enlightenment era version of Job in A.D. 1759 (Candide), and if he were honest about it he would have admitted it. Why is it, that all of these "very smart" people have so much *trouble* in reading the Bible? Voltaire had access to a KJB in 5th grade English during his lifetime. He also heard many a street preacher rant and roar from its pages. You can see that in Judges 1:19, the word **"he"** refers *to the antecedent*, which is *not* **"LORD,"** but **"Judah."** This means that **"Judah"** could *not* drive the inhabitants out as opposed to, "*God* could not drive them out." The critic will still ask, *"but if God was with them, shouldn't they have driven them out?"*

To dig deeper into the subject, in Joshua and Judges you first have to understand the *conditions for Israels success* in taking the land that was promised to them. We also have to understand the *assumption* made by the critic, which thinks that *if God is present somewhere then "all things" must be possible*, as in, Judah *should have* won the battle and driven out the inhabitants of the land since God was, well...*there*. This should go without explanation as to why that would not be true, but alas, we will dig, and dig we shall.

As with the explanation under Judges above, *we* are just as likely to assume that when God is present, or "with" someone, it does not necessarily mean that everything the person does will be a direct result from God's intervention or if he intervenes at all, such as winning a battle. Let's look at another example of God being present while not approving of the people/person he is present with; **"And the LORD was angry with Solomon, because his heart was turned from the LORD God of Israel, which had appeared unto him twice"** (1 Kings 11:9). This is Solomon who the Lord was supposed to be "with," **"As the LORD hath been with my lord the king, even so be he with Solomon, and** make his throne greater than the throne of my lord king David" (1 Kings 1:37).

What did he do? For the long list see 1 Kings 10:28, 11:1-10. God appeared to Solomon *twice* to try and talk some sense into the man, **"And had commanded him concerning this thing, that he should not go after other gods, but he kept not that which the LORD commanded"** (1 Kings 11:10). It was all *conditional* based on Solomons *actions*, **"And if thou wilt walk in my ways, to keep my statutes and my commandments, as thy father David did walk, then I will lengthen thy days"** (1 Kings 3:14). Solomon obviously broke just about everything written in Deuteronomy 17:14-20 in 1 Kings 11 and 10:28. Solomon was the wisest man to ever live according to 1 Kings 3:12-13, *but he still fell,* so is man.

Another example would be God dwelling *in* the believer during the Church age via The Holy Spirit.

After a person is saved, The Holy Spirit dwells within him, **"For by one Spirit are we all baptized into one body, whether we be Jews or Gentiles, whether we be bond or free; and have been all made to drink into one Spirit"** (1 Cor. 12:13). The means of baptism here is the Spirit, *not* water, it is receiving the Spirit *after belief.*

"But ye are not in the flesh, but in the Spirit, if so be that the Spirit of God dwell in you. Now if any man have not the Spirit of Christ, he is none of his" (Rom. 8:9).

"But the Comforter, which is the Holy Ghost, whom the Father will send in my name" (John 14:26).

"Nevertheless I tell you the truth; It is expedient for you that I go away: for if I go not away, the Comforter will not come unto you; but if I depart, I will send him unto you" (John 16:7).

"For ye have not received the spirit of bondage again to fear; but ye have received the Spirit of adoption, whereby we cry, Abba, Father" (Rom. 8:15).

"In whom ye also trusted, after that ye heard the word of truth, the gospel of your salvation: in whom also after that

ye believed, ye were sealed with that holy Spirit of promise" (Eph. 1:13) and so on.

After a person is saved, and given the New Birth by The Holy Spirit, they still have to deal with the *flesh*. There is the **"new man"** and an **"old man"** (Eph. 4:22-24) in the Christian: the flesh *and* the Spirit. The Spirit is what gives the believer a "spiritual circumcision" (Col. 2:11) so that you can, **"reckon ye also yourselves to be dead indeed unto sin"** (Rom. 6:11).

Paul says **"reckon"** as in, "I reckon he was a good man." People in the south use the word all the time and it still retains its meaning: to estimate something. Why is a Christian supposed to **"reckon"** himself dead to sin? It's because of that *duel nature* that is still in the Christian: the *old man* of the flesh and the *new man* in Christ. A Christian *can* sin (see 1 Cor. 6:15-20), but he *cannot* sin against the Body of Christ that he is now apart of, i.e. the sin is not counted towards *his soul* since he is of the Body (1 Cor. 12:13-27) and has had a "spiritual circumcision of the flesh" (Col. 2:11).

This explains what John meant in 1 John 3:9, **"Whosoever is born of God doth not commit sin; for his seed remaineth in him: and he cannot sin, because he is born of God."** (If you caught it, there was another *"contradiction"* solved.) Note the words **"born of God," "cannot sin,"** and **"his seed remaineth in him."** Who's seed—God's seed; which is The Holy Spirit that puts you in the Body of Christ. You cannot make Jesus Christ sin, so in that respect, you are sinless— because of Jesus Christ and what He did on Calvary. The *flesh is different* since the body has not been restored *yet* (see Rom. 8:23).

You are currently living in the flesh, but have the Spirit of God within you as a saved Christian. A Christian can have the Spirit but live in the **"old man"** his entire life though, he is *still* saved (Phil. 1:6; Eph. 4:30; Rom. 8:38-39; 1 Peter 1:4; 1 Cor. 1:8, etc.). Another example of this is in John 3:5-6 where Jesus is giving the revelation of the New Birth to Nicodemus,

"Jesus answered, Verily, verily, I say unto thee, Except a man be born of water and of the Spirit, he cannot enter into the kingdom of God. That which is born of the flesh is flesh; and that which is born of the Spirit is spirit."

"Born of water" means a *natural* birth, as mentioned in the next verse as **"flesh."** This is an example of the Bible interpreting itself, no clergy or priest needed. Catholics use this passage as a proof text for *"Baptismal Regeneration,"* where taking a bath saves people or sprinkling a baby with water—it never has and never will, according to *the Book*. Like Voltaire, some Catholics have trouble reading, or they don't read at all. Heck, the "first pope," Peter said baptism was a **"figure"** (1 Peter 3:21). A figure of what?—Death, Burial, and Resurrection of Jesus Christ and your new life in Him (Rom. 6:3-6).

To sum it up: The Christian has God within him via The Holy Spirit, but also has the flesh to deal with. Just because God is within you does not mean that He *approves of everything you do*, for the Spirit within can be grieved and lessened—**"And grieve not the holy Spirit of God"** (Eph. 4:30), **"Quench not the Spirit"** (1 Thess. 5:19).

The *conditions* for Israel's *success* in Judges were:
1. No worshiping of false idols (Deut. 30:17; Levi. 19:4; Josh. 23:7, etc.)
2. Believing with all your heart (Deut. 30:10, 6:5-6, 11:13; Josh. 23:8, 11, etc.)
3. Not being afraid (Deut. 20:1; Josh. 1:9, 23:6; Deut. 31:6, etc.)
4. Following the commandments, judgments, and statutes, which includes all of the above and more (Deut. 28:9, 14, 15, 25, 7:11, 11:1, 30:16, etc.)
5. Moses' warning against partial obedience in Numbers 33:51-53, **"Speak unto the children of Israel, and say unto them, When ye are passed over Jordan into the land of Canaan; Then ye shall drive out all the**

inhabitants of the land from before you, and destroy all their pictures, and destroy all their molten images, and quite pluck down all their high places: And ye shall dispossess the inhabitants of the land, and dwell therein: for I have given you the land to possess it." Also Deuteronomy 7:23-26, "But the LORD thy God shall deliver them unto thee, and shall destroy them with a mighty destruction, until they be destroyed. And he shall deliver their kings into thine hand, and thou shalt destroy their name from under heaven: there shall no man be able to stand before thee, until thou have destroyed them. The graven images of their gods shall ye burn with fire: thou shalt not desire the silver or gold that is on them, nor take it unto thee, lest thou be snared therein: for it is an abomination to the LORD thy God."

6. In addition to Moses's warning, there is Joshua's warning in Joshua 23:15-16, "Therefore it shall come to pass, that as all good things are come upon you, which the LORD your God promised you; so shall the LORD bring upon you all evil things, until he have destroyed you from off this good land which the LORD your God hath given you. When ye have transgressed the covenant of the LORD your God, which he commanded you, and have gone and served other gods, and bowed yourselves to them; then shall the anger of the LORD be kindled against you, and ye shall perish quickly from off the good land which he hath given unto you."

Israel broke *every single verse* mentioned above.
They *took gold* (Josh. 7:1, 20-21).
They *did not* destroy all the idols while in Egypt *or* after they left or when they came into the land (Josh. 24:23; Ezek. 20:8; Judg. 2:12).

More "Contradictions"

They were *scared* (Num. 13:31-32, 14:9; Judg. 1:19; Psa. 78:9; Judg. 1:29).

They did not keep God in their *hearts* (Psa. 78:11).

They *did not drive out* the inhabitants of the land but *instead dwelt with them* (Josh. 16:10; Judg. 1:29, also see Judges 1:27-33).

This would mean that they broke *all* commandments given to them hence, not loving God with all their hearts. There were Israelites worshiping idols as soon as they came to the land because they had been doing it *continually since they were in Egypt,* a type of the world (see verses above). The worshiping of idols and wanting to be like other nations is the equivalent to committing *"spiritual adultery"* against the Lord in Ezekiel 23, Hosea 2, and James 4:4, etc. They became friends with *the world* around them and wanted *to be like* the world; a big no no.

If you have noticed, Judges is not exactly in chronological order. Joshua dies in Judges 1:1, but then he is back in 2:6 and dies again in 2:8. Since Israel didn't do what the Lord said, everything written in Deuteronomy 28-30 *will* happen and *did*.

Judges 1:19 is the culmination of a long train of disobedience, put smack in your face so that the only way you could miss it is if you were just not paying attention while you read the previous Books, or you didn't want to see it, or you decided aforetime that you *weren't looking for the truth*. The thing is, if you are looking for a contradiction *without a desire for the truth*, you *will* find one, and the Lord will give it to you without any hesitation (see Ezek. 14:1-9 and 1 Thess. 2:11-12).

I'll give you a good one; **"For whosoever will save his life shall lose it: and whosoever will lose his life for my sake shall find it"** (Matt. 16:25). Do you realize how many people that verse has messed up?

You just don't get anything today that sounds even remotely negative, but that's Bible. Today you get a motion picture production with two Jumbotrons, Christian rock bands with girls wearing sluty outfits and a pound of makeup on; passive preachers who are too scared to even read you these verses because they only want to talk about one side of God. John 3:36 is not in their bible. Teachers who are too busy trying to "exegete *the* Greek" instead of their Bibles, they want to keep attendance up and have you *"feel good"* about coming to their church. They want to "create a safe environment for all people" instead of speaking *"plain"* they speak with great swelling words of flowery pastels. Why?—Because America has become so accustomed to being *entertained* by TV series on Netflix and watching the news that now people go to church for an escape from their lives instead of for a search for truth.

"And I, brethren, when I came to you, came not with excellency of speech" (1 Cor. 2:1).

"But though I be rude in speech, yet not in knowledge" (2 Cor. 11:6).

Israel got the land as promised, but it became a **"snare"** to them as promised, based on *their conduct* (see above). They "reaped what they sowed," all while God's promise was delivered and his words became reality.

Another verse our dear atheists *missed* was Hebrews 6:18 which states, **"it is impossible for God to lie."** Now, if **"all things are possible"** (Mark 10:27; Matt. 19:26) with God, then *why* is it saying there is something impossible for Him? How do you reconcile the two?

God could lie but does not, because if He did lie, He wouldn't be God. God would be a sinner. The context of Hebrews 6:18 is surrounding *a promise*. God keeps his promises in the Bible. You will find similar statements in Numbers 23:19 and Titus 1:2 surrounding promises and the nature of God. He will intentionally mislead someone *who messes with what he says*, such as with Voltaire earlier, and every person on modern bible translation committees (Ezek.

14:1-11), which in part, may explain their *inability to grasp English*.

Also, they (atheists.org) didn't give you what came *before* Matthew 19:26 which is, **"With men this is impossible; but with God all things are possible."** The idea here is that men are *not capable* of getting into Heaven *on their own,* given the proceeding verses, *but with God they are capable.* The verse is talking about man and his relationship with God. The Kingdom of Heaven being a *physical literal* land of dirt (Matt. 11:12) and Kingdom of God being *spiritual* (Rom. 14:17). That Kingdom of Heaven and its *landmass* is what Joshua and his congregation were going for in the book of Joshua and Judges, but in part, failed. It is the land *promised to the Jews* in Genesis 15:18-21. The land is *not* given to a Muslim who breaks Old Testament Law (Levi. 18:15). Notice how the religion of Islam is all about world *conquest*; convert or die, and Israel just wants their land back and has no use for killing those *who don't convert, as Muslims and Catholics are willing to do*.

They do get the land back (see Deut. 30:3-10; Jer. 32:42; Zeph. 3:12-20; Mic. 7:16-20; Ezek. 34:29-31, etc.), when the Savior comes back, **"And I will pour upon the house of David, and upon the inhabitants of Jerusalem, the spirit of grace and of supplications: and they shall look upon me whom they have pierced, and they shall mourn for him, as one mourneth for his only son, and shall be in bitterness for him, as one that is in bitterness for his firstborn. In that day shall there be a great mourning in Jerusalem"** (Zech. 12:10-11).

"And a voice came out of the throne, saying, Praise our God, all ye his servants, and ye that fear him, both small and great" (Rev. 19:5).

"And I saw heaven opened, and behold a white horse; and he that sat upon him was called Faithful and True, and in righteousness he doth judge and make war" (Rev. 19:11).

"And he was clothed with a vesture dipped in blood: and his name is called The Word of God" (Rev. 19:13).

"And he hath on his vesture and on his thigh a name written, KING OF KINGS, AND LORD OF LORDS" (Rev. 19:16)

"And ye shall tread down the wicked; for they shall be ashes under the soles of your feet in the day that I shall do this, saith the LORD of hosts" (Mal. 4:3)

"The LORD hath taken away thy judgments, he hath cast out thine enemy: the king of Israel, even the LORD, is in the midst of thee: thou shalt not see evil any more" (Zeph. 3:15).

"And I will plant them upon their land, and they shall no more be pulled up out of their land which I have given them, saith the LORD thy God" (Amos 9:15).

"So shall ye know that I am the LORD your God dwelling in Zion, my holy mountain: then shall Jerusalem be holy, and there shall no strangers pass through her any more" (Joel 3:17).

So, can God lie or not? He just said that it *was impossible* for Him to. As mentioned, if God chose to lie, He would no longer be God, since God is:

- Incorruptible (Rom. 1:23)
- Good (Psa. 25:8)
- True (Jer. 10:10)
- Upright (Psa. 92:15)
- Perfect (Matt. 5:48)
- None like Him (Exod. 9:14)
- Immutable/Unchanging (Psa. 102:26-27)

God is **"not a man, that he should repent"** (I Sam. 15:29), meaning, God is *not like fallen man*. Fallen man *needs* the help from God, not the other way around. Since God cannot change, *it would be impossible for God to no longer be God*. So, it appears that *there is something impossible for God*; He cannot stop being God. Man, on the other hand, *can* lie, is *not* immutable, *does* change, *is* corrupt, *is not* upright, *is not* good, and *far from perfect*. With the help of God (Matt. 19:26), *maybe* man has a chance.

Exodus 21:23-25 **"thou shalt give life for life, Eye for eye, tooth for tooth, hand for hand, foot for foot. burning for burning, wound for wound, stripe for stripe. "**
vs
Matthew 5:39 **"ye resist not evil: but whosoever shall smite thee on the right cheek, turn to him the other also."**

Problem: How can the law say an "eye for eye" but Jesus says the opposite?

Answer: Exodus 21:23-25 is a *civil law* which involves domestic problems, criminal problems, treatment of animals, marriage, and so on. They are all listed in what follows and in the preceding chapters of Exodus. We also see the same phrase in Deuteronomy 19:21. If you notice what comes before (verse 15-20), you will find it's *court conduct* in which *judges* and *witnesses* are involved. This is not far off from how we operate today. Every moral law we have today is based on the Ten Commandments found in Exodus 20:1-17. In Exodus 21:22 you will also see *judges* involved, leading up to Exodus 21:24.

Now that you have the context for those verses, what is Jesus talking about? In what context is he saying Matthew 5:39? In Matthew 5:38 you see, **"Ye have heard that it hath been said, An eye for an eye, and a tooth for a tooth,"** here He is referring back to Deuteronomy 19:21 and Exodus 21:24, where it's limited to the *courts* but obviously people have been applying it in person to person interactions outside of the courts. Jesus reiterates how people should treat one another, *before* it even enters the courts. If people treated each other like that, there would be no need of courts. If you notice in Exodus 20 where the Ten Commandments are, you will see a heavy emphasis on treating one's *"neighbor,"* in other words, *how to treat people,* Jesus is hitting home on that point.

Genesis 17:10 **"This is my covenant, which ye shall keep, between me and you and thy seed after thee; Every man child among you shall be circumcised."**
vs
Galatians 5:2 **"if ye be circumcised, Christ shall profit you nothing"**

Problem: Why is Paul saying circumcision *doesn't* matter when Genesis 17:10 says it *does*?

Answer: Again, we are dealing with *two different quotations from two different "Testaments."*
One is *under the Law* and the other is **"free from the law"** (Rom. 8:2). Circumcision is a *Jewish covenant* given to Abraham and his seed. After a Christian believes on Jesus Christ, a "spiritual circumcision," as mentioned before, takes place. **"In whom also ye are circumcised with the circumcision made without hands, in putting off the body of the sins of the flesh by the circumcision of Christ"** (Col. 2:11). You have a *physical* sign for the physical nation of Israel and a *spiritual* one for the Church.

As you can see, most of these "contradictions" *are from people who never adequately spent time in the Book and didn't care to go into the Book in any depth.* It's a lot like hearing someone talk about politics when they know nothing about it and are literally forming their opinion *on the spot* as they are asked a question. I believe Daniel Kahneman[1] wrote a book on the subject and that style of thinking. I would have guessed that

---
[1] Daniel Kahneman, *"Thinking Fast and Slow,"* 2011

Deuteronomy 27:22 **"Cursed be he that lieth with his sister, the daughter of his father, or the daughter of this mother"**

Leviticus 20:17 **"And if a man shall take his sister, his father's daughter, or his mother's daughter…it is a wicked thing"**

vs

([*Website comments*] But what was god's reaction to Abraham, who married his sister — his father's daughter? See Genesis 20:11-12)

Genesis 17:15-16 **"And God said unto Abraham, As for Sara thy wife…I bless her, and give thee a son also of her"**

Problem: Why did Abraham marry his close relative if it's against the Law in Leviticus and Deuteronomy?

Answer: Again, very *similar* to the separation from the N.T. and O.T., but this one is a little more difficult for some to pin down. This is an easy target for the Biblically illiterate.

Genesis and the story of Abraham was *before the Law. No one in the Book of Genesis had the Law of Moses.* The Law was given to *Moses* because people had become so lost without any directive will from God: the Law. There, of course, were some forms of civil law at the time of Abraham, such as The Code of Hammurabi and other systems of governance, but the Law given to Moses from Exodus 20 through Deuteronomy was *unknown* at the time of Job, Abraham, Isaac, Jacob, Noah, Adam, etc.

We do see some interesting occurrences before the Law, such as Abraham *tithing* (Gen. 14:20), he offers *sacrifice* (Gen. 22), as does Job, which is around the same period in time

(Job 1:5). This is a time of *trials* and *testings* from God towards individuals, as seen in Job 1 and Genesis 22.

Before the Law, people were judged *based on how they followed their conscience and how they acted on it* (Gen. 6:5, 9; Rom. 2:15, 1:21, 24-28). The world was wiped out due to *perversions* in Genesis 6; the Gentiles were given another chance, but soon given up in Genesis 11 because of their **"unnatural affections,"** burning lusts for one another, not being thankful, they bowed down to idols, and despite knowing God, they still did err and followed the darkness of their own hearts *instead* of their Creator (Rom. 1:21-24, 29-32). In Genesis 6 (before the flood) and Genesis 11 (after the flood) we have Gentiles *abusing* the lusts of their flesh and *abusing* the relationships of their kin, and in turn, their relationship with God. The union of man and woman is sacred in the Bible, ever since the very first husband and wife.

Despite this list of sins in Romans 1 and the sins listed in Leviticus 18 and 20, Sarah *is* Abraham's *half-sister*. She has a different mother (Gen. 20:12) than Abraham but shares the same father. *Jacob* also marries Rachel who is his *cousin*, as are *Isaac* and Rebekah. *Cain* takes his wife (most likely) from the children of Adam and Eve, or one of their children (Gen. 4:17). *It is evident that it was not considered sin to marry ones sister early on, half-sister, or a cousin at this time.*

What we have here is that, *as time went on*, people were not spreading out and stayed close, *marrying those of close relations when they didn't need to anymore*. Noah and his children were given the commission to **"replenish"** the earth (Gen. 9:1). They did, but obviously there were those who *abused* close relationships after the population of the world was brought back up; therefore, there would be little need to have close relations with a relative. From the time of Adam to Noah the relationship is *not* frowned upon. It appears that the Lord gave some leeway on the matter from the time of Abraham through Jacob, since *there was no Law* prohibiting it at the time from God; Jospeh marries an Egyptian native. After that, from *Exodus onward, it is* frowned upon. After God had called out for Himself a man (Abraham), and then a *nation* (Israel) *to be separate from the world* (Num. 23:9; Duet. 7:6, 14, etc.). That nation needed to be cleansed of the world they had just left (Egypt), where they had picked up bad habits. The Law was then established and part of that was God's desire for Israel to be separate from the other nations.

In Song of Solomon a wife is referred to as a *"sister"* (Song of Sol. 4:9-12, 5:1-2). The view that God had on this differed early on: *the first couple, Adam and Eve, were brother and sister —they had the same Father.* Having sexual relations with relatives became an issue *later* (see above), most likely from the time spent *in Egypt* (a type of the world), with those who were practicing idol worship, sex perversion, etc. The Law in Leviticus 18:6-20 deals with this very issue. There is a famous saying, a proverb rather: *"You can take them out of Egypt but you can't take the Egypt out of them."*

God's *dispensing* to man certain revelations *are given over time* in the Book. We tend to read Exodus and Leviticus and put everyone in the Book of Genesis in *that same category* when it is not so. Did Moses give the Law in Genesis 2?— No, he didn't. The people before Exodus 20 had no knowledge of God's thoughts on these matters unless they had a direct revelation, *like* those who did after Exodus 20.

To push the point further, *the line of Jesus Christ Himself* has a woman who committed *incest* with her father in law (Matt. 1:3; Gen. 38:18) *before* the Law, a whore Gentile *after* the Law (Matt. 1:5; Josh. 2:1, 6:25), and an adulterer who was also a murderer (Matt. 1:6; 2 Sam. 11:2-17) *after* the Law. The Bible is a very plain Book, but there they are, in the family tree of Jesus Christ, **"the man."** What are those kinds of people doing in a "Godly line"?

On the topic of incest and genetics, it's actually known that when a *new* pedigree is introduced, any genetic deformities may go away. That's a fancy way of saying that if you introduce more people from *another* population (Gen. 6) any mutations that may have occurred by sleeping with close relatives would go away. Abnormalities are more likely to occur between brother and sisters with the same parents *rather than* first, second, and third cousins.

One theory is that the genetic line *started out pure, and became more convoluted over time;* which could *also* be part of the reason behind Leviticus 18 (just speculation here); God *could* have been trying to protect a genetic line that was becoming more impure since the fall of Adam from further pollution and deleterious mutations; relations of incest or close relations would speed this up.

It's essentially backwards evolution hence, peoples lives being hundreds of years long in early Genesis and *reducing* in duration after the flood to present day. At the very least, the flood period marks a pivotal point. The average life span is right around 50-84[2] today, with an average of 73 years old, and has been for a while (Psa. 90:10). What brings the

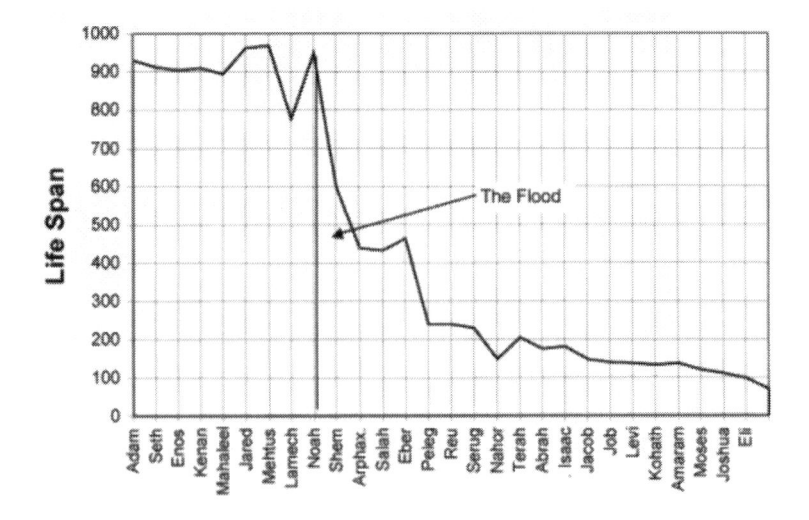

---

[2] Data taken from The World Health Organization, *"Life Expectancy,"* https://www.who.int/data/gho/data/indicators/indicator-details/GHO/life-expectancy-at-birth-(years)

average population age down in surveys today that were taken from the past (such as "life expectancy in 1000 B.C." being much, much lower) are babies dying, people dying of infections *without* antibiotics, and battles. A healthy individual has long been known to live around 70-80 years on average for some time now. It has come down from over 900 to around 70.

Proverbs 12:2 **"A good man obtaineth favour of the LORD"**

vs

(Now consider [*comments from webpage*] the case of Job. After commissioning Satan to ruin Job financially and to slaughter his shepherds and children to win a petty bet with Satan. God asked Satan:)

Job 2:3 **"Hast thou considered my servant Job, that there is none like him in the earth, a perfect and an upright man, one that feareth God, and escheweth evil? and still he holdeth fast his integrity, although thou movedst me against him, to destroy him without cause"**

Problem: If Job is an upright man, then why did he suffer so much? Didn't God say that, "the good will obtain favor?"

Answer: *Job did obtain favor and was rewarded, at the end of the Book of Job.* Job was in favor with God hence satan not bothering him *until* He gives *permission* to satan to do so.

Job was as perfect as a man could be, but sometimes those who the Lord *favors* get tested and chastened, **"My son, despise not the chastening of the LORD; neither be weary of his correction: For whom the LORD loveth he correcteth; even as a father the son in whom he delighteth"** (Prov. 3:11-12). Job's problem was self-righteousness.

"My righteousness I hold fast, and will not let it go: my heart shall not reproach me so long as I live" (Job 27:6).

To the atheist, *"God is love"* so why would God want to do anything even remotely *negative* to his creation? That is a twisted 21st Century mind binging on Netflix shows. Job asks these same questions throughout the Book of Job (see Job 10-11).

Besides the authors of the article not reading *the end of Job,* nor understanding the *basic premise of the entire book,* and its *fundamental questions*—other than the *core literary themes of the book,* they may actually have a problem.

This is the question that creates atheists (see above), that and, *"if God is all powerful, then why doesn't He do something about all this injustice?"* He did. You just don't like the answer. This was in part, what Job complains about in the Book. He says, *"Why am I getting treated like those who are unjust, when I do well and do so much for God? I am just!"* He acknowledged that people in the O.T. were well off and treated well by God *if* they honored Him, so Job was utterly *confused* by all of it, *just like those at the website who are having trouble with the same issue.* The only difference being that Job *continued* to worship the Lord.

"The tabernacles of robbers prosper, and they that provoke God are secure; into whose hand God bringeth abundantly" (Job 12:6).

Now, what is Job saying? He's saying you can rob a bank and it's just fine! Praises!—Just kidding. He is being sarcastic here, as he *knows* that they **"prosper"** only *temporarily* (see Job 15:34, 18:6, 14). How do I know he's being sarcastic?—see 12:1, 2, 3, 4, 5. You could *twist* the thing and *make it say,* "a thief prospers in the sight of God" and give no context other than the explanation of, *"a thief prospers in the sight of God"* and *someone* would buy it. There are many groups who take such measures concerning Scripture: the Mormons, Jehovah Witnesses, Seventh Day Adventists, Catholics, and what you are seeing first hand here with the atheists.

I have heard several people comment on the Book of Job who are atheists by degrading the entire Book to a "simple bet" between God and the devil. If it was a bet, then how is it that God is in complete control of the situation? The Lord gives satan instructions/permissions in Job 1:12, 2:6. There was one thing the devil never had permission to do with Job, and that was to *kill him*. Lucifer has the power to do it (Heb. 2:14) but that *power and authority is given to him by God Himself*. Furthermore, what does God have to gain from such a "bet"? Would God enter into a "bet" that He could lose? Did God and the devil shoot dice as well? Maybe Uno? God taught Job and the devil a lesson during that time: the devil learned that man can still surprise him even after 2,000+ years of studying man and what causes him to fall; Job learned of his self-righteous attitude.

Ecclesiastes 9:7 **"Go thy way, eat thy bread with joy, and drink thy wine with a merry heart"**
vs
1 Corinthians 7:30 **"they that rejoice, as though they rejoiced not"**

Problem: Aren't "holy men" not supposed to give in to excess and drink alcohol? Shouldn't they live a "holy" lifestyle? Moderation, or no moderation?

Answer: What they have *omitted* from Ecclesiastes 9:7 was the last part of the verse, which is, **"For God now accepteth thy works."** They complement each other, not contradict.
1 Corinthians 7:25-35 is centered on the subject of marriage and moderation, and interestingly enough, the next few verses after Ecclesiastes 9:7 get right into that. The idea is, *live while you can and enjoy it, but if you can't ask God to bless your beer or your marriage then something is wrong* and you

probably shouldn't get married to that person or drink that shot of tequila.

It is pretty amazing how Christians say prayers before meals but they never seem to say a prayer over a beer. "God, bless this Miller-Lite, I really need it." Maybe jokingly, but not seriously. Let us take a closer look in context of Ecclesiastes 9:7.

Verse 7 **"Go thy way, eat thy bread with joy, and drink thy wine with a merry heart; for God now accepteth thy works.**

Verse 8 **"Let thy garments be always white; and let thy head lack no ointment.**

Verse 9 **"Live joyfully with the wife whom thou lovest all the days of the life of thy vanity, which he hath given thee under the sun, all the days of thy vanity: for that is thy portion in this life, and in thy labour which thou takest under the sun.**

Verse 10 **"Whatsoever thy hand findeth to do, do it with thy might; for there is no work, nor device, nor knowledge, nor wisdom, in the grave, whither thou goest.** (Ecc. 9:7-10)

1. **"Go thy way,"** get up and get going. Get out there and apply it.
2. **"Eat thy bread with joy, and drink thy wine with a merry heart,"** many people use this as an *alibi to drink alcohol*. Bread is likened to the "word of God" (Luke 4:4), wine is likened to blood (John 6:54-58, 2:3-4; Matt. 26:28-29; Deut. 32:14). Now we have a prophetic application going on. The literal interpretation has *nothing to do with being drunk*. Does it say *"drink thy wine until drunk with a merry heart?"*—No, it doesn't. See, that Book will read *you*. Once a year Israel would have a "party day" and drink or eat whatever they pleased (Deut. 14:24-26). This isn't what is going on here. Notice how this *one* passage will just cut a person to pieces.

3. **"For God now accepteth thy works"** as in *now*, not tomorrow or yesterday. How do you achieve this without living a holy lifestyle?
4. **"Let thy garments be always white"** as in, *not* black in funeral garb, clean, unsullied from sin (Isa. 1:18). How do you achieve this without living a holy lifestyle?
5. **"Let thy head lack no ointment"** *oil* being a reference in type to The Holy Spirit (1 Sam. 16:13; 1 John 2:27). In other words, be filled with the Spirit of God (Eph. 5:18; Acts 2:4). How do you do this? Not by getting drunk as seen in Ephesians 5:18 but by singing songs to the Lord (Eph. 5:18-19). Notice that Ephesians 5:18 says, **"filled"** and not *"receiving."* How do you achieve this without living a holy lifestyle?
6. **"Live joyfully with the wife"** you chose each other in marriage, and made a bond with her, so continue and celebrate it.
7. **"Do it with might,"** anything you do, do it to the best of your ability. *"Give it 100%"* and *"turn up to 100."* Do the best you can and don't halfway-do-the-thing.
8. **"No work, nor device, nor knowledge, nor wisdom, in the grave, whither thou goest,"** you are going to die eventually and that's a fact, so the best thing you can do while you are on the other side of the coffin is the list above. This is *not* a doctrinal statement on life after death. This is what Solomon is *observing* of life on earth. For all he knows and by *his observations*, that could be so.

The idea there is that if God is accepting your works, your garments are white, you are living joyfully, and giving things your best effort, then being drunk all the time is not on the list or even drinking heavily every now and then doesn't make the cut.

You live and then you die. It is a *personal observation*. Paul had a personal observation that was quite different (2 Cor. 12:1-4). This verse in Ecclesiastes is used by Jehovah

Witnesses to prove that a person is *"unconscious"* in the grave until the White Throne Judgment of Revelation 20.

This is not so. In Luke 16:22-31 a person can *feel pain and wants water* after death; (Gen. 35:18) a *soul departs after* death; (Phil. 1:23) when you depart you are *with Christ,* for the Christian after death; (Psa. 18:5-6) a person can *feel sorrow* in hell after death; (Gen. 49:33) a person is *gathered with others before* their body is actually buried; (Isa. 14:15-19) bodies can be *gazed upon* after death; (Ezek. 32:21) and can *yell and speak after* death.

Why this group picked 1 Corinthians 7:30 for this "problem," I do not know, because Paul is agreeing with the verses above. They could have picked a much better verse. It's almost as if Paul had just finished Ecclesiastes chapter 9 as he was considering the church at Corinth in Chapter 7. Many people, like those from the website who generate these "discrepancies" are unstable and **"wrest, as they do also the other scriptures, unto their own destruction"** (2 Peter 3:16). Let's look at 1 Corinthians 7:29-31.

Verse 29 **"But this I say, brethren, the time is short: it remaineth, that both they that have wives be as though they had none;**

Verse 30 **"And they that weep, as though they wept not; and they that rejoice, as though they rejoiced not; and they that buy, as though they possessed not;**

Verse 31 **"And they that use this world, as not abusing it: for the fashion of this world passeth away."**

Paul is addressing **"brethren"** (vs 29) which are other *Christians.* **"The time is short"** for us, as Solomon said above, we have an expiration date. The difference is that a Christian is *not* looking toward the grave *or* fearing it, but *toward Jesus Christ* (Titus 2:13) who we will meet. If you have a wife or a husband it would be best to devote your time to God *rather* than the constant pleasing of each other (see 1 Cor. 7:34 and Phil. 4:5). It's not good to be unbalanced (Prov. 11:1) and especially in marriage and in things of *this world.*

Love and enjoy the time here with your wife and husband but our purpose is to **"Fear God"** (Ecc. 12:13), and to follow Christ, **"Be ye followers of me, even as I also am of Christ"** (1 Cor. 11:1).

This world is not permanent, it is *not* our home. We are **"strangers"** here with God (Levi. 25:23). We belong elsewhere, for follow Christ because **"the fashion of this world passeth away"** (vs 31) every breath you take, time passes by. As this time passes, how are you supposed to care for the Lord when you are spending all your *sadness*, **"they that weep"** on worldly things and all your *positive emotions*, **"they that rejoice"** on rejoicing over worldly pleasures that you may get from sex, children, personal achievements, and consumerism, material things, and *money*, **"they that buy"** on houses, cars, stocks, and the like, when you should be giving some of that to missionaries or a local church. The idea here is *balance and moderation*. In other words, *"a holy lifestyle."*

Ezekiel 18:20 **"The son shall not bear the iniquity of the father"**

vs

Exodus 20:5 **"I the LORD thy God am a jealous God, visiting the iniquity of the fathers upon the children unto the third and fourth generation"**

Problem: Does the iniquity of the father pass on or not?

Answer: Again, let us retrieve *the full verse* of Exodus 20:5, which yet *again and again* in our study of atheists verses the Scriptures, is so lovingly cut short by the "honest," just trying to "help a guy out," and of course, "evidence based" community at atheists.org.

"Thou shalt not bow down thyself to them, nor serve them: for I the LORD thy God am a jealous God, visiting

the iniquity of the fathers upon the children unto the third and fourth generation OF THEM THAT HATE ME"

"Bow down thyself" to *who*, and **"serve"** *who*? Well, other **"gods"** and "images" (see Exod. 20:3-4). God *will* and *does* visit the **"iniquity of the fathers upon the children"** to this day. We are talking about images and idols. Notice the punctuation in the passages. Think about alcoholics who leave their children in poor shape, with no money, and most likely to carry on the torch of alcoholism. They have made worship of the bottle. *Unless…they turn away from their fathers sin.* Even then it can be an uphill battle. Also, consider the deep seeded implications for Catholics concerning statues of Mary or other "aids in worship" inside their homes and churches.

What does the next verse say? **"And shewing mercy unto thousands of THEM THAT LOVE ME, and keep my commandments"** (Exod. 20:6). *He shows mercy to those who keep his commandments.* Now, doesn't that sound familiar, like Ezekiel 18:20? We shall read it *in full* instead of giving you a *sound bite,* after all, we want the *evidence* and not some shady work done by a group of Bible rejecting whitewashers.

This time, start it at the paragraph mark.

Verse 19 **"Yet say ye, Why? doth not the son bear the iniquity of the father? When the son hath done that which is lawful and right, and hath kept all my statutes, and hath done them, he shall surely live."**

Verse 20 **"The soul that sinneth, it shall die. The son shall not bear the iniquity of the father, neither shall the father bear the iniquity of the son: the righteousness of the righteous shall be upon him, and the wickedness of the wicked shall be upon him."**

Verse 21 **"But if the wicked will turn from all his sins that he hath committed, and keep all my statutes, and do that which is lawful and right, he shall surely live, he shall not die."**

Verse 22 "**All his transgressions that he hath committed, they shall not be mentioned unto him: in his righteousness that he hath done he shall live.**"

Verse 23 "**Have I any pleasure at all that the wicked should die? saith the Lord GOD: and not that he should return from his ways, and live?**"

Verse 24 "**But when the righteous turneth away from his righteousness, and committeth iniquity, and doeth according to all the abominations that the wicked man doeth, shall he live? All his righteousness that he hath done shall not be mentioned: in his trespass that he hath trespassed, and in his sin that he hath sinned, in them shall he die.**"

Verse 25 "**Yet ye say, The way of the Lord is not equal. Hear now, O house of Israel; Is not my way equal? are not your ways unequal?**" ...

Verse 30 "**Therefore I will judge you, O house of Israel, every one according to his ways, saith the Lord GOD. Repent, and turn yourselves from all your transgressions; so iniquity shall not be your ruin.**"

Verse 31 "**Cast away from you all your transgressions, whereby ye have transgressed; and make you a new heart and a new spirit: for why will ye die, O house of Israel?**"

The verse *right before* verse 20, in which atheists.org has so much trouble with, *asks the question and then answers it* from Ezekiel 18:20-24. It was just one verse *before* their "problem verse." If they didn't get that, it said it back in Exodus 20:5. It is *conditioned on the descendant either loving or hating God*.

If they follow the commandments and statutes, **"do that which is lawful and right,"** the man shall *live in his righteousness*. If he does not, then he will *die in sin*. God shows mercy on those who follow His ways, i.e. not **"visiting the iniquity of the fathers upon the children"**— just as you were told back in Exodus 20:5-6. This is nothing new, it can be seen throughout the Bible in practice.

The nation of Israel had become accustomed to assuming what the website itself assumed: *"the reason we are the way we are is because of our fathers"* (Ezek. 18:2). They are passing responsibility off, from themselves and on to their fathers and past generations. They are playing "the blame game." Just as God did not allow Adam and Eve to play the blame game, He will not allow His nation to either.

Also, notice how *this differs from the New Testament Body*. These verses mentioned all deal with *following commandments* and *working* the *Law*. Without the New Birth, a man is no different than the walking dead. As a Born Again Christian Paul says, **"Now to him that worketh is the reward not reckoned of grace, but of debt"** (Rom. 4:4).

"Not of works, lest any man should boast" (Eph. 2:9).

"Wherefore the law was our schoolmaster to bring us unto Christ, that we might be justified BY FAITH" (Gal. 3:24). (See the appendix titled, *"Faith & Works."*)

In Ezekiel 18:20 we read, **"the soul that sinneth, it shall die,"** just as Jesus said, **"I said therefore unto you, that ye shall die in your sins: for if ye believe not that I am he, ye shall die in your sins"** (John 8:24).

But in Christ you are to reckon yourself dead to sin: **"Likewise reckon ye also yourselves to be dead indeed unto sin, but alive unto God through Jesus Christ our Lord"** (Rom. 6:11).

Why? **"For sin shall not have dominion over you: for ye are not under the law, but under grace"** (Rom. 6:14).

How? **"But as many as received him, to them gave he power to become the sons of God, even to them that believe on his name"** (John 1:12).

"In whom ye also trusted, after that ye heard the word of truth, the gospel of your salvation: in whom also after that ye believed, ye were sealed with that holy Spirit of promise, Which is the earnest of our inheritance until the redemption of the purchased possession, unto the praise of his glory" (Eph. 1:13-14).

More "Contradictions" 123

"The scripture hath concluded all under sin, that the promise by faith of Jesus Christ might be given to them that believe"** (Gal. 3:22).

This is why **"Ye must be born again"** (John 3:7). This is what the Sacrifice of Jesus Christ did to those who believe as foretold by Isaiah in ~712 B.C., **"He shall see of the travail of his soul, and shall be satisfied: by his knowledge shall my righteous servant justify many; for he shall bear their iniquities. Therefore will I divide him a portion with the great, and he shall divide the spoil with the strong; because he hath poured out his soul unto death: and he was numbered with the transgressors; and he bare the sin of many, and made intercession for the transgressors"** (Isa. 53:11-12).

Back to the problem we face. A few other things to note in the dismantling of this "discrepancy" about Exodus 20:5-6 is that the **"of them"** in Exodus 20:6 *is in reference to the* **"generation"** *in verse 5*. This commandment has been slyly *removed* from Catholic bibles and the Catholic Catechism. I wonder why? *Could a statue of Mary be a* **"graven image"**?— Why yes, it surly is.

The explanation the Catholic Church gives for doing this is even more *ridiculous*. They make *two* commandments out of number 10 in Exodus 20:17 which states not to covet your neighbors wife nor his goods. Then they tell you the reason they got rid of number two (graven images) is because it was *redundant to the first commandment* of **"no other gods before me."** Now who's being redundant here?—Making two out of 10 is doing the same! Sounds like something was getting in the way of their own idol worship and their use of "worship aids."

Exodus 20:5-6 is in relation to *graven images*. As you can see from Ezekiel 20:8, Joshua 24:23, and Exodus 32:4-6, Israel had their share of iniquity visited upon them. (See Judges 1:19, 2:13 in connection to Joshua 24:23. Exodus 32:4-6; Ezek. 20:8 in connection with Numbers 14-16). It even continued much *further* than Judges 17 into *today* towards **"them that hate me"** (Exod. 20:5).

Furthermore, in Ezekiel 18:5-9 we are given an example. There is **"a man"** (verse 5), and a **"son"** (verse 10) and a "grandson" (verse 14). In the Bible, a good example representing Ezekiel 18:5-9 would be Hezekiah (2 Kings 18-20). In Ezekiel 18:10-13 we have the **"man," "beget a son"** in verse 10. This son did *not do* what his father did as far as following the Lord and be **"true."** His son was Manasseh (2 Kings 21). Manasseh was one of the worst kings in the later history of Judah and fits the description in Ezekiel 18:10-13: he did not follow his father Hezekiah but instead, did that which was **"abomination."** Then, our third example given in Ezekiel 18 is the grandson of the man in verse 5. To continue with our example, it would be Josiah (he is actually the *great-grandson*, but since his father Amon *did not* follow the Lord, the example still fits). Josiah led a revival for Israel (2 Kings 22-23). He is the son of Amon, grandson of Manasseh and great-grandson of Hezekiah. He fits the description in Ezekiel 18:14-18 who looked at his fathers sins (Amon) and **"doeth not."**

To summarize, we have three generations in Ezekiel 18: *a father, a son, and a grandson (or great-grandson)*. Each can be seen in the Bible given as examples in 2 Kings 18-23 with *Hezekiah* who loved the Lord (Ezek. 18:5-9), *Manasseh and Amon* who did not love the Lord (Ezek. 18:10-13), and *Josiah* who loved the Lord (Ezek. 18:14-18). It is nothing new. It was all *conditional* on what atheists.org conveniently left out of the passage: **"of them that hate me"** (Exod. 20:5).

James 1:13 **"Let no man say when he is tempted, I am tempted of God: for God cannot be tempted with evil, neither tempteth he any man."**

vs

Genesis 22:1 **"And it came to pass after these things, that God did tempt Abraham"**

Problem: I thought it said that God couldn't "temp" anyone?

Answer: This was already discussed in the chapter called *"A Bucketful of Contradictions."*

Exodus 20:12 **"Honor thy father and thy mother"**
vs
Luke 14:26 **"If any man come to me, and hate not his father, and mother, and wife, and children, and brethren, and sisters, yea, and his own life also, he cannot be my disciple"**

Problem: Are we supposed to hate our father and mother *or* honor them?

Answer: It is truly amazing what you can do with the Bible when you have absolutely *no idea* what is going on. You can make it say whatever you want. I'll give you an example: in Acts 2:44-45 you'll read, **"had all things common; and sold their possessions and goods, and parted them to all men, as every man had need."** Again, in Acts 4:32:-35 we see a very similar thing. This is *communism*. You could use these verses to support communism and wave around Marx's *"Communist Manifesto"* while quoting these Bible verses. Now, let's see *how this turns out* in the Bible, and if communism *is* actually Biblical.

In Acts 5:1-11 we see this communism *going horribly wrong* as it did *through the entirety of human history*. It only worked for a short amount of time in Acts before someone had to ruin it, and ruin it *they did*. Every Christian has the **"old man"** and the **"new man"** within them. After Acts 5, there is *no mention* of the Church acting this way, but instead Paul works *with his own hands* and tells others *to work* with theirs and *pay their own way* (2 Thess. 3:10-12; Acts 18:1-3).

The Bible is a very plain Book. What Church practices that from Acts 2 and 4 today?—Not one, except maybe a small commune somewhere in Iowa. Do you see the Billy Graham estate selling off all their possessions? People often say that you can make the Bible say whatever you want and that is true *to an extent*, but in all reality you just can't. Can you make any other book say whatever you want it to say? No, it says what it says when you get down to brass tax. The Bible, unlike the majority of books, has the keen ability to just completely mess a person up; strange Book, that one.

Back to the text. All that's going on in the issue between Exodus 20:12 and Luke 14:26 *is the idea that God comes first.*

Why are you to honor your mother and father in the first place?—Because it was *asked of you by the Lord*. The *number one* thing which takes precedence over *all* else is to **"Love the Lord thy God all thy heart, and with all thy soul, and with all thy mind"** (Matt. 22:37). Notice what *comes second* in Matthew 22:39. You will find this command in the O.T. as well (see Deut. 6:4, 11:13). To bring these passages "further into the light" using the AV of the Protestant Reformation, in Exodus 32:26-28 of the O.T. we have an example of *not* putting God first and relatives dying for worshipping the Golden Calf (Exod. 32:4-6) *in place of God*. For the Christian, the passage means that if you put your wife, daughter, mother, or husband, etc., *before* the Lord then you may as well have put Him in last place (Matt. 10:37). *"If you're not first, you're last"—Ricky Bobby, cir. 2006.* You may also see how the word **"hate"** is used in Judges 14:16 in the sense we are talking about.

What is paradoxical is that putting God in last invariably puts those you love in last, as was the case with Saul and Jonathan, where he and his son Jonathan were taken away due to Saul's heart leaving God (1 Sam. 28:18-19, 31:2). In David's case, his sin concerning Bathsheba and Uriah (2

Sam. 11) had dire consequences on his children in 2 Samuel 13. In a moment, it can change from keeping God *first* to the flesh being *first*. With you on the Throne instead of God, there are usually consequences, either here or at The Judgement Seat of Christ. *"You reap what you sow"* is still very much applied to the Christian.

Job 7:9 **"he that goeth down to the grave shall come up no more"**

vs

John 5:28-29 **"the hour is coming, in which all that are in the graves shall hear his voice, and shall come forth"**

Problem: Is there a resurrection or is there not?

Answer: Job 7:9 is also used to prove there is no afterlife by some. Now, Why would Job say this? If you notice in Job 7:15-16 the man is *suicidal*, **"So that my soul chooseth strangling, and death rather than my life. I loathe it; I would not live alway: let me alone; for my days are vanity."** Having noted the context in which Job is speaking in chapter seven we can now look at Job 33:30: **"To bring back his soul from the pit, to be enlightened with the light of the living."** Here, as well as Job 19:25-26 he *does mention a resurrection from the dead AND an afterlife.***"For I know that my redeemer liveth, and that he shall stand at the latter day upon the earth: And though after my skin worms destroy this body, yet in my flesh shall I see God."** Job will stand before God *after* his *body* has decomposed. What sort of *body* may this be? (See 1 Corinthians 15:39-44 for the *type*.)

You see how easy it is to confuse a *doctrinal* statement with a *personal* one. We have already viewed one a few pages back from Ecclesiastes 9:7-10 where Solomon is making an observation as he does throughout the book. Job was making a *personal* statement in chapter seven via the context, but in the passages from chapter 33 and 19 that we looked at, there is a *doctrinal* statement being made. Job had a similar revelation to that of Isaiah (Isa. 26:19-21) and Ezekiel (Ezek. 37) concerning a resurrection.

Matthew 16:28 **"Verily I say unto you, There be some standing here, which shall not taste of death, till they see the Son of man coming in his kingdom. "**
Luke 21:32-33 **"Verily I say unto you, This generation shall not pass away, till all be fulfilled. Heaven and earth shall pass away: but my words shall not pass away. "**
Romans 13:11-12 **"And that, knowing the time, that now it is high time to awake out of sleep: for now is our salvation nearer than when we believed. The night is far spent, the day is at hand: let us therefore cast off the works of darkness, and let us put on the armour of light."**
James 5:8 **"Be ye also patient; establish your hearts: for the coming of the Lord draweth nigh."**
1 John 2:18 **"Little children, it is the last time: and as ye have heard that antichrist shall come, even now are there many antichrists; whereby we know that it is the last time."**
1 Peter 4:7 **"But the end of all things is at hand: be ye therefore sober, and watch unto prayer."**
"These words were written between 1800 and 1900 years ago [*comments of the website*] and were meant to warn and prepare the first Christians for the immediate end of the world. Some words are those supposedly straight out of the mouth of the "Son of God." The world did not end 1800 or 1900 years ago. All that generation passed away without any of the things foretold coming to pass. No amount of prayer brought it about; nor ever so much patience and belief and sober living. The world went on, as usual, indifferent to the

More "Contradictions"

spoutings of yet another batch of doomsday prophets with visions of messiahs dancing in their deluded brains. The world, by surviving, makes the above passages contradictions."

Problem: Didn't it say that the day was *"at hand"* and Jesus was going to come back *before* anyone died? Why hasn't Jesus come back yet if He said He would, and other writers said He would come back soon, but hasn't? Why were they preparing for it? Why did they all talk as if it was going to be the very next day?

Answer: This is the last of the "contradictions" from atheists.org and they really went *all out*; rapid fire. I suppose they "saved the best for last." Given how many verses, this may take some time to get into. I will preface this section with **"But of that day and hour knoweth no man, no, not the angels of heaven, but my Father only"** (Matt. 24:36). Even though Paul had the gift of prophecy, Peter and John also had their visions, no man knows what day the Rapture will occur *or* for that matter, the Second Coming.

First, let's look at James 5:8 and 1 Peter 4:7. Both are saying **"the end of all things is at hand"** and **"the coming of the Lord draweth nigh."** The sense of both passages is that both **"the end"** and the "Coming of Jesus Christ" are **"at hand,"** and **"nigh."** You think, "oh, as in very soon" but let's see *how the Bible uses those terms:* does it mean "very close" or can it also mean "far away"?

According to Scripture (Isa. 13:6; Rev. 1:3; Joel 1:15, 2:1; Jer. 23:23; Matt. 3:2, 4:10; Mark 1:15; Deut. 32:35), **"at hand"** can mean 400-2000 years from that point, or it can mean a few minutes, days, or even a few years, (John 7:2, 11:55; Matt. 26:45; Mark 1:15, 14:42; Luke 21:31; 1 Sam 9:8; Deut. 15:9; Gen. 27:41). When we think of **"at hand,"** we tend to think of a hands-reach away, or a hands-breadth. As with all measurements, it depends upon the unit of measurement we are working with. In the case here, the question is how far away is the hand and what kind of a hand are we using. This is a good example of *the Bible dictating a measurement of time,* and as you can see, it isn't always the same.

As for the case of **"nigh"** in John 11:18 we do have an exact measurement, but in 1 Kings 2:1 you have a different use (as in Mark 13:29; Matt. 24:32, 15:8; Joel 2:1). It's used very similar to **"at hand."**

In Romans 13:11-12 Paul is talking about *the Rapture* of the Church, *which is also,* **"at hand."** The **"time"** in Romans 13:11 is the time of the Rapture and the **"salvation"** is of the Christians *body* (Rom. 8:15-23; 1 Cor. 15). The Christians *soul* is already saved. We are to be looking for Christ *today!*—Just as Paul was. The Rapture takes place *before* the "Day of the Lord." The Day of the Lord is what Jesus was talking about in Matthew 16:28 (**"Son of Man…in his kingdom"**). Paul and the passage in Matthew *are talking about two different things.*

Before you get all weird about the Rapture and start foaming at the mouth, saying that the Church *goes through* the Tribulation, and that *"the concept of the Rapture was invented around the 1700-1800's,"* let me just say that *Shepard* in A.D. 150, *Victorius* in A.D. 240, *Cyprion* in A.D. 250, and *Ephraim of Syria* in A.D. 350-390 all stated in their writings that the Church would *not* go through the Tribulation. *The idea was there well before the 1700's.*

1. The Church is saved from **"wrath"** (Rom. 5:9; 1 Thess. 1:10, 5:9).
2. The Body of Christ *is* the Church (Eph. 1:22-23; 1 Tim. 3:15; Col. 1:24) and is made up of saved individuals.
3. The Body of Christ *cannot* be broken or separated (1 Cor. 12; 2 Tim. 2:13)
4. The Tribulation is a time of God's **"wrath"** (Rev. 14:10, 16:1, 15:7; Isa. 6:11; Jer. 4:23-27; Isa. 26:17, etc.)

5. In the Tribulation saved Jew's and Gentiles are *separated* again (Rev. 7:4-17), which means the Church is *not* apart of it (see below)
6. There is neither Jew nor Gentile in the Body of Christ (Gal. 3:27-28) because it is *one* Body.
7. *Salvation* in the Tribulation is *by works and faith* (Rev. 12:17, 14:12). This is *not* a Christians salvation (Eph. 2:8-9; Rom. 11:6; Gal. 2:16; Rom. 10:13), it is *different*
8. There is *another Gospel* from an angel in the Tribulation (Rev. 14:6) consisting of *works and faith* (Rev. 14:6-13). This can not be for the Church since the Mystery of the Church was revealed to Paul and the dispensation of Grace (Eph. 3:2-3, 12) and if there is any other Gospel preached during that time, even *by an angel*, **"let him be accursed"** (Gal. 1:8)

In 1 John 2:18 we have John telling us what Paul is saying in 2 Thessalonians 2:7, about the **"mystery of iniquity."** There have been **"many"** "types" of antichrists throughout the ages (1 John 2:18): Hitler, *any* Pope, Caesar, etc. This goes back to Luke 17:1 which tells you that *"if the shoe fits, God will use you for that purpose,"* because his plan has to come to pass. All throughout the Gospel accounts Judas was a *thief*, the holder of *the money*, and *complains* when it was *spent unwisely* (according to him) but is spending a large amount of money on our Lord Jesus Christ *really* a bad means of expenditure (John 12:3-8)?

Judas was *a type* of the antichrist (John 17:12 Cf. 2 Thess. 2:3). None of these were *"the real thing,"* but each one at anytime could have been, *if* they were *allowed* to continue. This is what John is hinting at in 1 John 2:18, right after he gets done telling you the situation with the world in which the antichrist will *use to gain control* (Dan. 11:21-24). We know it **"is the last time"** (1 John 2:18) because of the level of corruption and deceit *keeps progressing*, as in 2 Thessalonians 2:3 where it says, **"there come a falling away...FIRST."**

Without the falling away, there will be no "Day of the Lord" *or* no Rapture. The falling away started in A.D. 33 as John is telling you back in 1 John 2:18 around A.D. 90. There were mass killings of Christians and persecutions of the most vile sort occurring around the time of A.D. 90. The emperors of Rome were *types* of the antichrist, and for all John knew, and as he was "hoping" (Titus 2:13), Jesus would come *today, not yesterday or tomorrow, but today!* **"Even so, come, Lord Jesus"** (Rev. 22:20).

Why were all these Christians preparing for Jesus to come back? For a Christian it is the **"blessed hope"** (Titus 2:13; Rom. 8:23-24) that He come back and for the redemption of our bodies. It is our **"hope."** Even with the advanced revelation given to Paul, he did *not* know when our catching up with Him would happen, **"the day of the Lord so cometh as a thief in the night"** (1 Thess. 5:2). A thief comes unannounced and without notice, **"Even so, come, Lord Jesus."**

You say, *"Okay, so what? 'At hand' doesn't mean what I thought it meant and it can have any number of events in-between…and some of the passages are about two different events…so what about Matthew 16:28 and Luke 21:32-33?"*

Could there be a more tricky Book on the planet?

First thing to note in Matthew 16:28 is that the passage says, **"till they see the Son of man coming in his kingdom."** Now, everyone has a bible that divides the Old Testament from the New Testament, yes? The division goes further, as noted by Shepard in A.D. 150, Victorinus in A.D. 240, Cyprion A.D. 250, and others when **"dividing"** (2 Tim. 2:15) up the Scriptures appropriately surrounding the topics at hand: the Church and the Tribulation. Papias A.D. 70-155, Justin Martyr A.D. 110-165, Irenaeus A.D. 178, Tertullian A.D. 190-210, and so on, were also avid in **"dividing"** with issues such as the Millennial Reign of Jesus Christ, the Tribulation, the Second Coming, and prophecies surrounding Jesus Christ's First Coming. You can count on this "practice" starting with Darby, like you can count on the pope renouncing his throne in the future. *You can not* **"study"** *the scriptures without* **"dividing"** *the Scriptures.* You will be as lost as Augustine and Joseph Boot when it comes to the issues we are about to face, you'll also wind up in a grade-A *mess* like atheists.org did.

The verse in Matthew 16:28 says **"kingdom,"** the question is *which kingdom*. The *Kingdom of God* and the *Kingdom of Heaven are two different things*. The Holy Spirit made a distinction between the two in *spelling* and when used in *reference*. Paul never says *"Kingdom of Heaven,"* because he was given the revelation of the Church; he says "Kingdom of God."

One can be taken by *force* (Matt. 11:12) and the other is strictly *spiritual* (Rom. 14:17). One is *external* (John 6:15) and the other is *within you* (Luke 17:20-21). The spiritual one involves a *new birth* to enter (John 3:5-7) and the physical one involves a *reign* (2 Tim. 2:12-13). One involves *land* that Jerusalem has yet to have (Gen. 15:18-21; Isa. 65:9, 66:13, 22; Amos 9:15; Obad. 21; Mic. 7:16-20; Zeph. 3:14-15, etc.), and the other involves a *spiritual* "plane" (2 Cor. 12:2-4; John 14:3; Eph. 2:6; 1 Peter 1:4). If you *deny* the difference, then further Bible reading is necessary.

Which kingdom is Jesus Christ talking about?

If it is the *Kingdom of God* then the passage *is true* without question due to the New Birth of his disciples *after* Calvary and the Holy Spirit descending at Pentecost (Acts 2) in which Peter, James, and John (the ones **"standing"** there in Matt. 16:28) *were alive* and thus, became part of His Body; entering the *Kingdom of God* (Eph. 2:6; Rom. 14:17).

If Jesus is talking about the *Kingdom of Heaven* then the passage would stand as partly *false* because Peter and James *did die* in their bodies *before* Christ set up his earthly Kingdom on a *physical, literal throne here on earth* (Rev. 19) which is yet future. They (Peter and James) did not live to see that in full, at their present state, and *did* **"taste of death"**

(Matt. 16:28). What about John that was there? John *did* see it, he wrote a book on the subject called, "Revelation."

If it's the *Kingdom of God* then they certainly saw Jesus when He was Resurrected and they certainly *were* Born again thus, entering into the *Kingdom of God* (see above).

What do the accounts of Mark and Luke record for the same event? **"But I tell you of a truth, there be some standing here, which shall not taste of death, till they see the kingdom of God"** (Luke 9:27).

What about Mark? **"Verily I say unto you, That there be some of them that stand here, which shall not taste of death, till they have seen the kingdom of God come with power"** (Mark 9:1).

When Jesus Christ comes back, He brings *both* Kingdoms back with him, the *Kingdom of God* (spiritual) and the *Kingdom of Heaven* (physical).

Given how many times Matthew says *"Kingdom of Heaven,"* it's no doubt miraculous that it *wasn't* penned here (Matt. 16:28); then that would *actually* be a booboo. How do you explain something like that? The way that "worked out" is something else—it's God's Book.

Now, what in the world, man? How is that possible? No human writer could have laid that thing out that smooth. It's as smooth as silk.

If you happen to get the two Kingdoms mixed up and say they are both the same, what ends up happening is a church-state regime tries to *"bring in the kingdom"* by force (Catholic Church) and murder anyone in their way. Read *any* church history book on the subject.[3] Other such *"kingdom builders"* are Islamists, who spread their faith *by the sword*, threaten slavery, and/or conversion in conquered countries.

What about Luke 21:32? First, it is a **"parable"** (Luke 21:29-33). Given that it is a **"parable,"** what can we draw

---

[3] The definitive work on the subject in a Biblical context is Dr. Peter S. Ruckman's *"The Sure Word of Prophecy."*

from it? The **"summer is now nigh at hand"** is in reference to Christ setting up his earthly Kingdom to come. The **"trees,"** which are often people, kings, and kingdoms in the Bible (Ezek. 15:6, 17:1-24, 19:10-14, etc.). God's **"determination"** is to gather the kings and kingdoms so that He may *destroy* them (Zeph. 3:8; Isa. 8:9-12, 30:28, 41:11, 66:15-16; Jer. 30:11; Joel 3:11; Matt. 13:30, 3:12; Rev. 17:2, 18:11, etc.). So that he may burn them. The **"fig tree"** was what Adam and Eve used as a "covering" for *themselves*. Further, it was the only thing Jesus ever *cursed* in the Gospel accounts (Mark 11:13-14). The fig tree has an apparent association with *self-righteous works* (Psa. 64:6 Cf. Gen. 3:7). The fig tree is Israel (Jer. 24:2-8) without God's "covering." Therefore God cursed Israel *until their redemption and restoration* at His Second Coming. Israel would rather *rely on their own works than that of Jesus Christ*. They stumbled at the stumbling stone (Isa. 8:14; Rom. 9:33). In A.D. 70 Israel was burned to the ground by their new "king," **"We have no king but Caesar"** (John 19:15).

It's also noteworthy that the Tribulation also goes by the name, **"the time of Jacob's trouble"** (Jer. 30:7)—Jacob is Israel—**"the LORD commanded the children of Jacob, whom he named Israel; With whom the LORD had made a covenant, and charged them"** (2 Kings 17:34-35).

"From following the ewes great with young he brought him to feed Jacob his people, and Israel his inheritance" (Psa. 78:71).

It is a time of humbling for the nation of Israel, just as the wilderness journey was when coming out of Egypt.

In Luke 21:31 Jesus is comparing the things He has said in the passages above and in the account of Matthew (Luke 21:25-28; Matt. 24:3, 5-8, 9-14, 15-16, 21, 24, 27-30) when referring to, **"when ye see these things come to pass."** Things *must* happen *before* Jesus Christ comes back. Undoubtedly **"this generation"** is in reference to the generation *in the parable* that Christ is talking *about, not* *talking to*. In other words, when x thing happens, y generation will not pass away until Christ's Kingdom comes into fruition, then Israel will bear its *fruit* worthy for God—the **"good figs"** (Jer. 24:2).

The passage is on the restoration of Israel and their New Birth and New Heart. The question really is: *when does that generation start?* What the thing is hinting at is that when the world will become *one integrated, "one world," global power,* (League of Nations, United Nations, Trilateral Commission, CFR, World Economic Forum, Bilderberg group, EU, etc.), united together, *summer is nigh* (Zeph. 3:8).

As for the **"words,"** they are settled in Heaven (Psa. 119:89) and are *also* on earth (Psa. 12:6-7), which will be renewed (2 Pet. 3:10-13) by the Originator of those words; as He will be right in front of you, *within speaking distance.*

This concludes the atheists.org "contradictions." As you have seen, most of them are reading compression problems, and a few are some deeper doctrinal issues that take some time to discuss. Some are questions relating to *study* of the Bible as opposed to just *skimming* through it. If anything, it shows the reader a proven track record of *how people hate to give God the benefit of the doubt, because they hate God.* You cannot claim neutrality on God because He doesn't claim neutrality on you. In Matthew 12:30 we read, **"he that is not with me is against me."** Does Lucifer claim neutrality? I think not. If you won't give God the benefit of the doubt then at least do your due diligence in presenting your claims scientifically and not as some half-baked professor of sociology who just got done tokin' on some "banana pancakes."

The next set of discrepancies I will be talking about will be those used by some of the more "well read" Islamists and Jews when being witnessed to "on the field." Later on, I will go into some deeper depths concerning more of those *"freshman classics"* from Christian seminaries, but first…let's check in with **"the world."**

Intermission

"Prophesy not unto us right things, speak unto us smooth things, prophesy deceits" — Isaiah 30:10

PEOPLE don't want the truth today. Most shy away from anything that even remotely sounds negative. Just as the verse above states, people want to hear **"smooth things."** Don't believe me? People would rather accept a lie if it means that they won't have to do something they don't want to do. Have you ever thought how crazy of a world we live in—I mean really thought about it? I'm sure you have in some fashion or another. Any world where Benny Hinn and Todd Bentley have people giving them *millions* of dollars in the name of their *"truth"* and *"healing"* is pretty crazy; insane actually. What if you aren't healed? Then *"you just don't have enough faith."* What a bunch of lousy no good **... So, it would be your fault that *his* healing abilities didn't work and then blame you for your *"lack of faith"* and in the process take your money?—Yes.

People actually pay for that stuff, you better believe it. If I had the gift of healing I'd be in a hospital somewhere winning souls to Christ, and so would *a lot* of other people, instead of putting on a show. Imagine how many people you could heal in every hospital. A great question for a *"healer"* is: *"can you drink anything poisonous?"* (Mark 16:18). I mean, this is one place where these people get some of their horrid doctrine. Try drinking Drano lately? (Caution: Do Not Do That. Given the "Tide Pod Challenge" of 2018, you just never know; better safe than sorry.) I doubt it, but it's a *sign* of an Apostle.

Paul had the signs and he healed many but later *after the book of Acts*, he seemed to have lost the *signs* of the Apostles. He traveled with Luke, a *physician* who cared for Paul, and Paul couldn't heal his best friend or himself (1 Tim. 5:23; 2 Tim. 4:20). *"But if you just believe enough…,"* listen man, go drink some Drano and we will see how much you *really* believe (*Don't Do That*). There's a reason "snake handlers" in churches don't seem to handle coral snakes or certain vipers; they would be really asking-for-it if they did. It's a big show, tickets, tickets, $5 a pop. *Read the Book.* The *Acts* of the Apostles are over. I'm *not* saying people don't have gifts, and I'm not saying I don't believe in healing, because I certainly *do*, but not from this bunch of rotten pomegranates. They take advantage of you *not knowing the Book*. They think you are a bunch of *suckers* who will pay for their next meal. Joel Osteen doesn't buy his own bit for a minute.

When you have a country full of people that actually go out and *buy* these peoples books and go to the seminars you have the *majority* being a bunch of wackos. To be normal is to be insane. As far as Christianity falling into apostasy one day at a time (2 Tim 3:1-7) and no body willing to face it for what it is, and the inevitability of the son of perdition (2 Thess. 2:3) coming into power, *what kind of a world does that look like*?

Each individual must conform, he must be part of the innumerable, immeasurable force of, We **"The People"** (1 Sam. 15:24; Exod. 32:1, 22-23). He must be molded and shaped into exactly what he *isn't* and be a shadow of the reality our ancestors saw up close and personal. Modern man is a candle flicker cast on a wall in a breezy auditorium.

Up is down, black is white, boys are girls, girls are boys, Christ is Buddha, Heaven is hell, men are animals, homosexual is normal (and should be *celebrated*), right is left,

left is right, true is false. People are willing to believe a fact checking site that was made by a politician to win an election. The majority of people are bonkers, insane, without hope, in darkness, in a dirty world with no soap (John 3:19; Eph. 2:2-3; Jer. 2:22).

There are the Mormons, who believe that the Jewish race migrated to the America's around 600 B.C., New Jerusalem is in Missouri, and Jospeh Smith before founding this cult was charged in court with fraud by using a "seeing stone" to help someone find buried treasure. He was a conman. Somehow, this man convinced others that an angel named Meroni told him all about the "lost" books of the Bible found on golden plates, that no one has *really* seen. The translation of this "unknown" language (which turned out to be Egyptian on one manuscript that Smith had passed off as being from the angel Meroni) which entails Jospeh Smith reading from a hat with a sheet over his head and thus, the Book of Mormon was born.

The Book of Mormon, in part, is plagiarized directly from a King James, which he had *under the sheet*, and in part is fabricated nonsense. Native Americans are not Jews, there has been genetic testing done. They believe that Jesus Christ was a created God and one day, *if they work hard enough*, they will become a god of their own planet; in other words, there are many gods (see Isa. 43:10). Anyone who has read a Bible and uses it as a final authority (or just *reads* it) knows that, like Muhammad, Jospeh Smith was a conman; deceiving millions of people into his cult. They will still try and convince you *that it's Biblical*. It's a cult with an agenda, just as *the world* has its cult.[1]

---

[1] Author's Note: For further reading and sources see *"Book of Mormon." "Doctrines and Covenants." "Journal of Discourses."* Fawn Brodie, *"No Man Knows My History: The Life of Joseph Smith, the Mormon Prophet,"* 1995. Also see the Mormon Articles of Faith. See the trial of Lori Vallow Daybell: the angel Meroni spoke to her about killing "zombies" (a spiritually dead person), who happened to be her children, 2019. See James Talmage, *"The Vanity of Mormonism,"* 1919. E. D. Howe, *"Mormonism Unveiled,"* 1834. Ellen Dickinson, *"New Light on Mormonism,"* 1885.

Intermission

What the world does is convince you that sexual perversion is okay, and if you don't accept that *(homophobe)* then you're a sinner *according to the worlds standards; you're a blasphemer*. You must *deny outright facts* or avoid topics such as: on average whites score higher on SAT's than blacks but Asians score higher than whites[2] *(racist, not allowed to talk about; off limits)*. Could this be because of income and available funds for SAT prep classes?—Not generally. Blacks are *more athletic* and have better abilities in that sphere than whites *(bigot; but can be talked about)*. You can't talk about these things, they are sins that *the worlds system* has created. The world will convince you that correcting a child by corporal punishment is sin *(child abuse)*; men should not enter into women's sports because men have different bone and muscle structure than women therefore have an advantage from birth *(sexist, transphobe)*, "SINNER! Go to HELL, YOU SINNER!"—They yell and yell. These are the sins *of the world*. If you step out of line, you *will* be labeled, cancelled, shadow-banned, or removed from the conversation on social media platforms all together.

How about this one: at the near end of the Roman Empire, the Ottoman Empire, and the British Empire (some of the largest civilizations in history), all incurred a rise in cases of homosexuality within their artwork and literature. **"Behold, this was the iniquity of thy sister Sodom, pride, fullness of bread, and abundance of idleness"** (Ezek. 16:49). People debate whether the rise in homosexuality and gay **"pride"** was actually due to a bigger "gay" population, or just that the culture had become "more accepting of gay's" thus, the art world began exploring it more. If we take the latter of the two, then there was a moral rot within the society which led

---

[2] The difference in black and white SAT scares was 100-200 points on average for accepted students into top private Universities as of 1993. Asians median score was 30 points higher than whites and blacks. See *"The Bell Curve"* by Herrnstein and Murray, 1996. Both authors have been deemed racist since the publication of their work, even though the statistics are undisputed and have not been debunked. If they were racist then Asians are the "superior race."

to its demise. In all cases the empires did not *start* that way. You will be called a bigot for even reflecting on these factual *observations*. Of course, the fall of an empire is multifaceted in nature: economics, war, food supply, over expansion, and so forth; but an *increase in liberalism and ideals that are in opposition to a nations founding principles* will cause a gangrenous smell from the bone of the organism. Whether it be from over-expenditure in times of war or drifting too far from the nations cultural starting point, a drift caused by multiculturalism. It is inevitable that a nation fall unless there be intervention from God Himself. People don't want to hear that, they want to hear people **"saying Peace, peace;...when there is no peace"** (Jer. 6:14).

What can one draw from such a stark observation? According to the average person today, we should just *ignore* it and *move on*; sweep it under the rug and *forget about it*. What does man ever learn from history?—Nothing. Why? It is uncomfortable, plain and simple. You would rather *"feel good"* than hear the truth. The measurement for truth is a yardstick of emotion. **"They speak a vision out of their own heart, and not out of the mouth of the LORD"** (Jer. 23:16).

Modern preaching has caught on to this way of **"the people"** and the attendance rolls have become sentient. You see the same thing happening in the States today in the media. You see a push from the media on certain topics. One being that homosexuality should be more acceptable and now fortune 500 companies are using them as chess pieces in *"brand awareness strategies."* Other times, politicians readily tap into the anger of middle-aged white men towards socially accepting the delusion of someone else's mind: that the man is a woman and vis versa.

Like relativism and post modern philosophy, these movements have their roots on college campuses. Institutions of higher learning have always been the seedbed of such movements. That's where Marxism took off and where the Antifa movement in 2016-2020 was most prevalent. Did you know Marx never worked a day in his life? He was a journalist, and for a short time, a librarian who surfed on Engles couch. *"Workers unite!"* Yeah right, man! Ever notice how hardworking people are *opposed* to communism but oftentimes professors and those who don't have jobs are in favor of communism? It's an intellectual, idealized movement without practicality or an honest view of history and the nature of man. Why else would young college students be at the spearhead of the movement?—Its fertilizer is romanticism and delusion.

The beloved Kant, Darwin, Hegel, Nietzsche, and Schopenhauer, all shared one thing in common: *"Man is the measure of all things."* This was said by Protagoras (490-420 B.C.) long before any of them were born. Descartes said it a little differently, *"I think, therefore I am" (cogito, ergo sum)*. These men and their ideals began to permeate institutions of higher learning. The complete mental psychosis of these individuals began to seep into the minds of others who considered themselves "intellectual" and "thoughtful." Men moved *away from* the Bible and *towards* Protagoras. Man had gone from Genesis 9 to 11 all over again. They moved *away* from Adam and Eve and *towards* Anaximander's fish[3] and Darwin's finches. They moved *away* from final authority of the Scriptures and *towards* the duel authorities of their own scholarship and the scholarship of their peers. Man was once again "on top of the world." He is his own master.

> Beyond this place of wrath and tears
> Looms but the Horror of the shade,
> And yet the menace of the years
> Finds and shall find me unafraid.
> It matters not how strait the gate,

---

[3] Author's Note: Anaximander (610-546 B.C.) was a Greek philosopher who is often credited with the idea that men evolved from fish long before the days of Darwin. Although, Anaximander's idea did involve fully pubescent humans hatching from the bellies of those fish.

How charged with punishments the scroll,
I am the master of my fate,
I am the captain of my soul.[4]

Throughout this chapter, you had opposites mentioned; two sides of the coin. What this new movement wants to do is get rid of the two sides of the coin and meld it, fashion it, work it, to get rid of its "impurities," and throw out the dross. These would be the impurities that the world deems as impure. Get rid of the differences, thats the key. That is the only way we can have *"true equality"* and an *"even playing field for the disadvantaged."* With everyone the same we can bring in *world peace* and "goodwill towards men of goodwill"[5] (Dan. 11:21, 24, 8:25). This kingdom will be brought in by man, as opposed to God. It is the kingdom of the antichrist.

Once you've thrown out the dross and melded the coin, what you have left is a mindless, drooling zombie who is wanting to constantly be entertained by news, media, movies, and television, just **"itching"** (2 Tim. 4:3) for that new thing. Who of which will succumb to the *spirit of the world* (Gal. 1:4) and help bring in this nightmare of a kingdom. Most Christians today are just as brainwashed and deluded already and will need very little re-education.

Here is a test: *Discrimination is good.* (Think about it)

What was the first thing that came to mind? Did you pass or fail? Did you say, *"no, it is not good"* because discrimination is bad?

Did you think: race, gender, trans, religious views, bigoted, xenophobic, chauvinistic?

---

[4] *"Invictus"* by William Ernest Henley, 1875

[5] This is the NIV, ESV, NLT, CSB, NASV, NET, etc., reading of Luke 2:14. The reading is found in all Catholic bibles and supports postmillennialism. What about the **"ungodly,"** who Christ died for (Rom. 5:6)? Peace on earth comes when the King comes back, not when man "brings in the kingdom."

Did you think: red light green light, arsenic or Pepsi, gasoline or oil, day or night, true or false?

Discrimination is being able to tell a difference from one thing or another, like the case of "affirmative action" and "no child left behind" have actually *harmed* our children and adult lives *more* than they have helped. The re-education process has made a seemly benign word into a fiery hot potato.

What does the Declaration of Independence say?

"We hold these truths to be self evident, that all men are created equal, that they are endowed *by their Creator…*"

What are they endowed with, Thomas?

"…with certain unalienable rights, that among these are life, liberty, and the pursuit of happiness."

Do you want the government giving you rights or your *"Creator"?*

No government can grant that to you. If they can then they *can just as quickly take it away*. They can provide *conditions* for that through *military* and *financial power*. It's granted by God alone. Look at any empire or government in the past 3,000 years; whatever the government grants, it can *take away just as quickly.*

Even though Thomas Jefferson was a Deist, the inspiration of the Declaration and Constitution was from a Baptist (Separatist's and Brownist's) inspired document called, "The Articles of Confederation" and later inspired the First Amendment. It deemed that Congress had to rely on the states to provide the necessary funds to carry out its functions. Congress had one vote per state, courts with limited powers, separation of Church and State, each state had its own currency and was responsible for its own fights. *It is modeled after a local N.T. church.* The Founding Fathers sought to improve upon this document.

It is no surprise given that preachers such as George Whitfield (A.D. 1714-1770), Gottlieb Spangenberg (1704-1792), who witnessed to John Wesley (1703-1791), were winning souls to Christ by the *thousands*. The Founding Fathers were exposed to *street preaching* on a regular basis and knew what sort of people they had to win over in their own country. Politicians will be politicians, no matter how you shake the salt.

> *"He said, 'My brother, I must first ask you one or two questions.*
> *Have you the witness within yourself? Does the Spirit of God bear witness with your spirit that you are a child of God?'*
> *I was surprised, and knew not what to answer. He observed it and asked,*
> *'Do you know Jesus Christ?'*
> *I paused and said, 'I know He is the Saviour of the world.'*
> *'True,' replied he; 'but do you know He has saved you?'*
> *I answered, 'I hope He has died to save me.'*
> *He only added, 'Do you know yourself?'*
> *I said, 'I do.' But I fear they were vain words."*[6]

In contrast to the US and *its foundation*, look at Saudi Arabia, Iran, Pakistan, Sudan, and Afghanistan. All of these nations have *modeled their governments after the Quran and the Hadith*. How dare I speak those words, we aren't supposed to mention it, we are all supposed to be "tolerant" and "accepting" of others culture; since when has Saudi Arabia been "tolerant" or "accepting" of anything other than an orthodox Muslim male?—I do not "accept" nor "tolerate." That would be "discriminating the facts," and we *can't* have

---

[6] *"The Journal of John Wesley,"* 1951, page 26

that in modern America: *to discern, to tell apart one from another*—this is unacceptable.

Look, do you want to live in a nation where a mans testimony is worth *twice* as much as a woman's in court (Saudi Arabia)? You women, do you want to be forced to wear a hijab and a burka? *Where are the feminists now?* How about driving cars? Do you want the freedom to drive yourself around and make decisions *without a mans approval?* That is a no-go with the Quran and Hadith. If you take your husband to court because he is beating you, *good luck!* They will ask, *"what did she do wrong?"* and likely dismiss the case because his testimony is valued *twice as much as yours. Feminists say...Nothing*. Silence. The front lines are quiet. There is no such thing as "religious freedom" in these places; if you leave Islam, you are tried in court and killed. You *may* get a second chance, you may not. *Don't take my word for it, read the Quran, read the Hadith, read about Saudi Arabia and Afghanistan.*

How about this exercise: *negative thinking is more helpful than positive thinking.*

Thoughts?

Your programming wants to say *"no, negative is bad... I need to think good things about myself, that's what my therapist says."*

It's true; negative thinking is more beneficial.

Run away from the lion cause it may eat you, stock up on food because it may not rain for a while, exercise so you don't get out of shape. Negative, negative, negative.

For a full discourse on negative thinking read Deuteronomy. These approaches are *how you read the Bible.*

The 20th-21st Century wants to rid you of these abilities. The *first step* into the *conditioned, insane thinking* is not being able to *discriminate*. Imagine a person who can't make a clear judgment on anything because they are so restricted and scared to make any sort of call due to "cultural norms" and not wanting to "offend" anyone. How will it sound or reflect on their "identity," or what would their peers think about them after they had been *honest?* They have entered a paralysis in proper decision making halted by *the worlds system.* Do you know what they would end up sounding like?—Just like every news reporter on BBC, CNN, NBC, et al. They would sound like a Fox reporter pandering to their audience. They would sound like the pope talking of ecumenical councils and "human rights." As for the person who is scared to "make a call" or be "plain," this is a good place to be and stay if another authority wanted to enforce an opinion on the person and *guide them in their thinking. The paralysis created a malleable mind* ready to be shaped by the hands of the potter. The metal worker is ready to throw out the dross. The old proverb is: *"If a person doesn't stand for anything he will fall for anything."*

Polarities shape us, the Bible tells us they are so. There are three schools of thought on the matter. *A dualist,* which God is certainly a dualist. *A monist,* which believes everything is connected, and the *non-dualist* which is duality and monism on acid. No one can give a decent definition of non-duality or even an easy way to understand what exactly it is; because it's *just experience.* Buddhists often refer to it and has made its way into the new-age scene. You are experiencing and *that's it*. No judgment, no reaction, just flowing through life as it comes. Blissfully "experiencing the experience itself," one breath at a time, as you are, in each moment. No judgments; just aware. Sheer awareness—you have now become a dog. Congratulations, you have just reduced yourself to thinking like an animal.

The world has been moving fast since the industrial revolution and even faster with the advent of the internet. At the turn of the Century in the early 1900's there was a river of new mass psychology being tested on patients and then found its way into the commercial atmosphere; adopted by marketers, companies, and even within the White House as ploys to change public opinion. *Sigmund Freud,* his nephew *Edward Bernays,* and *Walter Lippmann* all created a perfect storm of mob-psychology in 20th Century America. Freud largely views people as driven by base desires, such as sexual fantasies and urges, which his nephew then picked up on and made application to the marketing scene. Animals, more often than not base their actions on feelings and emotions, reward, gratification, punishment, wasted energy, energy consumption, life or death.

Bernays, who we can credit for how companies market to the people today, changed the sales pitch to *"you need this purse"* to *"you need this purse because it will make you feel better about yourself and will help express your true identity, your true self."* Hence iPhone, iPod, iMac, I, I, I, me, me, me, and many modern comfort luxury brands.

This man is responsible for making *"bacon and eggs"* a routine breakfast and telling you that *fluoride* is good for your teeth, after being asked by a metals company to figure out what to do with all the extra fluoride that was a byproduct originally bound for the garbage heap. Gotta' make a profit somehow, right? He had officials (dentists) to sign off on the lie because people are more likely to trust the *"experts"* in a given field on such matters than a company by themselves.

Bernays is also credited for changing the ghastly name of the U.S.'s "Propaganda Department" to *"Public Relations."* He was a master of *"double-speak,"* mentioned in the notorious novel "1984" by Orwell. It then altered "the peoples" view of the department because, well, *it just sounded nicer*. It didn't have the negative association that Adolf Hitler and Nazi Germany gave to the word "propaganda," it was new and fresh; it was rebranded and for all practical purposes, reborn in the public's eyes.

Authors such as George Orwell (*1984*) and Aldous Huxley (*Brave New World*) wrote about futures that they saw as having possible fulfillment in only a short time, based on such "advancements" in psychology and the sciences that was so prominent during the 20th Century.

Bernays called this act of mass manipulation, *"the engineering of consent."* The majority of Americans have no idea who this man *is* or *what* influence he had on modernity. He also used celebrities to make a "boring" and "disliked" president of the U.S. appear more accepting to the American public. He was a man in the shadows acting as puppet master.

Then comes Lippmann, who added to the theories of Bernays concerning mass psychology. He believed, as Freud, that people are animals, and no different than a dog: people run on suppressed urges, *if you can control the urges, then you can control the mob*. This of course, does work on the majority of people, but not anyone *who reads the Bible daily* and who has a source of *absolute truth*. Lippmann's theories were all based on the idea that a person has built in biases and that the person gets the majority of his information from news-media outlets thus, these media outlets could be used to shape mob mentality. You see it today in bright 4K technicolor, the news will always cover a story with an *"angle"* on it. Most recently the Capital Riots of January 6th 2021.

The news presented a very biased view in which made the viewer believe that these *"criminals"* went around vandalizing the White House when in fact, years later, footage was released that was *"uncut"* and *"unedited."* It showed the *"criminals" being escorted politely around by police* inside the White House, almost as if on a routine tour given by an elderly tour-guide while on a grade-school field trip. This is not surprising to most, but to some it may be a shock because they actually *believe* what the "black mirror" tells them. Now, how can we get **"the people"** of a population to do the same editing and manipulation in which the news media has done for decades—*only to each other?*

Enter Mao, he believed in *"political correctness."* He used it to police his own people into submission so his policeman would be present, even on their days off. Why spend millions of hard earned cash on police officers if you can have your own people do it for free, 24/7? Hitler used this tactic as well during World War II. He had people's own fathers, brothers, wives, and sons telling the government of their activity, and many were ultimately criminalized, sent to concentration camps, or "dealt with" by other means.

Political correctness is alive and well in the States. People love feeling empowered, they love being the "hero" and feeling like a "do-gooder." Most recently, the guilt-trip concerning a *certain vaccination* that had not been throughly tested on a population at the time. You don't have *"freedom of speech"* in Mao's system because you can't speak *freely*. The Constitution is out of the question.

Since you have the news media, popular movies, T.V. series, and celebrities *doing your thinking for you*, all that is needed next in the puzzle is *the abandonment of absolute truth and an absolute standard in which to judge the world.*

Americans rarely think anymore. When you see someone standing quietly in the corner, the most common response is, *"what's wrong?"*—Nothing is wrong, the man is just thinking. It's as if a wild, exotic animal had been spotted.

Enter stage left: *"Relativism."* You can have *your own* truth and I can have *my own* as well. We can both have *our own* truths and live our own "lifestyle," by doing whatever makes us happy and feel good about ourselves. A street whore is now a *"sex worker,"* a jail is now a *"corrections facility,"* a slut is now a *"liberated woman,"* a man-whore is now *"normal male behavior."*

The idea of a 20 year old female prostituting herself out online for all the world to see on Only Fans is a *"symbol of liberation and female freedom."* If you call it like you see it, then you are a "bigot" and "discriminating" against a *"valid work profession."* All things "must be equal" in this world, because everyone's "truth" is "their truth," and their truth must be *our truth*. If you do not accept this, then you are a "bigoted" and a "discriminating" pile-o-trash that should burn in hell.

Meanwhile, online "influencers" are pretending to be bisexual in order to virtue signal towards their clan, while they have a *boyfriend* holding the camera as they shoot their bisexual professions. Young women say, without any more thought on the matter than deciding what clothes to wear on a Monday, *"if my ***** can make me money, then why not?"*

"Having no hope, and without God in the world."

Are you a Bible believer or are you part of Mao's army? Are you a Bible believer or have you become victim to Bernays' and Lippmann's pursuit? Are you a Bible believer or an animal like Freud sees you? If you are just an animal as some say, then it's okay to practice eugenics and genocide. We are just animals after all; morals and ethics are nothing more than "cultural constructs" which ebb and flow through the ages.

The fact is, when a person reads the Bible today they bring all of this garbage and thinking along with them to the table. If there is no separation from the worlds system, there will be little progress. If you think modern scholars, who are on translation committees today are immune to this line of thinking then see examples *"pp," "qq," "rr"* and *"ss"* in the chapter called *"Oranges and Vitamin C."*

Here are some examples of how God thinks: *"good"* or *"evil," "right"* or *"wrong," "heaven"* or *"hell," "salvation"* or *"damnation,"* etc. He *"divides"* (Gen. 1:6, 14, 18 etc.), He wrote a Book in which you have to *"divide"* (2 Tim. 2:15)—not "get rid of differences" and "make things equal." One day even the **"goats"** and **"sheep"** will be *"divided"* (Matt. 25:32-33). Oh, the great swelling-words of our day! Jesus even **"divided"** families, friends, and loved ones, **"for I am come to set a man at variance against his father, and the daughter against her mother, and the daughter in law against her mother in law"** (Matt. 10:35).

He came to bring a **"sword"** (Matt. 10:34), that can *divide* **"asunder of soul and spirit, and of the joints and marrow"** (Heb. 4:12).

Jesus was such a pivotal figure that he caused **"division among the people"** (John 7:43, 10:19). He even tells you again, in case you missed it, in Luke 12:51. The *great negative word of the century is "division,"* we must "have unity!" How must this unity come? No one seems to consider it. **"Fulfil ye my joy, that ye be likeminded, having the same love, being of one accord, of one mind"** (Phil. 2:2). How? **"We have the mind of Christ"** (1 Cor. 2:16). Where do we get this sameness of mind and how do we **"speak the same thing"** (1 Cor. 1:10) if we are not all reading from the same Book?

Why would bible versions made after German rationalism, post modernism, and decades of decadence be better? Every period in the Bible ends in *apostasy* and *degradation;* why would the age of the Church be any different? It isn't (2 Tim. 3-4), it starts from within. The "Principle of Human Collapse" is Biblical, (renamed "Societal Collapse Theory") and historical. Not only that but it is observable.

Steven Pinker wrote a lengthy paper on the "decline of violence in human history" called *"The Better Angels of Our Nature."* His thesis states that over the course of history, humans have become less and less violent. He attempts to prove his hypothesis in like manner to that of Malcom Gladwell: by cherry picking the data and just out right lying.

The book by Pinker has since been debunked by numerous authors and bloggers. Why is it that the atheist and the "Christian scholarship" community *insists* that things are getting better and better instead of the Biblical viewpoint? Upward and onward (Gen. 11)! This "positive" attitude is killing the country and the world at large. *It is an avoidance of the truth, history, and the simple fact that without the Bible, mans destiny is one shut up with slime bricks and mortar building up the walls that lead to babel.*

The atheists shriek and say *"the Bible has killed millions!"* No man, humans have killed millions based on locking up the truth so evidently found in its pages (Catholic inquisition, Catholic conquests, Catholic crusades, Catholic book burnings, etc.). I do not paint the Roman Catholic church as the universal bogyman for Christendom but hey, if the shoe fits. With a Book yielding so much **"power"** (Ecc. 8:4) and its content mystifying billions by the hour, it takes the stage as a man with gun in hand. The gun without the man behind it is idle: a cold piece of metal and plastic with shimmering lead bullets. Drugs are just molecules of carbon, hydrogen, and nitric oxide until you add the drug user—that is when things get outright wild. Yet, this connection escapes some. Some want gun control while at the same time those same people want drug legalization.

Do you know the Bible well enough to know what is correct Christian *doctrine* and what isn't? Do you believe in *"soul sleep"* or that there is *"no hell"*? Do you believe the age old heresy (A.D. 140-155) that "the O.T. God is not the same as the N.T. God?

How did we end up here?

Blame yourself for *"going along to get along,"* blame yourself for *"being tolerant."*

WWJD? What would Jesus do? He would rip these people a new one just like He did in every Gospel record (Matt. 23; Mark 7:7-15; Luke 11:52-54; John 8:43-49, etc.) to the leading religious class of His day.

WWJD?

Chapter 4: The Witnessed

"He that winneth souls is wise" — Proverbs 11:30

WHEN engaging in discussions with Muslims or Jews, you may encounter individuals who are well-versed in their own religious traditions and may raise objections or point out perceived problems in the New Testament. These objections often stem from the views of modern Christian scholars or misinterpretations propagated by Imams, Ulama (essentially Muslim scholars), or Rabbis (Jewish scholars). It is worth noting that the Jewish people have a historical tendency of not heeding or comprehending their own Prophets and Scriptures (Jer. 37:15, 19:14-15, 20:1-2; Luke 4:24, 28; Mark 6:4; 2 Chron. 24:20-21), so naturally, it can present challenges when engaging with them.

Do you think Moses had any idea what he was writing when he wrote Genesis?

Moses: *"Lord, shouldn't it say 'God will provide for himself a lamb' instead of* **'God will provide himself a lamb'**? *It doesn't really seem clear to the reader."*

Lord: *"Moses, just write what I tell you."*

Moses: *"But Lord, you do see what I mean, right...Lord?"*

Lord: *"Well, Moses, one day God will provide himself as a lamb, so don't let the ways of the Egyptians get to you."*

Moses: *"What? I went to school in Egypt and I am learned of all their ways...they said to..."*
Lord: *Moses...MOSES!*
Moses: *Yes, Lord?*
Lord: *"Never mind, just write."*

You'll see this laid out, in detail, in 1 Peter 1:10-12 where, **"unto whom it was revealed, that not unto themselves"** is talking about *the O.T. writers.* If Abraham knew a man named Jesus Christ was going to take away the sins of the world by a sacrifice, *then why didn't he pass that information on?* It's because he didn't have any more of an idea than Samuel or Isaiah did. They just wrote what they saw and heard. You see, the Book is written in such a way that you will have to **"search"** the thing out and **"study"** it to see for yourself. One of the most famously disputed passages by Rabbis is Isaiah 7:14.

"Therefore the Lord himself shall give you a sign; Behold, a virgin shall conceive, and bear a son, and shall call his name Immanuel." (Isaiah 7:14)

The problem is the Hebrew word for **"virgin,"** which can also mean *"maiden"* or *"young woman."* The word in Hebrew in the text is עַלְמָה and is translated as **"virgin"** in the King James text, and is further *interpreted* in Matthew 1:23 as **"virgin."**

The verses that Rabbis appeal to in order to say that the King James text, or *any* Christian reading of the text is wrong, are Exodus 2:8, Psalm 68:25, and Proverbs 30:19. All of these verses involve a *"maiden"* that is *no longer a "virgin."* What they *don't show you* is the similar case of Rebekah, *before* she marries Isaac. **"Behold, I stand by the well of water; and it shall come to pass, that when the VIRGIN cometh forth to draw water, and I say to her, Give me, I pray thee, a little water of thy pitcher to drink"** (Gen.

24:43). The English word **"virgin"** in 24:43, if translated "formally," would be *"maiden."* It is the same Hebrew word used in Isaiah 7:14 (עַלְמָה). The English clears all of this up—she is obviously a **"virgin"** because you are expressly told this back in Genesis 24:16, **"a VIRGIN, neither had ANY MAN KNOWN HER."** Then she lost her virginity in Genesis 24:67 (Cf. Gen. 2:24). The Hebrew word in 24:16 literally means **"virgin"** (בְּתוּלָה).

You have cases of the Hebrew word for *"maiden"* or *"young woman"* being translated as **"virgin"** as in the case I just showed, *and* also the word for *"maiden"* in the use of those who are *not virgins* as in Proverbs 30:19. *A "young woman/maiden" COULD BE a virgin or COULD NOT BE a virgin*. The question is: *how is it used in Isaiah 7:14*—is it a "young maiden," who is *not* a virgin, *or* is she a young maiden who is a **"virgin"**?

Again, the Hebrew word used in Rebekah's case, *before* she is married in Genesis 24:16, means **"virgin"** (בְּתוּלָה). So, right there you have a case where an actual virgin is *called a maiden* in the Hebrew in 24:43 AND a *virgin* in the Hebrew in 24:16 —in both cases she is a **"virgin,"** *like* Isaiah 7:14 and Matthew 1:23. The texts interpret themselves without any need to go to *any* Hebrew or Greek. The AV is consistent in its translating because it recognizes *the use of the word in both senses.*

Examples of the Hebrew word for virgin (בְּתוּלָה), used as *"maiden"* or *"maid"* (or some variation thereof) *instead* of "virgin" in the English are Exodus 22:16; Judges 19:24; 2 Chronicles 36:17; Psalms 78:63, &c. This is something lacking from the modern day Tanakh.

One does not have to go outside the confines of the O.T. to find the proof if Jesus Christ really was "Virgin Born," for it can be found in Jeremiah 22:28-30 and Genesis 3:15. A woman cannot have a **"seed,"** as seen in Genesis 3:15. No descendant of David through Coniah's (Jechoniah's) **"seed"** will sit on that Throne. *Problem—Jechoniah is in the genealogy* *of Jesus Christ in Matthew 1:11, 16.* This means that Jesus Christ could never be the King (Matt. 2:2) *if* Joseph was His *real* father. His paternal seed must have come from *elsewhere hence, a Virgin Birth.* Further passages which indicate this are Jeremiah 36:30, 33:17, and Isaiah 22:22. **"David shall never want a man to sit upon the throne of the house of Israel."** What if this **"man"** was "God in the flesh" (1 Tim. 3:16)? Turns out, that's exactly what happened.

The Virgin Birth is one of the most misunderstood aspects of the life of Jesus Christ apart from the Resurrection. The two most compelling proofs that He was no ordinary **"man."** It is not a wonder the Virgin Birth and Resurrection **"shall be spoken against"** (Luke 2:34). It goes hand-in-hand with His deity. To this day, most Jewish Rabbis believe Jesus was born of a bastard, while Mary was a whore, just as they did in John 8:38-41. Here is a simple question: where is the body of Jesus Christ? Muhammad has a tomb where his body can be found, Siddhartha Gautama's (Buddha's) remains can be found; where is the body of Jesus Christ?—It's never been found.

It's easy to get discouraged when witnessing and sometimes the best thing you can do is *plant a seed* and move on. A word of caution: the Jewish people are *not* to be trifled with (Gen. 12:3; Psa. 122:6; Jer. 2:3; Isa. 41:11-12, etc.). God will have them all saved before it's over (Rom. 11:25-26). Sometimes it appears there is a **"veil"** preventing them from seeing what is in their own Scriptures (2 Cor. 3:14-15). Be careful in your dealings with them, **"They are beloved for the fathers sake"** (Rom. 11:28). There are many "fundamentalists" today that are spreading antisemitic literature and sermons to their congregations—don't make that mistake.

Others such as the Catholics will have you believe that Israel has been *replaced* with the Church in the same way that Muslims believe that they have replaced the Jews, and that Christians worship a false God. Clearly, they have not been "replaced" unless you *deny* the majority of the Old Testament, and a good chunk of the New Testament as well. Despite this "election" of God towards Israel, the *"holy"* Hadith (second only to the Quran in Islam) says that God turned Jews into rats bigger than monkeys.[1] The Jews were punished in many ways, but that is a new one. By its very nature, the Quran is antisemitic. This "holy" book (the Quran) contains 114 Suras (chapters) and is one of the most *unholy* books one may find—why? **"For God is not the author of confusion, but of peace"** (1 Cor. 14:33). The Quran is never clear on anything except that it is a mangled mess recited by someone who forgot what he said (Muhammad) in his previous sessions of dictations. Since Muhammad couldn't write, the Quran was written down by another as he spoke the "revelation" given to him by Gabriel—the 600 winged angel.

The Hadith, which is held in as high regard as the Quran consists of personal accounts of "the prophet's" sayings and actions. The Hadith and the Quran make up the rocky foundation of Islam as a whole. To pretend that Islam is a "peaceful religion" is deception at its best. Fundamentally it cannot be for one group claims it's peaceful and the other claims *"death to apostates and unbelievers."* One group must reinterpret the words of both the Hadith and the Quran thus defying "Allah." It is said that martyrdom, or *"istishadi"* will automatically save Muslims from hell and grant access to paradise no matter the sin committed.

> *"The person who participates in (Holy battles) in Allah's cause . . . and nothing compels him to do so except belief in Allah and His Apostles, will be recompensed by Allah either with a reward, or booty (if he survives) or will be admitted to*

---

[1] *"Holy Hadith,"* Bukhari, Vol. 4, Num. 524, 627

Paradise (if he is killed in the battle as a martyr)."[2]

"*And if you are killed in the cause of Allah or you die, the forgiveness and mercy of Allah are better than all that you amass.*" Sura 3:157

"*surely good deeds take away evil deeds.*" Sura 11:114

"*Allah guarantees him who strives in His Cause and whose motivation for going out is nothing but Jihad in His Cause and belief in His Word, that He will admit him into Paradise (if martyred) or bring him back to his dwelling place, whence he has come out, with what he gains of reward and booty.*"[3]

Muslims actually do believe in the Virgin Birth of Jesus Christ (Sura 66:12) but deny His Deity and Resurrection. If you don't believe that Jesus lived to an old age and instead believe that He died on Calvary, then you are plain stupid.[4] Jesus and the two men who were crucified with Him were *still alive* when they were taken down from the cross.[5] They claim Jesus Christ was sinless (Sura 19:19) yet Muhammad had to ask for forgiveness over and over.[6] Jesus Christ also *gives life* to a clay bird by turning it into a real bird (Sura 3:49;

---

[2] Bukhari, Vol. 1, Num. 35.

[3] *Bukhari*, Vol. 4, Num. 352

[4] Maulana Muhammad Ali, *"The Holy Quran,"* 1917, 2002 ed., Sura 4:159, footnote 159a

[5] Ibid, Sura 4:157, footnote 157a

[6] Bukhari Vol. 8, 335, 379, 407, 408 and also see Sura 40:55; 48:2; 47:19

5:110) but *somehow* Muhammad is superior to Jesus Christ *even though in their own "holy" book Jesus Christ is given abilities that Muhammad didn't have.* When did Muhammad ever give life to anything? He didn't. How is the act of someone turning an *inanimate object* into a *living object* something any prophet from the O.T. or the Quran could do? *You know who did that?* God did, in Exodus 8:16-17 when God turned dust into lice. *You know who could not follow and could not repeat the act?* The magicians of Egypt who then claimed, **"This is the finger of God"** (Exod. 8:18-19). You know who was behind the magicians in Egypt? Lucifer. It was an all-out battle of wits and abilities between the Godhead and the devil. God still prevails, even in the writings of the most *unholy* book conceived: the *"holy"* Quran.

You may be saying, *"well you are comparing two different religions so it isn't really the same—apples and oranges here."* Not really, because *the Quran states* that the O.T. and the N.T. were—*both—written—by—"Allah."* They are the very thing in which the—*"proof"—of—the—Quran—rests—or—fails. In other words, if the Quran doesn't line up with the Bible, then throw it out!* Allah said that, I didn't say that (Sura 10:94; 5:43, 47-48, 66, 68; 16:43; 6:37; 17:88). If you don't believe that, then you go to hell (Sura 5:86; 17:39-41).

These are all things you can keep in your utility belt next time you witness to a Jew or a Muslim. It's war out there and you aren't fighting **"flesh and blood"** but what is working behind the scenes (Eph. 6:12). Sometimes in Christian warfare a grenade in needed, sometimes a Glock 9mm, and sometimes an AK-47 to scatter the wolves surrounding a flock of sheep. When witnessing, you are in close hand-to-hand combat. So, you'll need a **"sword"** (Eph. 6:17) at your side. It isn't so much about offense, offense, offense. There is an opening, you make an offensive move, and then you *defend*. When an opportunity appears, you pull the **"sword"** out. An opening to battle could be as simple as a person saying, *"how are you"* and you say, *"I know Jesus Christ, so *pretty good. What about you?"* Talk about getting a strange look on that one. Another one you could use is when someone asks, *"what are you doing"* and you respond with, *"waiting on Jesus."* Watch that ruin someones day, or brighten a brother or sisters day.

Openers are always better it seems, rather than forcing it. Something as simple as having a conversation with someone and *they* bring up *"if there is a heaven"* or the topic of *"the afterlife"* or some such subject close to home-plate. It's surprising how much a topic like this is brought up by "agnostics" or atheists. Then you get the **"sword"** out (Eph. 6:17) and be not a **"hearer"** of the word only, but a **"doer"** (James 1:23).

You want to have someone get near your "wheelhouse" and then throw some jabs, then just defend and play off their responses. It's like Jiu-Jitsu in that the size of the dog in the fight doesn't matter; *technique always overcomes strength.* Some people just walk up to people and say, *"Do you know Jesus Christ?"* and it works, but this is a "cold call" approach and sometimes is forced, but still very effective at times. There have been many a book written on "soul winning/witnessing" so I won't go too in-depth here but I'll give you some ammunition and resources to have in your backpack when out in battle. Having a basic knowledge of someone else's religion can go far in some cases.

The next one is a classic in Muslim classrooms. Here is the problem: *"Jesus was not God because Jesus never said He was God. He said he was the 'Son of man'."*

Now, how this conclusion is made is from denying the Gospel of John, even though most Imams/Ulama/etc., will tell you that the **"comforter"** in John 14:16 is Muhammad. So, you know they *use it when it suits them.* They also *use* the New Testament the same way they *use* the Quran: by reinterpretation.[7] What in the world, man—aside from the obvious fact that the title of **"comforter"** is *interpreted* to be **"the Holy Ghost"** in John 14:26, most Imams still hold to this fantasy due to Sura 61:6 and Sura 17:81. Did Jesus Christ breathe *Muhammad* on the Apostles in John 20:22?

Read 1 Corinthians 12 and every time it says, **"Spirit"** replace it with *"Muhammad."* Apparently Imams don't read the Bible like they should according to what Allah says *in the Quran*.

Muhammad **"will guide you into all truth"** (John 16:13), will he?

Muhammad gives you the New Birth, does he (John 3:5-6)? Why, that would put him *equal with God*, a grievous *sin* in the Quran, *"Do not set up any other god with Allah lest you are rendered humiliated and helpless. Your Lord has decreed: Do not worship any but Him…"* (Sura 17:22-24). Muhammad himself said that he was just a man (Sura 41:6) that committed many sins (Bukhari, Vol. 8, 335, 408). In Muhammad's own words, *"O Allah! Forgive my mistakes and my ignorance and my exceeding the limit (boundaries) of righteousness in my deeds; and forgive whatever You know better than I. O Allah! Forgive the wrong I have done jokingly or seriously, and forgive my accidental and intentional errors, all that is present in me."*

A man would say that *who is guilty and full of sin*. What did Jesus Christ say? **"Which of you convinceth me of sin"** (John 8:46). **"I find in him NO FAULT at all"** (John 18:38) as said by Pontius Pilate, the very man who ordered his crucifixion. **"Have thou nothing to do with that JUST man"** (Matt. 27:19) as spoken by the wife of Pilate. **"This man hath done NOTHING AMISS"** (Luke 23:41) as spoken by the dying thief on the cross. **"I have betrayed the INNOCENT blood"** (Matt. 27:4) as spoken by Judas who sold Jesus out for a few coins. **"Certainly this was a RIGHTEOUS man"**

---

[7] Muhammad Ali, *"The Holy Quran,"* Sura 4:157, footnote 157a. This is the most mangled view of over ten New Testament quotations you will come across—it is pure absurdity and its masterful reinterpretation causes the reader to throw out 98% of the New Testament.

(Luke 23:47) as spoken by a Roman centurion. So far, that is 6 different witnesses, and all that was needed was two or three: **"At the mouth of two witnesses, or three witnesses, shall he that is worthy of death be put to death; but at the mouth of one witness he shall not be put to death"** (Deut. 17:6). There are even more than that: Acts 4:27-30; Luke 4:34; 1 Peter 2:21-22; 1 John 3:5; 2 Corinthians 5:21; Hebrews 4:15; 1 John 3:3, &c.). In *total* that is Mark, Matthew, Luke, Peter, John, Paul, Pilate, Pilate's wife, a dying thief, a Roman centurion, Judas, an unclean spirit recognizing Jesus, and Jesus Christ Himself. That is *twelve* witnesses if you don't count Jesus himself mentioned above.

What about Muhammad? *"So know, [O Muhammad], that there is no deity except Allah and ask forgiveness for YOUR SIN and for the believing men and believing women. And Allah knows of your movement and your resting place" (Sura 47:19),* also see 40:55; 48:1-2. That is Muhammad *asking* for forgiveness of sins for himself *and* his followers right out of the "holy" Quran.

"But wait, wasn't Muhammad "sinless" like Jesus was, like my Imam told me?" No, Muhammad was not, unless you are apt to *reinterpret the Quran any way you please.* The *Quran does state Jesus was sinless* in Sura 19:19; 33:35-36 and also the Hadith: Bukhari, Vol. 4, Book 55, 641; Vol. 4, Book 54, 506. Muhammad also claims the "sinlessness of Mary."[8]

Now, I wonder where he *got that idea in 600 AD*; perhaps, from *Catholics* in the area? Also, Mary has two brothers in the Quran—guess who they are? Only in the wildest imaginative mind would someone became so utterly mixed up in all of it, after hearing stories from Jews and Christians (*"people of the book"*) about their Scriptures would Muhammad cross wires such as these. Mary's brothers are *Aaron* and *Moses* (Sura 66:12; 19:27-28). Just as the Mormon

---

[8] Bukhari, Vol. 4, Book 55, 623; Vol. 5, Book 57, 113

church (or insert cult name here:___), Muhammadism takes advantage of peoples *ignorance* and a *desire* to do good.

Seems rather tragic to omit the sinless nature of "the holy prophet Muhammad" but include the sinless nature of a person who's followers you consider to be idol worshipers destined for hell; rather tragic indeed. Muhammad also needed the prayers of his followers, *"Indeed, Allah showers His blessings upon the Prophet, and His angels pray for him. O believers! Invoke Allah's blessings upon him, and salute him with worthy greetings of peace"* (Sura 33:56). When did Jesus ever need anyones prayers *for him*? He didn't.

Despite what the Quran *says*, tradition has set in around the *"sinless"* nature of Muhammad. "Yes, he committed sins but he was *forgiven* of those sins." Imams couldn't stand the idea of their "holy" book being wrong so they did what most religious institutions do when presented with a problem— *they make something up.*[9]

There is only one problem; in the Quran, *no one knows if they are going to heaven or not.* How does anyone know if their sins *are* forgiven or not? *They don't.* Allah can forgive anyone he pleases (Sura 7:89) if he *"wills it."* Wait, but isn't it all about doing good deeds and if you have more good deeds than bad (Sura 7:8-9) then Allah will forgive you as long as you ask and repent? *Only if Allah wills it* (Sura 6:39). Allah can keep anyone blind to the Quran as he so pleases (Sura 17:45-46). *There is no assurance about anything except that*

---

[9] Maulana Muhammad Ali, *"The Holy Quran,"* Sura 3:159, footnote 159a: The footnote calls the "holy prophet" "gentle" and holds him in such false high regard given the historical accounts of his life. Muhammad had the hands and feet cut off of an accuser, and the eyes gouged out with a nail (Our Al-Yakin Biography of Muhammad, ed. 24, pages 184-185). When Muhammad invaded the Jewish tribe of Khayber, he routinely slaughtered who he wished and took the women captive. He then captured Kanana ibn Al-Rabi'a who either owed Muhammad money or Muhammad knew that he was wealthy. Muhammad then proceeded to torture him by fire until Rabi'a told him where the money was (Ibn Hisham, The Biography of the Prophet, Vol. III, page 183). Muhammad killed 800-900 Jews who had surrendered from the tribe of Qurayza after denying Muhammads claim that Gabriel the 600 winged angel spoke to him (Ibn Al-Athir, The Perfect in History, Vol. II, pages 100-101). Muhammad called Jews "brothers of the monkeys" (Joseph Abd El Shafi, Behind the Veil, Vol. II, page 64). There are too many to list here, not to mention what he did to the elderly.

everyone on earth, even Muslim believers, will go to hell for some amount of time (Sura 19:71-72). At least John Calvin would have appreciated the "sovereign decrees" of Allah.

In the Bible God has "decreed" everyone to go to hell in this age since **"all have sinned"** (Rom. 3:23) and **"there is none righteous, no, not one"** (Rom. 3:10) and all are headed for **"death by sin"** (Rom. 5:12). Being **"children of disobedience"** (Eph. 2:2) and **"having no hope, and without God in the world"** (Eph. 2:12)—how does one change this "sovereign decree" of a hellhound sinner? How are the **"ungodly"** supposed to be justified (Rom. 4:5)?

"Christ died for the ungodly" (Rom. 5:6), **"but as many as received him, to them gave he power to become the sons of God, EVEN TO THEM that believe on his name"** (John 1:12), **"much more then, being now justified by his blood, we shall be saved from wrath through him"** (Rom. 5:9). All you do *is change the decree by believing on Jesus Christ*. God has no pleasure in those who do not accept his Son—**"For I have no pleasure in the death of him that dieth, saith the Lord GOD: wherefore turn yourselves, and live ye."** (Ezek. 18:32), **"The Lord is not slack concerning his promise, AS SOME MEN count slackness; but is longsuffering to usward, not willing that ANY should perish, but that ALL should come to repentance"** (2 Pet. 3:9). It appears that Calvin and Allah have a credibility gap.

Allah even commands his followers *to commit sin* (Sura 17:16). What a "just" and "merciful" god. Al-Zamakhshari understands Sura 17:16 to mean *"Allah commands those who live a life of luxury to disobey and commit iniquity."*[10] What follows by other commentators is a full on scramble to justify a lie and blatant contradiction to Sura 7:28, *"...Allah never commands what is shameful. How can you attribute to Allah what you do not know?."* They could have asked a Jew or a Christian about their own Book, as they are asked to do

---

[10] Seyyed Hossein Nasr, *"The Study Quran,"* 2015, comments under Sura 17:16

(Sura 16:43; 5:47). The *"people of knowledge"* or *"people of Remembrance"* or whatever variation in the English translation may be in Sura 16:43, refer to the people of the Gospel's and the people of the Torah, i.e. Jews and Christians. They don't ask, they only ask Imams and the Ulama which give a non-Torah/Gospel related response that validates Muhammad and his 600 winged angel. Echo chambers galore.

There is *no* assurance of salvation (see above) in Islam but there *is* assurance of salvation with Jesus Christ:

"For God so loved the world, that he gave his only begotten Son, that whosoever believeth in him should not perish, but have everlasting life" (John 3:16).

"For whosoever shall call upon the name of the Lord shall be saved" (Rom. 10:13).

"Who shall also confirm you unto the end, that ye may be blameless in the day of our Lord Jesus Christ" (1 Cor. 1:8).

"And I give unto them eternal life; and they shall never perish, neither shall any man pluck them out of my hand. My Father, which gave them me, is greater than all; and no man is able to pluck them out of my Father's hand" (John 10:28-29).

"For the wages of sin is death; but the gift of God is eternal life through Jesus Christ our Lord" (Rom. 6:23). Etc.

- *Paul* knew where he was going when he died (2 Cor. 5:8; Phil. 1:23)
- *Peter* knew (1 Peter 1:4-5),
- *John* knew (1 John 3:1-2, 5:13)
- *Jesus Christ* knew where he was going (John 14:2-3; Matt. 12:40-41; Mark 14:24; John 16:7, 16, etc.)
- *Moses* knew (Deut. 32:49-50)
- *David* knew (Psa. 23:6)
- Muhammad, nor *anyone who follows him* really knows where they will end up *"I know not what will be done with*

me or with you" (Sura 46:9). The most likely place is hell according to *their own book*.

That's what it says, I'm not making it up, nor am I being bigoted; it says what it says. It also says in the very next verse (Sura 46:10) that Muhammad was that prophet like unto Moses (Deut. 18:15). This is a blatant lie and anyone who has read either book can spot it right away. Moses was a Jew from the tribe of Levi, Muhammad was an Arab from Ishmael. Moses performed public miracles, Muhammad did not. God talked directly with Moses, Muhammad talked to a 600 winged angel named Gabriel. Moses made many (100's) prophecies (Gen. 3:15; Deut. 28-30 for example) that came *true* on the money, Muhammad was not a prophet, he was a coin flipper. *Jesus* on the other hand, did perform public miracles, did prophecy, did talk with God directly, was a Jew from the tribe of Judah.

The Quran acknowledges that Jesus is sinless, capable of creating life, and was born of a virgin. However, it categorically denies that Jesus is the Son of God or God incarnate (as stated in Sura 5:17, 72, 116; 9:31). Instead, the Quran portrays Jesus as a "prophet" who was born under a palm tree (Sura 19:29-30). According to the Quran, Jesus was created from dust (Sura 3:58) and did not die on the cross (Sura 3:56). Surprisingly, despite ample *evidence* dating back to A.D. 33 and numerous accounts from Church Fathers and early martyrs that contradict this view, many in the Islamic tradition continue to hold onto this perspective.

This perspective is believed despite available historical evidence from the greatest selling Book of all time which includes *four* historical accounts: Matthew, Mark, Luke, and John. There is also *Josephus* in A.D. 93 in *"Antiquities of the Jews," "The Babylonian Talmud"* A.D. 500, the Roman historian *Tacitus* in A.D. 56-120/115-117 who wrote of His death on the cross, the writings of *Mara Bar-Serapion* (philosopher) dated from A.D. 73-200, *Suetonius* A.D. 120, *Clement of Rome* A.D. 96, and so on. All of these sources document the life or death of Jesus, or both. Some are from believers, some from secular historians and non-believers. *Seems history is against the Quran*—especially the Gospel accounts which were *"written by Allah"*.

The Quran actually states that the Jews were in no way involved with the death of Jesus (Sura 4:160, 156-157). This goes *completely contrary* to the Biblical account; it was the Jews who brought Him to Pilate and the Romans who put the nails in His hands.

Other things to note in the Quran surrounding the *teachings of Jesus*, which *are to be followed*, but somehow have been supplanted by Muhammad's teachings such as: you are to *beat your wife* (Sura 4:34), and *kill those who oppose you* and *kill those who leave Islam* (Bukhari, Vol. 4, 260 and Vol. 5, 630; Sura 2:193; 9:5; 2:190-194; 9:73, 124, etc.). Here I will present two different English translations of Sura 2:193, *"Fight them until there is no [more] fitnah and [until] worship is [acknowledged to be] for Allah. But if they cease, then there is to be no aggression except against the oppressors."* Here is one from a more "progressive" translation: *"Fight against them ⌐if they persecute you¬ until there is no more persecution, and ⌐your¬ devotion will be to Allah ⌐alone¬. If they stop ⌐persecuting you¬, let there be no hostility except against the aggressors."*

Note the *"if they persecute you"* in the second translation. It has been watered down and "westernized" to be more palpable. In case there is any confusion on the matter of whether or not Muslims should be *offensive or defensive*, one need not look any further than *any history book ever written by anyone*, or just read the "holy" Hadith where it states that *offensive conquests were made* (Bukhari, Vol. 3, 495).

It's considered a *good deed* to kill an infidel (Christian, Jew, etc.). Wait a second... *don't you get to paradise by doing good deeds?* Yes. You also go to paradise for being a Martyr and fighting, i.e. suicide bombing (Sura 4:74; 61:10-12) where virgins await for your every sexual need. Heaven for a Quran believing Muslim is nothing but a sensual, fleshy place that can entice a man who is scared of fighting in combat: *"now remember those virgins."*

What did Jesus Christ say about all that?

Wasn't He a prophet in the Quran, and the Gospels were authored by Allah? Yes.

"Ye have heard that it hath been said, An eye for an eye, and a tooth for a tooth: But I say unto you, That ye resist not evil: but whosoever shall smite thee on thy right cheek, turn to him the other also" (Matt. 5:38-39).

"Love your enemies" (Matt. 5:44)

"Bless those that curse you"

"Pray for them which despitefully use you"

"For if ye love them which love you, what reward have ye?" (Matt. 5:46).

"Why beholdest thou the mote that is in thy brother's eye, but considerest not the beam that is in thine own eye?" (Matt. 7:3)

"For in the resurrection they NEITHER marry, NOR are given in marriage, but ARE AS the angels of God in heaven" (Matt. 22:30)

There seems to be a credibility *gap* between Muhammad and Jesus Christ, between the Bible in *both* Testaments and the Quran. What Muhammad did was take Joshua and Moses, cut out the conquest into the land that *God gave to Israel*, applied it to himself, and usurped that Kingdom for himself as an acting warlord all while having *sex with a nine year old*[11] and married her when she *was six years old*, and cutting the tongues out of those who talked back to him in the process. He did this all while having multiple wives and married his daughter-in-law named Zainab, making her his seventh wife.[12] That is breaking the law (see Levi. 18:15).

---

[11] Bukhari, Vol. 5 and 7; Ibn Hagar, Al-Isaba, Vol. 4, page 330, 348; Ibn Is-Haq, Al-Siyar Wa Al-Maghazi, page 255; Ibn Hisham, Al-Sira Al-Nabawiya, Vol. 4, page 66

[12] Seventh at the time. In total, some say 12 wives, some say 14. This does not include slaves.

Muhammad also changed the Sabbath from a Saturday which is the **"seventh day"** (Gen. 2:2) to *a Friday*,[13] he also allowed the rape of captured women[14] even if they were married. He also allowed camel meat to be eaten.[15] All of which contradict the Torah. But because Muhammad is *equated with Allah* (Sura 4:80, 59, 61, 69, etc.), *"Whoever obeys the messenger obeys Allah,"* he has to be obeyed or else you aren't obeying Allah and in danger of hell-fire. *"But whoever disobeys Allah AND His Messenger and exceeds their limits will be cast into Hell, to stay there forever"* (Sura 4:15). This can't be, no one can be *equated* with Allah. *No one is equal to Allah.* Muhammad *is* and *was* on equal grounds with Allah and it is all written down right in front of your face in the Quran. No one in Islamic communities wants to talk about it *for fear of death!*

Islam is also polytheistic *according to the Quran.*[16] There is more than one *creator* (Sura 37:125), and others were involved in what is *only* attributable to God alone: the creation of Adam, *authoring* scripture, and parting the Red Sea for Moses (Sura 2:50), etc. There is a constant reference to a *"We"* throughout the entire Quran—but Islam isn't polytheistic. No, no, certainly not. (Yea, right, okay.)

Furthermore, Muhammad *forbade* friendships between Christians and Muslims (Sura 5:51), which is now *"reinterpreted"* to mean exactly *what it does not say*, since Islam has found it's way in the West: *a place founded on Christian values.*

---

[13] *Bukhari*, Vol. 4, Book 56, 693; Vol. 2, Book 13, 1

[14] Sura 4:24. This goes against Deuteronomy 21:10-14

[15] Sura 6:142-147; 22:36 contradicts Leviticus 11:4

[16] Note the *"We"* and the plural *"creators"* in Sura 78:6-11; 77:20, 36; 23:49; 7:52; 15:16, 19, 22, 26-27; 37:125.

One of Noah's sons died in the flood according to Sura 11:43.[17]

A Muslim is *superior* to any Jew or Christian (Sura 5:82, 51, 41, 64; 2:65, 120; 4:47; 9:29; 3:110).

John the Baptist was "pure and sinless" which was stolen from the Roman Catholic Catechism of Immaculate Conception. It also contradicts 1 John 1:10; Romans 3:10, 23; Isaiah 64:6, etc.[18]

Muhammad gets mad when you *ask questions* (Bukhari, Vol. 2, 555; Vol. 1, 91, 92). It isn't good to ask questions.

Muhammad is forgetful of his own sayings (Bukhari, Vol. 6, 558).

Muhammad decided that *camel urine* was medicine (Bukhari, Vol. 1, 234).

The majority of hell is made up of women (Bukhari Vol. I, 28, Vol. 2, 161).

How can one go from saying that Jesus Christ was a prophet sent from Allah, and then claim His teachings are sound with Muhammad's teachings. *They are night and day, man!* You may say that the O.T. and N.T. are different, such as in the Church age, where the law has been done away with for the believer. Did you ever sit and wonder *why* that is?—It took the death of the *Testator* (Heb. 9:16-17). There was something that came *between* the O.T. and New Testament—*it was the death of Jesus Christ as a sacrifice*. What came between Jesus Christ and Muhammad? Why the change? *Nothing did, but 600 years of time.* It was all made up by someone worshiping a *"moon god"* called *"Allah"* (meaning "the god") out of 360 *other gods* of the early pre-Islamic religion, who tried *copying the Jewish and Christian texts into his own work* while saying he received it from a 600

---

[17] In *"The Study Quran,"* footnote 43 reads that "Yam" or "Kanan" died before entering the ark. "Yam" would be Ham and "Kanan" would be Canaan. Contradicts the Biblical account.

[18] See footnotes on Muhammad Ali Quran commentary under Sura 2:130; 40:55; 2:255; 89:29-30; 91:8; 33:21, etc.

winged angel[19] named Gabriel. (Jospeh Smith, the founder of the Mormon Church did a very similar thing.) He was smart, don't get me wrong. He won plenty of battles but Jim Jones was enough of a con-man to get his crew to drink the Kool-Aid. Hort was smart enough to get the RV passed by a committee. Hitler was smart enough to hide the slaughter of millions…for a time. Eventually things catch up with you— **"ye have sinned against the LORD: and be sure your sin will find you out"** (Num. 32:23). The Quran is unscientific and un-prophetic drivel; it was written by a power hungry warlord who wanted to be a god himself. Why is it, when these issues get brought up, followers of Muhammad kill, stab, or injure a person? There are numerous accounts of Christians witnessing to Muslims in predominantly Muslim countries and what usually follows is death. Their god is a god of hate whether or not some "well intentioned" Muslims want to admit it or not, and those are the fruits thereof: **"by their fruits ye shall know them."**

Back to the initial problem at hand—the claim that Jesus Christ never said that He was God *directly*.

Where does Jesus Christ claim that He is God in the Gospel accounts?

- John 8:58, where Jesus dubs himself **"I AM"** of Exodus 3:14. This is Jesus Christ *directly calling himself JEHOVAH*, which is why the Jews pick up stones to stone him right after. They knew exactly what He was saying.
- John 1:1, 14, the **"Word was God"** who **"was made flesh."**
- Matthew 22:41-46, Jesus calls *Himself* Lord from Psalm 110:1. He is calling himself God.
- John 20:28, Jesus accepts the testimony of Thomas and does *not* correct him when he calls Him Lord, **"my God."**

---

[19] Bukhari, Vol. 6, 380

The Witnessed

- John 9:38, Jesus allows a healed blind man to worship Him.
- Mark 1:1, **"Jesus Christ, the Son of God"**
- John 11:4, 3:36, 3:16, 13:31, **"Son of God,"** *all said by Jesus Christ Himself.*
- Mark 5:7, **"thou Son of the Most High God"** as recognized by an unclean spirit.
- Matthew 14:33, after Jesus walks on water, then causes Peter to be able to walk on water, He then enters the boat and the disciples begin to worship Him and say, **"Of a truth thou art the Son of God."** Jesus never corrected them even though He corrects anyone who needs it (Matt. 23). Also see John 6:69.
- John 5:21, Jesus claims powers of resurrection that only God has.
- John 5:22, Jesus claims God has given him judgment powers only God has.
- John 5:23, another statement putting Jesus in equal standing with God by claiming honor to *Himself* gives honor to God.
- John 5:25, the dead shall hear *the voice of Jesus Christ* at the resurrection.
- John 5:26, Jesus claims to have the same *life giving* force as God.
- Mark 2:27-28, here we have the famous "Jesus only calls himself the Son of man" statement made by Muslims and *in the same passage Jesus is claiming to be God, keep reading.* (Cf. Levi. 23:3—He's calling Himself LORD.
- John 14:6, Jesus Christ said **"I am the WAY," "the TRUTH," "the LIFE."**
- John 11:25, He said **"I am the resurrection."**
- John 10:7, He said **"I am the door."**
- John 10:11, He said **"I am the good shepherd."**
- John 8:12, He said **"I am the light of the world."**
- John 6:35, He said **"I am the bread of life."**
- John 15:1, He said **"I am the true vine."**

- Matthew 11:28, Jesus claims for himself what *no man can claim* (also see the previous seven examples).
- Matthew 18:20, Jesus claims to be *omnipresent.*
- Matthew 28:18, Jesus claims **"all power is given unto me," "all power,"** as in... **"ALL"** ... in **"heaven"** and **"earth"** He is claiming *omnipotence.*

There are many more examples throughout the Gospel accounts but those listed seem to be salient enough for this purpose. How can one honestly read Matthew, Mark, Luke, and John without seeing any of that? How can someone ignore blatant claims of deity? Simple, *they don't want to see it, they reject it, or they outright lie about what they read.* The Book is a two edged sword that swings both ways (Heb. 4:12). The Pharisees refuse to see the Son of God for who He is, but they don't have an excuse. Claiming to have "the answer" with it being void of truth is blindness:

"And some of the Pharisees which were with him heard these words, and said unto him, Are we blind also? Jesus said unto them, If ye were blind, ye should have no sin: but now ye say, We see; therefore your sin remaineth" (John 9:40-41).

Given what we have briefly gone over, the simple fact that Muhammad *never performed a public miracle* speaks volumes. Muhammad's *"sign"* was the Quran *itself* (Sura 17:88; 13:31; 2:23). Jesus Christ has performed many signs and miracles (Matt. 12:15, 14:13-21, 25, etc.). *Moses* performed signs and miracles (Exod. 4-12), as did *Joshua* (Josh. 10:12-13, 3:11-4:6).

The Muslim will often say, *"well, Muhammad was unlike any prophet known...he was different."* You can say that again, because *a mole* on his back was *proof* of his prophethood (Bukhari, Vol. 1, 189; Vol. 4, 741; Sura 33:40). A mole...on his back...was proof of his prophethood. It seems that *"prophecy"* would be the token of a true *prophet*—no?

Prophecies in the Quran are slim to none. There are more prophecies in the first forty pages of the Bible than the entire work of the Quran. That is the true test for any "holy" book: *did any of the prophecies come true or not.*

Muslims will cite the prophecy surrounding Sura 30:2-5 which states,

"The Romans [or Byzantines depending on your translation] *have been defeated in a land near by. Yet after being defeated they will prevail within a few years — unto Allah belongs the affair, before and after, and on that day the believers shall rejoice …"*

According to the vast majority of Muslim scholars and Imams this verse is talking about the capture of Jerusalem in the eastern Mediterranean region in A.D. 614 by the Persians. It had been under Papal rule (Rome) until then, and since Christians are *"the people of the book"* in the Quran Muhammad took sides (strategically) *with Rome* (the pope) who had control over the Byzantine area. The Muslims were not involved in this battle, but Muhammad was "upset" about it. Persians sacked and looted the city, destroying many Christian churches and other "religious" buildings. They also took many prisoners.

In case the reader forgot, *Jerusalem doesn't belong to the Papacy* or any other ruler, *it belongs to the Jews.* Jerusalem was a key position for the Papacy, mostly because of their religious reasons and piety of having Jerusalem as the "crown jewel" of Rome. They believed that "Holy Mother Church" had *replaced* Israel therefore, Jerusalem belongs to Rome—despite countless references and warnings in the Bible (Deut. 1:8, 21, 25, 35-39, 19:8, 26:1-3; Levi. 25:3; Josh. 1:2-3; Num. 35:34; Judg. 6:9; Zech. 12:2-3; Jer. 30:11; Zech. 14:12; Deut. 32:9, 43; Isa. 14:25; Hos. 9:3; Psa. 105:10, and about 100 more).

When Jesus was on trial before His crucifixion the Jews rejected God as their King and said, **"We have no king but Caesar"** (John 19:15)—that's exactly what they got from then on out. Ever since, they have had the Temple burned to the ground in A.D. 70 *by Rome* and have been under the dictates of the "pontiff" *in Rome* throughout the Dark Ages and other Gentile powers making political moves behind the scenes concerning their own land.

They have been subjected to the anti-semitic Catholic popes for centuries. Pope Gregory VI (A.D. 1045) said Christians shouldn't work for Jews. Pope Gregory IX (A.D. 1227) ordered that every copy of the Talmud be confiscated under penalty of death. Pope Paul IV (A.D. 1555) made ghettoes for Jews. The first ghetto for Jews was authorized by the Catholic Council of Breslau in A.D. 1266. Interestingly enough, the ghettos were governed by a board of Jewish elders, Rabbis, and judges. This is where Hitler got the idea during the Nazi regime in Germany. Hitler had elders and other Jewish leaders elected to run death camps, prisons, ghettos, work detail, file complaints, etc. This was called a *"Judenrat."* Jews were in charge of giving other Jews orders in the death camps and these Jews were in charge of such things as accounting for German companies (as made famous by the 1993 film, *"Schindler's List"*) and the military itself.

Hitler's *"Mein Kampf"* was published in 1925 and contains many of his malicious ideas concerning the Jewish race, mostly stemming from an anti-Jewish write-up he had read in his early years called, *"The Protocols of the Learned Elders of Zion"* written and released in 1864 and published again in 1918.

The German people knew who they were voting for if they read his work (*"Mein Kampf"*), which many *did*. No doubt, Pope Pius XII had read it when he was Cardinal, before he became the "holy father"—the big papa pope. In 1930 the previous pope, Pius XI, appointed him Cardinal Secretary of State, *responsible for foreign policy and state relations throughout the world.* Thus the election of Hitler was of course rigged in hopes of installing a pro-Catholic dictator soon to be in control of Europe (see footnote 21 in chapter 6). He then became the next pope, *Pope Pius XII* in *1939*—the start of WWII. The pope he worked under as Cardinal agreed to the concordant and was signed by and written-up by *Eugenio Pacelli* (see footnote 6 in chapter 9) with Hitler in *1933* and even "blessed" the Third Reich because they were so excited about their endeavor. The "blessing" was through the Vatican as an institution of course, since Pope Pius XI didn't want his *personal name* on the "blessing."—I wonder why?

You see, *Eugenio Pacelli* mentioned above who wrote up and singed the concordant *is Pope Pius XII* before he became "the vicar of Christ, and holy father, the Pope" when he was a Cardinal. Despite the monstrosity of what happened, the Vatican has never denounced or excommunicated Hitler *to this day* and most likely never will—even after the death of over 6,000,000 Jews (2 out of every 3 European Jews were murdered), and after soap was made from the fat of their bodies. Nothing—Just a bleak vague apology. Martin Luther is still excommunicated to this day and John Wycliffe is still a heretic. The Catholic Church is, and always has been anti-semitic and anti-protestant.

The other reason for the Muslims siding with Rome was strategic and political; we can expect nothing less from a church-state outfit similar to that of Islam (see pages 434-8). The eastern Mediterranean was a hub for trade and commerce, and it linked Asia, Africa, and Europe in trade routes during the time.

You see, *"the people of the book"* in the Quran are both Jews *and* Christians. All Muhammad did was pick what he thought the winning side would be. He was good at it, he knew *battle*. The Jews have always been against the Catholics; synagogues and temples were turned into Roman Catholic Churches and Jewish religious practices were limited by law. The Catholic Church was always willing to kill to have Jerusalem as *"a prize"* (11th, 12th, and 13th

Century Crusades). During the Crusades many Jews fought *alongside Muslims* in trying to defeat the Catholic Empire. In fact, this constant battle between *Roman Catholic's* and Muslims is what allowed for *a distraction from* the movement *of the Reformation* later on. The constant threat of the Muslims allowed the ideas and the text of the Reformation to flourish around the 15-16th centuries.

Persian occupation was short lived; the Byzantines were able to retake the city in A.D. 628, following a series of battles. This is what the "prophecy" is supposedly about. After the Byzantine recapture of Jerusalem, the city was once again under "Christian" control, and many of the destroyed religious buildings were rebuilt. However, the conflict between the Byzantines and Persians continued for several more years, with neither side gaining a decisive advantage.

After the death of Muhammad in A.D. 632, the "shook-up" Byzantine Empire around the eastern Mediterranean was soon *invaded* by Muslims in A.D. 637 (Jerusalem in particular). You had an all out war between Catholics and Muslims over a city who's *rightful owners are the Jews* (1 Kings 8:1, 44, 48, 9:3, 11:13; Psa. 2:6, 76:2, 78:68; Isa. 2:2-3, 60:14; Isa. 14:25; Deut. 32:43, 19:8, etc.). It was given under an **"everlasting covenant"**—meaning there is no end to it.

This patch of land was given to Abraham (Gen. 15) and passed on to Isaac (Gen. 26:1-4), then Jacob (Gen. 28:13-14), and then to the 12 tribes. The land has been fought over since the days of old and Jerusalem itself has been under siege or attacked many, many times. God has ironically ascribed the name *"Jerusalem"* to it which means, *"city of peace."* He named it that because *will be* in the future—**"in this place will I give peace"** (Hag. 2:9). That is where the **"peace"** in Luke 2:14 comes in.

First thing to note about this *"prophecy"* is that *the Quran was finished a few years later, after the victory*. Second thing to note is that depending on which translation of the Quran you have, it will read that the defeat of Rome will take place in *"a few years"* or *"ten years."* In either case it was wrong. It took 14-15 years for Rome to get it back and the starting point for *"a few years"* to the defeat of Rome has no reference point since *the Quran was finished in A.D. 632*. Two years from what point? *It was retroactively written.*

With this stated, some Muslims will then say the verse is actually talking about *"certain strategic moves"* as the starting point of reference, which then justifies the time scale. *This is their best foot forward.* On the other foot, the Holy Bible gives 48 specific prophecies down to the time, day, type of clothes, and place of birth about *one Man*, given 400 years or more *before* His birth. That isn't even all the prophecies. They number well over 500 (see the end of the chapter).

Good questions to ask and point out to a Muslim are:
- Sura 57:3 states Allah is the first and the last, just as Jesus Christ calls *Himself* in Revelation 1:17-18—what do you make of that?
- Sura 22:56-57 says Allah will judge the world. Jesus says that He will judge the world in Matthew 25:31-32, 46; John 5:27—what do you make of that?
- Sura 22:7 says Allah will raise the dead at the resurrection. John 5:25-29 says Jesus Christ will raise the dead at the resurrection—what do you make of that?
- According to the Quran, *only* Allah can make these claims.
- *Who is the real "Allah" and who is God?*
- By these standards above, Jesus Christ is God
- By these standards *Muhammad* was just a man
- Most modern Muslims will completely ignore or find a way around Sura 9:29 and 4:34 as well as many of the ones mentioned above; these regard Islam as a *violent* religion.
- Is Islam really based on *"evidence"* as most Imams claim, given the information in this chapter?

- Is Islam really a religion of *peace*? (They will say *"yes,"* with the caveat, *"if everyone were Muslim"*), if they respond this way bring up the **"fruits"** of Islam such as violence, condoning rape, beating wives, *promoting* slavery and encouraging it, Sharia law, the "anti-woman" nature of the religion, conquest, war, etc. If need be, then ask if they would rather live in the United States or Saudi Arabia, Iraq, Iran, etc., (comparing the Catholic Church-state regime to Islam will also do the trick).
- Muslims claim the Quran must be read in its *original language* and it is *commanded* to be read, yet a large potion of Muslims *do not speak or read Arabic*. 274 million people in the world speak Arabic yet there are 1.9 billion Muslims worldwide[20]
- Muslims are to pray five times a day facing Mecca and the prayers should be *in Arabic*
- The idea that there is only *one* version of *an Arabic* Quran is *false*. There is the Warsh, Qalun, al-Duri, Khalaf, and Hafs, for example. They all differ in places which proves that there isn't just *one* version of an Arabic Quran. This fact will get a person *stabbed*; it has happened before. There is a doctrine of preservation in Islam that says no syllable, vowel, word, or punctuation mark has ever changed—it's a bold faced lie.
- What are the **"fruits"** of Islam? This is a good question to allow the person to ponder over

Given the examples that I gave above, surrounding the deity of Jesus Christ in the Gospel accounts, a Rabbi will go back to Exodus 20:3, **"Thou shalt have no other gods before me."** They view Jesus Christ *as a separate god and nothing more than a falsely-worshipped idol.*

---

[20] According to https://www.encounteringislam.org/muslim-world-facts only 20% of worldwide Muslims speak Arabic.

Christians are nothing but heathen idolators to the Rabbi, he may not be as open about it but that is what most believe. Aside from Exodus 20:3, they will quote Exodus 20:4, **"Thou shalt not make unto thee any graven image, or any likeness of any thing that is in heaven above, or that is in the earth beneath, or that is in the water under the earth."**

As seen in the examples above, Jesus *does not* claim to be a separate god, but God **"in the flesh."** *He claims to be Jehovah Himself,* **"in the flesh."** Jesus was either the greatest sociopathic, self-obsessed liar who ever lived *or* He was telling the truth. Where are you gonna' put your chips? Who talks like Jesus did? Who says, **"I am the way"**? Who says, **"no man cometh unto the Father, BUT BY ME"**? I mean, who says that stuff?

Jesus Christ cannot be a **"graven image"** because He was **"made WITHOUT HANDS"** (Dan. 2:34 Cf. 1 Peter 2:8; Rom. 9:32-33; Matt. 21:44). The Jewish Rabbis and the Muslim Imams **"stumbled at the stumbling stone."**

"And he shall be for a sanctuary; but for a stone of stumbling and for a rock of offence to both the houses of Israel, for a gin and for a snare to the inhabitants of Jerusalem" (Isa. 8:14). Jesus Christ *is* that **"stone."** In the same manner, when a sinner is saved they have a **"circumcision made WITHOUT HANDS"** (Col. 2:11).

When a Jew or Muslim hears that Jesus is **"the image of God"** (Heb. 1:3) they believe He is *an idol made with hands.* They view Jesus as nothing more than Adam, who was created in God's image, who is now *fallen.* Now, *what* is often ignored is *what* Jesus Christ is an **"image"** *of?* If Jesus Christ is **"God manifest in the flesh"** then He **"is the image of the invisible God"** (Col. 1:15), since no one has **"seen"** or **"looked upon"** the Father, nor has anyone **"handled"** Him (1 John 1:1)—*that is, if He did no*t **"manifest in the flesh"** (1 Tim. 3:16; 1 John 1:2).

The next problem is the *Trinity*. Muslims and Jews alike have a very hard time with this very simple concept. A good way to explain it to a Muslim is that instead of it being 1+1+1=3…it's *1x1x1=1*.

Muslims see the Trinity as three separate gods which goes against their strong belief of "Allah is the only god." You may bring up the fact that *water* has three states, but it's still *water*. It has a *solid, liquid,* and a *vaporous state (gas)*. It is still H2O. It is best to *keep it simple* at times, depending on who you're talking to. A *family* has three parts to it: a mother, a father, and a child. That makes a family. The *sun* has three different types of rays: ones you can *feel* (infrared), ones you can *see* (light spectrum), and ones you *can't see or feel* (x-rays, etc.). It's still one thing—*the sun*. Man, do people have a hard time with that one. *Man has a spirit, a soul, and a body. Up, down, middle—hot, cold, lukewarm*…and so on. The concept of the Trinity, or **"Godhead,"** is so common in our day to day lives that they are **"without excuse"** (Rom. 1:20). It can be seen in such things as water and the sun.

Much of the confusion comes from the title given to this obvious Biblical concept, "the Trinity"; it isn't found anywhere in the Bible. The term "rapture" isn't found either but the *concept* is there with those figures such as Enoch and Elijah, groups such as the Church and Tribulation saints. The Trinity is simply that the **"Godhead"** has three distinct *persons* that make up the whole. They each have functions and describe a part of one God.

There are many passages in the Bible that show the Trinity in a clear light, one such being Matthew 3:13-17. In the passage we have the *Father* speaking **"this is my beloved Son, in whom I am well pleased."** Then we have *The Son* being baptized, when *The Holy Spirit* descends **"like a dove."**

When talking with a Rabbi or a modern day Jew, things can get complicated quick. Like Muslims, they believe the idea of the Trinity is polytheistic in nature and that the Doctrine of the Trinity was not set in place until the Roman

Catholic Council of Nice back in A.D. 325. They will most likely show you Deuteronomy 6:4 to prove there is no such thing as a triune God, which see. Today many believe that the Trinity was purely a Roman Catholic doctrine; this is false because it can be found throughout the entire Bible and in writings which predate the council. This is when the doctrine was established *"on paper,"* so to speak, by a council. The Jews also see the horrid and corrupt aspects of the Catholic Church, which can be a resting place of *common ground*, a place to explain some differences between Catholics and Biblical Christianity.

The Doctrine of the Trinity goes back *further* than A.D. 325. It is stated clearly in 1 John 5:7 and the text dates as far back as A.D. 170. Then there are the writings of Paul, John, Peter, Luke, James, Jude, Mark, and Matthew. There are Church Fathers and figures such as Polycarp (A.D. 69-155), Ignatius (A.D. 107-140), Theophilus of Antioch (A.D. 185), Tertullian (A.D. 155-220), Hippolytus of Rome (A.D. 170-235), and so forth that all write about the Trinity. As you can see, the Doctrine of the Trinity was established *long before* the Council of Nicea.

If God made Adam in *His own image* (Gen. 1:27) and Adam had a *body*, a *spirit*, and a *soul* (Gen. 2:7); would it not be logical to conclude that God *also* had a *body*, a *spirit*, and a *soul?* Adam had a body, **"God formed man of the dust of the ground"** and he has a spirit: God **"breathed"** the **"breath of life"** (Gen. 2:7). As mentioned before (see the *"Introduction"*), the spirit is the **"breath"** of God. Adam also had a soul, **"and man became a living soul."** You will see Paul's confirmation of the three-part man in 1 Thessalonians 5:23, **"And the very God of peace sanctify you WHOLLY; and I pray God your whole SPIRIT and SOUL and BODY be preserved blameless unto the coming of our Lord Jesus Christ."** It goes even further than that, *animals* have their own type of spirit (Ecc. 3:21) and soul (Job 12:10). They of course have a body.

Ever since *the fall* of Adam, man's spirit is *dead* in sin (Eph. 2:1) which is why, **"ye must be born again"** (John 3:7). It is a *Spiritual* Rebirth that causes a man to become "Born Again."

What about this soul? We know in Scripture from the O.T. that God indeed has a *soul:* **"my soul shall abhor you"** (Levi. 26:30), **"his soul was grieved for the misery of Israel"** (Judges 10:16), **"in whom my soul delighteth"** (Isa. 42:1). Freud was onto something when he wrote about the Ego, Id, and Super-Ego; he just happened to *deny* everything written before he was born in the Bible.

God indeed has a *spirit*, **"I have put my spirit upon him"** (Isa. 42:1), **"My spirit that is upon thee"** (Isa. 59:21), **"my spirit"** (Ezek. 39:29), **"the Spirit of God"** (Gen. 1:2), **"take not thy holy spirit from me"** (Psa. 51:11), etc.

What is missing is, the *body*. The body comes in the N.T. as **"JESUS"** (Matt. 1:25). God's Spirit is also *revealed in new ways* in the N.T. (John 14-16). This body is also revealed within the O.T. **"For he shall grow up before him as a tender plant, and as a root out of a dry ground: he hath no form nor comeliness; and when we shall see him, there is no beauty that we should desire him"** (Isa. 53:2). Isaiah 49:1 and 7:15 tell you that Jesus Christ was *raised like any other child* (Cf. Matt. 1:21 and Heb. 5:7-8). Imagine that. Imagine raising Jesus Christ as a baby—breast feeding, changing diapers, playing with toys, bumping His head, "don't do that Jesus...."

Many Rabbis believe the **"he"** of the passage is Israel. They also believe that Isaiah 53:10 is *about Israel* bearing the sins of the world, **"Yet it pleased the LORD to bruise him; he hath put him to grief: when thou shalt make his soul an offering for sin, he shall see his seed, he shall prolong his days, and the pleasure of the LORD shall prosper in his hand."** They do this by making the **"righteous servant"** of Isaiah 53:11 *Israel* instead of Jesus Christ. This of course, would make Israel the savior of itself *and* the world instead of **"thy Redeemer"** or **"the Holy One** of Israel" (Isa. 54:5). Key word there is **"thy,"** meaning "your (Israel's) redeemer," not Israel itself. Israel does not redeem anyone in this age and does not **"make his soul an offering for sin"** (Isa. 53:10) *for anyone.*

Israel is referred to as a **"servant"** in Isaiah 22:20, 44:21, 41:8, 37:35. **"Remember these, O Jacob and Israel; for thou art my servant: I have formed thee; thou art my servant: O Israel, thou shalt not be forgotten of me"** (Isa. 44:21). Now in 44:23 we have, **"the LORD hath redeemed Jacob, and glorified himself in Israel."** God is the Redeemer, not Israel. Israel has no active part in anyone's salvation today. God calling Israel His **"servant"** really messes with Rabbis in Isaiah 49:1-7. Remember, we are dealing with something that makes a person *"stumble"* (Isa. 8:14, 28:16; 1 Peter 2:8). The Book will make you stumble…it's written that way. In Isaiah 49:1-6 the trouble comes when Israel is called God's **"firstborn"** in Exodus 4:22. Rabbis believe God's son is Israel, and *only* Israel. Which, they *are* nationally, but Isaiah 49:5 shows that the one **"formed"** from the **"womb"** is a **"servant"** of God that will **"bring Jacob again to him."** The "**him**" being God. This cannot mean that **"the LORD hath called me from the womb"** (Isa. 49:1) is a reference to Israel —it's Jesus Christ. Again, verse 5 states that *the one who is brought from the womb will restore Jacob (Israel) to God,* **"And now, saith the LORD that formed me from the womb to be his servant, to bring Jacob again to him, Though Israel be not gathered, yet shall I be glorious in the eyes of the LORD, and my God shall be my strength."** The Redeemer of Israel is Jesus Christ who will restore them at his coming (Isa. 49:8-11). Israel has been awaiting a restoration and the land grant given to Abraham to be theirs as promised by the covenant from God in Genesis 15. They get it from God, not by Israel giving it to Israel, themselves (see the last 2,000+ years of history).

Another example is in Isaiah 44:1 where the **"servant"** is called **"Israel."** The servant is **"chosen"** just like in Isaiah

49:1-7 and Isaiah 42:1. In 44:3 the servant has the Sprit of God "pored out on him," just *like the one in* Isaiah 42:1. What is *not* observed is that the servant in Isaiah 42:1 and Isaiah 49 *is the one doing the restoring of Israel* and the one in Isaiah 44:1 is the one *being restored*. What a mess, goodnight Irene.

The confusion comes from not seeing that Israel *is restored later, at the Second Advent, by another party* (Messiah/Christ) and *does* have the Spirit poured on them *at that time, nationally* (see Joel 2:23-29). You couldn't have made a more perfect **"stone of stumbling"** (1 Pet. 2:8), watch your toes.

There is an amazing use of sentence structure in Isaiah, such as Isaiah 50:3-11. Who is the **"me"** in Isaiah 50:4? Is it the **"I"** of 50:3? That would make the Messiah or **"servant"** of verse 10 *God*, not to mention the prophecy of verse 6 that was *fulfilled in Mark 14:65*. You find out who this **"me"** is in Isaiah 51:1-6. It is the Lord, just as in Psalm 110:1. **"The LORD said unto my Lord, Sit thou at my right hand, until I make thine enemies thy footstool."** Jesus Christ quotes and brings this to the attention of the Pharisees in Matthew 22:42-45. Jesus asks the Pharisees what they think **"of Christ"** (Matt. 22:42). Their response is that the Christ (the Messiah) is, **"The Son of David."** People are calling Him the **"Son of David,"** as in Matthew 1:1, 9:27, 12:23, 15:22, etc. The Pharisees knew that the passage in Psalm 110:1 was *concerning the Messiah*, not Abraham (as most Rabbis today claim) because of what follows in Psalm 110.

Psalm 110:2 says, **"The LORD shall send the ROD of thy strength out of Zion: RULE thou IN THE MIDST of thine enemies"** (see all of Psalm 110 and Psa. 66:4-8; 72:6-9; Isa. 26:10-11). The **"day of thy power"** (verse 3) is in the **"morning"** (see Mal. 4:1-4; Hos. 6:3; Psa. 49:14; Matt. 13:43). "That ain't no" Abraham (Tennessee cir. 1999).

What Rabbis have done, just as the Pharisees did in John 8:39, is that they've replaced God Almighty with Abraham. Psalm 2 sheds light for us as to who this **"Lord"** is that is mentioned in Psalm 110:1 (in addition to Matthew 22:42-45).

"His anointed" in Psalm 2:2 means *"his Messiah,"* or Christ. The **"Son"** (verse 7) in the passage is the same **"Lord"** in Psalm 110:1 and the same **"Son of David"** in Matthew 22:42. (Read Psalm 2 and Psalm 110, see the *similarities*.)

The idea in Matthew 22 is that no father would ever call their son **"Lord"** in the Jewish tradition. That was disrespectful, and the Pharisees *knew that*—unless the **"Lord"** was more than his son, i.e. the Christ—the Son of David—God in the flesh. In Psalm 110:1 David is saying, **"The LORD"** (God) said to **"my"** (David's) **"Lord"** (God). Who might this be then? Modern Rabbis claim it is Abraham. Jesus claimed it was David speaking **"in spirit"** about *Himself* (Matt. 22:43-44, also see Mark 12:36; Luke 20:42), as did Peter (Acts 2:33-34). If you only had the O.T., Psalm 110:1 is concerning God himself (see above), but we have the New Testament revelation which clarifies it even further.

That Book is a Vietnamese spike-pit. After you have shown this to a Jew and they have conceded that the "servants" given in Isaiah are in fact *different*, the next question is, *"who do you think that other servant is?."* They will most likely respond with, *"the Messiah"* or some such response. Just keep going on with with how the Messiah *could* be God in the flesh, you will most likely run into the problem below.

Another issue that you will run into is that *God* could never be *"a man."* This is used by both Muslims and Jews while being witnessed to. What's usually quoted is Numbers 23:19, **"God is not a man,"** but they leave off what comes *after the comma*. The full passage says, **"God is not a man, that he should lie; neither the son of man, that he should repent: hath he said, and shall he not do it? or hath he spoken, and shall he not make it good?"** God *does not lie like a man* and he *does not have to repent like a man*. This is often quoted by Muslims online for the same purposes. Did Jesus Christ ever have to repent? *No.* Did He ever lie? *No.*

Remember, your concern is for *the persons soul, not to argue how much you "know" about the Bible*. Another verse to show them after this is Zechariah 12:10, **"they shall look upon me whom they have pierced, and they shall mourn for him."** Notice the **"him"** and **"me"** in the passage, it's referring to the Lord (Zech. 12:8-10).

As Nicodemus (John 3:1), who had a Ph.D in Old Testament Studies with a concentration in Hebrew, and a Masters in Theology didn't know about the New Birth: **"Art thou a master of Israel, and knowest not these things?"** (John 3:10). He missed Psalm 22:30-31 and didn't have the slightest idea about what Jesus was talking about. He assumed that one just went up and out the birth canal again. Like Nicodemus, some Jews will argue that they don't need the salvation offered by Jesus Christ because their sins were forgiven and are forgiven by various practices in Leviticus, Numbers, etc. This is a gross error. Within their own Hebrew text in Exodus 34:7 it says that God *will forgive* but **"by no means clear the guilty."** Again in Numbers 14:18, you will see the same thing.

A difference has been established between *forgiveness* and *clearing* a persons sins. Jesus Christ came to *clear* the sins of the world, not just *forgive*, **"In whom we have redemption through his blood, even the forgiveness of sins"** (Col. 1:14). To redeem a thing is to make an exchange for it, as in Leviticus 25:48, where a poor brother is bought back with *money*. Another example would be a simple visit to the local pawn shop. All the items may be *"redeemed"* with a *payment*. That is what Jesus Christ did on Calvary, He **"gave himself a RANSOM for all"** (1 Tim. 2:6). He *paid* the debt with his own blood, **"ye are bought with a price"** (1 Cor. 6:20), **"Forasmuch as ye know that ye were not redeemed with corruptible things, as silver and gold, from your vain conversation received by tradition from your fathers; But with the precious blood of Christ, as of a lamb without blemish and without spot"** (1 Peter 18-19).

In the O.T. *"redemption"* is never in reference to the *clearing of sin* unless it is a *prophetical* reference to Christ, such as in Isaiah 62:12, **"And they shall call them, The holy people, The redeemed of the LORD: and thou shalt be called, Sought out, A city not forsaken"** (also see Jer. 31:11-12; Isa. 52:3; Isa. 48:20, 35:5-10, etc.). There is an odd thing that happens after Isaiah chapter 40: *"redemption"* is mentioned over 20 times while it is only mentioned less than 4 times in chapters 1-39 (there's a nugget for ya). It is always in reference to something other than salvation in the O.T. for the exception of the *prophetical* references. On the other hand, in the N.T., sins are forgiven, remitted, *and* a person has been redeemed. **"Being justified freely by his grace through the redemption that is in Christ Jesus: Whom God hath set forth to be a propitiation through faith in his blood, to declare his righteousness for the remission of sins that are past, through the forbearance of God"** (Rom. 3:24-25).

An interesting thing I have run into with some Jews and Muslims is the idea that Jesus Christ's sacrifice on Calvary was *"pagan nonsense."* Surprisingly, I have actually heard many say: *"blood does not save anyone and the idea of a human sacrifice is demonic and pagan!"* This is from Torah reading, Tanakh reading, pork abstaining Jews mostly; which is bonkers to consider. A large portion of the Torah (first five books of Moses a.k.a. the Pentateuch) deals with *animal sacrifice*, feasts, and ceremonies.

What in the world is *that* blather: saying it's *"pagan nonsense"*? You are calling your own book *"pagan nonsense,"* are you? Have you lost your mind? You just called Moses and the Torah *"pagan nonsense!"* A Jew. Have you actually *read* Exodus, Leviticus, Job, Numbers, Deuteronomy, 1 and 2 Samual, 1 and 2 Kings…have you read *any of it*? That's the conclusion you came to—that blood used for atonement and redemption is *"pagan"*?

"For it is the LIFE of the flesh; the BLOOD of it is for the LIFE thereof" (Levi. 17:14), **"for the LIFE of the flesh is in the BLOOD"** (Levi. 17:11). *Moses sprinkled blood on* **"the book,"** *the people, and the alter* in Exodus 24:5-8 (also see Heb. 9:19).

Jesus Christ gives eternal life, His **"blood"** sacrifice can give that **"life."** The blood shed on Calvary was not from an average man, for it was *"God's Blood"* (Acts 20:28). Mormons believe that after baptism your sins are washed away but any sin committed after that baptism must be paid for *again*. In fact, certain sins must be paid for with the sinners own blood. If blood is a type of spiritual cleansing agent (1 John 1:7) how is unclean blood supposed to purify anything at all? If that is the case, then why did Jesus die?

"By the which will we are sanctified through the offering of the body of Jesus Christ once for all" (Heb. 10:10). The **"life"** that animals had could not, **"for it is not possible that the blood of bulls and of goats should take away sins"** (Her. 10:4). The act of animal sacrifice was to stay in *communion* with God, for the sins could not be *"cleared"* (Exod. 34:7). **"And every priest standeth daily ministering and offering oftentimes the same sacrifices, which can never take away sins"** There was a Sacrifice to end all sacrifices so that you may commune with God *daily* and not have to rely on *priests*, **"But this man, after he had offered one sacrifice for sins for ever, sat down on the right hand of God"** (Heb. 10:12). For a Muslim to say it was *"pagan nonsense"* would be the equivalent of calling "Allah" a pagan, since, *according to Allah, he wrote the O.T.* For a Jew, it would be to deny large portions of Scripture. Simple as that.

You will run into some "battle worn" individuals from time-to-time. Most "Muslim apologists" will get their information concerning the New Testament text from Bart Ehrman, James White, Bruce Metzger, Hort, Nestle, Aland, etc. *The same sources that Christian seminary campuses use to teach their students.* They will *not* look into Edward F. Hills, Pickering, Burgon, Fuller, Sturz, Letis, David A. Black, Robinson, Hodges, Hoskier, etc., in any more depth than Ehrman or White did when their teachers glossed them over.

Modern Christian seminaries face certain challenges that not only affect their own standing but also provide fuel for Muslim apologetics. Additionally, Rabbi Tovia Singer, a prominent critic of the New Testament, examines the works of what are considered some of the finest and most renowned Christian scholars today, and finds them unconvincing at best. In fact, he openly laughs at the arguments put forth by such scholars.

At times he has some great points, but eh, at others Singer is intellectually dishonest. He doesn't approach the N.T. in the same manner as he does the O.T., and he knows it. He does this for the simple fact that he doesn't *believe* the N.T. He has the same attitude as the destructive critic. He is *looking for solutions* in the O.T. because he is trying to prove *his* case, but when it comes to the New Testament, he is *looking for errors* to prove his case. This is a lot like the mentality of the atheist when he is looking for an alibi in order to not believe the Book, and God will give it to them (Ezek. 14) without hesitation.

Singer, how about those 700 horses in 2 Samuel 8:4, or was it 7000 like it says in 1 Chronicles 18:4 (*see Chapter 1*)? What are your answers for the alleged "contradictions" in the O.T.? You never seem to talk much about them.

Singer is also *a favorite in the Muslim community*. He often *panders* towards that community *as if they actually had something in common*. His stance is simple: "since Christians are idol worshippers, and Muslims are monotheists, then they (Muslims) are more like Jews" (despite Muslims taking over the land that was given to the Jews [*his people*], and despite violent attacks made on Jews regularly [*his people*], Muslims have more in common, since they don't worship "an idol").

What a bunch of embellished rubbish. Muslims aren't idol worshippers? What in the gobstoppers! What about the *"black rock"*? What about kissing that black rock and circling it seven times: the Kaaba? Is this not idol worship? Oh, it's just an "aid in worship" like the statues of Mary and the saints are for Catholics. Sura 2:158[21] states that a person must run between two rocks (hills) seven times. It was traditionally said to go back to Ishmael and Hagar, it was later discarded by many due to them believing that is was *"polytheistic"* in nature. If that isn't enough, which it won't be for many Muslims: why can't you draw a picture of Muhammad? Scared you might *worship* it? People have been killed over that. There was a case of a teacher in 2020 who was *beheaded* for it…*in France*[22] — *not Iran, Iraq, Afghanistan, or Saudi Arabia, but…in France.* Let alone what was said previously about the polytheism in the Quran itself.

Furthermore, *Muhammad himself was an idol worshiper*: "Allah's Apostle [Muhammad] said that he met Zaid bin 'Amr Nufail at a place near Baldah, this happened before Allah's Apostle [Muhammad] received 'Divine Inspiration'. Allah's Apostle [Muhammad] presented a dish of meat to Zaid bin 'Amr which he ate, *but* Zaid refused to eat of it and then said to the pagans, 'I do not eat of what you slaughter on your stone altars (Ansabs) nor do I eat except that on which Allah's Name has been mentioned on slaughtering'."[23] Why didn't *"Allah's Apostle"* say what Zaid said? It's because the man was a *raging lunatic* and is apparent after reading any biography, even those cherished by Muslims as being "an accurate representation" of his life.

---

[21] Syyed Hossein Nasr, *"The Study Quran,"* 2015, Sura 2:158 footnote.

[22] Author's Note: The European class that Samuel Paty taught was on "freedom of expression." Of course, hardly any major news media outlet reported on the subject for any length of time—it just doesn't fit the narrative. He was stabbed to death and then his head was severed from his body for drawing a cartoon version of Muhammad. Although, no one is equal to Allah, right?

[23] Bukhari 7, 407

He also *offered to idols*: "The Prophet slaughtered an ewe for one of the idols (nusub min al-ansab); then he roasted it and carried it with him."[24] Not only that, but the Kaaba was originally a site used to worship idols and spill blood used for that idol worship.[25] This goes against *both* the Old Testament and the New Testament (Exod. 20:3-5; Acts 15:29), supposedly written by "Allah."

Singer digs himself deeper by attributing the dates of the N.T. canon to the Catholic councils (Hippo A.D. 393 and Carthage A.D. 397). This is where the N.T. canon was *officially* canonized *by creed of a "council."* Guess what else was specified as Scripture at the Council of Carthage—the *Apocryphal books*. Many Christians had rejected those books years beforehand. Those books were *again* ratified as scripture by the Roman Catholic *Council of Trent* in 1545-1563. They are *still* deemed as scripture by the Catholic Church today.

The New Testament canon, as you have it in a King James Bible, goes back to A.D. 100-200 and before, where groups of Christians in the Body had accepted those writings as canon *long before* any Catholic council led by any Roman emperor sitting on any golden throne hellbent on control and power decided what they *should* be. They can be seen in the Old Syriac and the Old Latin. There was an *"unofficial"* dictum of what was Scripture and what wasn't; as deemed *by the Body* (1 Cor. 12:13; 1 Peter 2:5).

Singer is trying to prove that many other books had been around, making it difficult to determine what *actually* belonged in the canon and further, that by A.D. 393 it would be "too late" to really decide. So, who knows what should and shouldn't be in the N.T., right?—Wrong.

Singer *avoids* telling you that the Hebrew canon wasn't *"officially"* announced until A.D. *Second Century*, but its

---

[24] F. E. Peters, *"Muhammad and the Religion of Islam,"* 1994, pages. 126-127

[25] Alfred Guillaume, *"The Life of Muhammad,"* pages 8-9

writings *ended* around 400 B.C. with Malachi (which also means that the Old Testament Apocrypha is nonsense). That is of course, *500 years later.* Singer is trying to use the dating of the Councils of Carthage and Hippo as being *too late* for the decision of the canon to have any true impact or accuracy. That's only about 307 years from those councils compared with the 500 of the O.T., since the N.T. *was complete* by A.D. 90-96. By *Singer's standards*, he just lost the fight without even drawing his sword. The *actual standards* are given above (the Body decided on the N.T. canon long before the Roman Catholic councils).

Some date the *"official"* decision of the contents in the Tanakh (O.T.) around 150 B.C.. That would put the canonization of the Tanakh about 250 years out from its last writing. Still using the time frame above of 307 years from the *official* council declaration of the New Testament, it would only be a difference of 57 years between the O.T. and N.T. canonizations in respect to the distance of their last writing. It is hardly something to quibble over since the dating of the *unofficial* agreement on N.T. writings/canon took place 10-110 years after the last book had been written (Revelation).

The truth of the matter is that Christians had, believed, and read the N.T. as we have today as early as A.D. 100-200 which puts the date 10-110 years away. That is unheard of for *any* ancient document. You can see why Muslims like him: because they can't *think!* They aren't *allowed* to think for themselves. They hear, *"Christians are stupid"* and start to drool, foam at the mouth, and clap cymbals like a wind-up doll. When the Jewish Scriptures were decided upon, they were *divided* into *three* major groups. Jesus Christ already divided the Jewish Scriptures (Tanakh) up into three major groups in Luke 24:44.

Singer also blames Christians for "not knowing Hebrew," pastors in particular. He calls them liars for not understanding Hebrew, therefore, deceiving their congregations. One of his trademark attacks on the English Bible is found in Psalm 22:16, **"For dogs have compassed me: the assembly of the wicked have inclosed me: they pierced my hands and my feet."**

Here he says the King James translators (and every other bible version) were dishonest and down right deceptive in their work in translating the passage. He says this because the Hebrew word for "lion" is used instead of the word for **"pierced."** He will run to Isaiah 38:13 or some such place to prove it. He is partly correct, the Hebrew word for **"pierced"** does not occur in the passage directly. It is also verse 17 instead of 16 in the Tanakh.

The Tanakh reads, "For dogs have encompassed me; a company of evil-doers have inclosed me; like a lion, they are at my hands and my feet." Some translations include "[they maul]" or "[being crushed in the mouth of]" between "like a lion" and "they are at my hands and feet." There is just one issue with the addition of "crush": the Hebrew word used means "to dig, burrow, make a hole, open, bore" כָּאֲרִי (ka-ari). *That isn't "crush."* Lion is in the passage and it's part of the same word אֲרִי (ari). So, we have *"as or like a lion making a hole in my hands and feet."* Note the *"as"* and *"like"*: it's a similitude.

Within the Masoretic texts themselves, there are several renderings[26] of the phrase. Some include *"like a lion"* and some say *"dug"* (כרו). Some put *"dug"* in the margin. What happened is that some chose to focus on one form of the word and the others focused on another (dug/bore, *or* like a lion). Either way the King James gives exemplary *light* on the passage, and *"lion"* is already mentioned in verse 21. We aren't talking about literal **"bulls"** (verse 12) or "lions" (verse 21) here.

---

[26] Benjamin Kennicott *"Vetus Testamentum Hebraicum : cum variis lectionibus,"* 1776. manuscripts numbers: 39, 267, 270, 277, 288, 660, 283, 291, 539, 542, 649

Think about it; if a lion clamped down on your hands and feet, you would have at least one large gaping hole *"dug"* or *"bored"* into your flesh from one of the larger "fangs" in his mouth. *Sort of like a long iron nail being pushed through your hand.*

The more *modern* the Tanakh is, the *further* you'll get away from this rendering; it points too closely to Jesus Christ. They have a similar thing going on with their translations today as Christian translation committees and bible departments at seminaries do: an avoidance of objective truth. Rule number 1: if it hits too close to home, change it or get rid of it. See 1 Timothy 6:10 for an example in modern bibles. Anything that sounds too close to Jesus Christ or objective truth must *not* be true and needs to be rendered *differently*; see how modern Tanakh's rendered Zechariah 12:10 if you don't believe me.

The English interprets the word to be **"pierced"** as in John 19:37, **"They shall look on him whom they pierced."** Furthermore, the *lion* in Psalm 22:21 is the devil himself, **"Be sober, be vigilant; because your adversary the devil, as a roaring lion, walketh about, seeking whom he may devour"** (1 Pet. 5:8), this *lion* goes around **"to and fro"** (Job 1:7) **"seeking whom he may devour."** Who do you think was the spirit working *behind* the soldiers who shot dice for Jesus Christ's clothes in John 19:23-24?

Who was working behind these men? By what spirit were these men guided, in whom *crucified* the Son of God? **"…ye walked according to the course of this world, according to the PRINCE of the power of the air, the SPIRIT that now worketh in the children of disobedience"** (Eph. 2:2).

The same *spirit* that worked behind **"the PRINCE of Tyrus"** (Ezek. 28:1) who's heart was **"lifted up"** and said **"I am God, I sit in the seat of God."** The same *spirit* behind **"king of Babylon"** that said **"in thine heart, I will ascend into heaven, I will exalt my throne above the stars of God"** (Isa. 14:4, 13), the same *spirit* behind the **"prince"** **"Who**

opposeth and exalteth himself above all that is called God, or that is worshipped; so that he as God sitteth in the temple of God, shewing himself that he is God" (2 Thess. 2:4). That same *spirit* that God was talking to was also working behind the **"king of Tyrus"** (Ezek. 28:12-17) who was **"in Eden, the garden of God."**

Who do you think was there as the iron nail went through Jesus Christ's hands? **"Hereafter I will not talk much with you: for the prince of this world cometh, and hath nothing in me"** (John 14:30). That ain't *no Caesar*—it's *Lucifer*. He couldn't help himself but be involved with killing God in the flesh; after all, he wants **"to be like the most High"** (Isa. 14:14). Because of this, **"the prince of this world is judged"** (John 16:11). Lucifer sealed his own fate when he killed God's Son—**"God…manifest in the flesh."**

Another favorite, for both Jew and Muslim, are the *genealogical accounts* in Luke and Matthew. In the accounts there are two *different* sets of genealogies we will be discussing: (1) *Luke* traces Jesus Christ's genealogy from Jesus Christ back to Adam through Mary; (2) *Matthew* traces it from Abraham to Jesus Christ through the kingly line. Mark does not give a genealogy.

There are the other Gospels to consider, but they don't pick-bones with em'. Mark, who also goes by John (Acts 12:12), is a servant (Acts 13:5), who's Gospel reflects on Jesus *as a servant*. Since it portrays Jesus on this front, there is no genealogy. Servants don't have special genealogies such as the kingly one found in Matthew or the very human one in Luke who includes one of David's sons who wasn't king—Nathan (Luke 3:31), servants belong to their masters. John's Gospel gives the genealogy of the Creator as existing *before* time and space (John 1:1-3). Matthew's genealogy is a "kingly" one because his account is centered around Jesus Christ as *King of the Jews* hence, the genealogy going back to Abraham and through the kings.

Luke's Gospel takes Mary's line and goes back to Adam because Luke is centered around Jesus Christ as *a man* and it appears that he writes to Gentiles in cases. It becomes most apparent when the Parable of the Pounds (English weight) in Luke 19:11-27 is contrasted with the Parable of the Talents (Jewish weight) in Matthew 25:14-30. The "hard work" of modern scholars rids you of such references as this by placing "mina" instead of **"pound"** in the passage. *"Mina"* is a transliteration of the Greek word μvᾶ. They refuse to translate it, just as they do with **"hell"** by calling it "hades" throughout the N.T. in the NIV, ESV, NKJV, NRSV, NASV, NET, etc. The servant in Matthew 25 is *cast into hell* but the servant in Luke 19 has his *reward* of reigning over a place taken from him, but he himself *is just fine* (Cf. 1 Cor. 3). Further, Matthew uses the term **"kingdom of heaven"** almost exclusively, whereas Luke uses the term **"kingdom of God"** almost exclusively. The kingdom of heaven is a literal earthly kingdom (see Obad. 1:19-21; 2 Chron. 2:12 for example).

What is often said about Luke's list, by Muslims predominantly, is that *"Heli was not the father of Joseph."* One need not go very far to find out who Heli is, **"And Jesus himself began to be about thirty years of age, being (as was supposed) the son of Joseph, which was the son of Heli"** (Luke 3:23). Heli is *the father-in-law to* Jospeh—Mary's father. They will use that same verse above and then they will go to Matthew 1:16 to prove it. The *biological* father of Jospeh is Jacob. They are correct, Heli isn't his father...sort of. They usually stop there and then throw the Book out the window along with common sense. Matthew 1:16 reads, **"And Jacob begat Joseph the husband of Mary, of whom was born Jesus, who is called Christ.."** There you're told who Jospeh's father actually is: Jacob. Since He is Virgin Born, He cannot come from Jacob's seed, the **"seed"** is Mary's (Gen. 3:15) as discussed previously. This is why Matthew 1:16 reads as it does: **"And Jacob begat Joseph the husband of Mary, of whom was born Jesus, who is called Christ."**

We can note right away that this is not going to be an average genealogy since we have already come to a screeching halt in the very beginning. This is similar to the beginning of the genealogy in Matthew, in that *you know something is up* right from the get-go: *Jesus was not the literal son of David,* and *David was not the literal son of Abraham,* **"The book of the generation of Jesus Christ, the son of David, the son of Abraham"** (Matt. 1:1). We can note right away that this is not going to be your typical 23&me or ancestory.com family-tree.

What we have here in Luke 3 is **"Heli,"** being a *father-in-law to Joseph*, as mentioned above. You will see a similar thing in 1 Samuel 22:14, where David is called Saul's *"son-in-law,"* **"Then Ahimelech answered the king, and said, And who is so faithful among all thy servants as David, which is the king's son in law, and goeth at thy bidding, and is honourable in thine house?"** Because of this, David is called his **"son."**

You will see Saul calling David his **"son"** in 1 Samuel 24:16, **"And it came to pass, when David had made an end of speaking these words unto Saul, that Saul said, Is this thy voice, my son David? And Saul lifted up his voice, and wept."** If you haven't figured it out by now, by Jewish law Joseph would be Heli's *son*, since Heli is Mary's *father* and they are *married*, just like today, how your *wife's father would be your father-in-law* and *you would be his son-in-law*. It isn't uncommon for a father-in-law to call his son-in-law, **"son."** This also explains the next issue surrounding **"Nathan."**

Aside from this explainable issue, there is another in Luke's; *oh yes, the Bible is full of rocks to stub your toes and sand-burs to get caught in your socks*. There is **"Nathan"** in Luke 3:31; Jospeh descended from **"Solomon"** according to Matthew 1:6. In Luke's account Heli then descended from… Who in the world is **"Nathan"**? He isn't mentioned very much. He's the **"son of David"** according to 1 Chronicles 14:4, **"Now these are the names of his children which he had in Jerusalem; Shammua, and Shobab, Nathan, and Solomon."** Nathan was the *unknown son* and the neglected son who did nothing of great importance. He was probably an average son, doing what his father the king asked of him, unlike his brother Absalom or Solomon. Nathan found his way out of the shadow cast by his brother Solomon and into the genealogical line of Jesus Christ in Luke instead of his brothers. In the New Testament genealogical accounts Nathan is on-par with Solomon. That is quite miraculous. You're going though life feeling like a nobody, and come to find that your name has been inserted into the genealogical record of God in the flesh—my, my, what a day.

We aren't done yet. There are *two more* names mentioned that people find contention with: **"Rhesa"** in verse 27 and **"Cainan"** in verse 36 of Luke 3. Cainan is a doozy, for the LXX (Vaticanus, Alexandrinus, etc.) *added* the name of Cainan into Genesis 10:24, which normally reads, **"And Arphaxad begat Salah; and Salah begat Eber."** There is no **"Cainan"** in the verse which is where the issue arises in the account of Luke 3:36. Scholars will claim that since the LXX reads as Luke does, "Luke must have had and used an LXX in writing his Gospel." Yes, *or* the writers of the LXX went back and changed verses to better match New Testament writings, and is *highly probable* given the dates of all the available LXX's. It is the *same* scholarship that went into making the New Testament of Vaticanus B and Sinaiticus Aleph (א) (both of which are LXX's). See the chapter, *"Two Bibles"* for more details on those two manuscripts.

What we have here, given how the genealogies begin, is that Cainan is either a son-in-law to Arphaxad or he could have been of a more distant relation; as seen in Matthew 1:8 where Joram begat Uzziah. Joram did not *directly* beget Uzziah; Joram is his *great-great-grandson*. It is a little bit like Christ being called **"the son of David."** The same case may

The Witnessed

be said about **"Rhesa"** who was not included in 1 Chronicles 3:19. It is probable that they were just of distant relations or were not included, which does happen.

Remember how I said that Singer doesn't have the same mentality towards the N.T. as he does to the Old? Well here is a case-in-point: he attacks Matthew 1:8 for skipping over Joash, Ahaziah, and Amaziah, (the kings between Joram and Uzziah) but the Book dictates *it's own terms*. The idea is that the genealogy must be wrong since it doesn't include the three other kings; Joash, Ahaziah, and Amaziah. Well if that is the case then many genealogies in the O.T. *are flat wrong*. For example if you look at 1 Chronicles 3:17-19 and cross reference it with Ezra 3:2 you will see a very similar thing to what you see happening in Matthew. He didn't show you that though. *It skips clear over* **"Pedaiah"** in Ezra. *Why didn't he show you that?* Moreover, Ezra 7:1-5 skips clear over 1 Chronicles 6:8-10 and picks back up again from 1 Chronicles 6:11-14 with *the second* Ahitub and the *second* Amariah. *Why didn't he show you that?*

Does this make it *"wrong"*? No, of course not. Any author can write how he pleases and set rules to go by. It's *similar* to reading any book in that manner. The author has placed rules in which it is to be read. The rules are often discovered *as you read it.* These *"problems"* are from a Rabbinical Jew who is a *"master"* of the Hebrew language (Nicodemus). It's all right there in the Old Testament, *clear as day*.

A similar occurrence is in Matthew 1:11 where it reads, **"And Josias begat Jechonias."** Josias did not *directly* **"beget"** Jechonias, there is a generation missing. The missing king is the father of Jechonias, **"Jehoiakim"** (1 Chron. 3:15-16; 2 Kings 24:6). To complicate the matter even further, Jechonias has several names:

   I. **"Coniah"** as in Jeremiah 22:28
   II. **"Jeconiah"** as in Jeremiah 29:2
   III. **"Jehoiachin"** as in 2 Chronicles 36:9

IV. and if you want to count the different spelling in Matthew 1:11 as one **"Jechonias"**

Why is Coniah in Jeremiah 22:28 missing the *"Je"* from the beginning of his name? He was *cursed* and no one from his lineage *could sit on the throne of David*. God did not want to be associated with him, hence the *removal* of the **"Je,"** as in "Jehovah."

It begs the question: *"well, how is Jesus the messiah if he is from the lineage of Jeconiah?"* This was already talked about above in the chapter, but what it proves is *a Virgin Birth*; for how could Jospeh be the father, having descended from the cursed line of Coniah? This is, of course, denied by most Rabbis.

let's hear how Singer puts it:

> *"There can be little doubt that Matthew, like Luke, did not want the cursed king Yehoyachin* [Jehoiachin] *to appear in Jesus' ancestry* [well there he is in Matt. 1:11], *but confused* [!] *the two names and carelessly* [!] *removed his father Yehoyacim* [Jehoiakim] *instead* [which was then "carelessly" copied since the 2nd Century over and over in the vast majority of manuscripts...sure...]." [27]

Did he really? Sounds convincing, right? He isn't included because they're *two different genealogical accounts*. He got this idea, most likely, from Epiphanius of A.D. 4th Century. Singer, like most of his peers believes, that Matthew *"forged"* the genealogical account in order to come to an *even three sets of fourteen generations*. His thinking, *just as a practical atheist and destructive Christian bible critics*, is: just because a generation is passed doesn't mean that it was not there and does not count. Singer believes that the *"skipped"* generations

---

[27] Rabbi Tovia Singer, *"Let's Get Biblical: Volume 2,"* 2014, page 9

in Matthew's account should be there and were deleted for the sole purpose of coming out to an even 14, three times. As we have noted above, just because someone is not included in a genealogy does not mean that they don't exist.

To highlight the logic you are working with, Singer claims that the persons mentioned in the last set of fourteen (Matthew 1:12-16), must have had an average lifespan around *"fifty years,"* but states that in *actuality* the average life span was around *"thirty years"* during that time period. Therefore, Matthew's account would be false. Obviously he doesn't know that the *death of new born babies were counted towards the average life span* thus, bringing the average down and also that lifespan work is pretty "shotty" at best for anything in the 500 B.C. range.

Further, excluding all of the above information of average lifespan metrics, just because there is *an average does not mean there weren't those who were above that average*. There were, especially when we are dealing with a Book such as we are dealing with here. We are dealing with a *supernatural presence* in a personas life. In 600-100 B.C., if you made it past the first and then the fifth birthday, you were doing *pretty good* to say the least. Let's say the death of babies *were* factored in to Singer's statement.

> **"Contrary to the commonly held belief that in antiquity and as late as 1700 A.D. normal lifespan was about 35 years, there are indications that the ancient Greeks lived longer** [really?] **. In a study of all men of renown, living in the 5th and 4th century in Greece, we identified 83 whose date of birth and death have been recorded with certainty. Their mean +/- SD and median lengths of life were found to be 71.3+/-13.4 and 70 years, respectively."**[28]

---

[28] Menelaos Batrinos, PubMed, *"The Length of Life and Eugeria In Classical Greece,"* 2008

Before the captivity *David* lived past 30 (2 Kings 2:10-11; 2 Sam. 5:4; 1 Kings 1:1) to the age of 70, so did *Solomon* (1 Kings 11:42), and so did many other kings: *Jehoshaphat* was thirty-five when he *started* his reign (1 Kings 22:42), *Amaziah* (2 Chron. 25:1), *Uzziah* (2 Chron. 26:3), and so on. They all lived *long* lives. What about after the captivity—Daniel was in Babylon and lived long enough to see the Persian conquest of Babylon. That's roughly 47 years right there and on top of that, he was there and alive in Jerusalem before the Babylonian Captivity (Dan. 1:3; 2 Kings 20:18). Many Jewish traditions such as the Midrash date Esther at 40-74 years old as well as many other notable figures.

Singer says this is *"completely untenable."* Is it though? Singer has to, again, reject what he considers to be true in order to prove a false point. The Bible says, **"The days of our years are threescore years and ten; and if by reason of strength they be fourscore years, yet is their strength labour and sorrow"** (Psa. 90:10), that is 70-80 years old.

That is *what the Bible says about mans average age of death and it still applies to this day according to average lifespan research.*

The last problem in the genealogies is with Matthew, again. Those "even sets fourteen" generations I mentioned above *don't* come out to 42 but *41*, (and in some cases 43) according to Singer and the atheist community. I bet you didn't know there were so many *"problems"* in this Book. People spend a lot of time trying to find a way to throw the Book out the window and continue living without it. *There is no "contradiction" in the numbers given. They are figured by including both ends in each set*:

• Abraham is one and David is fourteen (Zara is *not counted* since Zara did not **"begat"**—Phares did)

• David is one and Josias is fourteen (Urias is *not counted*, he was the Hittite that David had murdered for his wife, the **"of her"** is referring to **"Bathsheba"** in 2 Samuel 11:3 who gave birth to Solomon)

- Josias is one and Jesus is fourteen (Jechonias is *not counted*, for he is *cursed*)

This works when Jechonias is omitted *manually by the reader*, by other **"study"** done *by the reader*, for Jechonias is cursed.

In case you are wondering where I got that from or if I just "made it work," *Matthew tells you how to count them in Matthew 1:17*. Abraham to David, David to the captivity, captivity to Jesus Christ. *You were told at verse one that this was going to be a unique genealogy.* Even if Matthew did goof, as Singer likes to think, you'd still have to omit one name. In that case, if his fathers name were put in *it would not work*. It must be Jechonias who is omitted on purpose by the reader.

The last subject in the chapter will be dealing with prophecy. This being the *number one reason* for any Jew rejecting Jesus as the Messiah. As a Christian who is well versed in Old Testament prophecy, you may be asking *how* or *why* given there are so many which were fulfilled. Rabbis believe that Jesus did *not* fulfill the prophecies surrounding the Messiah and they are *half correct*.

If He did fulfill all of them, then Israel would be restored and **"comforted in Jerusalem"** (Isa. 66:13) and **"remain"** there (Isa. 66:22). The inhabitants there *do say* **"I am sick"** (Isa. 33:24) and **"the wolf"** *does not* **"dwell with the lamb"** (Isa. 11:6). Neither has this happened: **"The LORD shall go forth as a mighty man, he shall stir up jealousy like a MAN OF WAR: he shall cry, yea ROAR; he shall prevail AGAINST his ENEMIES"** (Isa. 42:13). **"Judgement to the Gentiles"** has not been brought yet (Isa. 42:1). **"Judah"** does not **"dwell safely"** (Jer. 23:6) anymore than they did in Ezra and Nehemiah, which was very little; nor has the LORD made **"a FULL END of ALL the nations whither I have scattered thee."** Sadly that *includes* the United States (Jer. 30:11). Israel has *not* had her enemies cast out either (Zeph. 3:15), they're still there. Israel is *not* **"a name and a praise** among the people of the EARTH" (Zeph. 3:20); Jewish hate crime has increased over the years.[29] Jerusalem is not called **"a city of truth"** (Zech. 8:3).

Are you catching the way the wind blows? The Messiah was *supposed to restore Israel and put them at the head of the nations* (Deut. 28:13). What the Jews reject is that it actually happened in *installments* as opposed to *all at once*. A good example of this is in Isaiah 61:1-2 as discussed in a previous chapter called, *"A Bucketful Of Contradictions."* The Messiah *comes back* to take care of business; he first had to make **"his soul an offering for sin"** (Isa. 53:10).

You had to get the one who **"as a LAMB to the slaughter, and as a SHEEP before her shearers is dumb"** (Isa. 53:7), and who was **"wounded for our transgressions, he was bruised for our iniquities"** (Isa. 53:5), and who **"is despised and rejected of men; a man of sorrows, and acquainted with grief"** (Isa. 53:3) *before* you get the **"roaring LION"** (Prov. 19:12) **"the LION of the tribe of Juda, the Root of David"** (Rev. 5:5) who is a *King* in Jerusalem with actual hands and feet (see Zech. 12:10 and Ezek. 43:7).

"The LORD also shall ROAR out of Zion, and utter his voice from Jerusalem; and the heavens and the earth shall shake: but the LORD will be the hope of his people, and the strength of the children of Israel" (Joel 3:16).

"Behold, the days come, saith the LORD, that I will raise unto David a righteous BRANCH, and a King shall reign and prosper, and shall execute judgment and justice in the earth" (Jer. 23:5). (Hence, why He is called **"the ROOT of David."**)

The **"vengeance"** and **"wrath"** comes later. **"For the day of VENGEANCE is IN MINE HEART, and the year of my redeemed is come"** (Isa. 63:4). The Lord *comes first* as a *Lamb* and then he *comes back* as a *Lion*; I'll take the Lamb.

---

[29] https://www.pbs.org/newshour/politics/antisemitic-incidents-on-rise-across-the-u-s-report-finds

Are you really going to sit here and say that specific prophecies about *one Man*, made roughly 400 to 1700 years *before* He was born, which all come true "to-a-T" is not worth *noting*? Do you know the odds of that? No computer can calculate such a problem because there are just too many variables. The *closest thing* is using "compound probability" and it comes out to 1 in 10 to the 157th power; that is 1e+157; in other words, 1 chance in 10 with 157 zeros after it. Those are your chances of just 48 *specific* prophecies about one Man (and there are more than that). The Quran said what again? To give you some context, the known universe contains roughly 10 to the *80th* power of electrons, and roughly 10 to the 78th power atoms. If you had an inch long line of electrons and counted 250 of them per minute, it would take you 19,000,000 years to count the one inch. That is if you counted 24/7 with no sleep. Simply put, 10 to the 157th power is beyond astronomical.

What if I told you that I am going to be born in Nashville, and have a peculiar set of clothes that are taken from me before I die, then people make bets on my personal items using cards; I get offered a diet Coke on my death bed; the day of my death is Monday, in the evening; what gets me in this mess is a friend who betrays me for some money, $50 to be exact; am falsely accused of charges I didn't do and had no intention on doing; I get spit on by those same accusers; then I get buried in a coffin that I couldn't afford, and I was not going to have any bones broken before my death...

You would think I was absolutely nuts! You'd walk away from me as quickly as you could—but that's just what you have in the Bible concerning Jesus Christ except there are even more details about this one man written by some-odd 40 different authors from all walks of life, from kings (Solomon and David) to fishermen (Peter and John). Written on three different continents, all written between ~1700 B.C. (Job) and ~400 B.C. (Malachi), all of which were written 400 years *before His Birth*. There is *not one* "holy" book on the planet like that. Name it. I dare you. The "holy" Quran you say?—Get real, man! Wake up!

Given that we have spent much of our time on "contradictions" and "discrepancies" that may arise while witnessing and out soul-winning, particularly to Jews and Muslims, there are some conclusions to draw from the chapter now past. Many will say that some of these are "scribal errors" or "glosses" thus "solving" the discrepancy. These are the same people who claim to have "scripture" when they have never seen Scripture a day in their lives.

In a previous chapter we discussed some problems that *atheists* have found within the confines of the black-backed Book and in turn they are the same problems many seminary students face early on in the classroom from professors with little to no actual resolution other than changing the text, such as "going to *the* Greek" or *using* another translation to solve the issue at hand (for examples see *"Demolishing Supposed Bible Contradictions, Volume 1"* by Ham or *"Exegetical Dictionary of the New Testament"* or *"Theological Dictionary of the New Testament"* by Kittel. If the student had a *final authority*, then that is all he needs in order to solve any such conundrum that may arise. In all *practical* purposes, the average professor handles these issues no differently than an atheist or Muslim would.

In the next chapter I'll focus more on the lies told by Christian companies and translation committees, marketing of new versions, and eventually why one line of bibles is *not like another* line of bibles. Point out that one line of people is *not like the other* line of people, and show that one mentality is *not like the other* mentality. The primary source of discussion will be the English Standard Version (ESV): a *"cult"* classic, brought to you by *"conservative evangelical"* Christians, *used* by "conservative evangelical" Christians.

Chapter 5: Oranges & Vitamin C

"*Science falsely so called*" — 1 Timothy 6:20

REMEMBER that *"reeducation"* I was telling you about earlier? Marketing is powerful; it seeps into our subconscious and sometimes it comes across as "informative," as the students of David Ogilvy will hold to. Take T.V. commercials for instance. Sometimes they're goofy, sometimes they're witty, and other times annoying. Although, the best of commercials appear as though they aren't commercials at all. The best salesmen appear to not be salesmen. If the Dale Carnegie generation has learned anything at all, it certainly is that. Some are renown for their musical jingles of great swelling diapasons, and odes giving pleasure to the contemporary fleshy cochlea. Take the McDonald's song; everyone knows it. Random jingles you hear on commercials often stick with you, echoing around like a yodeler's lilts in the Swedish mountaintops, and sometimes with the same veracity and annoyance as the song, "*It's a Small World*" being stuck in your head. Well, marketing in the bible-world is like that too. Since about 1900 they've had advertisement campaigns which cost in the millions, but each version *doesn't seem to last more than 10-50 years in popularity*, if that. Marketing is manipulation no matter how much Ogilvy tries to say that it's not. The entire goal is to get a person to purchase a product by any means necessary. The only products that are not sold by means of manipulation, or rather to say in todays double-speak, *"to inform, persuade, and influence in a positive way"* are those that *promote themselves*, i.e., not spending millions of dollars to *"enlighten and inform"* the public. The best product sells itself.

Here are some marketing lines from the New King James Version:

- The NKJV makes reading the bible much *clearer*.
- It does not dilute the *truth*.
- There is no translation on earth that has the *beauty* of the NKJV.
- I am proud and thankful, at last, to have a *trusted* text that is *easy to read*.

•The translation comes from the Reformation *Textus Receptus* (same as the KJB) but with some *updating of archaic language*.
•The *boldest* and *most extensive* revision in the history of modern Bible publishing.
• The NKJV is the fifth major *revision to the beloved King James Version*.[1]

Notice the *italics*, that's buzz word paradise. Let's see if what they said is *true*. In Romans 1:31 the

---

[1] Marketing slogans can be found on "thomasnelsonbibles.com" and other Thomas Nelson promotional materials. Some webpages have been removed, as they come up "not found" as of 2023. Also see *"Holy Bible: NKJV"* (Nashville, TN, USA: Thomas Nelson Inc, 1990), page vii.

NKJV inserted the NIV reading into it, which the King James has had **"unnatural affections"** written in the text for over 400 years as ἀστόργους. So far, no looking too great. They already lied once. They did this *after telling you that they used the same Greek manuscripts as the King James* (Textus Receptus) but used the NIV reading *instead* when translating that Greek into English. *Sneaky, sneaky.* That's not all, the lies continue on. At Philippians 2:8 the NKJV inserted the RSV reading, which replaces **"humbled"** with *"emptied"* and has been considered an attack on the deity of Christ since the ASV came out in 1901. That's not all... This is the same *"trusted"* and *"clear" "revision"* of the King James that turned the antichrist into The Holy Spirit in 2 Thessalonians 2:7 by capitalizing **"he."** That is blasphemy if I ever saw it, plain as day. When they say, *"fifth revision of the King James"* they are flat out lying to you, again. It is not the *"fifth"* it is the 200th and something-or-another. Scrivener documented these revisions back in 1884;[2] there are actually *14-16* of the KJB (not the same kind of textural revisions done with the NKJV) depending on how you count them. What are you doing trying to say that there were *five*? It isn't a revision in the sense that it is the *same Bible*, it's a revision in the sense that it's a *new* version—just like the NIV, ESV, NASV, NRSV, NLT, NEB, etc.

These "revisions" to the KJ was the alibi given to convince themselves and others to accept the NKJV, but there is just one catch—*they aren't the same kind of revisions*. This is one angle they used as a launchpad for a marketing campaign. In one case, they sent out an ad with photocopies of pages of an original 1611 King James, comparing it to todays KJB. The idea is that because it doesn't match word for word (**"loved"** for loued, **"save"** for ſave, **"shepherd"** for ſhepherd, **"seek"** for seeke, **"feet"** for feete, **"me"** for mee) then it's okay to

---

[2] F. H. A. Scrivener, *"The Authorized Edition of the English Bible: Its Subsequent Reprints and Modern Representatives,"* 1884

change Romans 1:18 and 1 Timothy 6:5 to exactly what they *don't* say.

If it really is *"the boldest and most extensive revision"* in history, then what does that say about the King James? What does that say about *any* of the 300+ other versions available today? It says that the NKJV is *the best* and that all the others *fall short* of its "great and glorious achievements in the realm of scholarship." *It's marketing! They are lying to you!* They (ESV, NLT, NKJV, NIV, et al.) are saying, *"we are the best, so buy our book!"* Boy, there sure are a lot of *"the best"* translations out there. Which one *is* "the best"?—Oh easy, it's the NIV: the paraphrasing in it is much better than The Living Bible. They paraphrased things a little to much for *my taste*...no, I mean the ESV is better, if you are *preferring* something a little more *"literal"*...well, hang-on, actually, it's the NKJV due to its *"superb fundamental scholarship"* and the many *"good, godly men"* who backed the project. It makes the text "*clear so I can understand* it!"... annnnd...CUT!—That's a wrap folks, send in the video for editing, and tell Brando he did stupendous!

The picture shown a few pages back is an RSV advertisement from Life Magazine in 1952. Its marketing strategies are similar to the NKJV, and many others. "There is *finally* a bible *we* can *read*." Meaning you *couldn't* read any of the numerous other versions that came before it? What are you sacrificing for *"clarity"*? Is it really that much more *clear*? I know of people that flunked out of high school who have pulled more *"clarity"* and *"light"* out of a Dollar Tree King James Bible than most of the heads of bible departments have in a lifetime. What's wrong with *that* picture?

Before the RSV, there were some 32 odd versions already around since 1901. The advertisement calls the RSV, *"a new Authorized Version"*—it is *not* and is a blatant *lie* and *theft* at that. They are trying to "convey" and "inform" you that the RSV is just like your KJB, only *better*. The KJB had a kings stamp on it which made it *"Authorized,"* along with people calling it *"The Authorized Bible/Version."* It caught on over time—it's the *only* Bible that bears *that title and still goes by that title and is known by that title*, which is why everyone tried to *take* the kings crown—they want to pretend to be the monarch, when they clearly aren't. The history of kings throughout time is often marked by a dark tapestry of bloodshed, betrayal, and deception. Ambition drives individuals to vie for the throne, employing Machiavellian tactics and subtle manipulations in their pursuit of power.

"By what authority doest thou these things? And who gave thee this authority" (Matt. 21:23)—that is *the* question of the ages. It is *the* question now, at this very moment.

The definition of *"authorize"* means "to give *authority* or official *power* to." The term itself (Authorized Version) does not have much validity as to whether or not it was *officially* endorsed by any government, crown, or king since most of the 1600-1613 paperwork burned in a fire on January of 1619. The only thing king James *did* was have it *dedicated* in his name, and present a set of *guidelines for the companies* of translators to go by. Even those were not solely done by James. There have been many works written on the background of the king James Bible, the making, and the translators themselves so I will not go into depth here on the subject.

This *"Authorization"* is a point of contention for many, such as Luther Weigle, who was a translator for the RSV of 1952. He says,

> *"The term 'Authorized' has been applied to it as though it were the only 'authorized' Bible, or even as though this version has some special divine authorization which it does not share with other translations of the Word of God."* [3]

---

[3] Laurence M. Vance, *"King James-His Bible- and its Translators,"* 2016, page 199

Weigle never thought *any* bible was "some special divine" book. Roman Catholic Philip Schaff of the ASV of 1901 (ironically) says,

> "King James's Version can never recover its former authority, for revolutions never go backward. It is slowly but surly declining, and doomed to a peaceful death and honorable burial."[4]

The reason that was ironic, as said by the head of the 1901 ASV (Schaff), was because *everything in that quote happened to the ASV of 1901*, but the Authorized Version (AV) is *still* going strong in 2023. Also, as the Church falls further and further into apostasy, it's worth noting that the ASV was one of the first versions to open that door. The preceding version was the 1881-85 Revised Version (RV) by Westcott and Hort. The NKJV is the demonic bridge that allows a person to cross from "the kings English" to the text of Westcott and Hort. **"A little leaven leaveneth the whole lump"** (Gal. 5:9).

There is debate by historians surrounding the origin of the title given to the Book, but as the Christian world saw the *power* coming from that Book, the types of men it *produced*, and the greatest *revivals* ever seen by the world at large; the title "Authorized Version" caught on. **"By their fruits ye shall know them."**

Some believe that the KJB was actually translated *by* king James *himself*. That of course is *not* true in the slightest. In fact, many modern translation committees are modeled *after* how the King James Bible was translated. There were 47 scholars broken into six different companies working on the KJ. Some of those scholars could read and write Hebrew and Greek *by the age of 6* (John Bois).

---

[4] Ibid, page 200

Many in certain Christian circles don't even touch the Book because of the perpetuation of the lie mentioned above: they would rather read a an NIV. The reason given is, *"they [NIV, ESV, NASB, &c.] weren't translated by a king so they don't include the manipulative verses that the king put into the Book."* Yes, people actually say that.

This is said completely out of ignorance, and was most likely picked up by *hearing someone else say it and then regurgitated over and over:* "it sounds good...so...I'll believe it." There are many things wrong with the saying, but overall there are no *"manipulative verses"* found in a King James Bible that "slant" in the direction giving any sort of positive view of *any* king, aside from Jesus Christ. That Book shows you that *even* king David was a sinner; he murdered a person to get his wife. It shows you that *man is no good* (Psa. 39:5; Ecc. 7:20; Gen. 6:5, 8:21; Isa. 64:6), *including any king* (1 Kings 11-2 Kings 25) *or any judge* for that matter (Judg. 3-21). *Trigger Warning:* that Book is, for the most part, *against* humanity and our fallen nature. If (hypothetical) king James did attempt to "control the masses," he utterly *failed* due to the large portion of splinter groups and the "rugged individualism" which Bible reading creates.

There is one place you *could* actually try hanging your hat on, but it's in just about *every modern version as well*: *Romans 13*. Because of it being in every other version, you can't say the uneducated slur, *"it was put there by the government."* The chapter deals with the relationship of government and the Christian. **"Let every soul be subject unto the higher powers. For there is no power but of God: the powers that be are ordained of God"** (Rom. 13:1).

The chapter is a hard pill to swallow for many. King James did *not* "slip in the chapter" because he wanted people to follow him, or control them, or have people "bend the knee" to any such government entity: the *committee* translated it. The chapter overall is not disputed, since the vast majority of manuscripts *agree on the chapter,* going back to A.D. 150 in the

Old Latin and 𝔓46 (A.D. 175-225), for example. Many Church Fathers such as Irenaeus (A.D. 130-202), Origen (A.D. 185-254), Chrysostom (A.D. 347-407) and Augustine (A.D. 354-430) quote from Romans chapter 13 as well. This means that it is most apparent that the chapter didn't make its way "secretly" into the KJB.

There is not *one shred of evidence anywhere* that would suggest "king James" had his committee alter the text *so that he, his kingdom, or any king or government official that came after him would find favor, or to manipulate the masses towards a means of "mass mind control."* Show the evidence. There is none. Nietzsche was wrong and pathological.

This is, no doubt, where the ignoramus in the back raises his hand and says, *"didn't king James say that the translators couldn't use the word 'tyrant' when translating?"* That is true, in a way, but there is a reason and it *isn't* because "king James didn't want people to view him as a tyrant." The Geneva Bible (A.D. 1560) used the word "tyrant" *to the point of overkill* (over 400 times). To give you some scope as to how often that is, the word **"spirit"** (upper or lowercase "s") is used 505 times in the *entire* KJB and the word **"truth"** occurs 235 times. The Geneva Bible used the word as an eloquent middle-finger to the queen of France, *Mary Tudor* (1516-1558), who wanted to restore Catholicism. In her spare time she was burning protestants at the stake by the *hundreds* within her short reign. She's now known by the name *Bloody Mary*.

The question arises: *"does that exact word have to be there in order to understand what the text is really saying?"* The word "homosexual" isn't in the King James, but you get the sense when it is referring to it in Romans 1. The word "rape" isn't in there, but you get the idea when it's brought up in the Book; rape is taking a woman—*"by force."*

Lets look at Job 27:13, the Geneva Bible reads: "This is the portion of a wicked man with God, and the heritage of tyrants, which they shall receive of the Almighty." The KJB reads: **"This is the portion of a wicked man with God, and the heritage of oppressors, which they shall receive of the Almighty."** Was anything lost in that? A "tyrant" *is* an "oppressor."

Let's look at another—the first half of Job 3:17: "The wicked have there ceased from their tyranny." What about the KJB? **"There the wicked cease from troubling."** The Hebrew (רֹגֶז) behind the English word, **"troubling"** means just that—"agitation, excitement, trouble, turmoil." *Tyranny causes* trouble, agitation, and turmoil. Every time a word related to the above word "tyrant," does not need to be translated as *"tyrant"* or *"tyranny."* This is one of the many reasons why the King James wanted to get away from the Geneva Bible.

Back to the advertisement of the RSV. It says that the RSV is *"Easier to read," "more accurate," "preserves the timeless beauty of the King James,"* and then the advertisement gives you three quotes from religious *"leaders"* as to *why they "prefer"* the RSV over other translations—a tactic most famously used by Edward Bernays and popularized by Stanley Milgram called "Authority Bias." Reasons include: *"modern language makes the readings more clear,"* and the usual tongue-in-check setup you saw from the ASV and RSV decades earlier, and then the NKJV decades later used the same marketing ploys. The great bold header on the ad reads, *"greatest bible news in 341 years."* Must have been better news than the one before it, right? I'm talking about the ASV which came out in 1901, the RSV in the ad came out in 1952. That's only 51 years between two of *the most* heavily marketed (earlier) new bible versions. Note that the NKJV said the same thing, the NKJV was *"the boldest and most extensive revision in history."* Between the RSV and the NKJV there were over 150 different bible versions printed and sold to Christians in a similar manner. Many were abandoned but a few still stammer around waiting for another *update, so that the text is "more clear" and less "archaic."*

Why does every version that comes out *always compare itself with a King James Bible* in their advertisements? That is slightly odd, don't you think? What do you think? Is it because for 400+ years the living organism that is the Body of Christ had accepted the King James as *Scripture*? No? Maybe it's because the KJB has had the *majority of the market share since just a few years after it arrived on the scene, with no marketing campaigns and the majority of scholars since 1881 against it, the Catholic Church against it, and "non-denominational" local churches against it.* The cards *are* not, and *were* not in the favor of that Book being successful like it was and still is.

The bible market[5] in the US alone is roughly 430 million dollars annually (as of 2020) and with about 6 bibles selling every 10 seconds, it is a market full of $$$ and opportunity. The King James Bible is the best selling book *of all time* and as of 2022 had a majority 31% share of the market. Overall, the Bible has brought in over 5 *billion* dollars. *Could this be why* there is a new update on an average of about *every three to six months since the early 1900's?* The reader *must* have the *"newest, most clear, truest to the text, trusted version"* of the bible, right? Right? Can't miss out on the *most recent* finds and *discoveries* that will *"shed light on the text"* ($$$), getting those **"itching ears"** (2 Tim. 4:3) are we?

> *"We cannot do without an edition of the 'Bible' with critical commentaries from the Tubingen school and books on criticism of biblical texts, which could bring a very useful 'confusion into the minds' of believers."* [6]

---

[5] Danny McLoughlin, https://wordsrated.com/bible-sales-statistics/, February 2, 2022

[6] Authors Note: This isn't from a bible marketing scheme; its from Soviet-Russia. This is marketing at its best/worst and holds true today. These were some Soviet-Russia campaigns in public brainwashing. Their goal was to move away from religion altogether. Source: *"Letter From Gorky to Stalin,"* Library of Congress Soviet Exhibit at University of Illinois Urbana-Champaign.

If the NKJV only uses the Textus Receptus *as they claim*, "just *like* the King James" then what are all those RSV and ASV readings doing in there (Job 3:7, 8, 26, 4:4, 17, 13:18, 24:24; 2 Cor. 2:17; Rom. 1:18, 25; Acts 4:27, 30, 17:22; Matt. 20:20; Heb. 2:16, 3:16, 9:29, &c.)? They *lied* to you about using the Greek text of the Textus Receptus and when they *did* happen to use it, they *refused* to translate it (Acts 9:10; Rom. 11:22 &c., plus some 450 more alterations).

Arthur Farstad of Dallas Theological seminary, Dan Wallace of Dallas Theological seminary, Hindson, James Price a Greek professor at Tennessee Temple, Falwell, Curtis Hutson who took over *"The Sword of the Lord"* publication after John R. Rice, Henderson, Dobson, and Harold Ockenga who was the Evangelical president of Gordon-Conwell Theological Seminary and has a strong neo-orthodox position, were all involved in the NKJV committees and/or spokesmen for the new version.

None of these men were TR advocates, nor did any of them believe that God had preserved his words *anywhere* that you could *read*. Dan Wallace said,

> *"None of the translators, as far as I know, thought that the Textus Receptus was the closest text to the original. When the Majority Text (Hodges-Farstad) appeared, it deviated from the TR in 1,838 places. This leaves translation philosophy* [!] *as the sole criterion on which to judge it* [!]*. And there, I think it comes up short. It is not nearly as elegant as the KJV, but is far more pedestrian. In this respect, I found it to be just a bit more readable than the NASB. If one wants a more accurate translation* [note this well, he does not believe any translation are the Scriptures because they are only 'reliable

translations'], *I would recommend the RSV/ESV/ NRSV (over the NASB and NKJV), and the NET* [!] *over these* [although, none of them are the words of God, he recommends the NET because it's his version, he was the New Testament editor]."[7]

In fact, in Price's book, *"King James Onlyism,"* he does nothing *but side with Westcott, Hort, and Nestles* on many issues, which *is* anti-King James and *anti-TR*. He obviously didn't believe in the translation that he was apart of. He believes, "God has preserved the autographic text in *the whole body of evidence*"[8]—better get your seminary degree and learn from Price to see what God said, otherwise you're out of luck. The ridiculousness of what Price just said is beyond anything comprehensible. What he just said was… nothing at all—*you still have to decide what goes in the text and what doesn't*. What he said was—"I decide what He said."

These are the "men" involved in the translation of the "New-New-New King James Version." All of the participants had to sign a paper before committing to the translation: *"All participants in this project agree to sign the Statement of Faith that 'The Bible (both Old and New Testaments) alone, and the Bible in its entirety (plenary), is the infallible Word of God, and is therefore the inerrant (free from error), inspired (God-breathed) Scripture, in the autographs."*[9] This stated that they *must* believe that the "original autographs" were **"given by inspiration"**—the ones that don't exist (see the chapter titled, *"The Actors"*). Take note of the use of the term "THE

---

[7] http://www.reclaimingthemind.org/blog/2010/09/what-bible-should-i-own-dan-wallace/

[8] Malcolm H. Watts, *"The New King James Version: A Critique,"* Trinitarian Bible Society, 2008, page 6

[9] Arthur L. Farstad, *"The New King James: In the Great Tradition,"* 1993, page 70

Bible". According to their own creed, they don't have *"The Bible"*—it's some lost sheets of paper that no one has seen. I thought **"All scripture IS given by inspiration,"** not WAS given (2 Tim. 3:16).

They also state in the guidelines, *"This edition [NKJV] shall not corrupt nor diminish the original translation [KJB] but shall endeavor to speak in the late twentieth century as simply, clearly, and effectively as possible—all within the format of the original 1611 version—so that a reader of this edition may follow without confusion a reading of the original edition from the pulpit."*[10] Farstad then goes on to explain the use of the Textus Receptus and *not* Westcott and Hort's text (Nestles) even though they *did*. They also used "the" LXX in the Old Testament when they said that they would stick to the same text used by the KJ committee. *Lies!* Westcott and Hort *lied* in the same fashion when they were *revising* the KJB when they said they would *"make as few changes as possible"* to the text of the Reformation (discussed in the following pages). They only changed it to the tune of 36,000 alterations and 5,000+ changes to the New Testament. Their favored manuscript in doing so was Vaticanus B (discussed later).

Change of *"archaic language"* was it? Bring a *"more clear"* text was it?

Denying that **"money is the root of all evil"** was a *"better rendering"* of 1 Timothy 6:10, was it? Denying that **"gain is godliness"** (1 Tim. 6:5) helps the Christian *"understand"* does it? Removing **"study"** (2 Tim. 2:15) from a child of God's Book was *"beauty,"* was it? It allowed the reader to *"follow along from the pulpit"* did it? Removing the warning to the child of God about corruptions of the word of God (2 Cor. 2:17) is *"edifying"* is it? What a load of c-r-a-p!

The NKJV (*fundamentalist*) of 1982 was brought about in reaction to the NIV of 1973 (*liberal*) which was a reaction to the NASV of 1963 (*fundamentalist*) which was a reaction to

---

[10] Ibid

the RSV of 1952 (*liberal*)...on and on the pendulum swings. The reaction of the liberals in 1982 was the Readers Digest bible (*liberal*) which spawned the ESV of 2001 (*fundamentalist*) with its final version in 2016:

> "Beginning in the summer of 2016, the text of the ESV Bible will remain unchanged in all future editions printed and published by Crossway – in much the same way that the King James Version (KJV)"[11]

Well my, my, someone wants to be like big brother. They too compare themselves to the KJ (the standard). Here is Dr. J. I. Packer, "General Editor" of the ESV:

> "And in all these ways I think the ESV is going to go beyond its predecessors and establish itself as, in effect, the new [!] King James for the 21st century."[12]

So, the 2016 edition is the final one (see Appendix D). Here are some lies brought to you by a group of "god-loving," "god-fearing," "evangelicals" in *their own* introduction to the 2016 edition. They tell you that they use the RSV as a base text[13] (*read that again*...a "fundamentalist" translation is using a *"liberal" base text*...read that again).

I. "The ESV stands in the *classic mainstream* of English bible translations over the past half-millennium. The fountainhead of that stream was William Tyndale's New Testament of 1526; marking its course were the King James Version of 1611 (KJV), The English Revised Version

---

[11] See Appendix D

[12] J. I. Packer, *"English Standard Version: Introducing a Bible Translation that Doesn't Improve on the Original."* http://www.gnpcb.org/page/esv_video, 18, February 2003.

[13] *ESV*, 2016, Preface, page 19

of 1885 (RV), the American Standard Version (ASV) of 1901, the Revised Standard Version of 1952 and 1971 (RSV), *In that stream* [you already went off stream a while back], faithfulness to the text and vigorous pursuit of precision were combined with simplicity, beauty, and dignity of expression [oh, the piety]. Our goal has been to carry forward *this legacy* [which legacy] for this generation and generations to come." (*"Preface" of the ESV under "Translation Legacy."*)

They do this to convince you, the "conservative" bible reader, that it's *safe* and *trustworthy*. If the King James is good enough for them, (*which it wasn't*) then the ESV is good enough for *you*. They also lie to your face by conflating the RV with the KJB. *They are not the same and they know it. They are not from the same line of bibles*. This lie is actually sifted out in their own preface on page 22, where *they tell you the base texts in which they used: it's not the same Greek texts used by the King James translators*. So you have two translations using *two completely different base Greek texts*.

The RV of 1885 claimed a similar thing as the ESV and NKJV. They claimed it was only a *"revision" of the King James* when it *wasn't* at all—*it was a reconstruction of a new Greek text (Westcott and Hort)*, the very text that the entire New Testament is built upon. They lied in order to *"revise"* and just update a *"few archaic words"* of the King James, otherwise they would not have been able to do so. They did all of this in *the dark and in secret*.

> *"...the terms of the original resolution of February 10th, 1870, being the removal of plain and clear errors was alone contemplated, whether in the Greek text original adopted by the Translators, or in the Translation made from the same...only necessary changes* [!] *were to be made, Viz to introduce as few alterations*

224   Chapter 5

as possible [!] into the text of the AV consistent with faithfulness" [14]

If a man can *lie* about what he says he will do to the N.T. text and the very nature of the work involved, what then is his work really worth? The English that the King James committee resolved on differed in 190[15] places from the Textus Receptus (Greek text) used. There are 7,957 verses in the New Testament, *total*.

When *"revising"* the King James, Westcott and Hort's *new* Greek text changed the Textus Receptus in *5,788-6,000*[16] *places*. Again, there are only 7,957 verses in the totality of the New Testament. This was no *"revision,"* but a *reconstruction*. The ESV is based on a completely *different Greek text* (Nestles) than that of the KJB. That text, called Nestles Greek text, is in the main the same Greek text as Westcott and Hort's. The committees of the ESV and NKJV lied, just as the Revised Version (W&Hort) lied back in 1881-1885. You were told that they are just *"revisions"* and within the same *"stream"* of bibles when they are without a doubt *not* in that stream and is provable in a court of law. They use a different base text in translation and give more "weight" to readings from manuscripts that were previously *discarded* by the KJ committee—plain and simple, you were lied to.

> *"The Westcott-Hort text conforms verse division to that found in most English translations (though some exceptions occur). Certain verse numbers appear with no text following in the Westcott-Hort edition (often followed by the Nestle-Aland 26-27/UBS 3-4 editions) because the supposed*

---

[14] Dean Burgon, *"The Revision Revised,"* 1883, page 398-401

[15] Frederick H. A. Scrivener, *"The Parallel New Testament Greek and English"*, 1882

[16] op cit. Burgon, page 107

contents of such verses are NOT FOUND IN THE Alexandrian text type, early papyri, or in other manuscripts PREFERRED BY the specific editors."[17]

Notice the word *"preferred"* above, these would be the Alexandrian manuscripts that *omit* the majority of verses which are *omitted in new versions*. Alexandrian texts are known by omissions. The readings found in (or rather *not in*) modern versions were available to the KJB translators and had them on their bookshelf. They just chose not to incorporate them. They had them through *Catholic bibles* at the time. One line of bibles is not like the other like of bibles. The KJB line was cut off with the KJB. The other line of bibles started in modern times with the RV *(See Appendix B, Figure 1)*. The Nestles 28th edition even *tells you in the introduction about its history*. It used Westcott and Hort's text as a base.[18] Bibles produced from Nestles/Westcott and Hort differ in some 6,000+/- places in the N.T. from the King James. Of course, later on, *readings from the Textus Receptus were put back into Nestles 25-26th editions,* in some-odd 500 places, based on the *evidence* of KJ *"later readings"* actually found to be...*early readings*. Who would have guessed? How does a barge turn—very slowly.

II. ."..each word and phrase has *been carefully weighed* against the original Hebrew, Aramaic, and Greek."
Let's see...This also goes for the ASV, RSV, NLT, NET, NIV, AMP, NASV, etc. Check em'!

---

[17] Maurice A. Robinson, *"Introduction to the Greek New Testament: Westcott-Hort text from 1881, Combined With The NA26/27 Variants,"* 1995, Introduction

[18] Nestle-Aland, *"Novum Testamentum Graece,"* 28th Edition, 2016, Introduction

a) Isaiah 14:12 gives Lucifer the name Jesus Christ is given in 2 Peter 1:19. *"Day Star"* does not appear in Hebrew. Some render it as "son of dawn." Why **"Lucifer"**? Since a Christian has the New Testament revelation the idea is that the character brings, or reflects light, as in, it's *artificial* light and he's *not the source* of it, like the moon reflecting the suns light at night (Lucifer, lunar, lunatic). The Hebrew word here is הֵילֵל (heylel) and its root is הָלַל (halal) meaning, "to shine, to boast, to flash forth light, to praise." The root of the word is translated as **"shine"** four times in the AV: in Job 29:3 in reference to a candle casting light on a persons face, in Job 31:26 as a "moon walking in brightness," and Job 41:18 is a passage on Leviathin (the devil), and Isaiah 13:10 in reference to the "moon." Wonderful example of the *English giving light to the Hebrew*. The KJB translates the word as **"praise"** in some cases and **"glory"** in others. The word הֵילֵל (heylel) is only used *one time in the entire Hebrew O.T. and it is in Isaiah 14:12*. "Star" in Hebrew is כּוֹכָב (kokab), and is used over 35 times, therefore it cannot be *"star."* Do you know what sort of sick mind would make that alteration to "Day star"—what twisted, contorted, slithering sense of logic is that? "This Hebrew word does not occur anywhere else, but we are going to translate it as the *same name given to Christ."* Do you know how far removed one has to be in order to do that? **"Not given to filthy LUCre,"** **"red heIFER."** Now, who might be interested in attacking the deity of Jesus Christ and taking his title *any chance he gets?* Can you think of anyone? **"I will be like the most High."**

b) Matthew 5:22 removes **"without a cause"** therefore, turning Christ into *a sinner*. The horrid act of any translator to be able to do this means they don't read the Bible they have in English, let alone try and master Greek or Hebrew. (See Psa. 25:3, 69:4, 109:3, 35:7, 119:161, 78...thats just one book. Also see Lam 3:52; Prov. 3:30;

John 15:25 for the importance of the phrase and why *removing it is senseless*.) Jesus was *angry* in Mark 3:5, even the most Biblically illiterate would tell you about this story. The reading **"without a cause"** can be found in manuscripts D, E, K, L, M, S, V, W, 037, 038, 041, 042, 0233, *f*13, *f*1, 33, Italian, Syriac, and Coptic versions, Gothic bibles of Ulfilas, which puts the reading *before* B or ℵ. There are also over 28 Church Fathers who quote the KJ reading, placing the reading 200 years *older* than ℵ and B. The evidence *against* the reading is ℵ, B, 𝔓64, and cursives 01, 045. Siding with the *"oldest* and *best"* are we? The chart in the back shows (*see Appendix B, figure 2*) the *superiority* of the King James translation and the *foresight* of the KJB in Matthew 5:22. The removal of the phrase is a *direct attack* on the sinless nature of Jesus Christ. Why would anyone consider the *removal* of the phrase? It's one thing if you don't have the phrase as part of *any* evidence, but another thing altogether when it is *removed based on shady evidence and conjecture* amounting to a 1.9% favor of Greek evidence by the critics over 96.2% KJ reading. I can think of someone who would want it removed. Can you?

c) Matthew 5:44 omits **"do good unto them that hate you."** As usual the ESV follows the RSV (its base text that it's supposed to be improving upon). Siding again with ℵ and B (less than 1% of the Greek evidence) over the Majority of manuscripts, *f*13, and several other uncials, minuscules, and Church Fathers. This was no doubt thrown out because editors thought it was an attempt to "harmonize" Luke 6:27-28. If it was a harmonization, then it was a *poor attempt* because the phrase, **"and persecute you"** was not added to Luke's account.

d) Matthew 7:14 changes **"narrow"** to "hard," teaching a perversion of Salvation and staying in line with the Catholic texts of the Dark Ages. It is not *"hard"* to be saved; anyone can do it, but the path is **"narrow"** since

Salvation is through *one man* (John 3:16, 11:25-26, 10:11, 8:12; Matt. 16:25, 11:28, 10:39, 32-33, 28:18, &c.).

e) Genesis 2:7 **"soul"** has been replaced with "creature." It's the *first* verse in the Bible stating *the triune nature of man and God:* man was made in the **"image"** of God thus (Gen. 1:27)—God is a Trinity. In the verse you will find reference to a *body, spirit, and a soul*. In the ESV you will find a *body*, a *spirit*, and another *body* (creature), which ruins the cross reference to 1 Thessalonians 5:23 (this is *also* why Adam Harwood couldn't find *any* of it in his theological works[19]). The Hebrew word used in Genesis 2:7 is נֶפֶשׁ (nepesh). It is translated as **"soul"** *over* 400 times in the AV. It is so well known to be **"soul"** in English, that its New Testament counterpart is ψυχὴ (psyche/psookay) in Greek, meaning **"soul"** the *vast majority* of the time. Why on earth would anyone change that to *"being"* or *"creature"?*—"Creature," really? I can think of someone who would want to attack the *nature of God and also hates man*. Who could it be? Direct attack on the nature and personality of God and man.

f) Entire verses knocked out of the ESV based on Nestles and also Westcott and Hort's Greek text are: Matthew 12:47, 17:21, 18:11, 23:14; Mark 7:16, 9:44, 46, 11:26, 15:28; Luke 17:36, 22:44, 23:17; John 5:4; Acts 8:37, 15:34, 24:7, half of verse 6 and 8, 28:29; Romans 16:24; 1 John 5:7. These verses were also omitted in the RSV but added a vague footnote, "other ancient authorities insert...." All have copious amounts of manuscript evidence (*see the*

---

[19] Adam Harwood, *"Christian Theology: Biblical, Historical, and Systematic,"* 2022, pages 289-296. Author's Note: He decided that because new versions have translated נֶפֶשׁ as "creature" or "being" and the King James and others had translated the word in other verses other ways at times, just like ψυχὴ in the New Testament, that נֶפֶשׁ should not be "soul" but *"being"* in Genesis 2:7. By doing so, he just knocked out half the cross references to the trine God in the Old Testament and *basically* accepted Aristotle's view of man over the Biblical view by denying the image of God as presented in Genesis 2. That's how you *"go to the Hebrew or Greek"* to get rid of the truth. This entire book (800+ pages) could have been answered with a book from 1960 called, *"One Hundred Bible Lessons"* by Alban Douglas that runs under 300 pages.

next chapter) for leaving these in the text, without a footnote or a misleading and vague explanation. *Example*: 1 John 5:7 is often dismissed as only having evidence from the 14th century but it goes back to A.D. 170 in the Old Syriac, Tatian A.D. 180, Old Latin and Tertullian A.D. 200, Cyprian A.D. 255, Priscillian and Athanasius A.D. 350, Council of Carthage A.D. 415, Jerome A.D. 450, Cassiodorus A.D. 480, Fulgentius A.D. 510, Codex Waianbugensis A.D. 750, miniscule 88 (1150) four different Waldensian bibles A.D. 600-1400, miniscule 629 and 61. I wonder when it went missing? Enter, Westcott and Hort, now Nestles and that is the Greek text in which the ESV is based on. Every verse above is either completely omitted in Nestles Greek text or in double brackets. Furthermore, as part of the English *"translation legacy"* which the ESV wishes to stay apart of, Tyndale's, Coverdale's, Matthew's, The Great Bible, Geneva, and Bishop's *all contain* the verse in tact as opposed to the ESV's omission of the verse—it seems the ESV has departed from its English *"legacy."* But don't worry, the ESV wishes to soothe your soul by telling you on page 2,589, *"Just because a particular verse may not affirm a cherished doctrine* [!] *does not mean that the doctrine cannot be found in the NT* [and there it is: you can still find the fundamentals of the faith in the book, so it's okay that we have mutilated the text for your benefit, of course]. *In sum, although scholars may not be certain* [!] *of the NT wording in a number of verses* [!], *for the vast majority of the words in the NT the modern English translations accurately represent what the original authors wrote* [you sly dog], *and therefore these translations can be trusted as reproducing the very words of God."* …But it's not given by inspiration. You didn't mention anything about *that*. Very sly, very sly. They don't know what *"the original authors wrote"* anymore than Hort, Metzger, Ehrman, White, Hudson, Farstad, Wallace, or anyone that taught them knew. That quote above is *the* definition of what a *"reliable translation"* is, i.e. *not* **"given by inspiration."** "In sum," what you have is this: "we aren't sure on some of the passages because we don't have any originals to compare them to, *but* you can still trust *us* that *we* have reproduced the originals: the "very words of God." Only, some of them *may not* in fact, actually *be* the *"very words of God."* Since we have given you the *"very words of God,"* but it isn't the *"original"* very words of God, it's not given by inspiration; it's only *reliable* because some of the *"very words of God"* we have given you, may in fact, *not be...* *"the very words of God."* What in the wide world! That is the level of deception you are dealing with. It's a winding sense of logic that goes nowhere but backwards into the slime-pond it crept out of.

g) Colossians 1:14 omits **"through his blood."** Why? Westcott, Hort, Nestles, Metzger, etc. (See *"a"* Reads as the Douay Rheims.) 60% of the Greek evidence is in favor of the KJ and 40% against.

h) Matthew 6:7 reads "empty phrases" in place of **"vain repetitions."** Many Catholics use a rosary, which is very similar to a mala in Buddhism, to concentrate on *repeated* prayers. According to the ESV, if your prayer isn't "empty" then its okay to be like the heathen, right? The verse is explicitly stating that those **"repetitions"** *are* **"vain."** Catholics will pray the same prayer over and over and those involved with Catholic apologetics know this, which is why they are constantly having to defend their position and use the ESV reading to do so. You will find this same reading from the ESV accepted by any Catholic Bishop, Archbishop, or Pope (see the NRSV Catholic edition).

i) Matthew 6:13 shows an obvious and blatant attempt at "harmonizing" with Luke 11:4 in the ESV. The phrase that was left out is, **"For thine is the kingdom, and the power, and the glory, for ever. Amen."** Editors and critics *insisted* on changing Acts 9:5-6 *because* of "harmonization" in the KJ but then abandon their *"principles"* when coming to Matthew 6:13. The Didache written before Aleph (א) and B, the Apostolic Constitutions written before Aleph and B, Tatian's Diatesseron, church Father quotations, and all four "text-types" of manuscripts contain the King James reading with numerous witnesses. Critics favored 1% of the Greek evidence.

j) Philippians 2:6 denies the deity of Christ. In fact, the ESV states the exact *opposite* of what it's actually saying: **"Who, BEING IN the FORM OF GOD, thought it NOT robbery TO BE EQUAL with GOD."** Jesus Christ was **"in the form of God"** since He is the **"image of God"** (Heb. 1:2-3; Col. 1:13-15). Jesus Christ is **"equal with God"** as He claimed to *be God* (John 8:58; Matt. 25:31-32, 14:33, etc.). Furthermore, He was **"God... manifest in the flesh"** (1 Tim. 3:16). Now, that's what the AV tells you. Let's see *what the ESV says*: ..."who, though he was in the form of God, did not count equality with God a thing to be grasped [!]." This verse is supposed to be about *Jesus Christ* (see the previous verse Phil. 2:5). Jesus Christ also refused to *"grasp"* equality with God in the RV of 1885, the ASV of 1901, and the RSV of 1952. You could also take the verse to say that Jesus Christ thinks *you're* stupid, and you can't *"grasp"* that He was **"God... in the flesh,"** so, He *"emptied"* Himself—Philippians 2:7 reads as the RV, ASV, RSV, and Jesuit Rheims of 1582 does. What a grade-A mess, man.

k) 1 Timothy 3:16 attacks the incarnation of Christ with replacing **"God"** with "He," just like every other depraved "bible" since 1885. There are many people with the name "Jesus" in Spanish speaking countries. That *is* only a man. What saves a person is believing Jesus was **"God...in the flesh."** This is *the verse* about the Incarnation, of course, Muslims love the ESV's version because it does not say **"God was manifest in the flesh."** Reads similar to the Jesuit Dark Age bible. (*See Appendix B, Figure 1.*) There is *no evidence* for the reading *"He."* There is an issue with a "bleeding through Theta letter." The abbreviation for "God" in Greek (Θς) and the word "who" in Greek (Oς) look similar. The idea is that the line in the middle of the Θ bled through in uncial manuscript A to the other side of the page, making it actually an O instead of a Θ. The only issue is that when you actually look at it, the line from the Θ is not where it should be, which is in the middle: it's closer to the top of the Θ, but it still shows something in the middle, it's also very hard to make out today, even with high resolution photos. The other *"theory"* is that a "latter scribe" added the line to "correct it" because it looks different than a usual Theta. It also looks different because *the passage is half faded and gone from the page.* (Anti-Trinitarians use the ESV, NIV, NASV, etc., verse to prove that the Trinity doesn't exist. They will then go about doing the same thing that modern Christian "scholars" do to prove the reading of "He" instead of **"God"**—they lie about the evidence or give you just enough of a flowery exposition that you accept the reading of either "he" or "who" as being alright. For the reading of the KJB, **"God"** are Church fathers back to Ignatius who quotes the KJ reading (around A.D. 50-107/140) and Gregory of Nyssa (A.D. 335-395) who quotes the KJ reading about 20 times, and also Chrysostom (A.D. 347-407), Dionysius of Alexandria (A.D. 190-265) plus 16 more Church Fathers quote the KJ reading which are geographically diverse, uncials (A*), D, K, L, P, Ψ, Slavonic versions, Georgian versions, 300+ cursives/minuscules and lectionaries. The evidence for *"who"* instead of *"he"* would be ℵ, F, G, X, 33, 365, 1175, three lectionaries, Gothic versions, and church Fathers, who of which quoted both "who" *and* "God," such as Cyril of Alexandria (A.D. 375-444). Uncial C cannot be used as a reliable source for the reading due to it being unintelligible from constant chemical use, turning the pages blue-green in color. That is the "scholarship" you are dealing with—relying on manuscripts that you can't actually *read* what the *reading is* in 1 Timothy 3:16 (Uncials C and A which Nestles cites as *reliable* witnesses). *"He"* was decided upon despite *no evidence;* by pure *conjecture.* Furthermore, "mystery" (μυστήριον) is a neuter noun and can't be followed by the masculine pronoun "who" (ὅς).

l) 1 John 4:3 the ESV leaves out a very important component to *testing* a spirit to see if the spirit is of God or not. It omits **"is come in the flesh."** Attack on deity, hindering a spiritual *tool* for the Body of Christ. This is another example of removing **"God...in the flesh"**... *again.* Critics side with 2.5% of Greek manuscripts.

m) John 3:16 omits **"begotten."** I am a **"son"** of God and if you are saved, then you are a **"son"** of God, so were the angles in the O.T. (Gen. 6) called **"the sons of God"**: God has *more than one son.* Israel was his **"son"** (Exod. 4:22). Jesus Christ is his—**"begotten"**—**"Son."** Direct attack on the relationship between God and **"God...in the flesh."** Misunderstanding of the nature of the Born Again believer and their relationship to the Father. Misunderstanding on the relationship of Israel to the Father, etc.

n) Luke 11:2 omits **"which art in heaven....thy will be done, as in heaven, so in earth."** Reads as the Jesuit Douay Rheims. Critics follow 1% over 99% of Greek manuscripts.

o) Luke 2:33 **"Joseph"** is replaced with "father." Christ's "father" was the Almighty, *not* Joseph. Lines up with the dark age Catholic Douay Rheims. Evidence for "father": ℵ and B, D, L, W, 3 cursives and a few more. Evidence for the KJB reading: A, K, N, Θ, Ψ, and the majority of cursives. As with the majority of reading changes so far, they line up with the gnostic view, stemming from the school at Alexandria.

p) Luke 2:14 is a prime example of critics not understanding a prophetic verse or the *main theme of both Testaments*. The verse is centered on the Second Advent of Jesus Christ, *when he brings peace to man*. This is not the *inner* peace of a saved Christian, as it is used in Philippians 4:7. There has not been *world peace* since A.D. 33 despite every pope praying for it since. It's been nothing but *war* and *bloodshed*: two *world* wars, Vietnam, Cambodia, Korea, Genocides in Africa, Jerusalem and the Gaza Strip, Civil War in the U.S. and abroad, the Revolutionary War, The French Revolution, etc. *Postmillennialists* such as Origin, are torn on the passage. Augustine quotes the *postmillennial* ESV and Catholic versions, ℵ and B are against the King James reading but a second editor of the manuscript changes it to the King James reading as has happened many times. The ESV committee chose to throw out 1,700 Greek manuscripts and went with 6 for the reading. If you happen to have a vague footnote that says, *"some mss read..."* or *"other ancient authorities..."* those *"other"* and *"some"* are actually not *"some"* but the vast majority.

q) 2 Timothy 2:15 **"study"** has been removed, as well as **"rightly dividing."** *What* to do with the Bible and *how* to do it are both *removed (see chart in Appendix B, figure 3)*. Sounds like something a "good, godly, Holy Ghost filled Christian" would do, right? All you need to do is *"your best"* in *"handling"* the words. What sort of watered down soup is that?

r) Acts 2:47 **"be saved"** replaced with "being saved" which confirms Catholic doctrine of salvation by works in the Church age (see "d" above).

s) 1 Corinthians 1:18 **"are saved"** is replaced with "being saved" *again*. Salvation is "a process" since no one can really know if they are saved—said every Catholic

Bishop, Cardinal, Pope, Priest, Jehovah Witness, Mormon, Muhammadan, Seventh Day Adventist, Wicca practitioner, Norse Thor worshiper (they all believe that works = *some* form of salvation), etc. The 29th edition of Nestles Greek text has a Catholic on the committee which will be involved in the next round of "New-New" ASV's and RSV's.

t) 1 Corinthians 15:2 **"are saved"** replaced with "are being saved," see above.

u) 2 Corinthians 2:15 same thing.

v) Colossians 2:10 same thing, **"are complete"** is replaced with "have been filled." More Catholic doctrine.

w) Mark 1:2 **"prophets"** replaced with "Isaiah," which is in plain *error*. Verse 2 is from Malachi 3:1 and verse 3 is from Isaiah 40:3 so *it would be* **"prophets"***...plural as the text states*. No amount of intellectual roundabouts are going to get you around and about *that one*. Some people are educated beyond their intelligence. Many have spent pages in trying to justify the reading, "Isaiah." They do it by following Metzger's USB commentary where he tries to argue that the reading is "not original" and sides with the reading "Isaiah" based on a textural criticism principle to *"accept the harder reading"* (see the next chapter). This overlooks another "principle" which they deny in the reading: *"style of the author."* Mark's *style* is to *not name his O.T. quotations*. He quotes Isaiah in 4:12, 11:17, and 12:32. He also makes reference ten other times. The one place he does name him is a reference used when *Jesus is quoting Isaiah and Mark is quoting Jesus* (Mark 7:6). Further, Isaiah 40:3 is quoted in *three* other places which are parallel to Mark 1:2: Matthew 3:3; Luke 3:4; and John 1:23. They identify Isaiah *because there was no additional quote from Malachi in their Gospel accounts*. This is an example of Alexandrian manuscripts *"harmonizing"* Mark with the other three Gospels to make Mark read as *they* do. Ah, the scribes of Alexandria! They also side *against* about 97% of available Greek manuscript evidence and side with ℵ and B instead.

x) I'm running out of letters here. Another spiritual tool that is *taken* from you in the New Testament is found in Mark 9:29 and Matthew 17:21 by your *"friends"* from the ESV committee: **"fasting."**

y) Luke 23:42 removed the word **"Lord"** out of the dying thief's mouth *as he was about to get saved*. The change in the text teaches the heresy called *"Monarchism."* This taught that Jesus ceased to be called **"Lord"** on the cross. Apparently, new bibles are trying to bring it back "in-vogue."

z) The other command to **"search the scriptures"** in the N.T. has been altered in John 5:39. The ESV says, "you search the Scriptures *because* you think that in them you have eternal life"—you *do get eternal life from reading the Scriptures.* The King James reads, **"search the scriptures** (*command, notice the punctuation*)**; FOR IN THEM ye THINK ye have eternal life."** Jesus Christ is-*telling-them-to-***"search the scriptures."** *Why* is He doing that? Because they **"testify"** of Him. You *can* find eternal life in the Scriptures *if—you—search—them*, because they **"testify"** of Jesus Christ, who *leads to Salvation* by believing on the Man and what was said of Him—in—the—Scriptures. **"Being BORN AGAIN, not of corruptible seed, but of incorruptible, BY THE WORD OF GOD, which liveth and abideth for ever"** (1 Pet. 1:23). The ESV gives you a high-dive bellyflop. Everything you and I ever heard about Jesus Christ that was true came from *a Book*.

aa) Acts 1:3 "many proofs" is flatly stated in the ESV whereas the KJB reads, **"infallible proofs"** and is a solid statement that can't be trifled with. It is **"infallible."** Attack on the deity of Christ. The ESV reads just like the Catholic Douay-Rheims bible of 1582.

bb) Deuteronomy 32:8 the term "sons of God" has mysteriously found its way into the ESV, but *why*? The sons of God are angels in the O.T., and you and I in the N.T. (Gen. 6; Job 1:6, 2:1, 38:7; Matt. 22:30; 1 Cor. 6:3). Congratulations! You, in your new body (1 Cor. 15:50-51; Rom. 8:23) will be like Jesus Christ (Phil. 3:21) and become *as angels* who will then judge *the old angels* from Genesis 6 (2 Peter 2:4-5; 1 Cor. 6:3). So *why* then does the ESV make *the line of Seth* the "sons of God"? Tradition perhaps? It isn't Bible, that's for sure. The footnote of the ESV mentions the use of the *LXX* in the passage. The LXX is where people go to get the entire revelation of who the "sons of God" are/were all mixed up. The actual reading is **"according to the number of the children of Israel,"** not *"sons of God"* or *"angels of God."* If you don't believe me, then look at the next verse. Jacob *is* Israel: **"is the lot of his inheritance."** The *only* evidence for that in the ESV: *"The"* Septuagint, as in Vaticanus B and Alexandrinus A.

cc) Acts 7:45 translates Ιησοῦ as "Joshua," but everywhere else it's translated as **"Jesus,"** just not here and Hebrews 4:8. This is taking a God given revelation of the Scriptures from you. It's theft. It's **"Jesus"** that will lead Israel into the promise land and the Book of "Joshua" is *a picture* of that happening going into the Millennium. *Joshua* is another name for Jesus, just as *James* is another name for Jacob.

dd) Hebrews 3:16 is a flat out plain error (representing *"the original authors"* of course), **"not all"** were provoked or did all rebel (see Deut. 1:30, 29:1).

ee) Judges 16:13 words were added which are not found in any Hebrew, but instead from "the" *LXX* again. The seventeen words added are *"and fasten it with a pin. Then I shall become weak and be like any other man."* This is an example of another *lie* from the committee. They said it was from the same line as the Tyndale and the King James but it isn't, as you may have gathered thus far. The reading is found in Vaticanus B in the O.T. which is one of *"The"* Septuagint('s). Not only have they gotten away from the English line of N.T. bibles, they have also gotten away from the Hebrew text of the O.T. on numerous occasions.

ff) Matthew 1:25 omits the word **"firstborn."** This was also done in the 1885 RV and 1901 ASV for the same reason it was omitted in the RSV and NRSV; it teaches the *"Perpetual Virginity of Mary,"* a core Catholic doctrine. The "scholarly" work of "Textual Criticism" has done nothing but restore the Dark Age text of Roman Catholic Church. **"Firstborn"** implies *other children were born*, which they were born, after Jesus (Mark 6:3). **"Firstborn"** appears in D, C, Byzantine family manuscripts, and as early as A.D. 180 in Tatian's Diatesson making the reading *older* than ℵ or B.

gg) Matthew 16:3 **"O ye hypocrites"** has been removed.

hh) Matthew 22:30 has removed **"of God"** which can be found as far back as A.D. 180 (Tatian).

ii) Matthew 25:13 has deleted the most pivotal and important aspect of the verse.

jj) Mark 6:16 has deleted **"from the dead"** *(See chart in Appendix B, figure 4)*.

kk) Mark 13:14 omits **"spoken of by Daniel the prophet"** which gives *authorship to the writer* of the Book of Daniel directly from Jesus Christ Himself. Reads just like the Dark Age Jesuit Douay-Rheims. Again, critics side with 1%.

ll) Luke 4:8 **"Get thee behind me, Satan"** has been omitted, even though it's in the majority of Greek manuscripts. Reads just like the Jesuit Douay-Rheims.

mm) Hebrews 10:34 has no **"heaven"** for the saint. Reads just like the Jesuit Douay-Rheims.

nn) 1 Peter 1:22 you don't have to love the brethren **"through the Spirit"** anymore according to the passage in the ESV.

oo) 2 Peter 2:17 omits **"for ever."** Critics side with ~2%.

pp) 1 Timothy 6:5 reads, "imagining that godliness is a means of gain" in the ESV. That is the *complete opposite* of what the text actually is saying. The verse reads, **"supposing that gain is godliness,"** which means that just because you have a lot of material possessions, big Church building, lots of money in the bank, and high value stocks and bonds that have appreciated over the years, that does *not* mean this is a sign that you are *godly*. Godliness IS A MEANS OF GAIN, as you read *in the next verse*, **"But godliness with contempt is great gain."**

qq) Acts 17:26 sadly culture has made its mark here and for fear that people may think the Bible is *"too harsh,"* **"blood"** was changed to "one man." In case the translators didn't know: racial characteristics or phenotypes are not found *in* the blood, they are found in genes. Men share the same **"blood"** (aside from the obvious blood types such as O+, A+, A-, etc.), they do *not* all share the same *genes*. The *nations* did not come from Adam or *one* man—they came from *Noah's children after the flood. Three* of them: Ham, Shem, and Japheth (Gen. 10:1, 32. Also see Deut. 32:8). *Culture* is not a good way to "interpret" or dictate Scripture; *Scripture* should dictate your culture.

rr) Deuteronomy 23:17 **"sodomite"** was too "harsh" and "offensive" of a word to use, even though the Hebrew word used is קָדֵשׁ denoting a *male* temple prostitute... *which is a...sodomite*. The ESV does the same thing in 1 Kings 14:24, 15:12, 22:46; 2 Kings 23:7. Same Hebrew word used in every single case. "Let's not offend anyone," shall we. "Sodomy" and "Sodomite" have disappeared *entirely* from the ESV, as it appears. Throw it out of the Bible and into the world. The ESV's *"culturally acceptable rendering"* is a favorite with the "Christian-gay theologian" *Brandan Robertson*, who is a Moody seminary *graduate*. He also holds to the neo-orthodox view of Scripture (just as those at Moody, Tennessee Temple,

Fuller, Dallas, etc.), and attests that *"consensual male-male relationships"* are not frowned upon in the Bible. What bible are *you* reading?

ss) Song of Solomon 1:5 **"black"** has been altered to "dark." "We must be politically correct here." The "proper" word *is* **"black,"** as used in Leviticus 13:31. Oops, the ESV said "black" *there*, but oh-no, not when it's in reference *to someones skin; that is just unacceptable*. The **"tents of Kedar"** in Song of Solomon 1:5 were *black*, like *black* goats hair used in the Tabernacle (Exod. 26:7). You will see the same attitude from the ESV in Jeremiah 8:21. Except there, they just *refuse to translate the Hebrew altogether*. How "honest" and "transparent" of them. Footnote? No—Nothing. Furthermore, you will see in 2 Samuel 21:19 that they have taken a most *"literal"* stance on the passage in the "original" Hebrew making David *not* the killer of Goliath. They take this stance because it's not in the Hebrew, which is why **"brother of"** is in *italics* in your King James Bible. *Why didn't the committees take a "literal" stance on the previous verses mentioned?* I think you know the answer by now—*they only do it when it suits them and go so far as to create a problem in the text they are attempting to translate in order to "stay true to the text."* This is an example of the ESV using *"formal correspondence"* (word for word/literal) to get rid of the truth. Proper Biblical exegesis of the text involves comparing other Biblical passages. All one has to do to see the "literal" Hebrew rendering is to look at 1 Samuel 17:49-51 where it is said that David killed Goliath, and then look at 1 Chronicles 20:5. You will notice that **"brother of"** is *not in italics* (meaning it *is* in the Hebrew) indicating Goliath had brothers.

tt) Ephesians 1:6 **"he hath made us accepted in the beloved"** has been changed to a lighter and nicer way of putting it, "he has *blessed* us in the beloved." Now this may seem trivial, until you get to verses 11-12 and then

Oranges & Vitamin C 241

the true colors shine, and they shine! Saying **"accepted"** means that some *aren't* accepted—*who*? Those who did not trust in Christ (verse 12 Cf. ESV verse 12). You are **"accepted"** because you **"first trusted in Christ"** (verse 12). "Blessed" is not even in the passage, εὐλογέω means "bless." This is an example of the ESV using *"dynamic equivalence"* (thought for thought/paraphrase) to get rid of the truth. See Genesis 4:7 in the Bible for why *"blessed"* was a "poor choice."

uu) Micah 5:2 removes part of a prophecy surrounding the *deity* and *incarnation* of Jesus Christ by throwing out the phrase **"from everlasting"**—*meaning eternity, as in, no timeframe, beyond time and space*. In its place you will find —"ancient days." The Hebrew can mean both, "old" *and* "things yet future, something perpetually existing." The verse as it stands in the Authorized Version depicts the Messiah *as God*; **"Blessed be the LORD God of Israel from everlasting, and to everlasting"** (Psa. 41:13). The ESV depicts Him as just another man. There is another place this was done (see below). Micah 5:2 is also misquoted by a bunch of scribes and priests trying to show off for Herod in Matthew 2:6. The quote is a source for a "discrepancy," but it's simply a bunch of priests trying to show off.

vv) Mark 1:2 (again) Removes **"before thee"** (you) at the end of the passage. This is important because in the quoted passage from Malachi 3:1, the **"thee"** at the end of Mark 1:2 *is Jehovah* from Malachi 3:1. You have a messenger preparing the way before *Jehovah*. Jesus Christ *is* Jehovah in the passage. Not in the ESV.

ww) 2 Corinthians 2:17 You don't need to be concerned about the actual *words* being **"corrupt"** anymore; you just don't need to *"peddle"* them.

xx) John 1:49-51 is great example of how "thee, thou, thy, thine" *(singular)* and "ye, you" *(plural)* clear things up in passages, as opposed to just using *"you."* Also see John

3:7 where Jesus is talking to Nicodemus but says **"ye,"** meaning *"all of you* must be born again." In this sense, every new version including the ESV is *"less accurate"* and does not *"portray what the original authors wrote."*

yy) John 9:35 Like the majority thus far, the ESV follows the RSV by replacing **"Son of God"** with *"Son of man."* They took the confession out of the mans mouth as he was getting saved...*again* (see "y" above). This is exactly the kind of "scholarship" you can expect: *it's a violation of their own rules of textual criticism, which states to "choose the writing that best fits the authors style."* "Son of man" is *not* the *"style" of John*. The "style" of John is—**"Son of God."** To see the *"style"* of John, see: John 20:31 (the reason for him writing in the first place), and 1:18, 34, 39, 3:16, 18, 35-36, 5:19, 20, 21, 22, 23, 25, 26, 6:27, etc.

zz) John 4:24 reads **"God is a spirit,"** whereas the ESV reads *"God is spirit."* Why is the reading wrong? Well, the devil is *a spirit* (Eph. 2:2), angels are *spirits* (Heb. 1:14), and demons/devils *are spirits* (Mark 5:7-12), animals have *a spirit*, and *so do men* (Ecc. 3:21). This is a fine example of the English correcting *"the"* Greek, for there is no article in "the" Greek to give the reading with **"a,"** but it is possible to include it, and if it were not included then the reading would be incorrect for God is not the devil and vice versa.

The examples above are meant to be studied and pondered over. There are many more from other versions and even many more from the ESV itself, but those above shall suffice for my purposes here in this work. I would advise looking at any version the reader may have and run the checklist.

In the following chapter you'll hear more from "the scholars" i.e., *"the actors"*; why all this *"Catholic doctrine,"* and *the number one reason behind all revisions*. Later on, I'll discuss that 1-2% of manuscript evidence the critics side with.

In the chapter you just read, you were told that new versions oftentimes spend millions of dollars on ad campaigns and need the support of pastors touting them from the pulpit to local congregations to sell. The ASV of 1901 went bankrupt for this sort of scheme and so did many that followed. No one was interested in a Catholic version of their King James which had sufficed for about 300 years by that time for the Body of Christ. It was 300 years *"out of date"* but the Body was still reading it as if it had just come off the presses—denying the *"modern, more up-to-date"* ASV and RSV, even though almost every conservative "scholar" who graduated from any seminary in the nation promoted such versions. I leave you here, until the next chapter.

Chapter 6: The Archaic Arcade

"He that is of God heareth God's words: ye therefore
hear them not, because ye are not of God"
— John 8:47
"they that seek the LORD understand all things"
— Proverbs 28:5

AFTER examining the differences from the previous chapter you will still hear the standard line—here is Dan Wallace with the standard line: *"...when one examines the variations between the Greek text behind the KJV (the Textus Receptus) and the Greek text behind modern translations, it is discovered that the vast majority of variations are so trivial* [!] *as to not even be translatable (the most common is the moveable nu, which is akin to the difference between 'who' and 'whom'!)"*[1]

He is correct when it comes to the *"vast majority"* but he doesn't tell you anything about the verses shown in the previous chapter 5. This is *the standard line* you will hear from White (pages 39-40, 80-81 of *"King James Only Controversy"*), Metzger, and the gang. Wallace wants you to think that Nestles and the TR are basically *the same text* and that the differences are *not of any significance*. He wants you to be rest assured that the NET, NIV, ESV, etc., are all

---

[1] Daniel Wallace, bible.org, *"Why I Do Not Think the King James Bible is the Best Translation Today,"* June 2nd, 2004

"reliable." Let's hear what he has to say further on the subject:

> *"There are approximately 300,000 textual variants among New Testament manuscripts. The Majority Text differs from the Textus Receptus in almost 2,000 places. So the agreement is better than 99 percent. But the Majority Text differs from the modern critical text in only about 6,500 places. In other words the two texts agree almost 98 percent of the time* [!]. *Not only that, but the vast majority of these differences are so minor* [!] *that they neither show up in translation nor affect exegesis* [!]. *Consequently the majority text and modern critical texts are very much alike,* [!] *in both quality and quantity"*[2]

This is *the standard line* handed out by anyone who is willing, and people just eat it up on the receiving end. This, of course, means that the devil has *no interest in a bible* and that there are *no differences between a Jesuit bible of the Dark Ages and a Reformation King James Bible.* You are supposed to swallow that down like an orange sherbet ice-cream cone on a hot Florida summer day. **"By their fruits ye shall know them"** and liars produce **"after their kind"** so we need not be surprised here. The idea is, as stated before, that because *"the fundamentals"* are still *present* in *some way* within *a* book, then that means that it's *a* "bible," or rather, *"a reliable translation."*

It is true that, out of the "300,000" (it's estimated between 200,000-400,000 variants but no one knows for sure) variants, most of those are items such as spelling differences, which have little to no change in the meaning of the text from manuscript to manuscript—but then along comes a

---

[2] *"The Majority Text and the Original Text: Are They Identical?"* in Bibliotheca Sacra. April-June 1991, pages 157-158

manuscript like ℵ or B which disagree so much amongst themselves that *"there is no objective way of reconstructing an archetype."*[3] Manuscript B is known by a *"great number of its omissions."*[4] The Vatican manuscript B disagrees with 𝔓75 18% of the time. Those are two Alexandrian-type manuscripts. That 18% disagreement marks the *agreement with the Byzantine manuscripts* (KJB) in this case. 𝔓66 is about *half Byzantine* (47%) which means that it *disagrees with the Alexandrian readings* about *half the time,* yet is classified as "Alexandrian." These are the manuscripts used to change your Bible and give you Nestles Greek text; W&H favored manuscript B and Nestles is essentially W&H.

Facts: Westcott & Hort made 5,337 changes[5] from the Textus Receptus—there are only 7,957 verses in the New Testament. That would equal to about a 67% change. Considering *entire verses* were omitted in Nestles and Westcott & Hort's text, this is not too far off by any means. The text was *"strongly radical and revolutionary,"*[6] but somehow the changes are *"so minor"* that they don't matter? According to the changes made between the TR and W&H/Nestles text, you are to believe that none of those changes alter *anything* at all. Well, then—*why change any of it*?

Aside from already giving you over 40 occurrences where the sense *is altered*, in some cases by *one word*, there are many more than that. If you brought the math above to any accountant or banker, they would call you "a sucker" for believing that mess about the critical text (Nestles) and the Majority text agreeing 98% of the time. That is absurd—that would mean they only disagree 2% of the time. Note how he

---

[3] Wilbur Pickering, *"The identity of the New Testament Text,"* 2014, page 125

[4] Ibid, page 134, citing Scrivener

[5] David Otis Fuller, *"Which Bible,"* 1990, page 294, citing Everts, *"The Westcott and Hort Text Under Fire,"* Bibliotheca Sacra, January 1921.

[6] Ibid, page 293

didn't tell you the difference in the TR and the Critical text. He has a built in hatred for the KJB. People can't stand *that Book*. Why didn't he give you that number?

Major changes away from the Textus Receptus Greek New Testament amount to:
- 185+ verses (2.3%) which *do* affect doctrine and teaching.
- 3,323 differences with the TR (Scrivener's) and Nestle-Aland's (26th ed.) and averaging at about 20% *difference*.[7]
- USB 5th edition text marks 96 different readings in Matthew alone where Alexandrian readings were given precedence over Byzantine readings (even if they predated ℵ and B).
- The TR and the Majority text (Hodges & Farstad) differ 1,005 times.
- There were 36,000 changes in the Revised Version of Westcott and Hort made to the King James Bible (both testaments) and 5,337 in the New Testament.
- The ESV got rid of 25,698 w-o-r-d-s from the *entire Bible*.
- The NIV got rid of 64,098 words from the *entire Bible*.

None of these changes are of your concern though, *look the other way*. Let us rip up your Bible in *peace*. This is what they don't want to talk about and why they are always talking about *"the message"*—at the end of the day they don't have a Bible or Scriptures, they have *"a message"* which contains the *"fundamentals."* The mentality here is that, if the fundamentals are found *somewhere* within *the entire book,* then it's okay if some of the verses don't support them that are found *elsewhere within the same book.*

Example:
Virgin Birth validated—Luke 1-2
Virgin Birth denied—Luke 2:33
Ascension of Christ validated—Acts 1

---

[7] Andrew Messmer, *"Critical Text vs. Majority Text"*

Ascension of Christ denied—Luke 24:51[8], John 16:16
Blood Redemption validated—Romans 5-7
Blood Redemption denied—Colossians 1:14
Trinity validated—Matthew 28:19
Trinity denied—1 John 5:7

I'll give a live action example of how this is done while the person *professes to have a final authority* all while *condemning* those who *do have a final authority*, and how people readily *accept* it below:

Example 1:
> Blomberg: *"Some manuscripts* [doesn't tell you which ones] *add 'without cause' after 'anyone who is angry with a brother or sister' in Matthew 5:22 to bring out the probable* [!] *meaning of Jesus's statement.*"*
>
> *Footnote: *"Since elsewhere* [!] *he himself models righteous indignation.*[it's okay to turn Jesus into a sinner here because *"elsewhere,"* He isn't one]."[9]
>
> [For the manuscript evidence of Matthew 5:22, see "b" in chapter 5.]

Example 2:
> Blomberg: *"Contemporary 'King James Only' Christians often use this as a classic example of how 'liberal' modern translations are, because they 'delete' a text that makes a clear reference to the Trinity* [they do *'delete'* the text, how else would you word it?].*
>
> *Footnote: Discussed and refuted* [!] *in James R White's The King James Only Controversy...*
>
> *In fact, plenty of undisputed Trinitarian texts remain untouched* [there it is, there is the justification],

---

[8] For some odd 80 years (1897-1979) Nestles Greek text omitted **"and carried up into heaven."** It returned in the 26th edition along with ~500 other King James readings.

[9] Craig L. Blomberg, *"The Historical Reliability of the New Testament,"* 2016, page 633

The Archaic Arcade 249

and modern translations are not deleting anything [what are they doing then?]; *they are including* [oh, so deleting is now *"including"*] *what they believe* [!] *to was most likely* [!] *original without adding what later centuries scribes added."*[10]

Notice the critical thinking of Blomberg, professor at Denver seminary: *"most likely...," "they believe...," "are not deleting anything...they are including* [you must have a screw loose to believe that one]*," "some manuscripts...," "since elsewhere...," "probable meaning...."* These words do not resemble anyone who has *a final authority*.

What's Blomberg's final authority?—Himself and the opinions of his peers; certainly not the Bible. Yet, he is a member of the "Evangelical Theological Society," who's current president, Timothy George, is an *ordained* Southern Baptists preacher who, in order to get ordained, *must believe that the Bible is the inerrant final authority in all maters of a Christians life,*[11] which he happens to believe is the infallible, inerrant, plenary, verbally inspired *"original autographs"* just as Blomberg does. As the creed of The Evangelical Society goes: they believe that *"the* Bible" is *"inerrant in the autographs."*[12] This means that every time George or Blomberg says, *"scripture"* or *"the Bible,"* he is not referring to *any* tangible thing that you can see, touch, or read—he is referring to the phantom "original autographs." President George is also co-chair to *"Evangelicals and Catholics Together"*[13]—surprise!

---

[10] Ibid, page 630

[11] The actual creed is, *"The Holy Bible...without any mixture of error...the supreme standard by which all human conduct, creeds, and religious opinions should be tried"* as found on their website as "Southern Baptist Convention Creed." Where is this "The Holy Bible" if it's the lost "autographs."

[12] https://www.etsjets.org/about , under "Doctrinal Basis"

[13] https://www.etsjets.org/node/13623

Games, they play games. Another good one is, *"Erasmus had late texts, therefore the Textus Receptus is an inferior text"* when he did have "late manuscripts" but *the contents* of those physical manuscripts go back to the 2nd Century and further. They don't mention that part. More games. Enter Biblical illiteracy. *You would have to be Biblically illiterate to accept that smelly-jam sandwich.*

Ever notice how most "bible teachers" *don't* teach doctrine —see above. You can also see why "serious bible students" of the NIV and ESV often will ...*stop being serious bible students*—they then go *outside* the Bible they *have* to get answers or begin learning Greek from a professor at seminary to *"understand the true meaning of the text"* and who may have been on a translation committee that brought you that mess above; who then casts further doubt on *any* bible or *any* manuscript or *anything tangible at all that you can call "THE Bible"*—except one thing—*his opinions and the opinions of his friends.*

The "agreement" argument is that of a "majority rule" argument given by White, Wallace, and friends i.e., since all the texts *agree most of the time* then it *must* signify truth and correct readings (citing a "98% agreement"). What is most fascinating, is that modern scholarship actually focuses on *minority readings* within a *minority of manuscripts* (ℵ and B) that weren't discovered until about the end of the Dark Ages, but then turns around and *appeals to the validity of those manuscripts via a MAJORITY RULE* (98% agreement). Something is wrong with the front door alarm, man. It appears that something is awry with the "logical coherence of their arguments." Somehow, they can't think straight— they've been messing with those **"words"** too much.

Wallace then charges people who he thinks are *dumber* than him, with *fraud:* "[KJB or TR defense books such as those by Hills, Pickering, Fuller, Scrivener, Burgon, Ruckman] *written by people who have little or no knowledge of*

Greek or Hebrew, and are, further, a great distortion of the facts."[14] Facts? What facts? Your facts—or—*the facts?* White did the same thing when talking about people who believe the words in the Book: he called them *"anti-intellectual, anti-scholarship, and ani-freedom"* by holding the belief that there is *a Book* called Scripture; note this well (page 151, "King James Controversy"). This gives you some insight as to why "scholars" like Wallace, White, Metzger, and friends take the position that they hold: they are scared to be ridiculed for *believing what the Book says about itself,* so instead, they take the same view that allows for their careers to advance, get tenured, or a get published with gleeful appraisals by their idols written on the back covers of their publications by people *who think just like they do.*

Names? Titles? Authors? I have given *facts* thus far. I have misrepresented *no one.* I know of a professor of Greek, another with a Ph.D *in Greek,* and a B.D., B.A., M.A., and Th.M. There is another with an undergrad degree from Yale, a Th.M and a Th.B, a Th.D at Harvard, and doctoral work on "textural criticism." Then there is the dean of a School, professor of Divinity, etc. *Who* might they be talking about? Let's give Wallace a brief break, he went to Dallas Theological Seminary. (Break over)

He also *professes* he has "THE bible,"

> *"First, I want to affirm with all evangelical Christians that the Bible is the Word of God, inerrant, inspired, and our final authority for faith and life."*[15]

Where is it? Where is "THE Bible" you are talking about *"Did the scribes get it right when they copied the*

---

[14] op. cit., Wallace

[15] Ibid

scriptures?"[16] What *"scriptures"* is Wallace talking about? What Bible and what Scriptures?

> *"Is the Bible true? It is now the preliminary question, How do you even know that the Bible you have in your hands accurately represents* [!] *the original documents?"*[17]

Oh—that "Bible" and those "scriptures" that are the *"originals."* Those phantom, lost ghosts that no one has seen that you compare everything to. Why would Wallace bring the *"evangelicals"* into the conversation? He's posturing towards *"evangelicals"* by saying *"THE Bible"* to make them think he actually believes in what the Book says *about the Book*, like they do. Then he turns around and postures to "scholarship" by saying the "scriptures" are the *"originals."*

Maybe, God didn't intend on you having *exactly* what Matthew wrote. If He wanted you to have it that way, then you would have it. Keep in mind Wallace *lied again* about Papyrus 137, claiming it was a First Century manuscript of Mark, and that he was given a *"non-disclosure agreement,"* thus, causing a media frenzy (*see statements made by the Egypt Exploration Society. 4 June 2018* where they deny Wallace's account). It is actually dated A.D. 2nd Century to *possibly* A.D. 3rd Century, and contains Mark 1:7-8, 16-18. The textural character: *"Too small to determine."*[18]

Oftentimes those in leadership roles such as pastors or Christian "celebrities" will try to pass off all of these changes as *nothing to look at* (see above). Some are more worried about your *attendance* than actually giving you an honest answer and an honored text that you can call *Scripture*

---

[16] Daniel Wallace, danielwallace.com, *"Can We Still Believe the Bible,"* March, 2014

[17] Ibid

[18] Philip Wesley Comfort, *"The Text of the Earliest New Testament Greek Manuscripts: Vol. 2 Papyri 75-139 and Uncials,"* 2019, page 201

without bating an eye. They want you to *"feel good about yourself"* and for you to *"keep coming back."* They will do it in the name of having *"one mind in Christ"* just as Roman Catholics used to burn heretics at the stake in the name of Jesus Christ. Instead of a solemn look, modern Christians will do it with a smile.

Let's take a breather for a minute.

As a saved Christian you should have a **"sound mind"** (2 Tim. 1:7), not the kind of mind of White, Wallace, Metzger, Ehrman, Rice, Fuller, etc. When the Bible itself tells you, every time the word **"scripture"** shows up, it is never in reference to an "original autograph"; it's a copy of a copy (*see the Introduction*), and it's never in reference to the neo-orthodox position of *"the Word."* Despite this, many of these individuals speak of having a *"biblical worldview,"* but *not* in their "scholarly pursuits" or engaging in manuscript evidence.

Most of these men (and women) have their part from God and I'm not in *any* way, saying that *any* of them aren't saved. Like many of us, they have given in to the **"old man"** and would rather be **"highly esteemed among men"** by being like their idols rather than Jesus Christ who was **"outside the camp."** They would rather have their name on the inside flap of a bible translation to "get in good" with the community that they admire. Your Bible should be inline with *your Lord* (1 Cor. 2:16) and *you* inline with *your Bible*.

To muddy the waters further, those who do stand for a *"Biblical worldview"* from the Scriptures are oftentimes called "hell-raisers," "church spitters," "causing unwanted division in the Body of Christ," hateful," "problematic," "bringing unwarranted stress to pastors and their congregations," and so on.

I have a simple question for those who misrepresent the position: was *Jeremiah* liked by his own people? How about *Ezekiel*? How about *Isaiah*? *Moses*? *Malachi*? *Micah*? *Habakkuk*? They spoke *words* that caused **"division"** in congregations, but why? *It was because someone had already caused that division and these individuals were trying to bring their people back to what God said.* Even Jesus Christ caused **"division"** amongst the crowds (John 7:43, 9:16) because of what He was *saying*. These groups will quote Scripture to you, just like a Mormon or a Jehovah Witness does, as to *why it's bad to inform people about where the ESV, NIV, RV, ASV, NASV, RSV, NRSV/B, NEB, NET, and so son, came from.* They will quote 1 Timothy 6:20 and say that the things I say are **"profane and vain babblings"** and also 2 Timothy 2:16 to say it promotes **"ungodliness"**—respect for Scripture is now "ungodliness."

These are some truly *pious* and white-washing *Pharisees* who are more worried about *clean hands* and appearing *"spiritual"* to others than the state of *your heart and soul*. The people who *caused* the division in congregations were *the scholars teaching people out of their faith in the Book* back in 1881-present. They're the same group "teaching" today that taught you there is *no final authority except for your own opinions* about what the text *should say*. Is having reverence for the word of God promoting "vain babbling"? What a strange mentality. If they were thrown back in time, these Pharisees are the *same* people that put Jeremiah *in jail*, wanting to hear, **"Peace, peace"** (Jer. 6:14) instead of what Jeremiah had to say, and they are the same group who *murmured* against Moses.

This is how backwards things have become in the world of Christianity. The *very idea* that showing an attack on the deity of Jesus Christ in a new translation is "vain babblings" or that it leads to "ungodliness" is *exactly* the effects of reeducation which happens by *not reading the Book and listening to men*. Paul also said, in the same Epistle to, **"preach the WORD...REPROVE...REBUKE...EXORT...... with all long-suffering and DOCTRINE,"** why?—**"For the time WILL come when they will NOT ENDURE SOUND DOCTRINE."** Notice how that is neatly evaded.

Now, why all this *Catholic doctrine* mentioned in the examples given in the previous chapter? As I mentioned before, the texts used by just about every single new version are *Nestles Greek text* and *United Bible Society's text* (UBS). *Who* happen to be on these committees? Shouldn't it matter who is translating the book you hold in your hands and call *"the bible"?* Have the lines been blurred so much so that *anyone* can translate for a "conservative/orthodox" bible? Shouldn't it matter what doctrines they hold to? Obviously not everyone on a committee is going to agree on every single matter, which is one reason why they are beneficial, but what about fundamental beliefs that a "southern Baptist" church holds, for example—would they want a Mormon on the committee? Why would pastors of "fundamental southern Baptist" churches use and rely on an NIV or an ESV, who's base text *has had Jesuit's and Catholics in the committee?* What happened to John 10—**"the good shepherd"** who gets rid of strangers? There is also another type of shepherd mentioned who *lets the wolves have at it.* Which one are you?

Cardinal Carlo Maria Martini: a *Jesuit* who served as the *Archbishop of Milan.* He was also involved in the UBS's work on biblical translations and was known for his efforts *"to promote interfaith dialogue and cooperation."* He was also on the Nestle 27th and 28th edition committees.

Now let that sink in. Martini is wanting to create a sense of "ecumenicalism" *with what started out as a protestant organization* (the UBS). This is a farce if anyone ever saw one; every Cardinal and Bishop *must* believe what was decided in the Council of Trent (1547). The council was a *reaction* to the uprising Reformation movement which believed and relied on Scripture as their final authority, not the "Holy Mother Church." In that Council they decreed *every protestant who believed in salvation by faith alone to be damned to hell* (Sixth Session, Canon 9, 24, 30). Yet, he is known for his efforts, *"to promote interfaith dialogue and cooperation."* Jesuits are known for their "covert operations" in history.

You're a *heretic* and *cursed* if you don't believe what "Holy Mother Church" believes about the sacraments, purgatory, baptismal regeneration, and salvation *by works*. The decrees have *not* been revoked since their origin. When a bishop or archbishop gets on a stage and gives talks of everyone "getting along," he is a lying hypocrite of the worst kind; he is up there with Benny Hinn and Christopher Burns.[19] Religious fakes are the worst sort.

Ironically, the word Catholic means *"universal"*; they are *the least* "universal" organization in the world, aside from Islam, who only *pretend to be "accepting" and "openminded,"* when in fact, they are the most *bigoted and as close-minded as you can get* when you get down to what they are *supposed to believe*. What would *a Cardinal* be doing on a (self proclaimed) *Protestant* committee, claiming to be *open minded*? It's hard to take a man seriously when his beliefs are one thing, but his actions and statements are all together *another animal*.

Father Joseph Fitzmyer: was a *Jesuit priest* and a "leading Catholic scholar of the New Testament" (is that possible?). He was involved in the UBS's work on the Greek New Testament and contributed to several of the UBS's translation projects, including the New American Bible. **"And call no man your father upon the earth: for one is your Father, which is in heaven"** (Matt. 23:9).

Cardinal Albert Vanhoye: he was a *Jesuit priest* and served as a member of the "Pontifical Biblical Commission." He was involved in the UBS's work on the Greek New Testament and contributed to the 4th edition. This was published in

---

[19] Author's note: Burns defrauded Christians by the millions in scandals. Roys Report, *"Former Georgia Youth Pastor Put on FBI Most Wanted List for Alleged $10 Million Fraud,"* Josh Shepherd, April 29th, 2023

The Archaic Arcade

1993 and its corresponding text was Nestle-Aland 27th edition.

Father Jerome Murphy-O'Connor: was a Dominican priest and a "leading Catholic scholar of the New Testament." He was involved in the UBS's work and contributed to several UBS translation projects, including the New Jerusalem Bible (NJB), and the REB.

Father Roland Murphy: a *Jesuit priest* and a "leading Catholic scholar of the Old Testament" was involved in the UBS's work on the Hebrew Bible (O.T.) and contributed to UBS translation projects, including the New American Bible (NAB) and the NJB.

How is a "Catholic bible scholar" still Catholic? Every time a Catholic digs deeper into the Scriptures, they *leave Catholicism* or nail a thesis to some churches doors: Martin Luther, John Huss, John Wycliffe, John Calvin, Bruno of Segni, Robert Grosseteste, John Florence, John Knox, Menno Simons, Huldrych Zwingli, Philipp Melanchthon, on and on the list goes.

The new edition of Nestles text, 29th edition will have *Professor Dr. Stephen Pisano* from "Pontifical Biblical Institute" of Rome. He was *"Superior of the Jesuits* at the Biblical Institute."

UBS and Nestles is *non-discriminatory* and will work with anyone for a buck. They have no stance on anything, and their concerns are *"purely academic"* ($$$). They are essentially whores when it comes to biblical translation. It would appear they have no standing on anything.

With the advent of home television and now streaming services, the average American Christian is only aware of what he *hears* on the news or *sees* in the movies and the shows he watches. Unfortunately, you will not be seeing a TV series on Netflix about *the Jesuit order* and *why* they were founded, and *what* they still do *to this day*. That won't happen (although, it would make a great series); **"the prince of the power of the air"** (Eph. 2:2) won't allow it. To learn about the Jesuit order one must *read books*, many of which are out of print and others have been taken captive by Jesuits who have changed the text (yes, really), yet some remain such as the works by Edmond Paris and Malachi Martin. Many Jesuits *claim* that these works are, *"fabricated to ascribe a sinister reputation to the Society of Jesus."*[20] (*"THE* Society of Jesus"—how pious can one get?)

The leader of the Jesuit order has been dubbed *"the Black Pope,"* and for good cause: *its sole purpose is to undermine the Protestant Reformation and promote Catholicism*. It was them who set out to undermine the English Reformation bibles such as Tyndale's and Coverdale's *with the Douay Rheims bible of 1582;* it was the Jesuits who planned the *bombing of Parliament* to prevent the King James from being born in 1605; it was them who were behind *the rigged election of Adolf Hitler* in 1933;[21] it was them who *installed "Vatican II"* of 1962; it was them who *were,* and still *are behind the "counter-Reformation" movement* i.e., to get back to the *"true, one, Holy Mother Church"* and *"bring in the kingdom,"* which will rule the world politically and religiously while the pope sits on his golden throne as king over the entire world (yeah, seriously, that is their end game). This *"order"* supplies the propaganda and then carries it out into the world directly from Rome.

After all that, you *"prefer"* to read a bible that had a Jesuit *on the committee* for the underlying Greek text in which *that* bible was translated from? What in the world, man! That is one step away from the edge of madness, my friend. Is it any wonder why the King James Bible is *not "approved"* reading, but an NRSV and the "Good News" bible are? There's also a Catholic edition of the ESV; and *surprise!—There are hardly any changes in it,* other than capitalizing the word "council"

---

[20] John Gerard, *"Monita Secreta, The Catholic Encyclopedia, Vol. XX,"* 1911

[21] Edmund Paris, *"The Secret History of the Jesuits,"* pages 12-17. Also see John Toland, *"Adolf Hitler,"* 1976, pages 114, 307.

The Archaic Arcade

in various places, and then adding in the Apocrypha as part of the text as it's found in Sinaiticus ℵ and Vaticanus B. *My, what a surprise!*—no changes were made other than some *minor* ones, such as capitalization and ridding parenthesis around some passages. Who'd-a-thought?

III. "*Archaic* language has been brought into line with current usage." (ESV preface)

There are words in a King James that are out of use today and if the reader guesses, in most cases they can be figured out *by context*, or in some cases *a marginal note* may be needed to help the reader instead of changing the text.

These words include: **"affect"** in Galatians 4:17, **"ambassage"** in Luke 14:32, **"anon"** in Matthew 13:20, **"botch"** in Deuteronomy 28:27, **"bray"** in Proverbs 27:22, **"cast about"** in Jeremiah 41:14, **"crisping pins"** in Isaiah 3:22, **"cunning"** in Genesis 25:27, **"ensue"** in 1 Peter 3:11, **"fretting"** in Leviticus 13:51, **"glistering"** in Luke 9:29, **"hosen"** in Daniel 3:21, **"layeth at"** in Job 41:26, **"magnifical"** in 1 Chronicles 22:5, **"ouches"** in Exodus 28:11, **"ranging"** in Proverbs 28:15.

For a deeper look into the subject, obtain Laurence Vance's work titled, "*Archaic Words and the Authorized Version, 1996.*" In his work you will find the supposed *bedrock* that translators of the 19th-21st Centuries have relied on to build their foundation for revising the KJB. This combined with "new" discoveries of manuscripts (such as ℵ and B) and "advancements" in Textual Criticism (which we will get into shortly) all create a perfect alibi to put out a new version every 2-6 months. Is the language really changing every 2-6 months?

There is of course, the "*thee's* and *thou's* of the text in the Authorized Version (KJB). A lot of people are frightened by them—in actuality, it makes the text easier to read in many cases (see example *"xx"* in the previous chapter). Many make the mistake of calling the King James *"Elizabethan"* or *"Jacobean"* in referring to the type of English it actually *is*, when in fact, it's neither. Although, it's more Elizabethan than anything else, as protested by many. Here is Edmund Gosse, author of *"A Short History of Modern English Literature, 1898"*:

> *"It must not be overlooked that the English of the version of 1611, which is what was alone in use until the present generation,* [when he says 'was alone' he is referring to the RV of 1885 that came out] *was not truly Jacobean, or even Elizabethan, but an archaic and eclectic arrangement of phrases, the bulk of which had come down to Andrewes and his colleagues from Parker, and so from Crammer, and so from Coverdale and Tyndale, and so from Wycliffe and Purvey, and represented, in fact, a modification of a mediaeval impression of the Vulgate. The Authorized English Bible represents the tongue of no historical period, but is an artificial product, selected with exquisite care, from the sacred felicities of two centuries and a half* [of English]*."*

The Translators *intentionally* wanted to make the work unlike the modern speech of the day to *set it apart from what a person would normally hear;* after all, God's voice is unlike anything you would hear. The *"thee's"* and *"thou's"* do take some adjusting, if the reader has not been exposed, but once the reader has learned the language, it becomes *much easier* to see just who is talking to who, for *"thee, thine, thou"* is speaking to one person and *"ye"* or *"you"* is a group of people. This used to be taught in schools. Other languages still retain this informal and formal version of "you." English has since degraded.

After understanding the **"shew"** is the "show" of it, the King James is actually easier to read than any new translation on the market (the unbelief in this is from reeducation or not actually trying to read the KJB). It reads at a 5th-6th grade level and was *used to teach the English language* for a long time. For many-a-day it was where we *got our definitions* and in like manner, our first mainstream widely distributed dictionary: *"Noah Webster's Dictionary."* In it resides the definitions of words that Noah came to *by context in the King James text.*

The English language has been shaped by this Book and it's just as much apart of our subconscious psyche as a desire to be social (for the English speaking world). The KJB has been used *to teach* English to children in early schools[22] and Christian missionaries helped teach people of other nations how to read English *with* a King James as their English textbook.

Missionaries such as *John Geddie* (1815-1872), *John Paton* (1824-1907), *George Mueller* (1805-1898), *William Carey* (1761-1834), *Adoniram Judson* (1788-1850), and many others established schools and set up educational facilities for the common man. Of course, the Catholics were trying to stamp them out. The only reason the Catholics began to teach people how to read where their missionaries went, was because of their *"competition" with the Protestants.* Even ol' Saint Pat (5th Century) who was *opposed* to the Catholic Church in almost every way, was teaching people how to read and write and had set up numerous monasteries and institutions of learning.

The Catholic Church later turned St. Pat into a "saint" by taking credit for his work, despite his anti-Catholic stance (typical Catholicism). Without the missionaries putting their foot forward, using a Protestant Reformation text, literacy *would not have spread*—nor the beginnings of modern

---

[22] David Crystal, *"Begat: The King James Bible and the English Language,"* 2010

schools.[23] The greatest set of dates during this period is from A.D. 1650-1870,[24] and that launchpad *was the use of a King James Bible that came out in 1611*. They were *not* using the Latin Vulgate or the Jesuit Rheims; *they were using a black backed King James Bible*.

Idioms, or common expressions we use everyday come from this Book, and are still in use today: *"beer"* (Num. 21:16), *"light bread"* (Num. 21:5), *"scape goat"* (Levi. 16:10), *"the parting of the ways"* (Ezek. 21:21), *"eat a roll"* (Ezek. 3:1), *"that winds it up"* (Acts 5:6), *"blood, sweat, and tears"* (Heb. 5:7; Luke 22:44), *"teach him a lesson"* (Judg. 8:16), *"two cents worth"* (Luke 21:2), *"down in the mouth"* (Jonah 1:17), *"eat, drink, and be merry; for tomorrow we die"* (Isa. 22:13; Luke 12:19), *"feller"* (Isa. 14:8), *"right on"* (Prov. 4:25), *"from time to time"* (Ezek. 4:10), *"a good while"* (Gen. 46:29), *"nothing but the truth"* (2 Chron. 18:15), *"at the point of death"* (Mark 5:23), *"stole his heart"* (2 Sam. 15:6), *"apple of his eye"* (Deut. 32:10), *"land of the living"* (Job 28:13), *"handwriting on the wall"* (Dan. 5:5), *"east of Eden"* (Gen. 4:16), *"know for a certainty"* (Josh. 23:13), *"how the mighty have fallen"* (2 Sam. 1:19), *"the root of the matter"* (Job 19:28), *"to every thing there is a season"* (Ecc. 3:1), *"beat their swords into plowshares"* (Isa. 2:4), *"set thine [your] house in order"* (Isa. 38:1), and so on. David Crystal, a linguistics professor at the University of Wales wrote on the subject:

> **"This astonishing book has contributed far more to English in the way of idiomatic or quasi-proverbial expressions than any other literary source."[25]**

---

[23] Joseph Henrich, *"The WEIRDest People In the World,"* 2020, pages 7-16

[24] Ibid, page 8

[25] David Crystal, *"Begat: The King James Bible and the English Language,"* 2010, back cover. Authors Note: In his book Dr. Crystal goes into much detail on individual idioms found in the King James and how many are still relevant today such as appearing in sitcoms and advertising.

The Archaic Arcade

On the other hand, you have modern bible versions which use *just as many if not more "archaic" words* making the reader pick up a phone, use a personal computer, or Google the word at hand. In the case of the *"most easy to read"* version, the NIV has words like:

- *"goblet," "radiance," "not aquatinted," "obsolete," "skink," "supporting ligament," "revelry," "conscripted," "reimburse"* and reads at a 7-8th grade reading level. In order, here are the KJB word selections for those same words: **"cup," "brightness," "unskillful," "old," "snail," "joint," "play," "told," "repay."** Which set of words is more difficult? More words the NIV uses are:

NIV	Verse	KJB
abutted	Ezek. 40:18	over against
alcove	Ezek. 40:13	little chamber
blustering	Job 8:2	strong
colonnade	1 Kings 7:6	porch
dappled	Zeck. 6:6	gristled
goiim	Gen. 14:1	nations
satraps	Ester 3:12	lieutenants
terebinth	Hos. 4:13	elms
vassal	2 Kings 24:1	servant

There are many more examples, I suspect that you are seeing "the handwriting on the wall" (Dan. 5:5). What about the "archaic" words that the KJB uses? Have they been retained in the NIV? Why, yes, they have—**Abode, ancients, aright, asunder, away with, beckon, begotten, bier, bewitched, bowels, calved, celestial, coney, confections, cormorant, deride, distill, dung, effect, estate, forevermore, fowl, girdle, hallowed, haunt, heresies, infamy, laden, lance, lusty, mattock, naught, odious, osprey**, etc.

Same goes with the NRSV, NASV, ESV, NKJV, et al. The words retained or changed for a more *"up to date"* and *"clear"* translation are different in each version, but the pattern is the same. Each new version keeps words that are in the AV that were deemed as *"archaic."* Smell funny yet?

In some instances we see a more difficult or "archaic" word *replacing a simpler word*. For instance, in the NRSV we have *"augury"* replacing the AV's **"enchantments"** in 2 Kings 21:6, *"avarice"* replacing **"covetousness"** in Mark 7:22, *"bereave"* replacing **"rob"** in Leviticus 26:22, and *"bespattered"* replacing **"sprinkled"** in Leviticus 6:27. My personal favorite in the NRSV is the replacing of the AV's "archaic" word for "knob" or "nob" (sort of like a door handle knob) which is in the AV as **"knop"** and is replaced with *"calyx"* in Exodus 25:25. There is of course, *"the slime of the purslane"* found in the RSV, replacing **"the white of an egg"** in Job 6:6. No one uses the word **"wonders,"** as in Joel 2:30 anymore; people now say *"portents."* The word **"wonders"** was obviously *too archaic to use* in the RSV *and* its *"updated version,"* the NRSV.

Have you had any *"slime of the purslane"* lately? Need some salt on that? C'mon, where is your sense of humor? Did you lose it earlier in the chapter? As you can see, the *"updating of the language"* is far from what English people typically speak *today—so, why all the updating?* $$$ (1 Tim. 6:10). Think about it—why don't all the versions compare themselves against each other and look at their failures and successes? Surly, by *now* we would have a modern up-to-date translation that would be "understandable."

The same can be said about newspaper articles or other books the reader may have in his or her library as containing *"archaic"* or difficult words. Anyone that reads books knows that *at some point* they will have to look up a word. For anyone that reads publications such as *New American, The New York Times, Chronicles, Byte, Wired, National Review, Hot Rod, Forbes,* or the local Newspaper, knows that on occasion, a word will slip in there that you may not know. Words like, "jejune" in the *"Weekly Standard,"* Oct. 9th 1995, or "lucunae" from *"Reason"* in November of 2009, what about "doggerel" from *"The Atlantic"* in January of 2010, "blivet" from *"Chronicles"* in April 2010, or maybe "zaftig" from *"The National Geographic Traveler"* in June 2007—"zaftig"—look it up. Anyone who reads *any* amount of literature comes across difficult words at times. *So, why all the updating?* Why not just stick a note in the margin?

Take it from Smythe Palmer talking about the language used in the AV from his work, *"The Oxford and Cambridge Review"* (1844-1917):

> *"A certain aloofness from the familiar and banal language of everyday life is felt to impart solemnity and reverence to the truths which it expresses."*

I bring all this up because this is *the number one* reason for a new translation given to you by *any* translation committee. On average there is a new translation about every 2-6 months. *Why all the updating?* Surly by now all the "archaic" language has been removed? No?

See Jack P. Lewis in, *"The English Bible from KJB to NIV: A History and Evaluation, 1991"* and you be the judge:

> *"While a major portion of the KJB is understandable to any person who reads English* [just as any bible version is], *because of the choice of words and/or the change of the English*

speech since 1611 [here we go...], *some sentences in the King James will not be understood without help of a commentary* [what about prayer?]..."

Ditto the NIV, *and* NET, ASV, NASV, NRSV, NLT, NEB, NJB, RV. Has *anyone* understood *every verse* of an NIV due to its more *"clear"* and *"up-to-date"* language? I have never met *anyone* or read *anyone* that has mastered the Bible in *any* language or *any* version. Have you? I'll answer for you, "No," because *no one has.*

You see, this is the *number one reason for "revision"* today. The reason for a "revision" of the King James back in the late 1800's was because of some new manuscript "discoveries" and a "need for more modern language." The alibi for which the "revisers" used to change the text of the AV was, *"different editions of the King James differed, so why can't we revise it?...the King James updated the Bishops Bible, so what we are doing is the same thing!"*

They are referring to some 20,000 changes between the editions of different King James bibles to come out when they say things like that. Somehow, *you are to believe that these changes, made between the editions of the KJB and even changes between Martin Luther's bible and the KJB are the same changes made between the KJB and the RV, ASV, NASV, NRSV, NIV, NLT, ESV, et al.* The changes made between the KJB editions and modern versions of the bible such as the NIV or ESV are *not the same in character or nature; they are not the same as the changes made between the KJB and the previous editions of the KJB.* The editions of the King James include:

• 1612, 1613, 1616, 1617, 1629, 1630, 1634, 1638, 1640, 1644, 1660, 1675, 1680, 1701, 1762, 1769
• Editors include: Francis Paris 1762 with Cambridge, Benjamin Blayney 1769 with Oxford.

The Archaic Arcade

- These changes mostly consist of *spelling, printers errors, punctuation, changes in gender, and tense on occasion,* and *marginal notes.* The translators would often point out *printers errors* in the 1611 edition, but it's still the same Bible, which is why people refer to the King James as "the 1611." The vast majority of changes being that of *Germanic spelling* to what is now in your KJB and the *standardization* of spelling that came from the first accepted dictionaries.

More *severe* changes consist of:
- Genesis 6:5 "God" to **"GOD"**
- Jeremiah 52:31 "Jehoiakin" to **"Jehoiachin"**
- 1 John 5:12 "hath not the Son" to **"hath not the Son of God"**
- Ruth 3:15 "he" to **"she"** (*both went into the city see Ruth 4:1-2*)
- To see many more, check out James D. Price's work called *"King James Onlyism: A New Sect, 2006"* and the documented evidence from Scrivener called, *"The Authorized Edition of the English Bible: Its Subsequent Reprints and Modern Representatives"* which came out in 1884, a *good* hundred years before the work of Price.
- *None of the thousands of changes are anything like taking the words out of a man's mouth who is about to get saved (Acts 8:37).* You have already been shown another case from example *"y"* in chapter 5 of the same thing.
- It is also worth noting that the King James I have sitting on my desk at this moment, is *the Book* I talk about, not the 1611 edition (although, it still holds true, I have it on my shelf).
- Because the editions of the KJ differ in such a manner, you are to accept the 30,000-36,000 changes made in the ESV, NIV, NKJV, NET, NEB, ASV, NASV, RSV, NRSV, et al., such as: Mark 1:2 from **"the prophets"** to "Isaiah", attacks on the Virgin Birth in Luke 2:33, the Ascension in Luke 24:51-52, the Resurrection in Acts 1:3, warnings on Bible

corruption in 2 Corinthians 2:17, denial of the restoration of Israel (AMP) in 1 Thessalonians 2:16, the removal of the Blood of Christ from Colossians 1:14 and Acts 20:28, and the deity of Jesus Christ in 1 Timothy 3:16.

Any reading from Coverdale's Bible, Matthew's, Tyndale, Geneva, Bishop's, or the 1611 King James *would all be a better bible to use than the* ESV, NIV, NKJV, NEB, NLT, TLB, ASV, NASV, NRSV, et al. *For the changes in the former bibles are not the same kind of changes in the later versions.* That is critical to note. I *would* be in favor of a new version of the honored text, but sadly, I do not think it's possible in our present day. The time in which the AV was translated and published is *not the same* time period as today. Modernity has laid its burdensome load and has *influenced* us; we are too far removed from the *actual* persecutions of the Catholic Church (A.D. 500-1500) and Roman Empire (A.D. 33-313), for example.

For instance, there are large groups of "Christians" today that believe *hell is metaphorical* and it's just a *"separation from God."* In main-line Protestantism 88% believe in a heaven but only 69% believe in hell.[26] Imagine taking that poll in A.D. 1600—even *unsaved people* believed in hell. Tim Mackie, who is a *professor of biblical studies* at Western Seminary and co-founder of *"The Bible Project,"* doesn't believe in a literal hell, that God didn't make hell,[27] and also believes that it's okay to be homosexual in view of the Bible. *If he didn't he wouldn't*

---

[26] Pew Research Center, *"Views on the Afterlife,"* 2021
While most U.S. adults (non-Christian and Christian) also believe in hell, this belief is less widespread than belief in heaven (73%). Roughly six-in-ten American adults (62%) say they believe in hell…While roughly nine-in-ten (Christian) Protestants in the evangelical and historically Black traditions believe in hell, only about seven-in-ten *mainline* Protestants (69%) and 74% of *Catholics* share this belief. Jesus Christ spoke of hell more than any other.

[27] Tim Mackie, YouTube, *"Compelled: Speaking & Living the Gospel,"* time in the video: 31-42 min. Authors Note: God created hell, see Matthew 25:41. God also cares about your sexual orientation, see 1 Cor. 6:9-11; Levi. 20:13; Romans 1:26-28; 1 Tim. 1:10; Jude 1:7; Rom. 1:27-32; Gen. 19. This *"professor of biblical studies"* would have to throw out all of these verses and more, to come to his conclusion—some *"professor of biblical studies."*

have the viewers that he has, **"They are of the world: therefore speak they of the world, and the world heareth them"** (1 John 4:4). These are similar stances that Billy Graham took after befriending the Pope. **"If any man will come after me, let him DENY himself, and take up his cross daily, and follow me"** (Luke 9:23).

What do you know about being put in a bag with venomous snakes and thrown in a river? What do you know about having hot chains put around your neck? What do you know about being burned alive?[28] What do you know about being torn apart by lions in front of an applause? What do you know about hot iron taken to singe your skin until you die, or filleting flesh until you bleed out? We have become too convoluted by culture, commercials, TV, Netflix, movies, radio, podcasts, work, daily interactions, YouTube, music, extended amounts of time on a couch, and the news media.

This would certainly influence the text *(as it has)*, especially translations like the NIV, which is more of a *"though for thought"* translation and uses *"gender-neutral language"*—who's thoughts are you reading really? When do the translators become separate from their translation? I am afraid that it just isn't possible anymore, unless a new time comes. I do not see that happening due to *prophetic material in 1 and 2 Timothy*, being that, *apostasy* and *corruption* starts *within* the Body of Christ before the tribulation sets in. Every age in the Bible ends in apostasy—it starts with **"yea, hath God said"** (Gen. 3:1).

In the next chapter I will discuss the two different lines of bibles and a brief history of the separation between them. With one group of bibles comes a group of people, and with the other, another set of people. Each group is distinct and

---

[28] See *"Foxe's Book of Martyrs"* published by Hendrickson and *"The Bloody Theatre"* by Braght

yet they share similar qualities. Those who believe the Book are *not the same* as *those who critique it*. It has been this way all throughout the history of the Church. There have always been those who step in with *a second authority*. A man cannot have *two* authorities, which has been the status-quo for the Catholic Church throughout their history as an organization. When the Book doesn't agree with them, the church steps in and decides on the matter. This creates an opportunity for *more* authorities to creep in (a third, fourth, fifth), leaving the Book behind on a table while men decide on traditions and the fate of their congregations. At least Catholics are honest about their sources for authority. *Are you?*

Chapter 7: Two Bibles

"Now the Spirit speaketh expressly, that in the latter times some shall depart from the faith, giving heed to seducing spirits, and doctrines of devils; Speaking lies in hypocrisy" — 1 Timothy 4:1-2
"Are ye come to enquire of me? As I live, saith the Lord GOD, I will not be enquired of by you"
— Ezekiel 20:3

IV. On page 21 of the ESV, the Preface states: ."..It seemed best *not* to capitalize deity pronouns...there is nothing in Greek or Hebrew manuscripts that corresponds to such capitalization..."

WELL, why did you capitalize John 1:1 and 1 John 1:1? The capital "W" is a *revelation in the English not found in the Greek,* any Greek. They can't even follow their own rules. Nestles text has Mark 16:9-20 in double brackets indicating that it should't be in the text and John 7:53-8:11 as well, but they are too scared to go by the text *they recommend* and *use* for translation because if they didn't include the above passages, well, *no one would buy the book!* Do you realize that if the heads of these committees had their way, much of the Bible you know and love would be a mangled production of some ghost that no one has seen: the mythical, fantastical legend of the deeps—*"the originals."* The body of Christ has agreed for over *400 years* that the contents of the Authorized Version have been accepted as *Scripture*.

Essentially the ESV is just another book like the NIV, ASV, NASV, NRSV, NLT, CSB and 300+ other per-*versions* since 1885, brought to you by the *same types* that brought you the RV from Westcott and Hort's Greek text. Same types—they don't change; just the players do. **"O ye hypocrites"** (Matt. 16:3)

The motives, types of scholars, and time period were all different in the making of the King James. Most of the translators had a relative or knew of someone that had been burned at the stake for telling *the truth* about what the Catholic Mass really was: *a Baalite production that is anti-Christian and ani-Biblical*. As seen in the introduction of the King James Bible, the mens attitudes were different. The ESV, NIV, "reliable translation" crew wants to bring you back under the bondage of a Dark Age Jesuit text. Many were murdered for not *literally eating Christ* as a "communion wafer." They chose not to *cannibalize* Christ every Sunday at eleven, and for it, they were tortured and then murdered. All done in the name of Jesus Christ. (Side note: Where does Christ go after you eat him? There are only a few possibilities there.)

The Jesuit Rheims bible was accessible to the translators of the day which *contained many readings found in Vaticanus B and Sinaiticus* א. They chose *not to use* those readings where modern translators have and do *choose them*. Modern translators are so removed from history and the possible influence of corruption that they alter 2 Corinthians 2:17. Think about that for a little while. They never had a grandmother murdered by fire at the stake with metal chains around their hands and feet, scorching their skin as they slowly burned to death, or rats gnawing on sawed off limbs until they bled out. The hardest thing a modern scholar has to do is decide where he wants breakfast and where the iota subscript goes.

The modern scholar, *if* from Islamic decent, may have had it rough. For that culture is one where a person may be murdered for apostatizing from Islam or for just being a Christian in an Islamic country. Other than this group, and some other groups outside of the U.S., the *typical* Christian scholar has no room and little to no understanding of the capabilities that false doctrine and the insidiousness within it; the creeping vine, the stranglehold of what dark forces can do to a mind *who is oblivious to it and has no final authority* —a mind that views the Bible *"objectively and neutrally"* in their translating work (Matt. 12:30).

Church history did not stop at A.D. 1600 as some of the most *"renown"* Christian historians tend to stop writing. Christian history is *still* being written. There has been a line drawn in the sand which hardly anyone sees anymore. The King James translators *saw it*, groups of people from A.D. 33-1611 *saw it. Why not now? Why not you? Which side are you on?* —Oh, wait, there are no sides, it's all just *a—big—grey— mess*. We should all, *"work together and progress past our differences, join hands, and forget about the past."* Men never learn from history, let alone from the greatest history Book ever written: *the Bible.*

Here are the two distinct lines of bibles...but first *how does one determine such information and by what standard?* There are various kinds of evidence available, keenly dubbed *"manuscript evidence,"* that a person can use for determining such things. The categories are as follows:

> 1. *Uncial manuscripts:* Codices and scrolls written in block capital Greek letters. Usually signified by capital English letters or capital Greek letters such as A, B, C, D, T, Π, Φ, etc. When referring to Sinaiticus, it's denoted by the Hebrew letter Aleph (א) because it's *"special."* Uncial manuscripts are typically written on vellum. Vellum is a

strong and pricey form of paper made from animal skins. Total available = 299

2. *Cursive Manuscripts:* a.k.a. minuscules, written in lower case Greek letters. Cursives are denoted with numbers such as 1, 2, 13, 33, 69, 346, and so on. At times a zero will be placed in front of the number. They are sometimes grouped into families labeled *f*13 or *f*1 which consist of multiple cursive manuscripts. Since these are written in lowercase, they get the name *"minuscules"* and since the Uncials are written in big capital letters they are also called *"majuscules."* There are many names for the same thing, people like to complicate things. The favorite cursives used in Nestles are 33, 81, 579, 614, 700, etc. They agree with Alexandrian manuscripts most of the time. Total available = 2,911

3. *Lectionaries:* service books used in church worship which contain readings, writings, and verses of scripture. Usually denoted with a symbol, a lowercase italic-like "*l*" and then a number such as *l*2211. Total available = 2,484+

4. *Church Father quotations:* a.k.a "patristic evidence," references to verses or phrases of Scripture from the writings of the Church Fathers (e.g. Irenaeus, Clement of Alexandria, Origen, Polycarp, Tertullian, Hippolytus, Eusebius, etc.). Total available = roughly 36,000+

5. *Papyrus fragments:* a.k.a. *Papyri*, small pieces of paper, (scraps of paper), or what's left of a manuscript, sometimes several pages long which contain writings of Scripture such as Paul's epistles, the Gospel accounts etc. These are typically denoted by "P," more specifically a "Fraktur P" which looks like 𝔓, then add a number to it such as 𝔓60 or 𝔓10, 𝔓73 and so on. It looks

mysterious, but it isn't; the P stands for "papyrus" and the number is just the order of when it was registered so 𝔓1 doesn't mean that it's older than 𝔓52. The word *"Papyrus"* is where we get our word for paper from. It's essentially cheap newsprint and highly susceptible to fluctuations in weather and how much the print has been handled. The paper in most bibles today is not far off. One famous Papyri is 𝔓52 which contains parts John 18:31-33 and 18:37-38. It is *3.5 by 2.5 inches in size* and is dated A.D. 100-150, putting it very close to the initial writing of the Gospel of John (A.D. 90-96). Total available = 141

6. *Early Translations*: a.k.a. "versions," translations from the Greek N.T. into Old Latin, Old Syriac, Coptic, Herculean Syriac, Armenian, Georgian, Ethiopic, Latin Versions such as Palantinus, Latin Vulgate, Codex Bezae Cantabrigiensis (D) which is an Uncial with Latin as well, Sinaitic Syriac, Peshitta, Gothic by Ulfilas, etc. A.D. Second Century forward. Total = roughly 20,000+

7. *Sermons* of early preachers sometimes containing verses or mentions of scripture in Greek, Latin, Syriac, Coptic, and Armenian etc. These are numerous, some such examples are from Origen, John Chrysostom, Augustine, and Cyril of Alexandria, among others. These can also be found in their writings.

There is another category which involves the work of scholars and their critiques and conjectures. We can safely say that this category is the least helpful but it can be used from time to time.

Given all this evidence, manuscripts are then put into what are called *"Text-Types"* after they have been analyzed. Major text types are:

1.) *Alexandrian:* which has "outstanding" examples such as Vaticanus B, Sinaiticus ℵ, A, 𝔓45, 𝔓46, 𝔓66, 𝔓75, etc. What makes them "Alexandrian" is a theme of *omissions* and a "polished," *non-Kione* type of text. "Kione" is Greek, meaning *"common,"* as in "common, everyday language" used by *the average person.* The Alexandrian manuscripts "show the hand of professional scribes."

2.) *Western:* and examples include Codex Bezae Cantabrigiensis (D), Latin Vulgate, Codex Washingtonianus (W), etc. This group is often noted by its *additions* to the text.

3.) *Byzantine/Syrian:* includes the vast majority of cursives, some Papyri, some Codices, etc. What makes a text Byzantine is its use of Kione Greek (more common everyday style of Greek), minuscule/cursive writing style, "harmonization," and "longer readings." This group is seen as a *"later revision"* of the first two groups : the Alexandrian that subtracts and the Western that adds (more on this later).

4.) *Caesarean:* This group was initially proposed by Tischendorf and the brain-child of Krisopp Lake and Von Soden when they went through many of the cursive manuscripts. It is *disputed* as to whether this group should just be a part of the Byzantine/Syrian group or not. As you will see, it was most likely *placed to further separate the notability of the Byzantine witnesses from the Textus Receptus.* Now, many do not recognize the group but is still represented as two families in Nestles critical text; $f1$ and $f13$ which are groups of *Byzantine* cursives.

A note to heed on text types is that each group is not solely *one kind; they all contain readings of each other.* Instead of looking at one type as a solid color crayon, instead, each one is a multi-colored crayon; as if you were to take a blue, green, and red crayon and melt them together into a "crazy crayon." As mentioned in the chapter *"The Actors,"* there are readings *uniquely Byzantine in early papyri and Codices including Sinaiticus and Vaticanus.*

Now, after these manuscripts have been compared and put into their corresponding "text-types," what are the methods for figuring out what the author said in the *"original autographs"* and what the *"the original intent of the author"* was so we can produce a *"bible"*? This *"science,"* and I use that term loosely, is called *"Textual Criticism."* These theories are used to *"restore the original text"* of what the authors wrote. No one has the originals, so theories were *invented* to try and get back to what the originals *may* (!) *have* said. Most of it is purely *conjecture* and mostly *guesswork*. The *"science"* of the *"craft"* really took root in the 19th Century by proponents such as:

Brian Walton (1600-1686), *Father Richard Simon* (1638-1712) who is the *Roman Catholic* "father of textural criticism" and who decided that Moses did *not* author the Torah thus, turning Jesus into a liar (Matt. 19:7; John 5:46), *Richard Bentley* (1662-1742), *H. J. A. Bengel* (1687-1752), *J. S. Selmer* (1725-1791) often called "the father of German rationalism" and taught that anyone who believed in heaven, hell, or the Virgin Birth was *"prejudiced by dogma"* and taught *"accommodation theory," J. M. A. Scholtz* (1794-1852), *Karl Lachmann* (1793-1851), *Griesbach* (1809) who is most noted for the genealogical method (text-types and families), Tischendorf (1815-1879), *Hort* (1881), *Nestle* (1898), *C. H. Roberts* (1949), *Metzger* (1994), Ehrman (2005), and so on .

The "theories" are:

- "When two or more manuscript readings exist for a particular passage, *the more difficult or complex reading is more likely to be the original"*
- "When two or more readings exist for a particular passage, *the shorter reading is more likely to be the original"*
- "When two or more readings exist for a particular passage, *the simpler or smoother reading is more likely to be the original"*

- "The text of the manuscript or manuscripts that are *judged to be the most reliable and closest to the original should be given the most weight in determining the original text*"
- "The text that *fits best with the context and historical situation of the document is more likely to be the original*"

Some others that may be added are:
- "*Verses containing statements on Doctrine are controversial and suspect*"
- "*The reading is to be preferred that best conforms to the usual style of the author and to that author's material in other passages*"
- "*Vaticanus B should be given precedence*" (Hort)

Do you notice anything *strange* about those dates above and how many people show up *after* the Authorized Version came off the presses? *They all just crop up, just after the Book comes out.* Where were they before? There were many Catholic monasteries and places of learning. Why so many *after* the Book comes out? Also, contemporaries with these men include: *Spinoza, Darwin, Voltaire, Locke, Burke, Descartes, Hume, Marx, Rousseau, Hobbes, Jung, Freud, Nietzsche, Kant, Mill, Schopenhauer, etc.* The men listed above the textual criticism rules were going to *"restore the original text...with science"* (1 Tim. 6:20) not with The Holy Ghost. Could you imagine Luther saying that?

Quotes from "renown" scholars on textual criticism include:

1. *All* manuscripts were "actually reeking" and full of "dogmatic falsifications."[1] *Rendel Harris (1926)*

---

[1] Edward F. Hills, *"The King James Version Defended,"* 2006, page 87, citing *"Bulletin of the Bezan Club, III"*: November, 1926, page 5

2. "We shall *never know the original form* of the New Testament text."² *Krisopp Lake (1941)*

3. "The whole thing is *limited to probability judgments* [guesswork]; the original text of the New Testament, according to its nature, must be and *remain a hypothesis* [guessing]."³ *H. Greeven (1960)*

4. "The optimism of the early editors has *given way to that skepticism* which inclines towards regarding 'the original text' as *an unattainable mirage* [i.e. not possible]."⁴ *G. Zuntz (1960)*

5. "The primal goal of New Testament textural study remains *the recovery of what the New Testament writers wrote* [original autographs]. We have already suggested that to achieve this goal *is well nigh impossible*."⁵ *R. M. Grant (1963)*

6. "Great *progress* has been achieved, in recovering an early form of the text, but it *may be doubted* that there is *evidence* of the *original text to be recovered.*"⁶ *K. W. Clark (1966)*

7. "…it may be *doubted* that there is *evidence* of one *original text to be recovered.*"⁷ *Kurt Aland (1970)*

8. "Textual criticism is the technical and highly specialized discipline that works to *reconstruct the original text* and to figure out how, when, where, and why it got changed."⁸ *(2022)* "Scribes occasionally

---

² Ibid, page 86

³ Ibid, page 87, citing *"Der Urtext des Neunen Testaments,"* Kiel: Hirt, 1960, page 20

⁴ Ibid, citing *"The Text of the Epistles,"* by G. Zuntz, 1953, page 9

⁵ Ibid, page 87-88, citing *"A Historical Introduction to the New Testament,"* by R. M. Grant, 1963, page 51

⁶ Ibid, citing *"The Theological Relevance of Textual Variation in Current Criticism of the Greek N.T.,"* Clark, Vol. 85, 1966, page 16

⁷ Ibid, page 86, citing *"Bemerkungen zu den gegenwärtigen Möglichkeiten textkritischer Arbeit,"* Aland, 1970, page 3

⁸ Bart Ehrman Blog, ehrmanblog.org *"The Strange World of Textual Criticism"* Oct. 27th, 2022

altered the words of their sacred texts to make them more patently orthodox and to prevent their misuse by Christians who espoused aberrant views [passages with doctrine are suspect]"[9] *Bart Ehrman (1993)*

Further quotes include:
"The aim of textual criticism is *to establish the text as nearly as possible in the form in which it left the author's hands.*" *A. T. Robertson (1863-1934)*

"Textual criticism is *the science* of discovering the *original words* of the biblical authors." *Philip Comfort (1950-2022)*

"The New Testament can *only* be reconstructed through *conjectural emendation* [guessing]." *Karl Lachmann (1793-1851)*

Does any of this sound like "a science"? Words above include: "possible," "conjectural emendation," "doubted," "may be," "wellnigh," "impossible," "dogmatic," "falsifications," "hypothesis," "probability judgments," "may be doubted that there is evidence," "suggested." This is the least "scientific" field of study aside from "liberal dance theory." Mind you, the words listed above concern the very root of the "science."

Now, with the "theories" mentioned previously, a seminary student is well on his way to *completely ruining anyones bible*. In no way is this a *"science"* (1 Tim. 6:20). The rule of thumb in using this *"science"* (1 Tim. 6:20) is to be *"neutral and objective,"* but how can one be neutral when it comes to the Bible? *There is no such thing as neutrality in the Bible:* you're either saved or lost, Born Again or dead in sins, going to Heaven or going to hell. The moment an atheist such as Ehrman (or a *practical* atheist such as Hort) takes a "neutral stance" on the text he is working with, is the very moment *his mind goes to pieces* (Ezek. 14). *Luther* was not neutral, neither was *Paul, Peter, John, Matthew, Luke, Jude,*

---

[9] Bart Ehrman, *"The Orthodox Corruption of Scripture,"* 1993, Introduction

Two Bibles

Burgon, Tyndale's, Geneva's, Coverdale's, Matthew's, Bishop's, etc. The position of neutrality is a myth concerning the Lord or Lucifer—the world spins whether you agree with it or not or whether you claim a "neutral" stance that it may or may not be spinning.

By the *very nature* of the "science" of textural criticism, one *must believe* that the original wording is *lost* and that the scholar can restore it. The critic is trying to "restore what the original authors wrote," i.e. we don't have the inspired text as promised by Scripture. Right-off the bat the critic is taking an anti-Scriptural approach to dealing with the Bible. The very core of it assumes that the text is *lost* and begins with a state of disbelief in the word of God. By doing so the critic usurps the authority of The Holy Spirit in order to change the text based on his *"neutral theories"* of the "science"—and then adds his own conjectural emendations via *guesswork*.

Many times a translator is merely guessing at best, *"the basic principle...apart from accident...the simple example given assumes that the different lines of descent have remained independent of one another...imply...hypothesis...obscure...implies..."*[10] Did you catch that? I hope you did. A *"basic principle"* taken as scientific fact *is based on implication and assumption.* It's foundation is an *assumption*! Do you notice anything else strange about those rules above? Anything at all? *Not one says anything at all about the guiding light of Scripture: The Holy Spirit.* If you noticed, the *theories* are all based on *a theory* of later recension of the text—as in they are *anti*-Byzantine/Syrian. You would be working backwards from the "harmonizations" of *Byzantine* to the "additions" of the *Western* texts, and finally landing on the "oldest and best" which *have* "shorter," "polished readings," and are "complex in grammar," and non-Kione: the *Alexandrian* texts.

Considering that most textual critics believe that the "originals" were written in *simple Kione Greek* as opposed to

---

[10] Bruce Metzger, *"The Text of the New Testament,"* 2005, pages 207-208

a more "finessed literary style," *why would anyone favor a text that is written in a more complex, "literary style" of Greek as being closer to the originals?*

Since Alexandria was a hot bed of *philosophers* (Col. 2:8) and "sophistry," with the likes of: *Philo,* who was a Jewish philosopher that lived in Alexandria in 1st Century B.C. He is known for his *synthesis* of *Greek philosophy* and *Jewish theology*, and for his "influential writings" on ethics, metaphysics, and the "nature of God."

What is a Jew doing living in Egypt writing about Jewish things? According to *the Bible* he would be *an apostate* (Jer. 44:25-26, 42:13-22; Gen. 49:29, 50:25; Ezek. 32:2, 31-32; Isa. 19-20:4). The same Hebrew texts he was commenting on had those verses within them. You also have Callimachus the 3rd Century B.C. poet, Aristobulus (160-100 B.C.) the Jewish Hellenistic philosopher who attempted to harmonize Greek philosophy with Jewish thought. Didymus Chalcenterus (63 B.C.-A.D. 10) the Greek grammarian. Ptolemy the astronomer (A.D. 100-170), and Clement of Alexandria (A.D. 150-215). Also, Ammonius Saccas (A.D. 175-242) who is called the "father of Neo-Platonism."[11] Most notable being *Origen* (A.D. 185-254). Clement was one of his teachers who also learned from the "father of Neoplatonism" mentioned above: *Ammonius Saccas* (Col. 2:8).

Origen was the head of a *Christian University* in Alexandria, Egypt. He was also heavily influenced by *Philo's* work (see above). Greek philosophy of Plato and Socrates was *heavy* in the area and found its way *into* Jewish and Christian writings. A central theme in Platonism, and Gnostic thought stemming from it, is the idea of *God and matter* being separate, which poses a *problem* with the N.T.— **"God was manifest in the flesh."** We have a problem! See problems 1-8 below.

---

[11] The influence of NeoPlatonism heavily inspired the practice of the Catholic Mass which is a mystical experience via the practice of magic (Theurgy)—Transubstantiation.

1. Gnostics claimed to posses a *higher knowledge* than is contained in Christianity
2. They believed themselves to be *spirit*, while all other people were soul and body
3. They believed in an *"elect" few* empowered by God would receive salvation by God's arbitrary preselection.[12]
4. They believed *matter was evil*
5. Their views produced *asceticism* (Origin castrated himself)
6. They *rejected* the O.T., and its God, Jehovah
7. They *allegorized* the Scriptures in order to conform their Gnosticism to Christianity
8. They *invented* a creator who was a begotten creature who was an *inferior God*
9. They claimed the body of Jesus was *an illusion* hence their *corruption of Scripture* to destroy Him as equal with God[13]

Westcott and Hort, who admired the work of Origen, believed that the *"pure"* text must have come from Alexandria, a place of *higher education*, instead of the lower class, "common" folk of Syria and Asia Minor. Hort deemed the Textus Receptus a *"vile text"*[14]; so much for a *"neutral and scientific approach."* He also did *not* believe in Genesis 1-3 and accepted Darwinism as soon as it appeared; they believed that Mary worship was as beneficial as God worship, and that no literal hell exists.[15] In accord with Hort's theories on textural criticism, which are still widely used and accepted

---

[12] Kenneth Wilson, *"Augustine's Conversion from Traditional Free Choice to 'Non-Free Free Will,'"* 2018, pages 12-13

[13] This list and one like it may be found in and elaborated on by the work of Jay P. Green, Sr. called, *"The Gnostics, The New Versions, and The Deity of Christ,"* 1994, page vi and George Hodges, *"The Early Church: from Ignatius to Augustine,"* 1915 (2019 edition), page 28

[14] Fenton Hort, Hort, *"Life and Letters of Fenton John Anthony Hort, Vol I,"* 1896, page 211

[15] *"The Life and Letters of F.J.A. Hort,"* Vol. I, p. 149, Vol. 2, page 50, and a letter to the Archbishop of Canterbury, March 4, 1890

today, he did not believe in the preservation of the text, nor that it would be inspired.

Hort *denied* Scripture relating to the preservation of the words: 1 Chronicles 16:15; Psalm 119:89, 12:6-7; Isaiah 40:8; Matthew 5:18; Luke 16:17, 21:33; John 10:35, 16:12-13; 1 Peter 1:23-25; Luke 4:4, etc. In other words, Hort and Westcott are very similar to *the majority of textual critics and translation committee members today*. In all *practical* purposes, they were atheists when it came to believing the text of the Bible, for their starting point was believing that we don't have the text and that the original text is beyond recovery.

All it took was a few "highly esteemed," "good, godly," and "revered" Greek professors and theologians to jump on the bandwagon of Hortism, such as Warfield and A. T. Robertson. Both had powerful influence over other headmasters and professors around the world. Warfield, who was a champion of divine inspiration began to question inspiration of the text *after* accepting Hort's theories and the presumption that "the oldest *are* the best," namely the Vatican Codex B. He then became at odds with the fact that "the oldest and best" disagree amongst themselves a large portion of the time. Finally he could not accept his convictions on Biblical inspiration while at the same time accepting Hort's monstrosity of a "theory." He heard the same rubbish in the late 1800's that people hear today in the majority of seminary classrooms in 2023. In part, being that the text was "watched over and preserved"…at Alexandria.

> "The purer [!] text should be preserved at Alexandria than any other church would not in itself be surprising. There if anywhere, it was to be anticipated that, owing to the proximity of an exact grammatical school [Origen's school], *a more than usual watchfulness over the transcription of the writings of apostles and*

apostolic men would be suggested [!...or just the opposite]..."[16]

This *"school,"* which Origen was headmaster of, did *far more* than be *"watchful."* The intention was to *"improve the Greek, rather than degrade it."* (The old proverb goes, "the road to hell is paved with good intentions.") The Alexandrian manuscripts *just so happen* to favor this style of Greek: the polished scholarly Greek. *"Clearness"* is used more so than eloquence in early N.T. manuscripts; that is to say that the Kione was *earlier* than the "polished" Greek—those *earlier* than that of the "polished" B and ℵ. Sometimes the same word is even used twice in the same passage for sake of clarity (the Kione style).[17]

Origen (A.D. 185-254), being an "eloquent scholar" who had a reputation to uphold, saw many philosophers and intellectuals of his day making fun of the simplicity within the early Greek N.T. writings. He indicated a specific case with a man named Celsus.[18] In Origen's account he notes that the text *"should not merely convey the truth* [!]*, but which should be fitted to gain over the multitude."* He practiced what he preached, only his *"multitude"* would be his students and other intellectuals he surrounded himself with, for *after* A.D. Second Century is when these earlier Kione Greek texts went though *a revision*. The pinnacle of that revision being that of ℵ and B in the mid-Fourth Century.

> *"The consideration of the matter of style and the tendency of the Alexandrians to exceed the other text types in Atticising* [making it fancy] *suggests that 'two rules' of textual criticism be*

---

[16] Harry A. Sturz, *"The Byzantine Text-Type & New Testament Textual Criticism,"* 2022, page 108, quoting Hort

[17] Ibid, page 112, *"Demetrius On Style"*

[18] Ibid, page 113, quoting *"Origen Against Celsus"*

reconsidered: 1) 'prefer the shorter reading' and 2) 'prefer the more difficult reading'. These two rules are 'tailor made' to favor the more Attistic and less Kione (plain) type of text."[19]

It is also worth noting that Origen quotes the N.T. *more* than any other Church Father, a whopping 17,926 +/- times, but still *couldn't find the unlimited blood atonement of Jesus Christ, salvation by grace, proper local church offices, life after death, what water baptism is, or the doctrines surrounding the Second Coming of Jesus Christ.* He was a *postmillennial, purgatory believing,*[20] *baptismal regenerating,*[21] *priest naming,*[22] *salvation by works* (and believed that while at the same time believing all will be saved *after* purgatory, as in, *"universal salvation"*) type of *"biblical scholar."* He believed that the Apocrypha was inspired canon as well.[23] Are you smellin' the breeze yet? Are you seeing how the ball rolls? Stop picking daisies and listen for a sec, okay?

He was a scholar from Alexandria who did not take Genesis 1-3 seriously.[24] He also castrated himself.[25] Origen

---

[19] Ibid, pages 113-114

[20] De Principiis, Book III, Section 3 & 5,

[21] Philip Schaff, *"History of The Christian Church,"* Vol. II, page 222, 792

[22] Wilkinson, *"Our Authorized Bible Vindicated,"* 1930, pages 18-19, 216-220

[23] In his work *"Commentary on Matthew"* Origen refers to the book of Tobit as "divinely inspired," and in his *"Homilies on Genesis"* he describes the story of Susanna as "Scripture." Similarly, in his *"Commentary on John"* he speaks of the Wisdom of Solomon as "divinely inspired Scripture." Tobit supports the use of witchcraft (sort of like priests turning a wafer into the body of Christ). Wisdom of Solomon is written in the person of Solomon which is fraud at best since it was written way after the death of Solomon and has Platonism within such as "God created the universe from formless matter," pantheism is also taught. If you are Catholic you must accept these as "inspired scripture."

[24] De Principiis, Book IV, page 365, also see the same position by Hort in *"life of Hort,"* Vol. 1, page 78

[25] According to Eusebius of Caesarea, a fourth-century Catholic historian, Origen castrated himself as an act of extreme asceticism, using Matthew 19:12 as a proof text.

believed that salvation and Christ's Kingdom at his return would be *a gradual process* (evolution), and eventually *everyone would be saved—even the devil*. In order to do this he would have to throw out about *half* of the entire O.T. and N.T. (Matt. 13:40; Mal. 4:1-3, for a very brief example).

Origen influenced *Augustine (postmillennial,*[26] believed in *baptismal regeneration, and salvation by works)*. You then have Jerome who is Eusebius' and Augustin's friend. He believed in the "Holy Mother Church" and that the great pontiff sitting on the throne in Rome was the substitute teacher for God here on earth (*Vicarius Filii Dei*[27]). Augustine was dubbed *"the first Roman Catholic"* by Schaff. We are covering a lot, I'll slow down.

Jerome (A.D. 340-420) was commissioned by Pope Damasus to write the Latin Vulgate (A.D. 382-405). He had enough common sense to use the Hebrew Old Testament writings instead of Augustine's favored *LXX* which included the Apocrypha as *part of the text*. You will find many of the same readings from Jerome's Latin Vulgate in the RV of 1885 and consequently many new versions today support Catholic readings of this Dark Age text with the *intent* to undermine the Reformation. (Such a list includes: Matt. 1:25, 6:13, 12:6, 42, 20:22; Mark 6:11, 9:46, 15:28; Luke 2:33, 23:42, 24:51-52; Col. 1:14; Acts 28:29, etc. *To see a full list see Appendix*

---

[26] See Augustine's *"City of God"* Book 20, Ch. 9. Augustine believed in the heresy of joining the Kingdom of God and the Kingdom of Heaven, no literal 1,000 reign. He believed that both Kingdom's already existed and that the "Church" (Catholic Church) was the vehicle that would spread and bring in the Kingdom, in other words man would be bringing in the Kingdom instead of Jesus Christ. This is called "postmillennialism." All politicians are postmillennial by nature whether they believe the Bible or not.

[27] This Latin phrase can be found on the Papal Tiara which is a crown worn by popes. It has since fallen out of use due to controversy from the bold statement which means: *"Vicar of the Son of God, or representative of the Son of God."* In true Catholic fashion, apologist Patrick Madrid said there was never any crown with the inscription worn, but the Roman Catholic *"Our Sunday Visitor"* did claim there was such a crown. Despite the apologists claims, there are documents from A.D. 1000-1987 stating that *"Vicarius Filii Dei"* was a "common title" of the pope used within the Papacy (Johannes Quasten, *"Quasten Document"*).

288   Chapter 7

C.) This, of course, was the base-text of that which would come later: the *Jesuit Douay Rheims of 1582*.

What Jerome essentially did was take the Old Latin and reinfused it with Gnostic ideology and the best "scholarship" available. Consequently his text was the Roman text that brought on the Dark Ages (A.D. 500-1500).

Aside from Jerome, you have *Eusebius*, who was a Catholic historian (A.D. 260-339). Constantine ordered that 50 bibles, in Greek, be made for the Churches in the place Constantine *named after himself* (nice Christian), Constantinople. Many believe that Codex ℵ and B were of these 50 bibles, some do not.[28] They have many differences, but do show a similar hand was involved.

> *"This manuscript (Vaticanus) is supposed, as we have seen, to have come from the same place as the Sinaitic Manuscript [ℵ]. I have said that these two show connections with each other, and that they would suit very well as a pair of the fifty manuscripts written at Caesarea for Constantine the Great."*[29]

At the time of Origen up to Jerome we have a group who generally all agree, and are producing materials which show it to be so. Scrivener points this out over a hundred years ago—*"The readings approved by Origen, Eusebius, and Jerome should closely agree."*[30] On the other side of the fence we have the premillennial, non-baptismal regenerating, Scripture as a final authority, non-baby sprinkling, dispensational crew such as Polycarp (A.D. 69-155), Shepard (A.D. 150), Victorius (A.D. 240), the Montanists (A.D. 200-600), the Chilists

---

[28] A. T. Robertson, *"Introduction to Textual Criticism of the New Testament,"* page 80

[29] Caspar Rene Gregory, *"The Canon and Text of the New Testament"*, page 345. Note: Dean Burgon and Miller also agree: Burgon and Miller, *"The Traditional Text,"* page 163

[30] Scrivener, *"Introduction to the Criticism of the New Testament Vol. II,"* page 270

(another term for premillennial), the Novatians (A.D. 250-660), Donatists (A.D. 300-800), and the Paulicians (A.D. 600-1200). All of whom believed in the *"priesthood of the believer,"* and later would believe that the **"man of sin"** in 2 Thessalonians 2 was *the Pope*. In short, they were *anti-Catholic, anti-Origen, Anti-Augustine, Anti-Jerome*. This view can *still* be seen in the Introduction of the King James which no bible version has dared replicate.

There can be much said about the groups above, but for time sake we will briefly look at the *Montanists*. They first appeared in Phrygia, which is by Galatia in Asia Minor. They were given the name *"Montanists"* because instead of associating them with Jesus Christ, the Catholic church wanted to associate them with a man, to tar-and-feather what they actually stood for. They believed in the priesthood of the believer (1 Peter 2:5, 9) and believed that Jesus Christ was coming back to rule from a literal Throne, on the literal land during the Millennium.[31] They prayed for the Kingdom to come by praying "The Lord's Prayer" in its correct context, **"Thy kingdom come. Thy will be done in earth, as it is in heaven"** (Matt. 6:10). It is often said that they are the Quakers of their time. They saw the ecumenical councils of the Catholic church as a *"beginning of secularism"*;[32] they were right. The Montanists spoke frankly and openly, in harmony with the letters of Paul (2 Cor. 3:12).

> *"There were Christians who were in the church because they had been brought up in it; and others who had come because their friends or relatives were in it. Upon these Christians the burden of the rigorous life of the gospel lay rather lightly...the distinction, at first so sharp,*

---

[31] Philip Schaff, *"History of the Christian Church"* Vol. II Ch. 10, Sec. 111.

[32] George Hodges, *"The Early Church: from Ignatius to Augustine,"* 1915 (2019 edition), page 35

> *between the church and the world grew gradually obscure...They* [Christians who were not witnessing and living the rigorous life] *were adjusting themselves to their environment. They perceived that it was prudent to make some reasonable compromise..."*[33]

You see this in full swing today. They saw it brewing.

Tertullian (A.D. 155-220) *separated himself* from the clergy, who were part of the beginnings of Catholicism as we know it today. He was labeled a "Montanist" for doing so. Tertullian is quoted by saying, *"What kinship is there between Christ and Plato?"* He did not see compromise on the matter.

There appears to be two groups of scholars present thus far.

The second group says things like:
1. "The Bible is a warm letter of affection from a parent to a child; and yet there are many who see chiefly the severer passages. As there may be fifty or sixty nights of gentle dews in one summer, that will not cause as much remark as one hailstorm of half an hour, so there are those who are more struck by those passages of the Bible that announce the indignation of God than by those that announce His affection."[34] *De Witt Talmage (1895)*
2. "Old books go out of date...many of the national libraries are merely the cemeteries of dead books...not so with one old Book. It started in the world's infancy. It grew under theocracy and monarchy. It withstood storms of fire. It grew under prophet's mantle and under the fisherman's coat of the apostles...Tyranny issued edicts

---

[33] Ibid

[34] *"Dictionary of Burning Words of Brilliant Writers,"* 1895, page 30.

against it...but the old Bible [he is talking about a KJB] still lived..."[35] *Talmage* (1886)

3. "To alter the Authorized Version would unsettle the minds of thousands as to which was the word of God. There would be *two Bibles* spread throughout the land and what *confusion* this would create in almost every place. If new translations were to begin, *where would they end? The Sicilians would strike 'God' out of 1 Timothy 3:16 and struck out 1 John 5:7-8 as an interpolation* [all of which happened]."[36] *Joseph Philpot (1857)*

4. "We can only *conclude* with the *absolute* certainty, that the ancient text of God's inspired word both now and in the future will *remain* an object of God's special care. This certainly creates for us the obligation to treat the text that has been handed down to us *with great care*. This obligation lies in the confession of *the Reformation*."[37] *Jakob Van Bruggen (1976)*

5. "When the history of the New Testament text is interpreted in this way *[the majority text, closest to the autographs]* the widespread uniformity of the manuscripts at once becomes a potent tribute to the provenance of God in preserving His word."[38] *Zane Hodges (1932-2008)*

6. Methods of Hodges, Burgon, Hills, Pickering, Ruckman..."directs her attention to defining a conviction and does not lose herself, *like modern textual criticism*, in a quest for the unknown."[39] *Van Burggen (1976)*

7. "When we say the Holy Spirit guided the Church to preserve the true N.T., we are not speaking of the Church

---

[35] De Witt Talmage, *"The Monarch of the Books"* or also known as *"The King of Books,"* The Brooklyn Magazine, Vol. 4, Num. 6, September 1886

[36] Joseph Philpot, *"The Gospel Standard,"* 1857

[37] Jakob Van Bruggen, *"The Ancient Text of the New Testament,"* 1976, page 40

[38] Zane C. Hodges, *"A defense of the Majority Text,"* Unpublished paper, page 18

[39] Van Burggen, *"The Ancient Text,"* 1976, page 40

as an organization but of *the Church as an organism.*"[40] "*Naturalistic critics* will never be able to answer this question...how could it *[Byzantine text]* have so completely displaced earlier and better texts *[א and B]* in the usage of the Church [by *"Church"* he means the Body, as Paul uses it]?"[41] *Hills (1967)*

8. "The Lord spent all of human history writing the Bible and when it's finally done, no one wants to read it." *Anonymous (2022)*

9. "Merely reading the Bible is no use at all without we *study* it thoroughly, and hunt it through, as it were, for some great *truth.*"[42] *D. L. Moody (1895)* (The AV was almost 300 years out of date by the time of Moody's quote. When he says *"the* Bible," he is talking about a KJ.)

10. Men who *believed* and preached from an Authorized Version include: John Wesley (1703-1791) who used it when it was nearly 125 years out of date, George Whitfield (1714-1770), William Carey (1761-1834), Adoniram Judson (1788-1850), Samuel Mills (1806), Francis Asbury (1745-1816), Charles G. Finney (1792-1875), George Mueller (1805-1898), Charles Haddon Spurgeon[43] (1834-1892), D. L. Moody (1837-1899), Billy Sunday (1862-1935), Sam Jones (1847-1906), Thomas De Witt Talmage (1832-1902), *and many, many more.* Each of these men were Bible believing, witnessing, street preachers who sparked *national revivals.* They all used *one* Book.

---

[40] Edward F. Hills *"Believing Bible Study,"* 1991, page 107

[41] Ibid, page 104

[42] *"Dictionary of Burning Words of Brilliant Writers"* D. L. Moody, *"How to Study the Bible,"* 1895, page 40

[43] To show how far things have come from sanity; Rick Warren of Saddleback church is now (2023) chancellor of Spurgeon's College in London, England. The school was founded in 1856 by Spurgeon himself who adamantly opposed people such as Warren.

Given the previous information on Origen, it makes you wonder if Origen had another bible version that he was reading. He actually cited King James (TR) readings *and* Nestles readings about the same amount, since he originally had the TR/Byzantine readings before he then proceeded in corrupting them. Origen quoted the King James text 460 times and Nestles 491 times.[44] Overall, Church Fathers quoted the King James readings much *more* than the Nestles readings.

Papias (A.D. 95-110) with 1 KJ and 0 Nestles

Justin Martyr (A.D. 100-165) having 17 KJ and 20 Nestles quotes

Tertullian (A.D. 155-220) with 74 KJ and 65 Nestles

Cyprian (A.D. 200-258) with 100 KJ and 96 Nestles

Ambrose (A.D. 339-397) with 169 KJ and 77 Nestles

It appears that the King James readings go back to the time of the Apostle John and then *something* happened around A.D. 200-350, and again around A.D. 350-400. Tatian (A.D. 120-180) had a KJB, Polycarp (A.D. 69-155) had one, Chrysostom (A.D. 347-407) had one. One of these happenings would no doubt be the school of Alexandria's influence on the "original" text, by doctoring it up and making it palpable for those *in classrooms*. The other happening around A.D. 400 was Jerome and his new translation from the Old Latin (King James) into the Latin Vulgate of the Catholic Church (Nestles). It appears there are two *different* sets of bibles being used *and two different sets of scholars,* **"by their fruits ye shall know them."**

One group used the Latin Vulgate of Jerome to usher in the Dark Ages (A.D. 500-1500) while burning books *containing the writings of a what would later form the King James.* All of those premillennial, water baptism is a figure, salvation by grace through faith believing individuals and groups mentioned previously were then *deemed heretics* and

---

[44] Dean Burgon, *"The Traditional Text, Vol. I,"* page 100

burned at the stake for not accepting Catholic doctrine and teachings on matters, stemming from Origen and Augustine, and for not accepting Nestles Greek text (Jerome's Latin Vulgate). Some estimate the deaths of believing Christians by the Catholic Church range from 5 million to 50 million people. They were pushed *north* into northern Italy, France, and the surrounding areas where they then became the *Bogamiles, Cathari, Waldenses, and Anabaptists* (A.D. 800-1200).

Later after making their way to Germany and the surrounding areas came an uprising around A.D. 1517 with the likes of Martin Luther, Knox, Huss, Calvin and others leading the charge. Some just wanted reform of the Catholic Church, some wanted to challenge it out of existence, and some wanted to get as far away from it as possible. Revisions of bibles began. Martin Luther's German bible practically made the German language as its like companion did for the English (KJB).

Martin Luther believed in the inspiration of the Holy Ghost and believed in putting the Scriptures in the hands of his fellow man, as opposed to keeping it in the dark during the Roman Catholic height of power in the Dark Ages. His translation methods were *not like* that of Metzger and Ehrman. Luther was conscious of the Holy Spirit's **"power"** in every word of his translation; he relied on the Spirit and sought to put Jesus Christ in every corner of his work.[45] This is *unlike* the NIV, ESV, NASV, NRSV, NLT, etc., where they have deleted them in every corner (they are *"including"* them if you ask Blomberg). Luther was not an Alexandrian but of an Antiochian mindset.[46] There is a famous saying attached to the Reformation period: *"Erasmus laid the egg that Luther hatched."*

As the Reformation was really hitting home, the *Protestants* (1520) were born and then later on from the

---

[45] Leroy Froom, *"The Prophetic Faith of Our Fathers,"* Vol. V, 1948, page 32 & 127

[46] John Neumann, *"The Romance of Bible Scripts and Scholars,"* 1965, page 78

Protestants, came the *Baptists*. All of these groups had some major things in common: "the Catholic Church was the great whore" (Rev. 17-18), baptism was a **"figure"** and doesn't save anyone (1 Pet. 3:21), they were premillennial (this doctrine fell away for a time but came back later on), Scripture was their final authority, and they believed in the priesthood of *the believer* (1 Pet. 2:5, 9), not a pope or Catholic priest.

This is where we come to in History. After the reign of *Henry the VIII* (1509-1547) in England, who initially broke away from the Catholic hierarchy based on a sexual desire to be with another woman in marriage (*many* more). The pope didn't sign-off on it so Henry decided to become the head of the church of England instead. He began burning bibles and beheading wives, remarrying many times. After his death, his son *Edward*, who was trained up in the Scriptures, took the throne (1547-1553). He released John Knox from prison and was known as the *"British Josiah"* (2 Chron. 34:1-2).

One of Henry's daughters was *Bloody Mary*, who was trained and taught by Catholics: she burned bibles and killed those who opposed "The Holy Mother Church of Rome." Due to ovarian cancer her reign was shortened and Henry the VIII's second daughter, *Elizabeth*, began her reign (1558-1603). She allowed for bible reading and for many bibles to be printed (the Great Bible of 1539, Geneva of 1560, Bishop's of 1568). By this time England was becoming a superpower and grew significantly *after* the KJB had been produced, it remained one *until* shortly after the Revised Version of 1885 became public. They have not risen since. **"Blessed is the nation whose God is the LORD"** (Psa. 33:12).

The next ruler is the infamous *king James* (1603-1625), who is greatly attributed with the making of the king James of 1611 (his name is attached to it). Even though James was not on the translation committee, so-to-speak, he could recite any verse of Scripture on command and translate it into

Greek, Latin, or French; something no one before him, in his position, could do. The King James Bible of 1611 had a plot involved to kill king James, as surmised by the *Jesuits* (Gunpowder Plot of 1605), and before his reign, a Spanish fleet that was sunk which had plans to offset its production and crumble the English powers (Spanish Armada 1588) putting it back into the bloody hands of the pope. The Jesuits also had another strategy to offset the line of English bibles being made: *the Jesuit Rheims bible of 1582*. The Jesuit bible battled with the King James Bible for supremacy after its launch, and it is *still* battling to this day, through the means of Nestles, ESV, NIV, NRSV, NASV, NET, NEB, NLT, et al. When the odds were against it, *the Book* made it through—one against many.

The group of Greek texts that influenced the Reformation and Protestant bibles are listed below:

The Received Text of the Greek New Testament or a.k.a. the *"Textus Receptus"* which broke the chains of popery includes:

1.) Erasmus 1516 (who had writings banned by the Catholic Church even though he himself was of Catholic origin.)
2.) Colinaeus 1534
3.) Stephanus 1546
4.) Beza 1565
5.) Elzevir 1633

Which bibles came from these? *Martin Luther 1521 (German and his translations reached Holland, Denmark, Iceland, Yugoslavia), Erdosi 1541 (Hungary), Olivetan, Valera, Visoly, Gottshcalkson, DeGrave, Elizabeth Bible, Coverdale 1535 (English), Great Bible 1539 (English), Matthew's Bible 1537 (English), Bishop's Bible 1568 (English), Tyndale Bible 1525 (English), Geneva Bible 1560 (English), Diodati 1603 (Italian), King James 1611 (English). (These bibles produced revivals, millions saved, and the ushering in of the first nation that separated church and state in the world: the United States.)*

Erasmus is often accused of not having *"the best and most recently discovered new manuscripts,"* but did he really need ℵ and B and some more papyri at hand? He had the Latin Vulgate which "he extensively revised,"[47] Codex 1, the Complutensian Polyglot, and some other Byzantine manuscripts, which he went through. This accusation, (half truth, Gen. 3) is the common two-faced move in which many use to cast doubt on the text. Erasmus had later manuscripts and the readings that he chose were *anti-Latin Vulgate;* i.e. *anti-Catholic readings* i.e. *non-orthodoxically corrupted.* He threw Nestles text *out the window*. The Reformation had rejected it, and instead went with the Old Italic, Old Latin, Waldenseian type of text that goes all the way back to the Christians in Syria (Acts 11:26). Erasmus' text was also *banned* by the Catholic Church at the Council of Trent; banned to this day, as well as "The Hunchback of Notre Dame" for having a *priest* involved in *"salacious acts."*

Do not be confused, as I mentioned earlier, there are readings found in all different "text-types" from other "text-types." Likewise, there are readings in the King James which are from the Latin Vulgate. These readings are not the leavenous readings used to undermine the Reformation. Not every *reading* in a manuscript that is deemed rotten is bad, nor every reading in "a bible" of the same kind is deemed unusable.

Those bibles above started some of the biggest revivals known in the history of the Church. These bibles, which ignored the Latin Vulgate in many cases and restored those old readings found in early papyri and the Old Latin kept by the Christians at Antioch (Acts 11:26), the Paulicians, Novatians, Waldenses, Albigenses, etc., brought on the Reformation. There were hundreds of translations in

---

[47] Bruce Metzger, *"The Text of the New Testament,"* 2005, page 142

languages all over. When people ask the question, *"Where was the word of God before 1611?"* The answer is simple: *It was all over the place!*

This is what the King James translators meant when they said *"to make a good one better."* The King James translators *had access* to the same passages found in an ESV, NIV, NASV, et al., *by means of* the Jesuit Rheims bible. They outright *denied it*. They did not take Nestles text and "make it better," *they threw it out*. They were not referring to Roman Catholic bibles but to Coverdale, The Great Bible, The Bishop's Bible, and the like when they said, *"to make a good one better."* This excuse is used to make the KJB a *"better"* translation today by turning it into a NKJV or ESV.

To compete with these English bibles (e.g. Tyndale and Coverdale) Rome released its Jesuit Rheims bible in English. Its main competitors were just before the KJ: Coverdale's, Tyndale's, Bishop's, and Matthew's. This bible was used to gain Catholic control over recently lost ground. The basis for that bible was Jerome's Latin Vulgate (which included the Apocrypha as part of the text) via request of the pope. Jerome himself was questioning the Apocrypha as being inspired or not because he noticed that *none of the Jews considered it to be.*

The Apocrypha is always a place of contention for those wishing to "throw shade" on the early 1611 KJ. They will often say, *"the 1611 King James had the Apocrypha in it so how is it any different?"* By now the reader should know at least a few reasons of how the 1611 *is different*, but to be clear, *yes, it did contain the Apocrypha and so did many of the English bibles that came before it.*

Starting off with Wycliff who was the first to translate into English, he threw the Apocrypha out, and then it was later placed between the two Testaments. Coverdale's had the Apocryphal books inserted between the two Testaments with *an explanation saying they are not canon,* and the word *"Apocrypha"* as a header. Matthew's also contained them with similar notes and header. The Great Bible included them between the two Testaments *in the same way*. The Geneva Bible has a similar format to the former versions, and with the word *"Apocrypha"* as a header *on each page* all the way through the Apocryphal books. This made it obvious to the reader that this section was set apart from the rest of the bible. The Bishop's gets rid of some of the notes explaining the *uninspired* nature of the Apocrypha's section, but keeps the header *on every page*. Finally, the King James puts the books between the two Testaments, just as every other English bible had done, but *without* notes. They put a header *on every page that reads "Apocrypha,"* denoting that one is reading something *different than the rest of the Book,* since it breaks the regular format of headers throughout. You come to a section that reads, *"Apocrypha"* on every single page instead of the usual chapter, book title, and short summary readings. Given that almost every bible beforehand had given explanation to the Apocryphal books, the majority of Protestants shared the belief that the Apocrypha was only in the Bible for "edification" or "study" if one so pleased, but *it was not "canon."* This was common thought amongst the Protestants.

It was placed there for the purpose of examination. Eventually the King James Bible was printed *without* the Apocrypha, starting in 1826-1885. More fascinating is the fact that Sinaiticus א and Vaticanus B *both* contain Apocryphal books *as part of the text.* If these are the two "best" and most favored manuscripts, then why not translate Tobit and the additions of Esther, Bel and the Dragon, Ecclesiasticus, etc., into the text of the NRSV, NASV, and ESV? These versions (and more) all use the LXX in the Old Testament but then refuse to translate the entirety of the O.T. Sinaiticus and Vaticanus—If they're so good, then *translate them!*

We are covering a lot of ground here very quickly and not doing the period much justice, but for sake of the theme of this work and time, it will be kept short. There are many

Church histories written and many secular history books written on these time periods.[48]

The Received Text which blossomed into the King James has its roots in the Old Latin, Old Syriac, early papyri such as 𝔓66, 𝔓75, 𝔓45, etc. The Old Testament was in Hebrew and Aramaic, passed down through the Levitical priesthood and Masorites from 1500 B.C. and is now sitting in your King James Bible. After Malachi, there was a four-hundred year period of *silence* until Jesus Christ showed up on the scene, the silence was *about* 397/400 B.C. to the birth of Christ thus *further indicating that the LXX and its O.T. Apocrypha to be works of fiction.* Augustine *did* believe it to be inspired but his pal Jerome had his concerns. At least Jerome had enough sense to use the Hebrew O.T. when translating for the Latin Vulgate instead of *the* LXX. Another reason we know the Apocrypha is *not* inspired are *the words of Jesus himself*, **"which were written in the LAW of Moses, and in the PROPHETS, and in the PSALMS"** (Luke 24:44).

Jesus gives you the *three* divisions from the O.T. canon in the verse above; along with Matthew 23:35. **"The law"** being the *Torah*, the **"prophets"** the *Nabhim*, and the **"Psalms"** being the *Kethubim*. The Hebrew bible is in a different order than a King James O.T., or any Christian's O.T., and *ends with Second Chronicles as opposed to Malachi.* In Luke 24:44, Jesus is *giving authorship* of the first five books of the Bible to Moses. Modern scholarship does *not* agree with Jesus Christ thus, calling Him a liar. They *deny* Jesus Christ ever spoke it, it's a mystery in which is, *"yet to be solved"* according to most modern day "scholars." There are thousands upon thousands of manuscripts for the Hebrew bible (a.k.a. Tanakh). There is a famous tablet dated from 1000 B.C. containing a devotional of sorts with several scriptures (Isa. 1:17; Psa. 72:3; Exod. 23:3). This is why most of the debate

---

[48] Mueller, Schaff, Godspeed, Forbush, Fisher, Vacandad, Walker, Webber, Newman, Baker, Dolan, etc.

and squabbles revolve around *the New Testament*; the O.T. is pretty much set, except for the authorship of some of the books, because modern scholars *don't believe their own bible*.

If we go back in time to the period of Jesus Christ's earthly ministry, roughly 4 B.C. /A.D. 0 to A.D. 33,[49] He *had and believed* the *Hebrew* Scriptures, as mentioned above. After His death in the range of A.D. 33 to 95, is when the *"original autographs"* of the Gospels, Acts, Letters of Paul, General Epistles, and Revelation were written: the books comprising the New Testament. *Not one "original" exists; not one—not one from the Old Testament or the New Testament.* We have copies of copies of copies. These are what modern scholars are after. They want the originals that vanished long ago, hence an entire *"science,"* as I have briefly discussed, was invented to do so.

A total of about 5,700+ (closer to 5,835) manuscripts of the N.T. survive today. That is more than any other writing in antiquity. When you include different versions (Old Latin, Gothic, Syriac, etc.), the numbers are much, much higher. The originals were written in breezy prison cells from Rome (some of Paul's), some in Antioch of Pisidia (Acts 13:14, 49) where it was **"published,"** in Jerusalem (Acts 6:7), Antioch of Syria (Acts 13:1, 11:20, 26) where **"the disciples were called Christians first,"** by preaching and writing **"letters"** (Acts 15:23) to Antioch in *Syria* and Pisidia (yes, there are two places called Antioch), and Cilicia. We also have more from Derbe and Lystra where Timmothy read the **"scriptures"** as a child, which would be the *Hebrew* O.T. that he was reading (Acts 16:1; 2 Tim. 3:15). There is also *Philippi* (Philippians), *Thessalonica* (Thessalonians), *Corinth* (Corinthians), *Ephesus* (Ephesians), *Galatia* (Galatians), *Colossae* (Colossians), and the seven churches in Revelation 2-3 which are: Ephesus (as

---

[49] Some dispute the dates within a few years. Instead of His death being in A.D. 33, some place it in A.D. 27. You will find that many chronologists differ in their findings surrounding dates, *most* of the time the debate is over a few years.

named before), *Smyrna, Pergamos, Thyatira, Sardis, Philadelphia, and Laodicea* all located in *Asia Minor*.

From *the Bible* we know that The Holy Ghost *forbade* the *going further east into Asia* at this time, around A.D. 50-55 (Acts 16:6) but was instead moving up *North* from Jerusalem through Syria and the surrounding area *over west*, towards Asia Minor, to Greece, and then Rome. From these places is where the hunt for "the originals" *should be* according to the Bible, *not in Alexandria*.

From here, *two major groups began to form*, which always form: (1) *apostate* and *allegorical* interpretation of the Scriptures; (2) *believing* and *literal* interpretation of the Scriptures. From this point on is when corruption (2 Cor. 2:17) entered into manuscripts.

The New Testament was written by a hodgepodge group in the Body of Christ. Some of it was written, or spoken by (while someone else wrote), **"unlearned and ignorant men"** (Acts 4:13). Could you imagine *a fisherman* from the deep south writing a page from the best selling Book of all time? Some by Luke, who was *a Physician*, which is apparent in the way he writes (Luke, Acts), and also Paul who could speak multiple languages, but it's he who counted *all his good learning* and *acts of the law* as **"dung"** (Phil. 3:4-8). There is Matthew, who wasn't a fisherman like John, Peter, or James, but wasn't a Physician like Luke: he was a tax-collector—one of the most revered Books in the N.T. canon was written by someone from the IRS. How does that make you feel? God entrusted his words to a diverse group; it was not just one group of learned men, or scholars from Alexandria who he gave **"the oracles of God"** (Rom. 3:2). They also were all *Jews*.

The next movement is *northwest* to escape Roman persecution of the 1st Century to 4th Century into *northern Italy, Austria, and France*. Then further into Germany and its surrounding areas. We then keep going *west* to Britain, England, then later to the Americas, and now on its way *back around to Japan and Asia to the place it all started, Israel.* The Holy Spirit moves across the globe as the **"Sun"** (Mal. 4) rises and sets: *east to west.*

The Syrian/Byzantine area is where most of the manuscripts are found that were put to use in the Geneva Bible, Bishop's Bible, Matthew's Bible, Luther's, Coverdale's Bible, and so forth; eventually leading to the King James. *If you believe what the Bible says about these places* then you don't need to go much further. Scholars think that we *don't* have what God said, but we will get there *eventually* with *new discoveries* and the "science" of *textual criticism.* In other words, God didn't preserve his words because He would have preserved *"the originals,"* but *"we"* will figure it out in time, *"we"* being the scholars of today. By definition, *practically* speaking, they are atheists.

If I know anything about God, it would be his sense of humor. He has a wild sense of humor, **"come to Beth-el and transgress,"** He is saying come to the house of God and *sin.* Here's another one: San Francisco is built right on a *fault*-line. It could cause a massive earthquake at any moment. That *fault*-line existed *long* before it was inhabited by the current, *"rainbow flag"* waving residents...its foundation is on a *fault.* Who's *fault* was Sodom and Gomorrah? Now, that is a *weird* sense of humor right there, but there it is.

The Lord is being sarcastic, and I am not saying this is what He did, but if I could imagine it, I'd say God made the *late* manuscripts the *representation* of the *"originals"* and made the *early "best"* manuscripts (which they really aren't the earliest and best) the most corrupt and furthest away from the "originals." Couldn't you see Him doing that? I could. Make the late ones early and the early ones late. What a mind-grenade. After all, the **"mystery of iniquity"** was already at work in Paul's day (2 Thess. 2:7) and back then there were already those who chose to **"corrupt"** God's words (2 Cor. 2:17). People were even writing in Paul's name to churches trying to tear it down *from the inside,* which is where you get the incentive for Paul writing the second letter to the Thessalonians.

It's amazing that the Church was not brought down early on from the inside. That which was thought an error will in fact be proven *not* to be an error over time. Just as the King James committee, *used faith* in the text of 1 John 2:23, with no evidence at the time: *half the verse is in italics.* Years later, it was proven to be right based on manuscript *evidence* and the reading also happens to be in Vaticanus and Sinaiticus, the two *"oldest and best."* Are you catching the way things drift yet? Are you feelin' the summer breeze?

As opposed to fishermen, like Peter and John (the **"unlearned men"**), we then have the type from **"Alexandria,"** who is **"eloquent"** and "learned" in the Scriptures (Acts 18:24), but who still is *not quite there yet in his learning and Biblical understanding* (Acts 18:26). Paul had to go over his teaching with a fine comb afterward wherever he went (Acts 18:24 Cf. Acts 19:1; 1 & 2 Corinthians). Let us not forget that the Church at Corinth was the *most fleshy Church in the N.T.* Let's hear it from an *"Alexandrian"* type, shall we? James White says:

> "Most also believe the Byzantine represents a later period in which readings from other text-types were put together ('conflated') into the Byzantine reading...Since the Byzantine text comes from a later period (the earliest texts are almost all Alexandrian and not Byzantine), it is 'fuller' in the sense that it not only contains conflations of the other text-types, but it gives evidence of what might be called 'expansion of piety.' That is, additions have been made to the text that flow from a desire to protect and reverence divine truths..." [50]

---
[50] *"The King James Controversy,"* 2009 edition, pages 71-72

He shares ideals and sentiments with almost all modern day Christian scholars in trying to tell you that the *"earliest are the best"* and the Byzantine manuscripts *can't be,* since they are from *later dates.* The thinking is that since a manuscript from A.D. 350 is closer to the "original," it would have *less errors* due to the copying process. Sounds good, right? This has been proven *wrong* time and time again. What if the copyist is starting out with something that is *garbage*? What if the text was *intentionally* mishandled as with the case of the gnostics, or in the case of Eusebius, Jerome, or Origen? They wouldn't do that, no—they are *"good," "wonderful"* men, who were *"champions for the cause"* —Yea…okay.

Starting out as *"Lucianic Recension Theory,"* Hort tried to prove that the later manuscripts went through revisions to fit Christian doctrine of the day (around A.D. 300). The Lucian Recension Theory is the idea that the text around A.D. 300 went through a major revision which led to the Byzantine manuscripts, then leading to the Received Text (Textus Receptus), and then later on the translation of the King James Bible. Why were people so adamant on getting rid of that Book? So, if it went through this *"major revision,"* then it does *not* represent the original autographs closely at all— that's the thinking. The theory still permeates much of modern scholarly communities even though many have abandoned ship. These groups still view the Byzantine/ Syrian manuscripts to be of a *later* origin (despite the early attestation by Church Fathers and earlier manuscripts such as the papyri) than *"the great Uncial Codices ℵ and B."* This is believed *despite absolutely no historical evidence of a revision.* With a revision this large and vast, surly it would be found *somewhere* in the annals of history—*no,* nothing. Regardless, you *will* hear:

Chapter 7

"The Byzantine Text likely traces back to the work of Lucian of Antioch."[51]

"Lucian's work was the first major recension of the Greek New Testament. This recension involved a great deal of harmonization (especially in the Gospels), emendation, and some interpolation."[52]

"There was far less tampering with the text in the Alexandrian text type than in the Lucian [straight up lie!], *and the underlying manuscripts for the Alexandrian text type were superior* [!] *than those used by Lucian."*[53]

"From the fourth century onward, Lucian's recension became the most prevailing type of text throughout the Greek-speaking world. In fact, it became (with minor modifications) the received text of the Greek Orthodox Church. From the fourth until the eighth century, the Byzantine text was revised even further until it was nearly standardized. From then on, almost all Greek manuscripts followed the Byzantine text, including those manuscripts that were used by Erasmus in compiling his edition of the Greek

---

[51] Philip Wesley Comfort, *"The Essential Guide to Bible Versions,"* 2000, page 90

[52] Ibid

[53] Philip Wesley Comfort, *"Encountering the Manuscripts: An Introduction to New Testament Paleography & Textual Criticism,"* 2005

Two Bibles

New Testament (which became the basis of the English King James Version..."[54]

"Lucian was proposed by Hort as the father of the Byzantine text [which has now been proved wrong]. This proposal, incidentally, was by no means necessary to Hort's theory, but was a decent hunch [!] that may well be correct."[55]

"Hort's threefold argument against the Byzantine text is still [!] a good argument that demonstrates the Byzantine text to be secondary, late, and inferior."[56]

All of the quotes listed above are from destructive critics. All would take your Bible and cut it to pieces if they were given the opportunity. Imagine if you heard that over and over in school without getting *the opposing side of the issue... i.e. the evidence.*

Next we have James Price, who worked on the NKJV and is a supporter of the *Critical Text*. A Critical Text, such as Nestles, takes all manuscripts available and applies the *"principles of Textual Criticism," "weighing the evidence,"* and views of their peers in deciding on a reading. The proponents of the Critical Text say they "weigh all the evidence" in order to make revisions to the text of the Bible, but as we have seen already, they talk out of both sides of their mouth and are mentally unstable.

They do not *"weigh the evidence"* properly, since they give credence to א and B as well as many more Alexandrian

---

[54] Ibid

[55] Daniel Wallace, "*Mark 1:2 and New Testament Textual Criticism,*" bible.org, 2004

[56] Daniel Wallace Interview, evangelicaltextualcriticism.blogspot.org, 2006

manuscripts *over any other*. Even in cases where the Alexandrian texts *agrees* with the Byzantine texts, they will *not* side with it. Anything that agrees with ℵ and B, especially such manuscripts as 𝔓66, 𝔓75, which agree in portions, they will side with those *readings*. It's what "the collective" believes in academia. The progression of *"science"* (1 Tim. 6:20) has a long history of being wrong. The NKJV was *supposed* to be just an *"updating of archaic language"* while *"staying true"* to the Received Text according to its own translation committee. *It was not and did not*. Take it from James Price, who was on the NKJV committee and is paraphrasing Metzger:

> "The Antiochan text corresponds to Westcott and Hort's Syrian Text. The text is supported by Antiochan Greek manuscripts, quotations from Syrian Church Fathers, and the Syriac translations. It is the ancestor of the Byzantine text which is the result of a fourth century recension..."[57]

> "The Byzantine tradition seems to have developed in two stages. Probably in the late third century, the Christian community in Antioch, in Syria, attempted to restore the text of its Greek New Testament. This restoration may be likened to the recension Lucian made of the Greek Old Testament..."[58]

---

[57] James D. Price, *"King James Onlyism: A New Sect,"* 2006, page 192. Authors Note: It is interesting given the title of Price's book mentioned—part of the title says, "a new sect." Believing the KJB is Scripture has never been and never will be "a new sect." You would have to throw out Finney, Mueller, Mills, Whitfield, Talmage, Jones, Moody, and Sunday just to name a few, who's ministries date to the 18th Century. There is nothing "new" about it.

[58] Ibid, page 143

Then we have Nestles text, the height and beacon of light in Christian scholarship, *going back on all of this* in their own introduction to their 26th edition. Nestles reads:

> *"The view is becoming increasingly accepted today that neither Codex Bezae nor the Old Syriac derive directly from the II century. Similarly the idea of a 'Neutral Text'* [this is Westcott and Hort's idea that Vaticanus B was a "pure" text and to be viewed as free from corruptions] *has been retired* [!]. *Neither Codex Vaticanus nor Codex Sinaiticus (nor even P75 of two hundred years earlier) can provide a guideline we can normally depend on for determining the text. The age of Westcott-Hort and Tischendorf is definitely over!* [!!!!!]"[59]

This was only after about 80 years of accepting a theory *with sparse evidence behind it*. Nestles text is *still* largely based on Vaticanus B and Sinaiticus ℵ *despite* the claimed pivot. It is still generally W&H's text to this day! They are lying, just as Hort, White, Wallace, Dr. Pufferfish, Blomberg, et al., did. Nestles made the pivot due to *pressure* put on them *after numerous individuals* took Dean Burgon's work, Hills work, Pickering, and the "dreaded" Dr. Ruckman's work, and began to see the *error Hort had made and therefore Nestles had made* for following *his* text.

Many scholars today still hold Alexandrian manuscripts to be the *"best"* in determining the *"original text."* That's the accepted stance by the majority of scholars, even though Burgon and his works are still widely *undisputed* and to this day (over 100 years later) still stands largely *correct*. Those

---

[59] Nestle-Aland *"Novum Testamentum Graece,"* 26th edition, 1979, page 43* of the Introduction

who attempt to refute Burgon always go after his *"theological"* stance instead of his *evidence presented* thus, white-washing him and keeping him out of the conversation: he is shadow-banned. Unfortunately, Nestles is still full of **"leaven"** and even Ehrman in 2011 *admits*[60] that *Nestles text is still largely Westcott and Hort's Greek text from 1881* (*which is based on false, disproved, discredited, "science"*).

What Hort did was,
a.) *Assumed* a Syrian Recension.
b.) *Invented* the cause of it.
c.) *Dreamed* the process by which it was carried out and created *a cult* following, all based on *conjecture* without substantial *evidence*.

Dr. Hort detected *eight* instances within the Gospels of the Textus Receptus, where the Alexandrian reading was combined with the Western reading to give a third "new" reading that's now found in the TR hence, "Lucian Recension".

For example:
"And the people saw them departing, and many knew him, and ran afoot thither out of all cities, and outwent them, and came together unto him" (Mark 6:33)

- The Western reading is *"and came together there"*
- The Alexandrian reading is *"and came before them"*
- The TR reading is *"and came before them and came together to him"*

Hort called this a *"conflate reading"* and found *eight* verses (Mark 9:38, 6:33, 8:26, 9:49; Luke 9:10, 11:54, 12:18, 24:53) in order to prove Lucian Theory out of the *entire New Testament text*. I'll run that by you again: Hort had *eight* verses to prove

---

[60] Bart D Ehrman, *"The Orthodox Corruption of Scripture,"* 2011, page 333

his theory. With these verses, he would go on to *"prove"* that "a third editor took the Western and Alexandrian texts and put them together into one major edit that came after the Alexandrian (א, B) texts and after Western texts (D)."

It took *thirty years* to find these eight verses out of *the entirety of the Gospels.*[61] Out of these verses, *five failed to show this alleged agreement between* א, B, and D (Mark 6:33, Mark 8:26; Luke 9:10, Luke 11:54, Luke 12:18). Of the five verses previously mentioned, 2-4 words are *omitted between themselves* in א, B, and D. *They didn't even agree amongst themselves.* Leaving *three* verses out of *all* four Gospel accounts to *actually* work with.

This is *not* scholarship, but it fooled a lot of people. There have been other "conflate" readings found since the time of Hort, but many have been like *disproved* due to readings having early papyri support and/or the *fact that ALL text-types have conflated readings*! Early papyri support for readings completely demolished Hort's theory of a "later Syrian/Byzantine recension" and all of his cloned friends I mentioned earlier.

Despite this finding in the late 1800's, Hort's "scholarship" had many *notable* and *influential* proponents in the 20th-21st Century such as:
- Casper Gregory
- Burnet Streeter
- Bruce Metzger
- Ehrman
- Wallace
- Kurt & Barbara Aland
- James White
- and almost all faculty and staff at seminaries around the nation

Lucian Theory was a vicious virus in 20th Century Christianity. Dean Burgon was an avid opponent to Hort's

---

[61] Dean Burgon, *"The Revision Revised,"* 1883, page 262, footnote

theory of Syrian Recension (Lucian Theory). Metzger used some of Burgon's work from *"Revision Revised"* (1883), which is a collection of articles from the London Quarterly Review that downright *bashed* Westcott and Hort's Revised Version (RV) of 1885. Metzger tried to cast doubt on the *actual* scholarship that Dean Burgon had accomplished many years ago. His scholarship is still undefeated and only high brow slurs have been attempted to bamboozle audiences of fresh faced seminary students away from his work.

Ehrman and Metzger pass his work off as a *"basically theological and speculative"* argument.[62] Does this argument sound familiar? It's the same one White uses in his book *"King James Only Controversy"* in order to bash people who actually *believe* the preservation of the Scriptures. Metzger further cast doubt on a serious scholar of the text by putting words in Burgon's mouth, *deceptively*. (Just like Hort in his commitment to *only alter a few places in his revision;* **"after his kind."**) The quote is what follows.

> *"It is significant that Bishop John W. Burgon, who ardently and, at times, acrimoniously opposed Hort's estimate of the secondary character of the Syrian text, nevertheless acknowledged that Lucian revised [!] the text of the New Testament; see his volume, The Revision Revised (London, 1883), p. 29."*[63]

The actual quote (from page 29), that Metzger is citing says, "We know that Origen in Palestine, Lucian at Antioch, Hesychius in Egypt, 'revised' the text of the N. T. Unfortunately, they did their work in an age when such fatal misapprehension

---

[62] Bruce M. Metzger & Bart D. Ehrman, *"The Text of The New Testament: Its Transmission, Corruption, and Restoration,"* Forth Edition, 2005, page 181

[63] Bruce M. Metzger, *"Chapters in the History Of New Testament Textual Criticism,"* 1963, page 17 footnote 3.

Two Bibles 313

prevailed on the subject, that each in turn will have inevitably imported a fresh assortment of monstra into the sacred writings."

That is the Dean calling the Lucian revision of the text an *"assortment of monstra"*—why would he be calling it that if he is *a proponent* of what other critics call the "Lucian/Syrian recension"? Why would he lump it with Origen?—*He's making fun of the idea, at the very least:* "revised" is in *quotations*. See, Metzger made you believe that just because Burgon *mentioned it*, he then must *believe it*—that is the level of deception that you're working with, from a "good," "godly," "champion of the cause." Here is Burgon again:

> *"Apart however from the gross intrinsic improbability of the supposed Recension—the utter absence of one particle of evidence, traditional or otherwise, that it ever did take place, must be held to be fatal to the hypothesis that it did. It is simply incredible than an incident of such magnitude and interest would leave no trace of itself in history."*[64]

Why doesn't Metzger discuss *that*, instead of quoting Burgon *deceptively* in order to make him side with Metzger's own *opinions;* or even consider what Colwell says, *"—the Byzantine or Alpha text type—had in its origin no such single focus as the Latin had in Jerome."*[65] How about Geerlings, who says about the Byzantine/Syrian text, "Its origins as well as those of other so-called text-types probably go back to the autographs."[66] There is also a major issue brought to the table

---

[64] Burgon, *"Revision Revised,"* page 293

[65] Colwell, *"The Origin of Text Types,"* page 137

[66] Jacob Greerlings, *"Family E and its Allies in Mark,"* 1967, page 1

by Pickering[67] who also looks at *evidence*. The name of the man that this "revision" is attributed to Pickering states: *"Lucian was an Arian."* If he was an Arian, *then how would he accept his own revision?—It was anti-Arian at worst.* Newsflash: there was no "Lucian Recension." Not to mention, Metzger's NRSV and RSV *bring back* the Arian reading in John 1:18. It appears Metzger is more *"Lucian"* than Lucian was!

Hort invented a theory that involved the Byzantine text being an "official text" with backing by councils that was an "ecclesiastical" Constantinopolan text—therefore its fourth Century origin—there would be historical evidence if this were so. What a loaded bag, man! Furthermore, Vööbus says about Hort's *theory: "—this kind of reconstruction of textural history is pure fiction without a shred of evidence to support it."*[68]

Now, what none of these individuals infected with the need for applause from their peers and **"having men's persons in admiration because of advantage"** (Jude 1:16) saw was the fact that there are earlier texts than the "Lucian" revisions. The Peschito which for a long time was dated to the 2nd Century but has now been placed 4th-5th Century (*after* the theories of Hort became widespread), other ancient Syrian versions from Asia Minor, and the Old Latin date from the 2nd Century (A.D. 100-200) that do not contain the same changes made in ℵ, B, and D, let alone other Uncial manuscripts such as C. The Old Syriac is dated A.D. 150, the Old Latin is dated A.D. 150-157, and papyrus readings from A.D. 150-400. *How can there be a great recension when there were manuscripts and Byzantine readings predating the "recension"?*

Metzger and friends missed the forest for the trees. It appears that the recension was *actually* amongst the Alexandrian manuscripts themselves. Now, isn't that something? For this reason, and for the somewhat "unexplainable sudden explosion" of Byzantine texts around

---

[67] Pickering, *"The Identity of the New Testament Text,"* page 86

[68] A. Vööbus, *"Early Versions of the New Testament,"* 1954, page 100

Two Bibles 315

A.D. 400, and also the proof that there actually *were* Byzantine readings from the *same time and before* "the oldest and best" manuscripts (ℵ, B, etc.), many modern scholars have abandoned the "Lucian Theory" ship. Some still hold to its railings *in practice*, such as Nestles text and the UBS text. They view the ship as a *"renovated"* ship instead of a sinking one. A better term would be a *"new updated version"* of the ship which will *"shed light on the text."*

Meanwhile back in Rome, that is exactly what Catholics were doing in their own productions, see the Jesuit Rheims bible. Catholics would intentionally change verses to fit around their narrative. When was the Catholic church on the rise?—A.D. 76-500 with it's fall starting around A.D. 1500. Most of the Catholic doctrine was conjured and settled between A.D. 76-400, in time for Jerome's translation and just in time for our two *"best and most renown manuscripts"*: B and ℵ. Rome received her knowledge and cherished doctrines from Origen, Augustine, Jerome, and friends who had degrees from Alexandria, Egypt.

These "learned" and "eloquent" types banded together in Alexandria. There was a well developed "scholarly discipline" of textual criticism localized at Alexandria (see Metzger's *"The Text of the New Testament,"* 2005, page 198). Zenodotus and Ephesus (325-240 B.C.) were making comparisons of the many manuscripts of the Iliad and Odyssey in the famed library of Alexandria. The guidelines that were made are: 1.) *eliminate verses regarded as spurious*, 2.) *mark some as doubtful but leave them in the text*, 3.) *transpose the order*, 4.) *introduce new readings into the text*. These are not far off from the guidelines of modern Textual Criticism today.

This would later be the same location and bastion of scholarship who's graduates include: *Philo, Clement of Alexandria, Marcion, Origen, Augustine, Eusebius, Jerome, Gresbach, Hort, Nestle, White, Metzger, Ehrman, and sympathizers.* It is known by *allegorical* interpretation instead of *literal*. The literal arose from *Antioch* (Acts 11:26), known as the *"Antiochian Method."* If you would like to hear what "Alexandrian" interpretation sounds like, listen to *Jordan Peterson's* work online covering Genesis or *Augustine's* work in *"City of God."* Peterson gives it a good try, but sadly, he has no idea what he's talking about the vast majority of the time. He is mostly appealing to "Jungian archetypes" when referring to Scripture, which is similar to what *Philo and Origen did in applying Platonism and Greek philosophy to Scripture in their day.* The only difference being that Jordan Peterson has not attempted to write a manuscript or translation. Philip Schaff, our Roman Catholic ASV friend, has a few words on the Antiochian Method:

> *"The Antiochian school seeks to explain the obvious grammatical and historical sense, which is rich enough for all purposes of instruction and edification. It takes out of the Word what is actually in it, instead of putting into it all sorts of foreign notions and fancies."*[69]

A few things that make a manuscript *"Alexandrian"* in its classification is its *"eloquence,"* and how *"polished"* they are, as mentioned previously (see pages 277, 283-6). In other words, it was written by the same bunch of people that are today now involved with revising bibles, which is why scholars favor these manuscripts. They were written *by* scholars *for* scholars, and scholars love reading other scholars' work. Seeing the *"hard work"* and *"amazing amount of time"* spent *on the work itself* reminds them of…*themselves.*

Don't think for a minute that this crew is simply "admiring" the work of the past; it's *self* admiration. The library of Alexandria was burned twice in history, once in 48 B.C. by the Romans under Julius Caesar and again in A.D.

---

[69] Philip Schaff, *"Prolegomena: The Life and Work of Chrysostom,"* ch. XIII

Two Bibles

642 by Caliph Omar ibn Al-Khattab, after the Muslims had taken the city. Much of what was there was lost in both occasions. While the Body of Christ was *at work preaching* and *witnessing to souls* using the Old Latin, Syrian, and the like such as Ulfilas, Sinaiticus ℵ was hidden away for over a thousand years, until someone came upon it in *a waste basket half burned*. B was *collecting dust on a Vatican shelf* for roughly the same amount of time. The Body of Christ, in it's greatest years of *revivals* and *street preaching* knew nothing about either manuscript. They were dead in a coffin.

The Roman Catholic years of corruption of the text began through Origen (A.D. 185-254) who believed that the Apocrypha *was inspired* and wanted to place two of the books before the N.T. books for children's learning as canon, LXX Septuagint (A.D. 200-450), Eusebius (A.D. 260-340), Council of Nicaea (A.D. 325), Jerome (A.D. 340-430), and Augustine (A.D. 400). Whereas, on the other side of history, we have faithful protectors of God's word in which many are still living today, with this same attitude as the Waldenses and Anabaptists; who of which *studied*, *protected*, and *cherished* the letters of Paul, the Gospels and other writings leading to Ignatius (A.D. 107), Polycarp (A.D. 155), and later, people like the Waldensians (A.D. 1100) coming from the Novatians, Montanists, Paterines, Bogamiles, Cathari, Paulicians, and the Vaudois bridging the gap from A.D. 200-1100—all carrying and *believing* the TR (KJB) in various forms.

These groups also shared the belief that *water baptism was a figure, infant baptism was unscriptural, salvation by grace, the Law of Moses was not N.T. doctrine, the church was a local assembly instead of the "Holy Mother Church."* Pope Innocent the III (A.D. 1198-1216) started a campaign to wipe them all out and burn their books. The Montanists (A.D. 200-600) viewed the Catholic Church as "carnal," while they viewed themselves as "spiritual"; often calling themselves *"the pneumatics"*[70] which essentially means, "those operated by the Spirit."

The Waldensian line of the Old Latin and Syriac made it all the way to the Textus Receptus and thus, tapping the watering hole in which the wellspring of the King James sprung. *The buck stopped there.* It appears that God is not interested in *"preserving the original"* anything. He seems to be more interested in making sure you have his *words* in a completed Book that you *believe*. If you had the *"originals"* now, you wouldn't know what to make of them and scholarship would be too busy altering and "polishing" them anyhow.

The Bible shows you the movement of God and his *adversary* throughout *history*. God's Book is a *history Book*, why is present day or from A.D. 33-1611 any different? *Scholars do not make any note of Lucifer through history or in evaluating manuscript evidence*. It appears to be *off their radar*; I am strictly talking about "Christian scholars" here. They do not concern themselves with such childish things as Lucifer or The Holy Spirit bearing witness to a text in history. Why not factor in *the second most powerful being* in the universe aside from the Godhead?—Because they are mentally unstable and Biblically illiterate.

The deplorable lineage of corrupted biblical texts stemming from the influence of the so-called "new scientific tenets of textual criticism," to which I alluded earlier, has begotten a host of Greek Texts that warrant close scrutiny. Among these ill-fated offspring, we encounter an array of names that echo their ghastly foundation: Bentley 1720, Hug 1808, Doedes 1844, Mattaei 1782, Mace 1729, Bengel 1734, Griesbach 1805, Semler 1756, Harwood 1776, Alter 1787, Birch 1789, Lachmann 1850, Tregelles 1870, Hort 1881, Wordsworth 1890, Nestle 1890, Souter 1910, Aland-Metzger 1966—their works serving as catalysts for the erosion of

---

[70] Philip Schaff, *"History of the Christian Church, Vol. II,"* Chapter 10, Sec. 110

textual fidelity. **"There is a way that seemeth right unto a man, but the end thereof are the ways of death"** (Prov. 16:25).

Semler, Griesbach, and Nestles, in their pursuit of intellectual novelty, have recklessly abandoned the bedrock of Scriptural preservation. Their texts, tinged with the impurities of subjective judgment and misplaced rationalism, stand as testament to the dangers of intellectual hubris unfettered from the reverence due to sacred texts.

The subsequent generations, including Hort, Metzger, White, and Ehrman continued down this treacherous path, sowing seeds of doubt and discord within the realm of biblical scholarship. Their collective legacy is one of disarray and instability, as they "neutrally" disregarded the sanctity of the sacred text in their relentless pursuit of speculative reconstructions. **"Lean not unto thine own understanding"** (Prov. 3:5).

These Greek Texts, conceived amidst an intellectual milieu intoxicated with the hubris (if even that) of textual criticism, have insidiously propagated a lineage of distortion and manipulation. Those Greek texts produced these "bibles": New World Testament, Rotherham, Fenton, NIV, Weymouth, RV, RSV, NRSV, New Jerusalem, AMP, NEB, The Living Bible, ASV, NASB, NRSV-CE, ESV and over 250 more.

> *"The editions of Sephanus, Beza, and the Elzevirs all present substantially the same text (TR); the variations are not of great significance and rarely affect the sense. However, in the nineteenth century numerous scholars set out to produce Greek texts which would reflect new principles of Textual Criticism. The resultant texts DIFFERED INCREASINGLY from the long-accepted texts of previous centuries and resulted*

Chapter 7

in a new English version [!], the English Revised Version (RV) [of W&Hort]."[71]

Some of the *"earliest and best manuscripts"*—enter stage left —Vaticanus B, Sinaiticus Aleph (‭א‬), Septuagint (LXX), Alexandrinus A, C, and D are among a few. The favorites are usually the "great uncial codices" ‭א‬, B, C, and D and now along with them, some assorted papyri, or *even* some Byzantine witnesses. As long as they *disagree* with KJ readings since the KJ readings are "late" due to that "Lucian Recension," then the readings are favored by critics, *even over papyri dated 100+ years before* ‭א‬, B, C, or D. (ex. Romans 5:6, 8:11, 9:3, 10:15, 12:1, 15:15, 21, etc.). Are we catching how the snow drifts yet? Most people who side with the Textus Receptus or King James tend to make a villain out of those manuscripts above, but *for good reason.*

B and ‭א‬ are both "Codices," which is a fancy word for *book* (like "codex") and written in *"Uncial"* form, which is a fancy way of saying capital Greek letters. They both contain a Greek Old Testament with Apocryphal books and a Greek New Testament. Both are dated around A.D. mid-Fourth Century. The Greek O.T. is what would be called *"The"* Septuagint by Christian scholars—those shrouded by tradition. Notice the singularity of *"The"* becomes splintered into multiplicity, as we find ourselves faced with the existence of two Septuagint's. There is no *"The"* Septuagint, **"And they shall turn away their ears from the truth, and shall be turned unto fables"** (2 Tim. 4:4). The only copies we have that are available of this "pre-Christ Greek Old Testament," possibly used by and quoted by writers of the N.T. are from around A.D. 150-340. How Paul could have used them in A.D. 50 is a mystery shrouded in the mists of time.

---

[71]Scrivener, *"New Testament in Koine Greek,"* Trinitarian Bible Society, 2022, Preface, page ii

The Uncials ℵ, B, C, and D often celebrated as the relics of ancient Christian literature, stand as formidable pieces of garbage within the labyrinthine realm of manuscript evidence. Their notoriety, however, extends beyond mere reverence, for they possess a certain degree of infamy that raises eyebrows and leaves one questioning the enduring allure of possessing the title of *"the oldest and best."* How is it that the fervor surrounding these manuscripts, and the scholars who champion them, such as Hort and Tischendorf, has yet to wane? Perhaps it is time for these enthusiasts to descend from their intellectual reverie, shaking off the drowsiness that accompanies their slumber atop open books, particularly those pages that expound upon the "new methods in textual criticism."

For example, with the addition of uncial A, in Luke 8:35-44, B stands alone 6 times; ℵ 8 times; C 15 times; D 93 times; and A 2 times. A and B stand together 1 time; B and ℵ 4 times; B and C 1 time; B and D 1 time; ℵ and C 1 time; C and D 1 time. Not once do all five agree against the majority. Yet, somehow these are all in the same *"text-type."* A "scholar" weighs these manuscripts more heavily "in terms of his own prejudgments."[72] Hort based his text on B while Tischendorf based his on ℵ. Since Nestles is *still* largely Hort's Greek text, it relies on B and these uncials above. Hort relied upon Tischendorf and Nestle relied upon Hort. Are we getting the picture yet? I'll continue. The very man who collated them said they were *corrupted*:

> *"So wide are the variations in the diction, so constant and inveterate the practice of expanding the narrative by means of interpolations."* From Scrivener's Introduction to Codex D

Let's look at the *facts* surrounding these manuscripts:

---

[72] Pickering *"The Identity of the New Testament Text,"* page 155, citing Colwell, *"External Evidence,"* page 3

Codex Vaticanus B: (mid-fourth Century) doesn't have much of a history really, or anything to hang ones hat on *other than its antiquity*. There are 7,578 changes in B from the Received Text of Erasmus, Elzevir, Colinaeus, and Beza. That amounts to about one change every verse (7,957 total verses in the N.T.). It has 197 readings found in *no* manuscript. B omits 2,877 words in the Gospels, adds 536, transposes 2,098, substitutes 935, and modifies 1,132.[73] The least bit of care went into its writing. The notion that א and B were meticulously crafted, possessing the imprint of scrupulous professional scribes, starts to fade into insignificance when subjected to *rational* scrutiny. It requires a **"sound mind"** (2 Tim. 1:7) to assess these manuscripts without being captivated by their illusory allure brought about by their propagators. Omissions range from single words, to two, or three words, or *entire clauses and verses, at an amount of 1,491 times* (Scrivener). That's just in the Gospel accounts alone. The biggest omission being that of the *last twelve verses of Mark* completely missing, when manuscript *evidence*, even from *before* Codex B, includes the passage.

The last twelve verses of Mark are in *every known Greek manuscript except three*; א, B, and 304; every Syriac except the Sinaitic; every Latin except k (which contains a slightly longer ending, going beyond verse 8 called "the shorter ending of Mark"); it's in all Coptic, and Gothic versions. It does *not* appear in the Armenian or Georgian versions. Irenaeus attests (~A.D. 150), as well as the Diatessaron to the last twelve verses going back to the 2nd Century. It has further witnesses and Church Fathers such as Hippolytus (A.D. 170-235) going back to the 2nd Century. Clement of Alexandria, Eusebius, and Origen are cited as *against* the passage, but they also don't comment on Matthew chapter 1

---

[73] Burgon, *"Revision Revised,"* page 12

so should we exclude that as well? *"...codices B and ℵ stand convicted of containing 'poison'."*[74]

This is why Burgon said things like, *"The foundation of your work is essentially rotten."* (Revision Revised, page 516) Westcott and Hort wouldn't listen to him because his speech was...*harsh*. Truth is truth, sugarcoated or not. Take it anyway you can get it.

Direct tampering of Codex B is *evident* in Luke 22:43-44, where Jesus Christ's "agony and bloody sweat" and ministering angel suffers omission in B but is included in ℵ, making B and ℵ *disagree amongst themselves*. Nestles text *follows* B by putting *brackets* around the text. Still not favoring *"the oldest and best"* now are we?—Yes, they are, and do. The text of Luke 22:43-44, as it stands in the AV, is quoted by a great number of Church Fathers such as Justin Martyr, Tatian, and Irenaeus in A.D. Second Century thus *predating* both ℵ and B. How about that "polished" text of B?—*"...no small portion of these are mere oversights of the scribe seems evident from the circumstance that this same scribe has repeatedly written words and clauses twice over..."*[75]

Codex Sinaiticus ℵ: has *"sinister resemblance"*[76] to B and probably originated from the same *"corrupt original."*[77] It contains 8,972 changes from the Receptus, which is more than one change per verse. It *disagrees from B* in 3,000 places in the Gospels alone, and this number *does not include spelling or variants between synonyms*. It has 60 changes in Matthew *chapter 1* from B alone. John 1-14 contains about 48% of the Receptus readings. It omits 3,455 words, adds 839, substitutes 1,114, transposes 2,299, and modifies 1,265. It has 443 readings found in *no manuscript including within its own*

---

[74] Pickering, *"The Identity of the New Testament Text,"* 2014, page 315

[75] Scrivener, *"Plain Introduction To the Criticism of the New Testament,"* Vol. I, 1894, page 120

[76] op cit., Burgon

[77] Ibid

324   Chapter 7

"Alexandrian" text-type. It was discovered by Tischendorf in a garbage can, half burned, at a Mt. Sinai monastery. He was not allowed to take it, but he ended up *stealing it*. ℵ dates around the same time as Codex B, and like it, *omits the last twelve verses of Mark* and in like fashion shows horrendous signs of tampering such as the alteration to the ending to John. Codex B keeps the text making the two *"oldest and best"* in disagreement with each other *again*, while the majority of texts agree on keeping the passage. These blunders are more than *"scribal error."* The omission of our Lord saying **"forgive them; for the know not what they do"** and the inscription on the cross **"in letters of Greek, and Latin, and Hebrew,"** is an obvious sign of the scribe altering the text to try and have it match other places or resolve "discrepancies." The spear that pierces Jesus' side is done *while he is still alive* in both B and ℵ.

What sort of "scribal errors" are those? *"As for Codex ℵ, the folded sheet containing the end of Mark and beginning of Luke is, quite frankly, a forgery."*[78] He said this because even the discoverer of the manuscript (Tischendorf) warned that those pages appeared to be written *by a different hand* with *different ink*. This is quite an admission from someone who superciliously and superstitiously favored the text of ℵ. The lines of Mark leading up to the ending at verse 8 is shown to take up more space *on purpose* to try and fill as much space as possible in order for the manuscript to *appear as if the Gospel of Mark had ended at verse 8*. This makes ℵ an invalid witness against the omission of Mark 16:9-20.

The ending of Mark (Mark 16:9-20) is a very interesting passage to omit; do you know what's *in* that ending? Mark gives you *the signs* of an Apostle, **"And these signs shall follow them that believe; In my name shall they cast out devils; they shall speak with new tongues; They shall take up serpents; and if they drink any deadly thing, it shall not**

---

[78] op cit., Pickering, page 312

hurt them; they shall lay hands on the sick, and they shall recover" (Mark 16:17-18). Now, wouldn't this be utterly *convenient* for a church *that based its hierarchy on Apostolic Succession?* According to the Catholic Church, Peter was the first Pope who passed "the keys" down a long line of later Popes *in Apostolic succession*. This would make every Pope an *Apostle. Papa does not have the signs.* Many were actually poisoned by their "allies" while in office during the Dark Ages in attempts at sitting upon the golden throne. No signs of an Apostle, no worries! *Delete it.* How convenient for the *"Holy Mother Church."*

Further on the subject, why on earth would a scribe end it with "ἐφοβοῦντο γάρ" at verse 8? If you are to believe Metzger, White, Ehrman, YouTube personalities, Hort, Wallace, etc., you would have admitted that The Holy Ghost would leave the disciples **"afraid"** after an angel said **"be not afrightened"** in verse 6, and that Jesus would leave them **"afraid"** in verse 8 by *not* appearing to bear witness of His own Resurrection, *in His own Gospel account...about Him.* Does that sound like a Holy Ghost filled scribe? The Holy Ghost who **"proceedeth from the Father, he shall testify of me"** (John 15:26). Nestles text *still* has it in double brackets and new versions use vague footnotes casting doubt on the passage.

Many critics will convince the public that because there is a "shorter ending" of Mark out there, and that the "longer ending" (16:9-20) was written in a *"different style"* than Mark usually writes, then that means (despite credible *evidence*) that the ending does *not* belong in your Bible. Is this true?

How did Irenaeus accept the passage as genuine, when he himself was a speaker of Kione Greek? Surly he would have noted the "change in style" or passed it off as a non-valid part of the Holy text. All the other Kione speaking scribes which copied the passage didn't seem to think twice about its genuineness, but somehow the modern destructive critic, who thinks he has *more knowledge* of Kione than its *own native speakers from the time period* will tell you: "it's *not* genuine." Irenaeus knew Polycarp personally who knew the Apostle John, who knew Mark *personally.* Irenaeus says that Mark wrote it.[79] It did not seem to be an issue until it reached the "trained" scribes of Alexandria, Egypt.

To sum up Mark 16:9-20 we have every Greek manuscript except 3 (א, B, and 304) containing the passage, but א disqualified itself (see above), so really only 2.

Every Greek lectionary except one.

Every Syriac (~1,000) except one (Sinaitic).

Every Latin manuscript (~8,000) except one (k).

Every Coptic except one.

Church Fathers quotations, and the passage has evidence going back to the 2nd Century.

Not in the Armenian or Georgian versions.

Those are *deliberate* changes based on the scribe's knowledge, intent, and presumptions of the text he is working on—just as the critics who work on Nestles and Metzger's texts do *today*. This is no *"copyist."* Both B and א, again change Matthew 11:19 to fit James' **"faith without works is dead,"** by replacing **"her children"** with "her works" in a blind attempt at making sense of Church Age doctrine. Both B and א change Peter's denial in order to make the **"cock crow"** *make sense to themselves* and the reader (obvious alteration). These are signs of *obvious collusion* and *tampering*.

The simple fact that the text you hold in your hands as a King James Bible is attested to having so many supposed "errors" is just *further proof* that there was *no collusion* in the making of its text. It's pure, unadulterated, unedited, "Parental-Advisory needed" content. I will get more into *Peter's denial* in the chapter called, *"Saving Private Ehrman."*

The account in Matthew's Gospel of the angels in chapter 28 was also *altered in a blind attempt to make sense of the text*

---

[79] Ibid, page 314

(see above). To bring Matthew 27:34 into agreement with Mark 15:23, "wine" was used instead of **"vinegar."** A few Geographical issues were given-a-go at being *"corrected"* in Luke 1:26, 14:13, and Mark 1:28 etc. That's a few in the N.T. alone, from the *"oldest and best"* manuscripts. How could anyone who is *sane* admit that these are either *"pure"* or *"neutral"* or the *"best"*? You can't, unless you are insane. By the very *fact* that א and B disagree some *3,000* times means that one of them is *wrong* 3,000 times, or one of them is *right* 3,000 times, or they are both wrong. If you brought א and B to a courtroom as one testifying against the other, you would be laughed out of court. The witness would be deemed unusable in a court of law. These are *facts*, not "scholarly conjectures."

Some *heretical readings* found in א and other "Alexandrian" manuscripts that either *deny* or *subtract* from the deity of Jesus Christ are:[80]

- Mark 1:1 which omits **"Son of God"** (in א)
- John 1:34 which reads "God's chosen One" instead of **"Son of God"** (in א)
- John 3:13 omits **"who is in heaven"** (in א, also in B and 𝔓75, 𝔓66)
- John 6:69 reads "the Holy One of God" instead of **"the Christ, the Son of the living God"** (in א, also in B and 𝔓75)
- John 9:35 reads "Son of man" instead of **"Son of God"** (א, also in B)
- John 9:38-39 omits **"And he said, Lord, I believe. And he worshiped Him."** (א, also in 𝔓75)
- John 19:5 **"Behold the man"** (is omitted in 𝔓66)
- Luke 23:42 eliminate deity (א, also in B and 𝔓75)

---

[80] Edward F. Hills, *"Believing Bible Study,"* Third Edition 1991, page 76-77. Authors Note: The first six are from Hills, the additions were not taken from his work.

- Romans 14:10 **"Christ"** is omitted (א, also in B)
- Luke 23:45 has a *regular* eclipse occurring (א, also in B and 𝔓75)
- Luke 12:31 **"God"** is omitted (א, also in B)
- John 10:29 has the Father losing his greatness (א, also in B)

The evident *tampering* and obvious *corruption* of these texts have made "scholars" come up with new ideas on what *"scribal errors"* are, **"For the time will come when they will not endure sound doctrine; but after their own lusts shall they heap to themselves teachers, having itching ears"** (2 Tim. 4:3).

One, which I find fascinatingly dull is that the scribes *weren't* "professional" scribes in the beginning (A.D. 33-300) so there are *more* errors between manuscripts; in other words, they were dumb and didn't know how to copy a paper. How then does one explain the *total depravity* of א and B? These are supposed to be highly educated *"professionals"* who graduated from Alexandria seminary.

To tally everything up:
- א drops 10-40 words on certain passages, letters and words, even whole sentences are written twice.
- 7,578 changes in B from the TR.
- 8,972 changes in א from the TR.
- 𝔓66 varies from the TR in 694 places and has over 900 "clear, indubitable errors" in John.
- 𝔓66 disagrees with B in 620 places and from א in 852 places.
- 𝔓66, B, and א only agree 264 times in 615 verses.
- B has 589 readings in the Gospels alone that are unique to itself which affect 858 words.
- א has 1,460 unique readings in it that affect 2,640 words.

- 𝔓45 has 90 itacisms, 275 singular readings (unique readings with no other manuscript support) and 10% are nonsensical.
- 𝔓75 has 145 itacisms, and out of the 257 singular (unique) readings, 25% of them are nonsensical
- 𝔓66 has 216 careless readings as well as 400 itacisms, 482 singular readings which 40% are nonsensical and "plain errors."[81]
- 𝔓66 shows a 44.6% agreement with ℵ, and 50.4% with B, and 47.5% agreement with the TR, and 51.2% with 𝔓75.
- 𝔓45 shows 42% agreement with B, and 40% agreement with the TR.

"If you were asked to write out the Gospel of John by hand, would you make over 400 mistakes? (Footnote...I am trying by the suggested experiment to help the reader visualize how poor these early copies really are.)"[82]

One cannot help but question the suitability of presenting the aforementioned witnesses as credible evidence in a court of law. The pinnacle of Christian scholarship seems to lie in the perplexing task of deliberating (after meticulously considering glosses, additions, dittography, substitutions, interrelationships, homoioteleuton, erroneous abbreviations, accidental omissions, and amalgamation of texts) whether Mark 1:2-3 should read "Isaiah" instead of **"prophets,"** despite the fact that the passage in question quotes from two

---

[81] Dean Burgon, *"The Last 12 Verses of Mark,"* 1871, pages 73-86 and *"The Revision Revised,"* pages 11-14. Also see Wilbur Pickering, *"The Identity of the New Testament Text,"* pages 129-132, 151. David Fuller, *"True or False."* Ernest Colwell, *"Scribal Habits in Early Papyri,"* 1965, pages 374-376, 378-379, 387.

[82] Pickering about 𝔓66 and other early papyri, , *"The Identity,"* page 131

prophets. Such an endeavor appears utterly baffling, bordering on the realm of insanity!

Do you see how the wind blows, yet? You have to be *mentally unstable* or *demon possessed* to get that, man. That is far-out, wild stuff right there. What in the word.

Sometimes they even will put the reference to Malachi in the margin! Oh, the *"light"* of the new versions! What would I do without the *"newly shed light"* on such passages? Oh my! Do you know how *mentally depraved* one has to be to do *that* and then *rationalize the "correction" to the text?* It's the same type of person that believed the Vatican Codex B is one of the *"best"* manuscripts after noting all the above. What the Christian scholar has is a collection of Greek texts in which agree some 55-70% of the time, and *take the agreements* as the *"Word"* of God, and then hide then rest from the *"lesser common folk"* who just don't understand without accepting the *"advanced theories of Hort"* or taking 6 years of Greek in seminary. You wouldn't want to be *"identified with the arrogant superstition of Bible-belt fundamentalism"* now would you?[83] Not a fine scholar like yourself? No, no, we can't have that. Meanwhile, the TR has geographically diverse attestation from before ℵ and B and coming through the likes of the Paulicians, Novatians, Montanists, Waldenses, Albigenses, etc.

They have no final authority but themselves. They are their own gods, Genesis 3:5, **"ye shall be as gods."**

Having said all of this, Metzger responds:

> *"In light of the striking similarities in text between the fourth-century B and early third-century 𝔓75, it is clear* [!] *that the Christian scholars* [!] *of Alexandria worked assiduously to preserve* [!] *an accurate* [!] *form of the text... Alexandrian witnesses today are classified*

---

[83] See footnote 1 in *"The Actors"*

according to whether they preserve the excellent [!] 𝔓75-B line of text...the carefully [!] preserved and relatively pristine [!] Alexandrian text."[84]

Metzger thinks that the *scholarly* scribes of Alexandria *preserved* the "original" text when all they did was *alter* the texts they *did* have into mangled blasphemous pieces of garbage only to resurface later to usher in the apostasy of the Church in the form of Nestles and its accompanying "bibles." How could you take that data above and *honestly* say what Metzger did? He leaves all that information out in his work cited. He teaches the line he gave in his book to all of his students, *and they believe it*. It never seemed to occur to Metzger that the Vatican Codex B and the waste basket Sinaiticus א were *"pristine" in appearance* because they were *shelved* for much of Christian history...BECAUSE NO ONE READ THEM. Sinaiticus has more than 10 different hands correcting the text according to the man that collated it; Scrivener.

Tischendorf's Greek text had a built in bias for א, because he *"discovered"* it. Westcott and Hort had a built in bias for Vaticanus B, Nestles Greek text has a built in bias *against the Textus Receptus* (KJB). The bias for the Alexandrian text is built *into the the very fabric of textual criticism.*

Some points of study found in Nestles Greek text for the Greek student or the pastor of the local church to look further in their own studies are listed below. It's the Greek text behind the ESV, NIV, NRSV, etc., that a portion of your congregation is no-doubt using in their study.

a. John 6:47 ὁ πιστεύων εἰς ἐμὲ (**"He that believeth on me"**) has ~99.5% of the evidence behind it yet Nestles

---

[84] Metzger, *'The Text of the New Testament,"* page 278

sides with ὁ πιστεύων ("the one believing/who believes").

b. John 7:8 οὔπω has ~96% of the evidence including 𝔓66, 𝔓75, and B, *f*1, *f*13, and 𝔐, yet οὐκ is used by Nestles siding with ℵ and D which disagree between themselves a great bit. Favor has been given to ℵ over older papyri/manuscripts and a vast line of witnesses.

c. John 1:18 Nestles contains the gnostic reading of two gods, *"only begotten god"* (μονογενὴς Θεὸς) with ~0.1% support and siding with 𝔓66, 𝔓75, ℵ*1, B, C*, 33. Hardly any modern translation will actually translate what Nestles text says anymore because of the backlash from previous translations which did translate it. The reading ὁ μονογενὴς υἱός (**"the only begotten Son"**) has ~99.6% of textural support. Favor has been given to the older papyri and uncials (see "b" above for "scholarly emendation" at work).

d. 1 Timothy 3:16 still has ὃς (who) instead of Θεὸς (**"God"**), which has ~98% of support behind it and pre-dates "the great uncials." New versions use the reading with *no* evidence whatsoever, "He."

e. Luke 23:45 still contains the natural "eclipse" (ἐκλιπόντος) instead of **"was darkened"** (ἐσκοτίσθη) which has ~98% of the evidence.

f. James 5:16 where **"faults"** has been changed to "sins." This has been changed on the basis of manuscript ℵ and Jerome's Latin Vulgate after he had edited the Old Latin for Pope Damasus in the late A.D. Fourth-Century. This verse, when changed to "sins" is the very verse in which Catholics use for "confessional." The Greek word for "faults" is παραπτώματα which the TR reads and Byzantine manuscripts. The Greek word for "sins" as found in Nestles Greek text is ἁμαρτίας. They are *not the same word* nor do they share the same Greek *root*. This can be found in the RV, RSV, ASV, NIV, etc. It agrees with

Westcott and Hort's 1881 Greek text. The AV agrees with Tyndale, Geneva, Bishop's, Coverdale, and Great Bible. The NKJV says "trespasses" while claiming to be just an updated KJB to rid it of *"archaic"* language. It gives a vague footnote that says, *"some mss say therefore confess your sins,"* as if that is going to help the Bible reader discern anything useful at all. Nestles sides with ℵ and B over 90% of Greek evidence.

g. James 4:9 the TR μεταστραφήτω is substituted with μετατραπήτω in Nestles Greek text with *no evidence whatsoever* behind it thus violating their own rules of textural criticism, going *against* ℵ and B because…you get one guess—ℵ and B agree with the Textus Receptus in this case. They side with religious fanaticism: Westcott and Hort and Tischendorf's Greek Text.

h. 2 Corinthians 4:6 **"Jesus"** has been omitted. The KJB reading of **"Jesus"** may be found in ℵ, and 𝔓46 which predated B. It was omitted in B. Favor has been given to B over older readings such as 𝔓46. Nestles 28th edition still has **"Jesus"** in brackets.

i. Acts 28:1 Nestles has changed ἐπέγνωσαν into ἐπέγνωμεν with *no evidence* behind it whatsoever, violating their own rules for textual criticism and thus based on conjecture, ἐπέγνωμεν may also be found in Westcott and Hort's text.

j. 1 Corinthians 4:14 νουθετῶ was changed to νουθετῶν which goes against B, 𝔓46, D, and many others but is suggested by ℵ, A, C, and a few others. 𝔓46 predates ℵ and B. The reading of "νουθετῶ[ν]" in Nestles was only put into brackets *after* the 25th edition. Previous to inserting the brackets, the reading change away from the Textus Receptus was given *with all evidence against it*. The evidence being for the TR reading is 𝔓46, B, D and others. No evidence was given at the time to suggest a different spelling other than Westcott and Hort and Tischendorf which had access to ℵ.

k. In Matthew 26:22 ἕκαστος αὐτῶν which has support from 𝔓37, 𝔓45, A, K, W, Γ, Δ, Π, Θ, Σ, Φ, *f*1, 565, 579, 700, 1241, *l*844, *l*2211, 𝔐, sy-h, and sy-p. Westcott and Hort's Greek text reads just as Nestles does with the reading of εἷς ἕκαστος. Its support is, ℵ, B, C, L, Z, , 33, 102, 892, 0281, and sa. Here, Nestles favors the W&H reading over the TR, even though the TR reading is *backed by numerous "ancient" authorities*. (Exemplifies the built in hate for the KJB.)

l. John 6:10 reads ὡσεὶ in the TR and has support from, 𝔓28, 𝔓66, A, Γ, Δ, Θ, Λ, Π, unc9, and 𝔐. The Byzantine tradition *agrees with the oldest* and making it an unbroken line of transmission, but watch what Nestles does next; the Nestles text, again agrees with W&H in the reading of ὡς. Its support being 𝔓75, ℵ, B, D, L, N, W, Ψ, 579, and 892. It favors Vaticanus and Sinaiticus over the reading in which the oldest line up with the Majority Byzantine text (𝔐). That was W&H's attitude. He did say it was a *"vile"* text. We are supposedly in a new age and the *"age of W&H is over"*—yeah, okay.

m. Mark 8:13 reads εἰς τὸ πλοῖον in the TR with the support of 𝔓45, D, H, K, N, U, W, Γ, Π, 0131, *f*13, sr-sp, bo-pt. The W&H and Nestles reading is... *nothing*, with the evidence of ℵ, B, C, L, and Δ.

n. We again have Nestles and W&H lining up with the reading of *(blank)* in John 13:23 and its supporting manuscripts of B, C*, L, Ψ, 3, 80, 87, 892, 1424, f-scr, sy-s. On the TR side we have the much *"older and better"* reading of δε with its supporting manuscripts, 𝔓66, ℵ, A, C(2), D, W, X, Γ, Δ, Θ, Λ, Π, unc8, *f*1, *f*13, 33, 579, 700, a, c, f, ff2, q, bo, sy-p and 𝔐. The reading goes back to A.D. 200 *at least*. This time Nestles and Hort sided with B against the praised ℵ, *because* ℵ *agreed with the Majority-Byzantine text,* in these cases it's to be disregarded as having any credibility. It appears that there is little "method" to "textural criticism" (1 Tim. 6:20), it is little more than guess-work. The little of it that *could* be called *"science"* is nothing more than a rotten foundation that the entire house is built upon: the "Alexandrian" witnesses.

For further study, these verses should be taken into account: Luke 4:44; John 7:53-8:11; Mark 16:9-20; Luke 3:33; Matthew 19:17; Mark 6:22; John 6:11; Acts 19:16; Matthew 1:7, 10, 5:22, 10:10, 21:5, 1:25, 6:13; 1 Corinthians 5:1; John 18:24; Mark 6:8; Luke 2:33; Luke 22:43-44; Mark 15:39. Not only from a basis of textural evidence but from how they would affect the text as a whole; **"a little leaven...."** They no doubt have a cumulative negative effect on the text.

All "textural criticism" has done is reinstate the Catholic text of Jerome and the Dark Ages. That is the height of man when he disregards God and claims neutrality in working with the text of the Bible.

The rot continues on and on.

As mentioned in the *"Introduction"* of this work, where in the Bible does it mention an "original" anything being referred to as Scripture? It isn't there. It is explicitly absent! It appears that the concept of *preserving* God's words took precedence over an emphasis on the *"originals."* To say that God doesn't know how to handle the mistakes through the copying of manuscripts is to *deny* the historical account of the Bible itself. Yet, surprisingly, this is what is taught and propagated in every seminary across the nation. Men have been making mistakes since the fall of Adam and Eve, God has had *to deal* with those mistakes, and they have not hindered His plans—or do you think they have? Do you honestly think that an all powerful Being who **"made the stars...ALSO"** is worried about the "mistakes of men" getting involved with His *promise* of preservation? That somehow God cannot provide you an inerrant Book? God's plans involve *preserving* His **"words"** (Psa. 12:6-7; Prov. 30:5-6; Psa 119:89; Matt. 5:18, etc.), *not the "fundamentals," or the "theories," or the "message."* W-O-R-D-S.

The reader will also note a constant theme: people appear to be trying to rid the world of *one* Book. There were many bible versions just after the King James came out, and before. Why did this Book stick and *not* the others for some 400 years? Why did the ever-so-popular Geneva Bible and Bishop's Bible fall out of favor by the English speaking world? What made it the accepted, no, *"Authorized"* Bible of the Protestant Reformation—*even after the old English within it had fallen out of use*?

People went through many attempts of shutting it down (Jesuit Gunpowder Plot, Catholic Spanish Armada, Jesuit Rheims bible, etc.), and even *after* the Book came out, it was under such fierce attack. Somehow, with all odds against it, it became *the worlds number one selling Book of all time* (including the combined sales of the other top 5 best selling books of all time). How does one explain that? It became the *Authorized Version by the Body of Christ*. **"Where the word of a king is, there is power"** (Ecc. 8:4). It has **"power"** behind it.

All one has to do is believe what the Book says about Rome (Matt. 2:16, 27:2, 31; Acts 12:1-6; 2 Tim. 4:6, etc.), Egypt (Gen. 50:5; Exod. 13:19; Matt. 2:15; Acts 6:9, etc.), and Antioch, Syria (Acts 11:26, 13:1-4, etc.) *to have a better understanding of "textural criticism" than 90% of seminary students and graduates.* That's what the whole thing comes down to—do you believe what the Book says about itself?

Let me ask you a question dear reader: What are the **"fruits"** of new versions? You may say, *"More people are Christians than ever before."* You would be right, but aren't there more people than ever before, on earth? Now, what about all those people who are *leaving* Christianity for the world since, say *1885*? There are people leaving it in groves and have been in increasing numbers since 1885.

In the days of the Roman Empire, people left it for fear of being martyred. Many dying a martyrs death while "sticking to their guns." Why are people leaving it today? You say, *"Well, that is a many faceted issue."* Why, its fear. People are scared of believing in a "fairy tale" story and because people like Dawkins make more rational sense to them than their own teachers did who "teach" them *about* Bible. They are lulled back into the world by the very institutions and leadership that they trusted to teach them *Truth*.

When speaking in terms of the seminary student or the Christian who has a desire for study, they *are taught right out of the faith*. If they aren't taught out of the faith, then they are *taught how to lie when it comes to matters of final authority* and become *cloned* stormtroopers who end up *in local churches* or being a tenured professor *teaching* another generation of students on *how to lie*. They go on to perpetuate the deception—to reeducate en masse. The fundamental principles of modern textural criticism, as practiced today, are *doubt* and the *denial* of Scripture at its very core—the denial of preservation and acceptance of the *"lost"* originals.

If the reader would like to look further into the subject mentioned in this chapter, there is a wealth of information in the books mentioned within the footnotes, which are kept out of many seminaries *intentionally*. The authors are doctors, professors, schoolmasters, and writers; some with more than four earned degrees from such institutions as Princeton, Harvard, and Yale, who either side with the King James or the Textus Receptus behind it and by doing so become outcasts from the castle of "academia."

In the next chapter I delve into the details surrounding a student and the *"master"* who taught him everything he knows. The student could not come to terms with *"the oldest and best"* manuscripts and their differences, nor could he come to terms with the *"inspired originals"* being *"lost."* He could not come to terms with the promise of preservation in the Bible given his *"education."* He saw all the variants in Greek manuscripts and then decided that the *"originals"* are unattainable. This revelation left him devoid of *any* "original" or *any* bible in *any* language or version that could serve as a reliable final authority. With his foundations shattered, he eventually abandoned his faith, subsequently rising to become the most influential figure in the field of textual criticism in our time. I give you—Bart D. Ehrman.

Chapter 8: Saving Private Ehrman

"Holding faith, and good conscience; which some having put away concerning the faith have made shipwreck" — 1 Timothy 1:19

MARK 2:26 "How he went into the house of God in the days of Abiathar the high priest, and did eat the shewbread, which is not lawful to eat but for the priests, and gave also to them which were with him?"

vs

1 Sam 21:1-6 "Then came David to Nob to Ahimelech the priest: and Ahimelech was afraid at the meeting of David, and said unto him, Why art thou alone, and no man with thee?...So the priest gave him hallowed bread: for there was no bread there but the shewbread, that was taken from before the LORD, to put hot bread in the day when it was taken away."

Problem: Did Abiathar or Ahimelech give David the shewbread to eat?

Answer: This is one of the last threads pulled from Bart D Ehrman's faith at Princeton Seminary by a Greek professor. He was shown this "discrepancy" and then decided to be an atheist after years of pounding in Greek classrooms about "errors" and the such as I have pointed out thus far.

Ehrman[1] either never got the answers, or he chose to not believe them. Pickering appeared to have worked it out just fine, and he graduated from Dallas Theological seminary just like Wallace did. Again, we see this division amongst the scholars just as it was in A.D. 200-400. This is a serious *"problem"* (if it's actually a problem) because it would make Jesus Christ a *liar*. Since **"God is not a man, that he should lie"** (Num. 23:19), Mark 2:26 would make Jesus Christ a bold faced liar.

Let's see what Ehrman got himself into and how he tried to make a liar out of God Almighty. We should know better by now, and shall stick to the old proverb when concerning ourselves with the likes of Ehrman and friends: **"let God be true, but every man a liar"** (Rom. 3:4).

So, what's the light on the passage? In 2 Samuel 8:17, it says, **"And Zadok the son of Ahitub, and Ahimelech the son of Abiathar, were the priests; and Seraiah was the scribe."** Abiathar was a high priest *with* his father and his father died at the hand of Saul (1 Sam. 22). There can be *two* high priests (Jer. 52:24; 2 Kings 25:18; Luke 3:2).

If we look at the *English,* as it stands, you see **"in the days of"** in Mark 2:26. Abiathar and Ahimelech were certainly *in the same time period*, for **"the days of"** denotes a *period of time* in the Bible: Genesis 10:25, 11:32, 14:1, 25:7, 26:1, 15, 18, 30:14, etc. Abiathar was Ahimelech's son. It is wise to note that **"Abiathar"** has *a father* of the name **"Ahimelech"** *and* he named his own son the *same name* of his father, as seen in 2 Samuel 8:17 (c.f 1 Samuel 22:20, 11). Using the same name was common amongst Levitical priests (see 1 Chron. 6). There is no issue there.

---

[1] According to the book, Ehrman is still saved (2 Tim. 2:13; 1 Cor. 12:13). He's just causing a lot of harm in the Body of Christ.

The question is: *why* is Jesus Christ bringing your attention to the time period of **"Abiathar"** in Mark 2:26? Why would he want to bring that up in front of a bunch of Pharisees? The text, as it stands in the English is *correct* and there is no issue seen with it as it stands in the AV. As said previously, Abiathar *was* **"in the days of"** his father who gave David the shewbread. The passage is actually quite revealing.

David is one of the greatest *types* of Christ in the Bible aside from Joseph. David is in exile from Saul, who is trying to kill him (1 Sam. 19:10). David is the rightful heir to the throne and king via his anointing (1 Sam. 16:13). This happens to be just what Jesus is going through at the time of the Gospel accounts: just as Jesus Christ is the rightful heir to the Throne and He too was anointed (Luke 3:22), He is also in exile from that Throne; He has yet to sit upon it and the Pharisees are trying to kill Him (John 5:18, 7:1, 30, 10:39, etc.). He has to deal with all this to fulfill Scripture. He must be plotted against and be given the Throne, but not sit upon it yet, just as David's case in 1 Samuel.

If a Jew, at the time, went back to read 1 Samuel 21-23 and its surrounding context again, they would come across a few things of notoriety. They would find that Saul was a raging demon-possessed usurper of the priesthood, who was trying to kill David, who of which was *innocent* (1 Sam. 14:35, 7:17, 16:16, 19:9, 24:9-15). Saul kills Abiathar's father (a man of God) in his rage to find David and kill him (1 Sam. 22:16-17). The Pharisees were *also* a demon-possessed priestly class (Matt. 23) trying to plot the murder of an innocent man—Jesus Christ.

What about "the" Greek? Both the Greek in Nestles and the TR of Mark 2:26 say the same thing (ἐπὶ Ἀβιαθάρ). Pickering states, "the preposition here, epi, [ἐπὶ] is *the most versatile* of the Greek prepositions, and one of its many meanings/uses is 'toward'. The standard lexicon, BDAG, lists fully *eighteen areas of meaning.*"[2]

In no way was the AV text in error in its translation. *What was Ehrman learning in seminary? How could something so simple trip him up?* He certainly *was not* learning Bible by any means of the imagination. He is a fantastic philologist—but what happened? *What* on earth was he doing there? Let's take a closer look...

Ehrman originally went to Moody Bible Institute, which is traditionally "conservative." He then went to Wheaton College for a degree in English literature. He then makes a last pitstop at Princeton Theological Seminary to study under a Greek professor that was recommended to him by another professor of Greek while attending Wheaton.

This professor's name was *Bruce Metzger (1914-2007)*. You have heard a lot about him thus-far, but he is, quite possibly, the most *destructive New Testament critic* who has ever lived in the 20th-21st Century. Hort took the cake in the 19th Century. Like Hort and Origen, he believes that *Genesis 1-3 is a myth*.[3] He, like Hort, believes that the *"oldest and best"* are א, B and other uncial codices of the "Alexandrian" variety. He also propagated many of Hort's theories.

Ehrman writes about his teacher that he was, *"relatively certain that the original text probably survives among our manuscripts somewhere* [!], *almost certainly in our oldest and best manuscripts* [!]*."*[4] He also believes that there are mistakes in the Bible, but after all of this he calls himself biblically "conservative." Metzger also believes[5] that the Shepherd of Hermas and the Epistles of Clement are inspired.

---

[2] Pickering, *"The Identity of the New Testament Text,"* 2014, page 216

[3] Bart Ehrman's personal blog: https://ehrmanblog.org/why-dont-you-believe-like-your-teacher-dr-metzger/

[4] Ibid

[5] Bruce M. Metzger, *"The Canon of the New Testament,"* 1997, page 256, 211.

Metzger believes that 1 Peter 3:19 is most likely an error. *Why?* He doesn't understand in the slightest as to what it's talking about. *So, its an error.* He learned that from his teachers. He says it's based on *"style"* yet, in *2 Peter 2:4-5* you have your answer (Cf. 1 Peter 3:19-20). Jesus Christ went to hell after his crucifixion (Acts 2:27-31; Eph. 4:9) and preached to some *angels* and also some other *people* when He was there (1 Peter 4:6). That is *two* different epistles by Peter talking about the *same thing*. Those *angels* were in the days of Noah, which would place them at Genesis 6 (Cf. Jude 6)—they were **"disobedient"** because they **"kept not their first estate."** They **"saw the daughters of men that they were fair."** He gave the two groups two different sermons while He was down there in hell.

Metzger doesn't *believe* what he reads so he missed the whole thing. He passed this on to his students. Conveniently, Metzger believes that 2 Peter was not written by Peter.[6] He is also a member of the "Catholic Biblical Association," this is not surprising given the NRSV and its many Catholic readings (Matt. 1:25; Luke 2:33; Col. 1:14; 1 Tim. 3:16, and about 40 more) which Ehrman *uses as source texts to quote from in his book when he isn't translating the Greek himself* (*"Jesus, Interrupted,"* preface, page xii).

Ehrman says in his book, *"Jesus, Interrupted,"* (2009), *"I realized that I was pretty good at Greek,"* so logically to continue his studies further, he wanted to study under *"the most revered scholar,"* I would also want to do the same; so would most for that matter, but Metzger, who just *"happened to teach at Princeton."* "Just happened" to teach there? Surly, your prowess, and aptitude of grasping sequential events can explain the phenomenon of this synchronism? I do say old boy. Well, Metzger was at Princeton because Princeton housed some well-known destructive critics of the N.T., and Metzger is *a liberal* who generated the RSV and the NRSV

---

[6] op cit, Ehrman

(both *liberal*) which destroyed the Reformation text by favoring Vaticanus and Sinaiticus *against* TR readings, just as Hort did.

Graduates include: *B. B. Warfield, John Gresham Machen, Archibald Alexander Hodge, Eugene Carson Blake, Caspar René Gregory, William Henry Green*, etc.

All the names above are "recognized, distinguished scholars of the first rank." None of them believed any book on this earth was "*the* Bible" anytime they mentioned it and were their own final authority.

For Example: *Warfield,* who was a professor of theology at Princeton says in, *"The Person and Work of Christ"* (1950) that Jesus came for "social health," and Christ would never sit upon the Throne of David, that Jews would never regain Palestine, no Millennial reign of Christ, and no Judgment Seat of Christ. Some *"theologian."* Like Schaff, (See the *"Introduction"*) he believed that the **"leaven"** of Matthew 13:33 was "the Gospel." The leaven was destined to improve the structure of society, *without* Jesus Christ returning.[7] Leaven is never a reference to improving *anything.*

Ehrman is *an atheist having the same approach to the Bible and to final authority as the modern day "conservative" or evangelical.* He learned it from Metzger and Metzger learned it from Warfield, Hort, Streeter, Griesbach, Augustine, and Origen. Ehrman was also on the NRSV committee *with* Metzger.[8] Some colleagues of Metzger's will call him *"conservative,"* but that was when it was in-fashion to be "a conservative" and a Christian. He clearly holds a liberal view. A *"conservative"* Christian Biblically is not the same thing today as it was in the 1930's-50's and before. A "conservative" today is essentially "liberal" in their views. This is why White and many others *call themselves, and each other, "conservative."* They aren't when it comes to the Bible. They

---

[7] Also see Ruckman, *"The Christian Liar's Library,"* 1997, pages 12-13

[8] https://ehrmanblog.org/bruce-metzger-and-my-loss-of-faith-a-blast-from-the-past/

have adopted the very view in which the early conservatives *fought against*. It mirrors politics in the States as many "conservatives" are actually just "classical liberals" or somewhere along those lines, and the "liberals" are mostly just socialistic Marxists. This is not "progression," this is *decadence*. These are the small steps into moral and societal collapse. It is the rot of an untreated wound that leads to death.

Ehrman says about his scholastic career, *"faith commitments are irrelevant to scholarship."*[9] There is that good old *"neutral approach"* that Hort had. He also tells us about his teacher Metzger, *"it was the research that mattered, not the personal faith commitments."*[10] In all the time that the two spent together, *"Metzger and I never talked about either my faith or his."*[11] They did spend a lot of time together according to Ehrman, *"We had an exceptionally close relationship. I was closer to him than any other student he had over his long and illustrious career."*[12]

How could two adamantly committed students of Greek and the N.T. *not talk about their own faith when going over the N.T. together?* This is the "academic" setting where new translations are made. Metzger made Ehrman's career, according to him.[13] These professors who are "well established" and "revered" can make or break someones career with a stroke of the pen, as Metzger has done to many with his *opinions* while teaching, writing, or presenting on certain matters such as Burgon or Sturz concerning the Byzantine tradition.

Education in the world of academia is *almost* as important as politics. Ehrman goes on to give you insight into what

---

[9] Ibid

[10] Ibid

[11] Ibid

[12] https://ehrmanblog.org/why-dont-you-believe-like-your-teacher-dr-metzger/

[13] Ibid

really happens in some of the most well-known seminaries in the country. He isn't wrong. He even admits to the vast amount of students going to seminaries with absolutely *no bible knowledge* and *relying on their teachers as guides*, then they come out thinking like clones (Ehrman didn't say they "come out thinking like clones" because he doesn't believe that, he doesn't believe that because *it's what happened to him*; almost). These students then either go off to a church and get into ministry or teach. Some even *lose all faith in a final authority* and believe that Moses never wrote Genesis and Matthew, Mark, Luke, and John never *really* wrote the Gospels, as Ehrman does and likewise the teachers that taught him. They were written by *"unknown"* authors in early Christianity, and of course no one *really* knows what Jesus taught.

At least Ehrman was honest and true to his training; he became an atheist instead of playing mental gymnastics like White in trying to reconcile what he learned from his teachers with what the Bible *says*.

Go to a forum[14] on Reddit under "bible scholars" and they will recommend Ehrman's books for you to *"learn the current state of Christian biblical scholarship,"* and have a *"better grasp of where the field is."* Half of the people on that forum are in the same boat as Ehrman, they are either atheist or agnostic. The other half claim to be Christian or of "other faiths." How do I know?—*I asked them*, and then nicely asked them to make it known on the front page of their forum that the information is *not* coming from people that actually *believe* the Bible, but rather from people that just "study" *about it*.

In true form of openminded scholarly discussion, they blocked me for it. Couldn't say I didn' see it-a-comin'. Why did I ask them to do it? Well-meaning people who were new to the Bible were going on there asking *this group* for book recommendations by scholars *"who are Christian"* that have

---

[14] r/AskBibleScholars

resolved some of the very same matters we are discussing here and have been for the last seven chapters. They recommend Ehrman, who hasn't solved a thing; he only presents more problems, problems that have existed since Jerome was on the baby bottle. How is one *"a bible scholar"* when one doesn't *believe* the book in which he is supposed to be a scholar *of*? Especially when its main premise and revelation to this age is *belief*? Thats like being an evolutionist with an earned degree in the field reading Dawkins, Darwin, and Henrich all while not believing anything you're reading about it. I understand there are scholars who study, say, Greek Mythology, but this is my point: *the same mentality is being applied to biblical studies as is applied to Greek Mythology, where Santa Clause originated, the origins of the Easter Bunny, Star Wars film analysis, and breakdowns of Stan Lee's comics.*

Seminaries have moved away from teaching the Bible and instead teach *textual criticism of* the bible. They tear it to shreds, then throw it at you like confetti in hopes of you thinking how smart and earned they are of their degrees. This is *the best* Princeton can offer, a bunch of *babies* (1 Cor. 3:1-3) in the word of God, and *destructive critics* that master a dead language before they have even learned the basics in an English Bible—their own language.

That's the group, **"by their fruits ye shall know them"** (Matt. 7:20). They want to teach you *about* the Bible instead of what's actually in the thing, hence Metzger's idea that 1 Peter 3:19 is in "error." This group, like White, has no idea what's in the Bible because *they don't have one,* yet they want to tell *you* what should and should not belong in it. What in the world...I mean, c'mon, man. Here we have an example of a once dedicated believer of the word of God that has been *corrupted by* a "good, godly, well meaning, well established, revered" Greek professor. Metzger may know his first and second declension nouns, and if putting the circumflex accent on the antepenult is correct Greek grammar, but White and the man *does't know what's in the*

Bible[15] *anymore than Origen or Muhammad,* as you can see from Metzger's *ghastly* translation of the RSV and NRSV brought to you with the help of *The National Council of Churches (NCCC)* which had to "rebrand" itself just as many companies like Facebook have done after *bad publicity.* They rebranded in 1950, previously the *Federal Council of Churches of 1908.* They are a political front for the advocacy of a Catholic version of socialism still, to this day. The NCC (for short) bought the copyright of the *failing* ASV, RSV, and the NRSV. They are all about ecclesiastical and ecumenical movements, which they took directly from the Roman playbook. The simple description of an NRSV will tell you it's *"Ecumenical, but generally mainline Protestant and Roman Catholic in respect to public teaching and devotional use."*

You mean to tell me that if Roman Catholics used a bible and it was *approved*, that the Protestants would want to use that one too? Have you lost your mind? The Catholic church even has it's own edition called the *NRSV-CE,* just like the ESV has theirs. Again, not much changed from the "standard" edition of the ESV or NRSV to the Catholic version—*because it's already a Catholic bible.* (See chapter 5.)

Anyone hear of the Gunpowder Plot? The Inquisitions? The book burnings? Could you imagine the looks on the Protestants faces when you told them *"oh yea man, this bible here is Catholic approved AND we can use it too…just don't look at* Col. 1:14; Acts 1:3; Rom 16:1; Matt. 17:21, 18:11; 23:14; Mark 7:16, 9:44, 46, 11:26, 15:28, Mark 16:9-20; Luke 23:17; John 5:4; Acts 8:37, 24:7; Rom. 16:24; James 1:8; the removal

---

[15] Example: See how White handled 2 Timothy 2:12 on page 132 of *The King James only Controversy* (1995), and John 6:47 on page 261, John 1:18 on page 258, John 7:53-8:11 on page 262 where White says it is a *"near certainty"* that those verses should not be in your bible. He handles 2 Timothy 2:12 where he believes it teaches "works-salvation" when the object is **"reign,"** not salvation from hell. White does not understand English nor does he understand that by changing **"suffer"** to "endure" you will be forced to cross reference it with tribulation passages such as Matt. 24:13 and Heb. 3:6, 14. Yet White has the audacity to tell you what should and should not belong in a bible. The very next verse (2 Tim 2:13) is telling you that you can not separate the Body of Christ. As you will see, Ehrman has no place to say what should and should not belong in any bible in any language.

of **"Christ"** 87 times, **"Lord"** 91 times, **"God"** 138 times, **"Heaven"** 88 times, **"hell"** 41 times, and **"Lord Jesus Christ"** 22 times. *You see none of that really matters, because the fundamentals are still in there."* Newsflash: the Catholic church also believes in the Trinity, Jesus as the Son of God, that He was born of a Virgin, the Death and Resurrection, etc., and *so does Lucifer* and his **"devils."** (See Matt. 8:29 and Acts 19:15.)

You are insane! In what world? In fact, in an early edition of the New American Bible Hebrews 10:12 was altered so that the **"one sacrifice"** *was not* **"for ever"** by changing the comma to read: *"after he had offered one sacrifice for sins, for ever sat down on the right hand of God."* Jesus isn't going to "for ever" sit on the right hand of God; *He stands* (Acts 7:56), and He *comes back* on a horse (Rev 19). If that isn't enough Vaticanus B omits from Hebrews 9:14 on, to exclude the entire chapter 10 which deals with the *One Sacrifice of Jesus Christ and the uselessness of priests offering sacrifices daily*, (it's saying that the Catholic Mass is *useless*). It also omits the *ending of Mark* which would be convenient for a pope (see the chapter *"Two Bibles," pages 321-327*). Someone does't want you to know the truth.

By the way, are you noticing anything (aside from my negative sounding tone) familiar about only one tenth of the verses presented here? Possibly *a pattern* in which the ESV also fell into by following *the same manuscripts* and *poor scholarship*? Maybe, a pattern[16] of similar verses in which the NRSV and ESV share along with the NIV, NLT, NEB, CSB, et al.? No, no way. Nothing to see here. Look the other way. Stay blind—it's more comfortable since that's what you are used to.

I'll tackle some of Ehrman's *"discrepancies"* and *"contradictions"* in this chapter from his book mentioned

---

[16] Run the same verses mentioned in chapter 5-8 with any bible version. One Book is not the same as the others. There is the 21st Century King James, which is "safe," but would you want a watered down beverage, or the actual thing?

earlier ("*Jesus, Interrupted*") as we go along. First, I'd like to throw something at you, the reader. You can see a debate between Ehrman and James White on YouTube. It's in two parts, and what you learn is *very telling*:

1. White and Ehrman believe all the same things, except one came out still being a Christian and the other atheist. Both are "textual critics" and have worked on translations (NRSV-Ehrman and NASV-White).
2. James White is critical of Roman Catholicism *but uses a Catholic bible.*
3. White and Ehrman *were taught all the same things* and look up to all the same people, minus a few that White looks up to.
4. *Neither one* can point you in the direction *of what God said, as in, the "words."* It's *somewhere* in the mass of Greek, Hebrew, and Aramaic texts and has made its way into the various 300+ English translations, according to White. This means every time White says *"the* Bible" he is not referring to anything you can touch, see, or read—it is somewhere amongst the mass of Greek manuscripts and some parts are undiscovered. Every time he says "Scripture" he isn't referring to anything he's ever seen or handled. "We" have "reliable translations" which will give you "the message," but not the words—all while claiming to be biblically "conservative."[17] Ehrman is at least honest with his position and says "we don't have them"—his reason? Because, *"words matter"* and where there is a different reading in one translation verses another, to say it *doesn't matter* is just foolish. One must be right and one must be wrong. Finally some honesty… from an atheist instead of the Christian? My, My, what have we here?

---

[17] See footnote 5 in chapter two, *"The Actors."*

Saving Private Ehrman 351

5. Both are *destructive critics,* but one is a *liar* who tries to angle his arguments (White). The other just does't know how to handle the evidence or able to reconcile it (Ehrman).
6. I would trust Ehrman with watching my home before I would ever trust White.
7. Both contestants try to oust each other with scholarly jargon in an attempt to depreciate the others argument, Ehrman's specialty.
8. After two hours of the debate you learn *absolutely nothing* of what's in the Bible. Only confusion as to what *may* or *may not* belong in it.
9. White believes (as do all of his colleagues) in the pre-Jesus Christ LXX, and believes it's a *good source to use.* He favors a non-Jewish text that contains the Apocrypha in which Jews have *condemned* for a source in translating the Jewish Old Testament.
11. White, just as most in this arena surrounding Scripture, is a hypocrite who will give the cloned party-line he learned in his re-education: he believes that God's *"Word"* is in the *commonalities in all the texts we have available*, i.e. cursives, uncials, fragments, codices, etc., but when it comes to *the differences in them*, he says they are *not important* and *none take away from "the message"* of any book (individual books of the Bible). What White *means* is that the *"message"* is the same, i.e., the Gospel of Jesus Christ, and the *"words"* are *not* of importance—they can be settled with a footnote in translations. Do you realize that you can fit *"the message"* on a small business card? The Bible is about 1,200 pages in nine to ten point font. What are all those *"words"* doing in there?
12. Ehrman shows the *power of words* by giving the example of Hebrews 2:9 where *"apart from God"* derives a totally different meaning than **"grace of God."** "Apart from God" would indicate God was no part of it. Thus, trying to catch White in his hypocrisy of saying he "has

the words of God," when in fact he does not, nor does he show reverence towards *words* and has *no idea what they are or where to find them because he has never even seen them.* At least Ehrman is honest about it.

13. White gives the same degraded argument presented to you by the faculty and staff of every major seminary in the U.S. and Europe today: *"Well, there are other places in the book of Hebrews that would still indicate the grace of God was with Jesus."* This would be another example of the totally depravity of this mindset. *"Just because one verse is different does not change the fundamentals of the faith."* If they were all changed you *wouldn't buy the book.* Why insist on one depraved change in a place when there is support for the doctrine elsewhere? *It's as if that gives credence to the change.* Do you see that mentality? *"Well the King James has changed over time!"* Yea it has, *"forme"* to **"form,"** *"voyd"* to **"void,"** *"vpon"* to **"upon,"** *"deepe"* to **"deep,"** *"mooued"* to **"moved."** Well, that must mean we can remove the **"blood"** of Jesus Christ from Colossians 1:14!—Insanity.

14. Ehrman stands at the pulpit with the veracity of an angry child waving his hands, demanding to be shown the *"original autographs"* so that he may have something to hang his hat on in his search for what God said. His view of inspiration is: *"If God wanted you to have His words then why didn't He preserve them?"* See that? He is being *honest with himself and his training.* White believes God preserved His words, *but only about 70-95% of them.* As for the left over percentages, he and his bedfellows will tell you what they should be. White and Ehrman are not that different after all. With all the waving about Ehrman *still believes he knows what is in "the original,"* even after saying *for a few hours* that "no one knows what the originals said." Ehrman falls victim and claims he knows what was *"written by the original authors"* on his blog

(ehrmanblog.org) when talking about 1 John 5:7, John 7:53-8:11, and Mark 16:9-20.

The debate is very telling indeed, and White does't really have an argument. It wasn't really a debate, but rather two people agreeing on all the same things except the final outcome of the evidence presented to both men when in seminary. The final outcome being still believing or not believing, given the one sided view in most seminaries.

When asked a question from an audience member, *"how do you know if the third copy has mistakes in it from the original?"* Ehrman responds, *"Well, we actually don't know."* There you have it—the ridiculous *"logic"* of modern Christian scholarship. What he said was that a third copy from one of the originals *could* represent it 100% or 0%. A valid admission to make, but the frog is still in the pot. It's *all conjecture*. Neither White nor Ehrman believe John 7:53-8:11 (a.k.a. the *Pericope de Adultera*) belong in your Bible. Of course White doesn't, he was a "consultant" for the NASB/NASV which put the passage in brackets in some editions and an asterisk mark in others. The NASV now goes by the NASB. They think that by changing "Version" to "Bible" that it will sell better.

Does John 7:53-8:11 belong in your Bible? This is a very famous passage in which a woman is "caught in adultery" and brought before Jesus by the Pharisees to try and catch Jesus off guard and make him contradict himself. During it, He stoops down and writes with His finger on the ground. Jesus ends the passage by saying, **"He that is without sin among you, let him first cast a stone at her."** He then goes back to drawing in the sand.

What's the evidence *for* and *against* the Pericope? The evidence *against it* are...you guessed it, "the *oldest* and *best* mss"Sinaiticus ℵ, Vaticanus B, Alexandrinus A, and Ephraemi C. Along with them are other witnesses: 𝔓66, 𝔓75, L, N, T, W, X, Δ, Θ, Ψ, 33, 157, 565, 1241, 1424. The Coptic church bibles, Sahidic, sub-Achmimic, some of the Bohairic,

Old Latin a, f, and q. Metzger throws out A and C for obvious reasons: they are *"defective at this point."*[18] Netsles 28th edition adds A and C to the witnesses against the text as W&H did, but says *"apparent reading, but not certain (vid)."* "Apparent reading," is it? How does one get an *"apparent reading"* from A and C? Codex A has two leaves *missing* from John 6:50-8:11 making it *not a valid witness at all.* Codex C is beyond *damaged* and it also excludes much of the Gospel's passages in John so it is hardly a valid witness to even include. You can expect such "scholarship" from Nestles text which spawned the NIV and ESV.

Burgon took the time out to measure[19] the amount of lines/letters from the two missing leaves from Codex A based on other leaves present. He postulated that a carless scribe (such as from ℵ, B, C, and D) could have begun to copy the passage but then caught himself and scrambled to correct himself on the next visible leaf which shows the bunching of letters (f47r/marked pg. 73 of the mss) where the scribe writes smaller than the surrounding text. Burgon's explanation may be found in the cited work on footnote 19.

With A and C out of the picture we have ℵ and B which we have seen the character of each already (see the chapter *"Two Bibles" pages 316-331).* Given that they do *not* contain the Pericope, nor do they contain the ending of Mark and many other blunders, this only confirms that their beautiful outward appearance is deceiving at best. Hort says that the Pericope would be, *"...fatally interrupting the course of St. John's Gospel, if retained in the text."*[20]

---

[18] Metzger, *"The Text of the New Testament,"* page 319

[19] Dean Burgon, *"The Causes of Corruption of the Traditional Text, Vol. II,"* 1896, pages 244-245, also see the entire appendix on the subject.

[20] Ibid, page 238, citing *"Westcott and Hort, preface to the revised text of the New Testament,"* page xxvii

Metzger follows Hort's opinion by saying it, *"interrupts the sequence of 7:52-8:12."*[21] Within the half-hour we will see how Hort, Metzger, White, Wallace, et al., "follow the leader" and have trouble with following basic story plots.

L and Δ contain a blank space after John 7:52 which testifies *to the existence of* the passage. As Burgon says, "These are therefore witnesses *for*,—not witnesses *against*."[22] We now only have left N, T, W, X, Θ, Ψ of the Uncial Codices to work with out of the now disqualified originally cited witnesses א, B, C, D, A, L, and Δ. So, we don't have too much to work with anymore concerning *doubting* the passage as compared to previously. We can also throw the cited Church Father Origen out because his commentary containing those parts of John was lost.

Nestles *lied* about L and Δ, and Metzger *lied* about א, B, L, and Δ, then they actually *lie* to you again on page 319 of their work titled, *"The Text of the New Testament"* by telling you, *"Even more significant is the fact that no Greek church father for 1,000 years after Christ refers to the pericope as belonging to the fourth Gospel."* Metzger has been repeating this *lie* since ~1964. As Burgon pointed out before Metzger was born, and Hills in 1967, you can drop that number by three centuries at least. There are Greek manuscripts containing it from the 8th and 9th Century so for the manuscripts to be *in Greek* the later part of Metzger's "1,000 years" can readily be chipped away by 300 years.

Notice the *tone* of the quote and the *assuredness* of Ehrman and Metzger. If Metzger didn't believe it should be in your Bible, then why did he allow it to be, given he was the head of the NRSV? White doesn't either, who was a consultant for the NASV. Surly, omitting the passage would at least be consistent with their "evidence based, scientific findings,"

---

[21] United Bible Societies *"A Textual Commentary on the Greek New Testament, 4th ed.,"* 1994, page 220

[22] op cit. Burgon, page 245

no? Why do they relegate it to a footnote? Why not get rid of this Holy Scripture if the findings are so robust as Metzger makes them out to be?

Now, what about the evidence on the other side, *in favor of the pericope de adultera?* Uncials (now with L and Δ from above) D, U, Γ, K, Π, M, Λ, and H. Cursives 118, 209, 1071, 28, 700, 1010, 264, 13, 69, 124, 174, 230, 346, 543, 788, 826, 828, 983, 1689, and 1709, 15 copies of the Bohairic, Old Latin b, c, e, ff, g, h, and j dating the passage to the *Second Century*. The Harclean Syriac, Palestinian Syriac, Ethiopic, Georgian, Arabic, Slavonic, Armenian, the majority of manuscripts (~85%), and further *where Metzger and Ehrman lied by omission above:* Church Fathers, Jerome (A.D. 385), Ambrose (A.D. 374) and Augustine. It was Augustine and Ambrose who, in effect, said:

> *"'Be it known to all men' (they say) 'that this passage is genuine: but the nature of its subject-matter has at once procured its ejection from MSS., and resulted in the silence of Commentators'"*[23] *(A.D. 396).*

> *"Certain persons of little faith, or rather enemies of the true faith, fearing, I suppose, lest their wives should be given impunity in sinning, removed from their manuscripts the Lord's act of forgiveness toward the adulteress, as if He who had said 'sin no more' had granted permission to sin."*[24]

Then Pacian (A.D. 370), Faustus (A.D. 400), Rufinus (A.D. 400), Chrysologus (A.D. 433), Sedulius (A.D. 434), and

---

[23] Ibid, page 259

[24] J. A. Moorman, *"Early Manuscripts, Church Fathers, and the Authorized Version,"* 2005, p. 212

others. You see, those in the list I gave are *Latin* fathers, not *Greek*. So, they gave you a *half-truth* (Gen. 3:5), by saying "no *Greek* fathers," but *did not give you any other evidence of Church fathers to look at*. Classic modern Christian scholarship.

Furthermore, what Metzger and Ehrman are alluding to is called the *"silence of the Fathers"* in relation to Byzantine readings such as the one we are looking at here. I have already given *Latin* fathers who quote the passage and many other versions in other languages distributing it geographically and it represents a long line dating back to the Second Century, but this issue goes bone-deep, to the marrow. For this is a passage once present and then removed —why? *Why are the early Greek Fathers silent on the passage?* Metzger and friends assume that just because some earlier *Greek* Fathers were "silent" on the passage, then that *must* mean it doesn't belong in your Bible and was not "original." Yet, *Old Latin* manuscripts b and e, for example, together date between A.D. 200-400. *They were translated from Greek.*

Aside from that blunder, as Pickering, Hills, Burgon, Sturz, etc., point out, there *are many* early Church Fathers which quote other King James readings such as Clement (A.D. 150-215), Tertullian (A.D. 150-220), Origen (A.D. 185-254), Marcion (A.D. 85-160), Justin Martyr (A.D. 100-165), etc. With these, plus the early papyri readings, they give solid evidence for the Byzantine/Syrian text (KJB).

The fact that they are silent on the Pericope (John 7:53-8:11) *does not disprove its existence*. By this logic *"Lucian Recension/Theory"* would have been *proven wrong long ago* due—to—the—*historical—silence*. Make note, the silence of the recension is *not* the same kind of silence seen in the Greek Fathers on John 7:53-8:11 for obvious reasons (see the chapter, *"Two Bibles"*). A huge revision of the text by ecclesiastical powers or the like would leave a trace in history. There was never *any* solid proof of the recension and it was the *cornerstone* of Hort's theory. Hort never cared for insurmountable evidence.[25] Did the silence of the pericope leave a trace in history? Yes, it did, but even more is that the evidence *presented* by the manuscripts has more *"weight"*[26] than does the "silence" of patristic evidence (Greek Fathers), because *many wrote about what they would preach*. This is why there was "silence" concerning the passage. The passage in John may have been a little "tricky" for some to preach, due to Jesus *forgiving an "adulterous" woman*. It may not have been *"good preaching or Sunday school material"* at the time when it was supposed to be preached according to the lectionaries (it was the lesson for the time of Pentecost!).

Oh, yes. What about those *lectionaries* that Metzger and friends oh so conveniently leave off? The passage is in the history annals of *the Eastern Church*.[27] With that in mind, it is no wonder that Chrysostom passed over the passage and why "no early Greek Father" quoted the passage; he was part of the Eastern Church. Most of the Fathers commenting on the passage were from the Western Church.

This lectionary lesson began at John 7:37 and continued to John 7:52, at which point the orator designated to read the Scriptures for the church services *was to skip to 8:12*. The eastern church was *not silent* on the matter, for it is seen *clearly* from the lectionaries. This also explains why the passage is *"moved around"* in a few manuscripts.

White follows Wallace, Wallace follows Metzger, Metzger follows Hort, Ehrman is a new "text-type" with a branching arm from Metzger and an old style made new by atticism. None represent the "original" text.

Here is the marrow from the bone. What you have by these *"highly educated scholars"* who believe that the *"oldest"* are always the *"best"* (all while *not really* believing that, since

---

[25] Colwell, *"Genealogical Method: its Achievements and its Limitations,"* 1947, page 111

[26] Edward F. Hill's, *"Believing Bible Study,"* 1991, pages 128-130. Also see Pickering, *"The Identity of the New Testament Text IV,"* 2014, pages 67-68.

[27] The Eastern Church predominantly spoke Greek whilst the Western Church spoke Latin.

many King James readings *predate* ℵ and B by *150+ years*) is Jesus continuing a conversation with the same group of people from John 7:52 to 8:12...*but there is a problem.*

If you are to believe them, you have Jesus leaving the scene and *somehow*, He speaks to them **"again"** (8:12)?

a) You have two groups of people at the temple, a **"division"** has occurred amidst the people (vs. 40-43),
b) **"some of them would have taken him"** (vs. 44) but they didn't, not even the officers.
c) Note the paragraph mark on vs. 45.
d) The Pharisees were assembled with Nicodemus and the officers approach them *without having detained Jesus, which leads to a dispute* (vs. 45-52). Jesus is not present.
e) Then Jesus is supposed to speak **"again"** unto them, but he was never with them to begin with.

To put it another way, you have John 7:52:

"They [Pharisees] answered and said unto him [Nicodemus], Art thou also of Galilee? Search, and look: for out of Galilee ariseth no prophet."

"Then spake Jesus again unto them, saying, I am the light of the world" (John 8:12).

What is the antecedent of **"them"** in 8:12 and what is meant by the word **"again"**? These are the simple and overlooked questions by the Pharisees such as Metzger and friends. Jesus was *not* with them from verse 45 on, and the Pharisees *do* respond to what Jesus said in 8:12. By removing the passage, a real conundrum is created that did *not* exist before. Metzger and friends have created an aberration in the text as they have likewise done in many other places, such as: Luke 4:44, 23:45; John 7:8, 6:47; Acts 28:13; John 1:18; Jude 15; 1 Timothy 3:16; Matthew 5:22, and so on. We can expect such work by the United Bible Societies, Nestles text, and those who work on them.

For example, in Luke 4:44 Jesus was in **"Galilee,"** *not* Judea. They introduce a contradiction in the text. Given the context of Luke 4:44, how then could He be in Judea? The work of Nestles text is the same type of scribal work achieved in א and B (see pages 320-8).

Now, what actually happened in the Pericope? They disappeared because **"every man went unto his own house"** in 7:53. After this account a *new* account in chapter 8 begins on the proceeding morning, starting at verse 1 where **"all the people"** came to the **"temple"** to hear Jesus. He **"sat down"** and taught them (verse 2). The **"scribes and Pharisees"** (verse 3) then joined him *where He was in the temple*. Jesus makes the famous statement found in John 8:7 to everyone in the temple, and they leave one by one *after reading the writing in the sand*, thus pointing out the hypocrisy of the Pharisees (Deut. 17:6-7; Levi. 20:10; Deut. 22:22).

Where is the man she was with when she was caught **"in the very act"**? Why is she alone? That isn't Jewish Law (see references above). In this scene, only two individuals remain: the woman and Jesus, with Jesus standing (8:10). Notice the new paragraph starting at verse 12? Notice how some of the most educated people have trouble with English? Jesus spoke to them **"again."** *Who?* They all left in the scene from 8:1-11.

Notice again, that you are told *who* He is speaking to and *where* He is in 8:20. He's now in the **"treasury,"** which is in **"the temple"** but not where He was in the beginning of chapter 8 when He was teaching. We have a change of scenery. Jesus followed them into the treasury to tell them off. There were other Jews in the treasury since **"many believed on him"** (verse 30). How fitting for the Pharisees to go to their *place of comfort after being under conviction*. The discussion ends up back outside, *probably* around the time of 8:43-56 and He leaves in verse 59.

If that weren't enough, notice in John 7:37 that it is **"in the last day, that great day of the feast."** *What feast?* The feast of **"tabernacles"** (John 7:2). Tabernacles is a feast of *seven* days, beginning on a sabbath day. It ends *on the eighth day*, which is *also a sabbath* (Levi 23:33-44; Deut. 16:13-15). **"SEVEN days shalt thou keep a solemn feast." "On the FIRST day shall be a sabbath, and on the EIGHTH day shall be a sabbath," "and ye shall keep the feast unto the LORD SEVEN days."** The feast of Tabernacles is in total *eight days long* with a special *sabbath at the end*. It lasts Saturday to Saturday. An example of how Israel practiced according to the Scriptures is found in Nehemiah 8:1-18. In Nehemiah 8:18 we read that the **"last day"** is not the sabbath day, also that they *held the feast seven days, and on the eighth day was a sabbath.*

Back to John. The **"last great day"** of the *feast* was the *seventh day, not the eighth*. In John 8:1-2 we read that it is the same day, **"early in the morning."** We have to know that Jewish time is different. The new day beings at 6pm and ends at 6pm. Our Gentile time is 12am to 12am. That new day is *still* the seventh day of the feast of Tabernacles, which in John 9:4 you read that a new day is approaching, **"while it is day: the night cometh."** This new day (or evening/night to us) *is the sabbath or eighth day* (John 9:14). If you make **"the last day, the great day of the feast"** the sabbath which all the "correctors" and "commentators" do, then you have a problem with john 9:4 since Jesus healed the blind man on the sabbath (John 9:14), which is the *eighth day of the feast of Tabernacles.*

So, what we have in summary is: (1) the last day of the feast starting at 6pm (John 7:37), (2) everyone going to their own houses possibly around 9pm (John 7:53), because why would a bunch of Pharisees suddenly leave a great feast in the middle of the day with lots of people noticing when they are *all about appearances*? It had to be evening/late at night for people to not ask questions. (3) Then the next day, **"early

in the morning," which is still the seventh day of the feast, possibly 3-6am (John 8:1-2). (4) Next is 3-5:59pm **"night commeth, when no man can work"** (John 9:4). (5) Directly following is 6pm, **"the Sabbath"** (9:6-14), the *eighth day of the feast*.

White, Ehrman, MacArthur, Metzger, Hort, and friends all believe this should't be in your Bible. The greatest portion of the feast would have been *in the evening* for this is still when the majority of the world holds large activities such as these and for other reasons which I will discuss. The Jews would also need time to clean up and *prepare for the sabbath*. This "wind-down" day would be the daytime following the **"last great day of the feast."**

If you make the last great day of the feast the sabbath, like the commentators do, then you have a week of time missing in a continuous line of events from 7:37-9:14 because you go from sabbath to sabbath abruptly. Even if you took the pericope out, it would still be a continuous line of events, but you would be going from evening to another evening rather abruptly as well, given that the last great day would be a sabbath (eighth day of the feast), implying that there was an entire missing week between the last great day of the feast and when He healed the blind man. This ruins references to the Second Advent of our Lord Jesus Christ. Time in the Gospels does jump around but in this case it is continuous which would make omitting the pericope a blunder from a fool.

If you were to take it out, you would destroy a reference to the Second Advent of Christ for He comes back **"early in the morning"** (Matt. 14:25; Mal. 4; Psa. 19:3-4; Matt. 13:43; 2 Peter 1:19; 2 Sam. 23:4) on the **"Mt. of Olives"** (Zech. 14:1-4; Acts 1:11-12), around the time of the feast of Tabernacles. Of three main Jewish feasts, the *Passover* was associated with Christ's crucifixion (1 Cor. 5:7), *Pentecost* was the birth of the Church (Acts 2:1-5), the feast of *Tabernacles* is connected to the **"Sun"** (Mal. 4:2) coming into His Kingdom (Matt. 16:28), and the **"blind"** Jew who can now **"see"** (John 9:25; Isa. 35:5) will be representative of the nation of Israel after the Second Advent when they are restored at that great day (see Zech. 12:10, 2:10-12; Zeph. 3:5; Haba. 2:14, 20, Isa. 11:4, 9; Deut. 30:3, 5-6 etc.). There is, of course, the spiritual application of the blind Jew being that of a Christians salvation...."*I once was lost but now I am found...was blind but now I see...Amazing Grace how sweet the sound...*"

Ehrman and Metzger wrote a textbook together called *"The Text of the New Testament: Its Transmission, Corruption, and Restoration,"* which covers outdated and false forms of Textual Criticism, amongst other monstrosities. Ehrman himself has written many textbooks on the subject of N.T. manuscripts and the *"historical critical approach"* which are used in schools today around the country. Students coming to a town near you who have been taught all the same things as Ehrman, White, Custer, MacArthur, Aland, Hort, Wuest, Gregory, Norris, Kittel, Sumner, Wallace, Price, et al.

How does a man lie to his congregation about these matters? A "bible believing" church? Are you really? Or are you trying to be *fashionable and keep that attendance up* because you know if you told your congregation *what you really believe* then half of them would walk "right out the door." The other half would stay because they have become as deluded as you, who took the pounding and gave in to those professors that are like **"Demas"** (2 Tim. 4:10). You care more about your *image* than the Truth. When you get on that pulpit, you don't know what God said do you? Beyond the *"message,"* you haven't got the slightest idea. Be honest. Really, be honest. This is a "safe space."

How does this three step process work?
1. Start out as a born again fundamentalist.[28]

---

[28] Bart D. Ehrman, *"Jesus, Interrupted,"* 2009, page 16

2. Go to a place with destructive critics and incubate yourself amongst them. Immerse yourself in the echo-chambers. Have a destructive critic as a guide (Metzger) who will rid you of a final authority so you and your teacher may become the final authority. Become "increasingly liberal" by seeing the Bible as more *"metaphorical"* and *"less literal."*[29] [30]Study and *believe* Westcott and Hort's theories on Textual Criticism at this institution, because you were never presented enough evidence to the contrary.
3. Have *philosophical* (Col. 2:8) differences in how God handles things because you believe you could have done it better yourself.[31]

- *Final Product*: <u>Leave the faith</u>.[32]

That's the three step program of almost every seminary in the nation. Beats Alcoholics Anonymous' twelve-step program. Maybe it makes you think twice about sending your kids to one of these schools? Which is why these "great institutions of learning" *tried to hide it all* throughout the 70's, 80's, and 90's. They want that money, man $$$, "keep sending those checks (I mean, students)—we need to pay for our indoor pool and gymnasium."

The position, still held in some circles, used to be that those who *professed* to be believers in the inspiration of the Bible actually only considered the "original autographs" as inspired. However, this viewpoint has been increasingly criticized as it is seen as unreasonable and lacks a solid basis because the very things being compared to *don't exist!* As a

---

[29] Ibid, page 3, 17

[30] Machen wrote a book on this subject that is as good as prophecy called, "*Christianity and Liberalism*" which predicts this phenomenon and a well worth read at that.

[31] op cit. Ehrman, page 17

[32] Ibid

result, a shift or rather a pivot has occurred within the same group of people towards *"a broader understanding of inspiration,"* stating that the entirety of God's Word is inspired. According to this perspective, the inspired *"Word"* can be found in the commonalities found throughout different bible versions and manuscripts. Then you have Ehrman's class, which doesn't believe either and views it strictly in a historical fashion, devoid of anything else. This is the pivot people are taking in his circles: away from inspiration and preservation and towards "historical applications" and the "societal norms in which the writers lived." His circles are the future "circles" of textual criticism. Are we seeing how the wind blows yet?

If you think the three steps mentioned above are an isolated case, then I direct you to a work by Jonah David Conner called, *"All That's Wrong With the Bible" (2017)* where he deals with similar issues that Ehrman does, such as "contradictions" and "discrepancies" but like Ehrman, *also* with no actual solutions. You will read on pages 5-8 that Conner (note the process):

- *was* raised "conservative Protestant" (as 1 above)
- then went to a very conservative Christian institution
- Next, he went to Liberty University whose founder is Jerry Falwell. His son Jerry Falwell Jr., who was the president after his father in 2007, has resigned in 2020 due to "sexual scandals" (as 2 above)
- Then Conner finished a Ph.D in *Linguistics* with a *concentration on translation* (as 2 above)
- He began to *"question his beliefs"* over a period of years involving *"a detailed study of Textual Criticism"* leading to his new found higher state of knowledge (**"knowledge puffeth up"**) (as 3 above)
- Then *atheism* (final product)

You see, he went to Liberty and was pounded so hard in a Greek classroom by phrases like, *"a better translations would be," "the original probably reads," "here, the King James chose a very unfortunate verb," "the King James did not translate the article here,"* and so on. He was shown *"scribal errors"* made by "poor candle light" and told that ℵ and B were *"the oldest and best"* so many times that he began to believe no words of God were anywhere to be found—lights out. In his studies of textual criticism, he couldn't tell up from down with the Greek, Spanish, Latin, or *any* language, including English so he walked "right out-the-door."

In your average Greek classroom (after some introductions and basic Greek grammar) you'll find your professor saying:
- "The NASV can be considered a *more accurate translation compared to* the NRSV due to various factors in its translation methodology and *textual basis*."
- "In certain instances, the AV *fails to capture the precise meaning* of the text, demonstrating its shortcomings in terms of word choice."
- "The King James *chose a poor word choice* here…"
- "At times, the King James Version diverges from *the Greek text*, which can affect the *accuracy* of the translation."
- "The King James *follows no Greek text* at times."
- "You *must understand Greek* to get the *true* sense of the text."
- "A thorough understanding of Greek *is essential* to grasp the *true essence* of the text, particularly in passages such as (insert Gospel chapter here_____), where the *nuances* of the Greek language provide *crucial insights*."
- "It is worth acknowledging that the translators of the King James Version *did their best with the resources and materials available to them at the time*."
- "In examining *the tense* of the participle, it becomes apparent that corrections or adjustments should be made to *accurately reflect the intended meaning*."

That's how it's done. *Over and over again.* You walk out of 2-6 years of Greek and now have a choice to believe everything your teacher has taught you and his teacher that taught him, *or* to follow the Spirit and word of God. Choosing the former of the two, you have *no final authority* other than a Greek lexicon or Nestles text (until a new edition comes out), your own opinions, and those of your peers. You are forced to believe in the "Scriptures" *publicly* as a pastor or preacher, but *deny them privately* as either being the "original autographs" or the neo-orthodox position of Barth and Brunner's *"Word"* of God. You've been taught out of your faith by people who claim to be Christian, but in all *practical* purposes, are just like Ehrman: an atheist with no reverence for the word of God. This destructive approach is directly responsible for *Biblical illiteracy*, loss of respect and reverence of the AV or for calling *any* bible version "Scripture."

All translations do the same things that the KJB is accused of in Greek classrooms and are often reasons given for a new translation (while blaming the KJB).

a) The highly esteemed NASV has used the *wrong tense* in: Matthew 3:1, 12; Acts 7:51, 10:11, 18, 13:11, 1 Thessalonians 1:10, 2:3, etc.

b) Words that were *added*, which came from *no Greek text* at all are found in: Luke 1:25, 31, 20, 29: Acts 10:16, 13, 34, 13:47, 39; Titus 1:1, 3; Hebrews 1:10, 2:2, etc.

c) None of these passages can be translated *literally* in English *without being complete gibberish*: Luke 2:5, 5:12, 36; John 3:22, 16:17; Acts 2:29; Romans 4:2, etc.

All of the above are okay when another translation does it, such as the NASV, but when enemy number one does it (KJB), then it must be thrown out and "revised." *All translations add, subtract, alter tense, add articles, and so forth. It will never not be that way. Why then is the AV vilified and a new version appears every 2-6 months?*

The bunch that believes the *"Word"* finds it by deciding what *you* want (page 364-366 in *"The English Bible, From the KJB to NIV" by Jack Lewis*). After you have all 300+ translations, you still don't know what God said (Ibid, page

363), and you need as many as you can get. This sounds a lot like what Ehrman says on page 7-8 about the Gospels in his book *"Jesus, Interrupted," "between the Gospels the interpreter has to write his own Gospel."*..This is Ehrman insisting that the *"discrepancies"* between the four Gospels make the reader come up with *his own picture of the Gospels* in which is *"right" only* to the reader, therefore making the actual Gospels wrong. What sort of demented thinking is that? First off, it's the Body deciding and not one single reader, secondly you *have to* form the full storyline by doing so; there is just no other way around it. Historians do a similar thing when looking at different accounts of history. They look at archeology, eye-witnesses, written accounts, and so on to piece the whole story together.

Let's tackle some of these discrepancies in order from his book. I will not go into all of them in his work because this isn't a refutation on Ehrman himself. I will go in order so the reader doesn't think I'm cherry picking the "easy" ones.

Problem: How did Jesus cleanse the temple once if He cleansed it in His early ministry (John 2) and his later ministry (Mark 11)?[33]

Answer: Ehrman presents a false claim here. He argues that since each of the accounts (Mark and John) only have Jesus cleansing the temple once, then He must have only done it once. With that logic we can assume that Jesus doesn't have a genealogy because Mark didn't include one in his Gospel.

What he fails to grasp is his insistence on each Gospel affirming Jesus' temple cleansing twice as a requirement for accuracy. That's how *he* wants the Bible to be written. It reflects his reluctance to challenge the prevailing views of his

---

[33] Ibid, page 7

peers, thereby confining his thinking within familiar boundaries of his own echo chamber. However, the truth is that the number of times Jesus performed this act is not explicitly mentioned. As we'll soon discover, the Gospel accounts are not intended to conform to such rigid expectations. Instead, they complement each other, *supplementing* the narrative rather than contradicting it.

The answer is very simple. John 2:12-17 is around the time of the *first* Passover mentioned in John (2:23). There are *four* Passover's mentioned making his ministry three and a half years (5:1, 6:4, 13:1) since it began around the feast of Tabernacles (three years plus six months). John 2 is his first cleansing of the temple, *in his early ministry*.

In Mark 11:15-18 we have Jesus cleansing the temple around *His third year in his ministry*, which matches with Matthew 21:12-13 and Luke 19:45-46 in the timeline. The second temple cleansing occurs just 3 days before His crucifixion—the fourth Passover in the Gospels.

What is different? A similarity in three of the accounts is the phrase, **"den of thieves"** in Luke, Mark, and Matthew. John uses the phrase **"an house of merchandise"** followed by a realization *not found in the other three* by his disciples **"the zeal of thine house hath eaten thee up."** In Matthew, Mark, and Luke Jesus calls the temple **"my house"** as in, He is God; that's *His house*. In John we see the confirmation of that meaning when He calls it **"my Fathers house."** The confirmation being that He is God in the flesh (1 Tim. 3:16). Further, in John, Jesus **"made a scourge of small cords"** to whip the people out of the temple which he didn't have or use in Matthew, Mark, or Luke. *God did not write His Book the way you wanted Him to.*

The reason why Ehrman finds it so challenging to reconcile is due to the longstanding distinction between the Gospel of John and the synoptic Gospels (Matthew, Mark, and Luke). The synoptic Gospels are deemed "historical" as they bear similarities, while John's Gospel is regarded as a separate entity, labeled as "a theological account on the divinity of Christ" by "highly regarded" seminaries across the United States. Did you catch that? It means that the Gospel of John is not a factual depiction, but rather a persuasive discourse aimed at convincing readers of Jesus' divine nature, as propagated by numerous Christian institutions. It's just verbal jousting concerning theology trying to convince the reader that Jesus was the **"Son of God."**

Aside from the Quran, Muslims like to use Christian academia as source material and for their view on Jesus. Due to this view, Muslims view John as non-historical nor worth the time to read it, and use **"the Son of man"** title of Jesus mentioned in Matthew, Mark, and Luke to say that Jesus was *not* God but was just human, or rather only "a prophet" as they teach. (They forget about Mark 1:1; Matt. 22:41; Mark 12:35-36; Luke 20:39-44; Matt. 1:23; Mark 2:5, 7; Matt. 28:18-19, 18:20; Luke 8:24; Mark 4:39; Matt. 14:25-26; Matt. 28:6; Mark 16:6; Luke 24:6.) Did Muhammad do any of those things? Did he perform miracles in front of witnesses? Did he talk directly to God? Was he sinless? Why did he have to pray for his sins if he was sinless? Was he resurrected? Was he even a Jew like Moses? The answer to each question is a resounding N-O. Then how in the world was he *"a prophet like unto Moses"* (Deut. 18) as all Muslims claim? He wasn't, he was a sex-crazed war-lord who started a cult (see chapter 4).

Problem: Did Peter deny Jesus three times before the cock crows twice or before the cock crows at all?[34] (Matt. 26:34; Mark 14:30.)

---

[34] Ibid

Answer: This is what is commonly referred to as a "freshman classic" within the seminary realm. Its purpose is to mold students into believing that they ought to possess the same level of ignorance as their professors, a misguided notion that holds sway in many academic institutions. It's another case of an "expert" who is at work in "the field" of Christian scholarship.

Ehrman cites reading a work by Johnston Cheney, where he has Peter denying the Lord *six times* in trying to get this "contradiction" straightened out. That approach is actually from Bullinger, and it happens to be a good attempt but ultimately wrong, as it does not make the slightest bit of sense.

You would have two sets of three denials each i.e. *set one* being John 18:17; Matt. 26:70 with Mark 14:68; Luke 22:56-58 and Matt. 26:71-72 with John 18:25-26.

Set two is Mark 14:69-70; Matt. 26:73-74 then Luke 22:59-60, making six rooster calls.

Pickering also finds *six denials* by breaking up John 18:15-27 and Luke 22:54-62. Inventive and confusing. What was not taken into account was the term **"cockcrowing,"** as in Mark 13:35 which Ruckman found. It's *used as a period of time*. A "watch" in Jewish time is a set period, such as, **"even," "midnight," "cockcrowing"** and **"fourthwatch"** (Matt. 14:25) a.k.a., **"morning."**

Jesus Christ our Lord tells Peter that before this "watch" (**"cockcrowing"**) that he will deny Him (Matt. 26:34, 75). In Luke, the phrase **"this day"** (Luke 22:34) is there to show the watch called **"cockcrowing"** extended until 3am when the morning watch began. In Mark 14:30, 72 you see that it refers to the actual amount of sounds emitting from the beak of the flightless bird. (Could you imagine the Lord looking at you in Luke 22:61 after you had denied him three times? Man. Those are the eyes of the one who created the universe staring back at you. If He never had become a man, how in the world would anyone be able to relate to Him?)

Chapter 8

You have an actual time period *and* the amount of rooster crows in the passages. Does this discredit the Gospel accounts? Why, no. It shows that Ehrman was beat over the head so many times with "discrepancies" and "contradictions" that the man just plain gave up. He told himself that he came to a "logical" conclusion based on the "evidence" presented.

Problem: "Do they see a man, as Mark says, or two men (Luke), or an angel (Matthew)?"[35]

Answer: Apparently Ehrman didn't have literature written in 1845 or 1958, nor had he ever read Pickering's work on it. He never cites Pickering. This had been solved since 1845 and most likely before. As I've highlighted before, the Gospel accounts are designed to *supplement* one another, much like the testimonies of four credible witnesses, each proclaiming their **"word is truth"** (John 17:17), and we know that God does not lie (Num. 23:19). With this, we find our answer whereas Ehrman's failure to acknowledge this stems from intellectual laziness on his part. How easy it is to point the finger, but how difficult it is to point it at yourself— **"knock, and it shall be opened unto you"** (Matt. 7:7).

Here it is as follows:

Before we begin, let's get one thing right: angels are *men* without wings in the Bible, in every case. They appear as men; *no wings* (Judges 13:3-21; Gen. 18:2; Acts 1:10; Gen. 32:24, 30). The sequence is listed below.

1. Saturday the guards seal the stone and set a watch
2. Jesus **"is risen"**
3. Two woman come to the tomb on Sunday early in the morning (5-6 AM); Mary Magdalene and Mary Cleophas (Mark 16:1). Others, who are unnamed come with them (Luke 24:1); Joanna is one that is named in Luke 24:10

---

[35] Ibid, page 8

and Salome in Mark 16:1-2. On the way they worry about the stone (Mark 16:3).
4. The stone is rolled back by the angel of the Lord and there is an earthquake (Matthew 28:2)—this is happening at the same time as Matthew 28:1, when they are on the way there. By the time they made it to the tomb the sun had risen.
5. They arrive and see the stone rolled back, the angel of the Lord is no longer outside the tomb (Mark 16:4; Luke 24:2; John 20:1). They go in.
6. (Matt. 28:5 notice **"women"** plural, not *"woman"*) receive the message from the angels (plural) inside (Luke 24:3-8; Mark 16:5-7; Matthew 28:5-7). There are two separate messages from the angels implying two of them (Matt. 28:5 and Mark 16:6 is one angel and Luke 24:5 is a saying from both). Angels look like men so Luke 24:4 says **"two men."** The women depart immediately in fear to go tell those outside (with the spices) what they have seen (Mark 16:8; Matt. 28:8). The "watch" (guards) leave (Matt. 28:11-15).
7. Mary Magdalene exits the tomb before the others and runs off first to tell the disciples (John 20:1-2) Mary Cleophas and Joanna run after behind her (Luke 24:10).
8. Meanwhile, Peter and John as told news by Mary Magdalene, arrive and look in. Peter goes fully in the tomb and observes the clothing followed by John (John 20:3-8) and comes back out (Luke 24:12). (Since they don't see angels they suppose that the two women were lying when they get the report (Luke 24:11, 23).
9. As the Apostles and the women leave the tomb, unable to embalm and anoint a body *that isn't there*, Mary Magdalene returns and stays weeping, at this point the Lord appears to her as the first post-Resurrection appearance (Mark 16:9; John 20:11-17).
10. Jesus presents the Blood in Heaven (John 20:17; Heb. 9:22-24)

11. Mary Cleophas and Joanna return, after this with the women they have contacted. They meet Jesus immediately after He has appeared to Mary Magdalene (Matt. 28:9-10; Luke 24:9-11).
12. Mary Magdalene goes and tells the disciples (Mark 16:10-11; John 20:18). Later, Jesus appears to Peter and to others (Matt. 28:9; Luke 24:34, 13-35; Mark 16:12-13) and so forth.

Given that the Resurrected body of Jesus Christ can become *invisible* (Luke 24:31) and *pass through solid objects* with ease (John 20:19, 26), other discrepancies from the account melt away. It seems our esteemed colleague has made a grave error—the four Gospels are *like* the four accounts of the Tribulation in the book of Revelation, and they are also *like* the books of the Prophets. They are *like* that because they are *supplementary of one another to get the whole picture*. It's as if a painter placed pieces of his paining all around. Some pieces go on top of others and some on the sides as if it were a giant puzzle. The Lord uses *similitudes* in His Book in case you don't get it the first time. This is not the same as having 300+ new versions on your bookshelf and going through each one to see what God said simply due to the contradictory nature between the versions. Those "bibles" are *not the same*. They actually *do* present real contradictions between themselves and within their own text that cannot be settled. I have given references to some of these created contradictions in new versions already (see pages 355-60, examples "dd," "b," and "ss" in Chapter 5 for instance).

The Gospel accounts can be likened to a policeman conducting interviews with multiple witnesses to gain a comprehensive understanding of a particular event. As the reader, you play the role of the policeman. Ehrman takes the stance that each Gospel account should be examined independently, focusing on its historical accuracy. According to this viewpoint, any deviation or difference among the accounts would imply errors or inaccuracies. For instance, Luke provides unique details, such as an advanced perspective on the afterlife during the time of the Law (Luke 16), while John offers a more detailed account of Jesus' early ministry (John 1-2), which the other three Gospels lack. You've seen this in action with the post-Resurrection narrative (see above).

He views it as reading four different history books on the same event, which they are, but he is forgetting a crucial ingredient: **"the testimony of Jesus is the spirit of prophecy"** (Rev. 19:10). You aren't reading Will Durnat's take on the Roman Empire here, nor are you reading *"The Rise and Fall of the Third Reich"* by Shirer. It is not a human book but meant for humans to read. Sometimes I think that God wrote the Book that way just to mess-up a person like Ehrman. **"I the LORD will answer him that cometh according to the multitude of his idols"** (Ezek. 14:4). I know I am not alone in this thought. He will let you do it too (Ezek. 14:1-11; Jer. 13:16). In fact, the only thing Jesus *rejoiced* over in the Gospel accounts was hiding things like this from the very same types of people (Luke 10:21; Matt. 11:25; Psa. 8:2). He succeeded in his work (Isa. 29:14).

The Gospel accounts are *supplementary* to one another, just as many historical documents and reports can be. That Book is put together like the human body. I mean, why not just have everything laid out and explained already? Why the long list of names everywhere? Why have to hunt everything down? Why give the making of the Tabernacle in Exodus more chapters and writing space than the very creation of the Universe?—Odd book to say the least. Nothing like it.

Ehrman would fit into the category of Malachi 2:6-10, but today *we are under grace* (Eph. 2:8-9; Rom. 4:4-5).

In respect to the prophets, when considering the major themes in each book, you get something like this:

- Isaiah (760-698 B.C.) saw: First Advent/The Birth of Christ, Calvary/Crucifixion of Christ, Return of the Jews, Antichrist/Son of Perdition, The Tribulation, Second Advent, Armageddon, The Millennium/Restoration and Conversion of the Nation of Israel, New Creation/ New Jerusalem

- Jeremiah (629-562 B.C.) saw: First Advent/Birth of Christ, return of the Jews, Tribulation, Second Advent, Millennium

- Ezekiel (593-573 B.C.) saw: First Advent, Return of the Jews, Antichrist/Son of Perdition, Second Advent, Armageddon, Last Revolt of Satan, Restoration of the Nation of Israel/and earth/Millennium

- Moses (1451 B.C.) saw: First Advent, Second Advent, Return and Restoration of the Nation of Israel... (Moses prophesied in *the First Book* practically everything that was to happen)

- Malachi (397 B.C.) saw: The First Advent, Second Advent

- John (A.D. 90-95) saw: The Antichrist/Son of Perdition, The Tribulation, Armageddon, Second Advent, The Millennium, Last Revolt of Satan, Renovation of the earth, New Creation/New Jerusalem

- Daniel (606-534 B.C.) saw: Calvary, Destruction of Jerusalem in A.D. 70, Times of the Gentiles, Antichrist/Son of Perdition, The Tribulation, Second Advent

- Samuel (Possible writer of Judges) saw in Judges *chapter 5 alone* (1296 B.C.): Armageddon, Second Advent

None of the writers had the slightest idea as to what they were seeing or writing. They were told to write, so they did. These are *broad strokes* of only a few examples in the Bible. The Book is a *prophetic book as well as historical.* For instance, many things in Deuteronomy 28 happened to Israel in the book of Second Kings but they *also* continued beyond that into World War II during the Holocaust, and they will happen again in the future. **"The testimony of Jesus is the spirit of prophecy."**

It becomes evident to anyone who delves into the *study* of the Bible that the writers of the Gospels incorporated certain elements, subtly interwoven by the Holy Spirit. Imagine that. God is a character, man. The Old Testament writers had no idea what they were writing (1 Peter 1:10-12).

Imagine being told to write all this mess about a shepherd and a gardener (Gen. 4), and about a tent in the wilderness (Exod. 25), or some dreams that a guy had (Gen. 36). Imagine having to write that odd prayer *supposedly* about Samuel when he was born (1 Sam. 2). What about this guy named "Joshua" leading Israel into the promise land with huge lists of names and places...what is all that doing in a "Holy Book"? It's all important and it's how God writes, for he has written a Book (Exod. 32:32-33).

What kind of a book would you expect God to write? Maybe something like the *"Bhagavad Gita"? "The Vedas"? "Tibetan Book of the Dead"? "New Age Geometry"?* Maybe the *"holy Koran"?* If God were to write a book intended for earthly accessibility, it would take the form of a King James Authorized Bible—a text that can be freely printed without seeking anyone's permission (a valuable convenience later on in the future). It would be remarkably straightforward, comprehendible even to a fifth-grader. However, it would also be intentionally complex to the extent that even the most esteemed "scholars" would falter tripping over their own hubris, resulting in their perplexity and contradictory interpretations. They would be cut-up (Heb. 4:12). There is no way man can get 40 some authors together over ~1700 years on three different continents and have the continuity that the Bible does—There is just no way. It has never been done by anyone else.

Only problem is...people have forgotten how to read it and have *traded career advancement for the truth.* I mean, ask yourself why write the Book in such a way that you really have to study and search the thing out to see even the broad strokes, or even just to answer a simple question? A question like *"Do they see a man, as Mark says, or two men (Luke), or an angel (Matthew)?"* Why not just make it clear for the Ehrman "text-type"? Why would God write a book like that?—This is the real question Mr. Ehrman failed to "exegete." "Why didn't God make things easy?" "Why didn't God write it the way *we* write?" "Why didn't God write it the way *I wanted* it to be written?"—He wants you to get to know Him. He's like a Father who is watching His toddler draw a picture—nothing is in the lines and the house is smaller than the people, and all the lines are crooked, but He offers help and says, **"Herein is love, not that we loved God, but that he loved us, and sent his Son to be the propitiation for our sins"** (1 John 4:10).

First, it helps to know the author. Having a relationship with the one who has given inspiration to it really goes a long way. Second, the Christian walks by faith: **"for we walk BY FAITH, not by sight"** (2 Cor. 5:7).

Problem: "It's amazing how internal problems like these, if you're not alerted to them, are easily passed by when you read the Gospels, but how when someone points them out they seem so obvious. Students often ask me, 'Why didn't I see this before?' For example, in John's Gospel, Jesus performs his first miracle in chapter 2, when he turns the water into wine...and we are told that 'this was the first sign that Jesus did' (John 2:11). Later in that chapter we are told that Jesus did 'many signs' in Jerusalem (John 2:23). And then, in chapter 4, he heals the son of a centurion, and the author says, 'This was the second sign that Jesus did' (John 4:54). Huh? One sign, many signs, and then a second sign?"[36]

Answer: In John 2:11 we have, **"This beginning of MIRACLES did Jesus IN Cana of GALILEE...."** Next we have Jesus leaving to go *to Jerusalem* (John 2:12-13). In John 2:23 we read **"miracles"** plural, *in Jerusalem*. Then in John 4:3 we are told that Jesus *left Jerusalem* (Judaea) and *went again into Galilee*. To get to Galilee, which is north, Jesus had to cross through Samaria. So, Jesus is going from Judaea (south), through Samaria (northward), to Galilee (north). We have it again in John 4:45 where you are *expressly told* that Jesus is now in Galilee where His *second* miracle is performed *in that location*. It is a *location* specific issue.

It even says it in the very verse and chapter in which Ehrman cited (John 4:54). You have a *set of miracles Jesus did in Jerusalem* in John 2:23 and the **"beginning"** of them in Galilee (John 2:11), and a **"second"** one *in Galilee* (John 4:54). Why so quick to title this a mistake when you, the reader, were just told He had done many **"miracles"**? This guy is a *professor teaching kids about the New Testament* and he can't seem to read English. He has been blinded by his ambitions. The next one is a similar issue.

Problem: "In John 13:36, Peter says to Jesus, 'Lord, where are you going?' A few verses later Thomas says, 'Lord, we do not know where you are going' (John 14:5). And then, a few minutes later, at the same meal, Jesus upbraids his disciples by saying, 'Now I am going to the one who sent me, yet none of you asks me, Where are you going?' (John 16:5).

---

[36] Ibid

380   Chapter 8

Either Jesus had a very short attention span or there is something strange going on with the sources for these chapters, creating an odd kind of disconnect."[37]

Answer: There is definitely *something* disconnected. Perhaps it's time to unplug the TV for a while, as it seems to be deteriorating your mental faculties. Observe how readily he suggests a solution to his own quandary—the solution being *"the sources for these chapters,"* namely the manuscripts.

I should remind the reader that Ehrman is using his *own* translations of *"The* Greek" and also using Metzger's NRSV. Given that I have covered the vague meaning of *"the Greek text,"* not much will be said about it here. At least Ehrman was in such high standing in Metzger's eyes *as to write a textbook together.* **"By their fruits ye shall know them."**

What is going on here in the text? I mean, you really do *have to be taught how to be this dumb.* In case the reader is upset with my language, may I remind them that I will show no quarter to a wolf when attacking sheep. Let us now analyze Ehrman's *"attention span"* shall we? After all, we are only covering three chapters of writing here.

In John 13:36 we have Peter asking Jesus, **"whither thou goest"** because of what Jesus says in verse 33, where the context is the future crucifixion (verse 31). In 14:5 we have Thomas asking Jesus *the same question* after hearing 14:1-4. Thomas asks for, **"the way"** when Jesus then responds with, **"I am the way"** (John 14:6). You also have Philip unsure whether or not he has seen the Father (14:8-9) *after* hearing John 6:46, and 12:45, etc.

The disciples are still having a bit of trouble with *understanding.* The key to Ehrman's debacle is what happens *in-between 14:5 and 16:5.* The only disciple to interrupt is Judas (not Iscariot), at 14:22. Everyone else is *quiet* and *listening.* What makes everyone *really* quiet? Why, it's what

---
[37] Ibid, page 9

Christ says in 15:18, 19, 20, 24, 16:1, 2, 3, 4. Then we read in 16:5, **"But now I go my way to him that sent me; and none of you asketh me, Whither goest thou?"** If you had heard those things in 15:18-16:4 you would have had **"sorrow"** fill your heart too (John 16:6), and you probably would have shut your mouth in *sheer amazement* by what He was saying. In fact, one of the things his disciples did was *stop asking him the same question that Peter and Thomas both asked previously, even after Christ had repeated Himself.* Christ is saying, in that moment, that no one has asked the original question that they wanted to know, because of everything He just laid on them—*they were speechless,* and Christ is pointing that out.

Look at the next verse (John 16:6)—Jesus told them the world would *hate them* and they would *be killed* (16:2, 15:18) —they were, they will be *persecuted* (15:20)—they were, people will *hate Jesus* (15:23)—they did, and people will hate them for loving and following Jesus Christ—they do. What kind of a *fool* would ask "wither goest thou" after *that*? They did not question again until 16:17.

If you don't believe the complete asinine stupidity of Dr. Ehrman yet, then maybe this next one should allow you to cash in your chips. You will find on page 9, *"Problems turn out to be even more common in the Old Testament, starting at its very beginning. Some people go to great lengths to smooth over all these differences, but when you look at them closely, they are very difficult indeed to reconcile."* Indeed Dr. Ehrman, indeed. When one takes a *"look" "closely,"* yes, what he said. Why doesn't Ehrman publish a novel on his proposed solutions to the text instead of just pointing out "problems"? Simple—he would no longer have the approval of his academic friends.

What Ehrman means is that people go to great lengths to *reconcile their biases,* which is exactly what he is doing now. He has, in fact, made an entire career out of it, just as Singer did which we talked about in the chapter, *"The Witnessed."* His house of cards rests on the work of other destructive critics such as White, Metzger, Origen, Hort, and Nestle. This group *aspires* to be like one another, and to appear "smarter" than the next.

Problem: "The creation account is different from the account in Genesis 2...Are animals created before humans, as in chapter 1, or after, as in chapter 2? Are plants created before humans or afterward? Is 'man' the first living creature to be created or the last? Is the woman created at the same time as man or separately?..If 'light' was created on the first day of creation in Genesis 1, how is it that the sun, moon, and stars were not created until the fourth day?"[38]

Answer: So, do we see Ehrman's problem here? *He never got past the first chapter, and on to chapter two.* No wonder he's made a blundering mess of it. What we have in Genesis 1 is a creation account as described in days, and in chapter 2 a *summary* of the account in chapter 1.

Firstly, the **"light"** in Genesis 1:3 and the **"Day"** and **"Night"** of Genesis 1:5 are *absolute* darkness and *absolute* light. You can gather that much from there not being material objects emitting light until the fourth day. The Gospel of John gives you the key to interpretation (John 1:4-6), also notice that John 1:1 begins how Genesis 1:1 does. The Holy Spirit is taking you back to Genesis 1:1 when you read John 1:1-3. Did Jesus have a physical, literal sun 864,000 miles in diameter and burning at 10,000 degrees Fahrenheit inside Him? No—it was **"the true Light, which lighteth every man that cometh into the world"** (John 1:9).

It's the *"Light"* and *"Darkness"* used in the same sense as it's used in 1 John 1:5; Matthew 8:12, 22:13, 25:30; Daniel 2:22; and Psalm 104:2. It is *not* a twenty-four hour period of light and darkness. The twenty-four hour period starts in Genesis 1:14-19, which is where the twenty-four hour solar-

---

[38] Ibid

cycle starts. This is also where Jewish time comes from: **"evening and the morning."** A new day begins in the **"evening"** so a new Jewish day begins in the *evening* (6pm-6pm).

The layout of chapter 1 is as follows:

- *Day 0*: original creation destroyed; new creation is about to be made (Gen. 1:1-2); creation of the third Heaven (Cf. Gen. 1:28, 9:1; 2 Peter 3:5-6; Psa. 148:1-12. This truth is hidden in every other new version). This is one of the unique revelations only found in a KJB.

- *Day 1*: the creation of absolute **"light"** and **"darkness"** (Gen 1:3-5) as given by the titles **"Day"** and **"Night."**

- *Day 2*: the creation of the second Heaven, which is the universe contained in the **"firmament"** (Gen. 1:6-8)

- *Day 3*: the **"land"** and the sea of earth; plant life (Gen. 1:9-13)

- *Day 4*: moon, sun, activity in the universe such as other planets and **"stars"** and the like; finishing of the first Heaven which is the atmosphere (Gen. 1:14-19)

- *Day 5*: **"Fish,"** aquatic life, whales, birds (Gen. 1:20-23)

- *Day 6*: Animals *and* **"man"**/woman were created (Gen. 1:24-31)

Beginning in chapter 2, we have the **"seventh day"** in which God **"rested"** (Gen. 2:1-3). We then go into a summary and elaboration of the events that happened *in chapter one*. 2:5 is where Dr. Ehrman got stuck, again. In 2:6 we have our answer as to what was going on with the plants on earth.

They needed water to grow. You see a similar thing in 2:8-9, **"And the LORD God planted a garden"** with **"And out of the ground made the LORD God grow every tree that is pleasant to the SIGHT, and good for FOOD."**

"Food" for *who*? **"Pleasant"** to *who's* eyes?—Man. We have a breakdown of events from chapter 1 in 2:4-7, where God is putting the *seeds* in the ground, *watering* the earth, the plants *grow*, and man is created to be a caretaker.

In 2:8-15 we have God making a *certain place on earth specifically for man*, with *unique vegetation, and animals fit for man*. It's a close-up view concerning a particular place of interest for God.

We see Ehrman stumble again in 2:18 where you read, **"it is not good for man to be alone"** and then in 2:19 we see God forming *more* animals and birds that are **"a help meet for him."** This is not the same as **"And God made the beast of the earth"** (Gen. 1:25). These are animals and birds *in the garden of Eden, not the entire earth*. If God brought every single bird, beast, creeping thing, cattle, fish, etc., to Adam to name them, they would have been doing that for much longer than 24 hours. We know that man and woman were created on day six. This would mean that Genesis 2:7-20 all took place *before* the seventh day. God wants him to name the **"help meet for him"** that he *just created* (Gen. 2:18-19).

This obviously doesn't work out so God makes woman out of man (Gen. 2:20-22) on *the same day he made man and beast*; the sixth day. Notice also that it says that **"every thing that creepeth"** was made in Genesis 1:25 but *not* **"every"** beast or cattle. It also says **"every living creature"** in the seas and air in 1:21. Why not "every" beast or cattle?—God does say **"every beast"** in 1:30 *after man and woman are created* and the specific vegetation in the Edenic paradise. Genesis 2:7-25 took place in Genesis 1:26-28. 1:29-31 took place in ~2:23-25.

Ehrman even mentions since chapters 1 and 2 use a few different words, that there *must* have been two different authors. All modern "scholars" of Ehrman's caliber believe that the first five books of Moses were *not* in fact written by Moses: *"moses did not write the Pentateuch (the first five books of the Old Testament) and Matthew, Mark, Luke, and John did not write the Gospels."*[39]

It's a mysterious author "X." Scholars would assign a letter such as "J" or "E," or other letters to "unknown authors" who used different words like "Elohim" (אֱלֹהִים) in Hebrew instead of "Jehovah" (יְהוָה). This is called *"Astruc's Clue,"* brought forward by a French *Catholic* named Jean Astruc (1684-1766). Astruc's Clue has been proven to be incorrect by numerous people over the years but the concept is still regurgitated with new names. One of those who debunked it being Robert D. Wilson of Princeton, who spoke 45 languages. The "new updated version" of Astruc's Clue is called, *"The Four Source Hypothesis."* This is used by "brilliant scholars" to try and understand the "problems" of the Gospels; often dubbed "the synoptic problem"—how they differ in some places, and how they are similar. "The Four Source Hypothesis" creates more problems than it solves.

It is as follows:

1. Mark is the earliest Gospel, so he is safe.
2. Matthew gets his stuff from Mark and the mystery author "Q" as well as mystery author "M."
3. Luke gets his stuff from Mark and "Q" and another mystery writer "L."
4. What you have there with "Q," "M," and "L" are three completely unknown authors/sources influencing the Gospel accounts which is what makes them "different." —*Not* that they were written by three different people. The presence of "Q," "M," and "L" in the Gospel accounts signifies the influence of three unidentified sources or authors. These elements supposedly contribute to the

---

[39] *"Jesus, Interrupted,"* page 5

distinctiveness of the Gospels, that is, *not* because they were *written by three different individuals.*

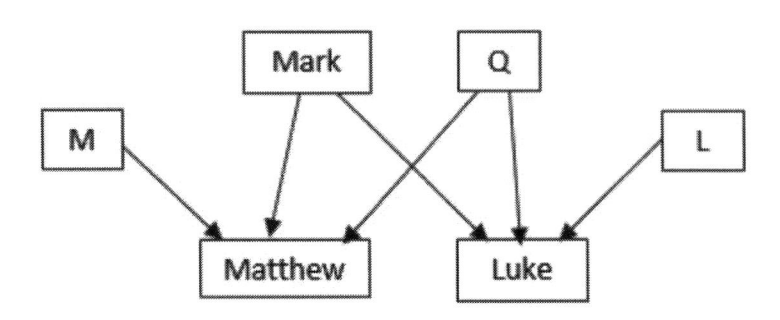

```
        Mark        Q
  M  ╲  ╱  ╲   ╱  ╲     L
      ╳      ╳
  ╲  ╱  ╲  ╱  ╲  ╱  ╲
   Matthew      Luke
```

Now, do I need to really explain that any further? It is pure conjecture. Do you know what kind of an idiot you have to be to make that mess up? That is about as effective as just throwing your hands up in the air and saying, *"dang it, man I don't know!."*

Clearly, Mark the servant wrote Mark, Matthew the tax collector penned Matthew, Luke the physician authored Luke, and John the fisherman likewise wrote John. The same style of writing is used in the Gospel of John as in the Epistles of First, Second, and Third John. Likewise, the book of Acts, who's writer is Luke, has the same style as the Gospel of Luke—it comes across in Greek and in English. For instance, the Epistles of Peter exhibit bad grammar; what you would expect from a fisherman that fished on a boat naked (John 21:7)—he was a "good-ol'-boy." These examples can be seen in 2 Peter 2:22, 1 Peter 5:8, and 2 Peter 3:16 amongst others. Nevertheless, there are church Fathers such as Papias (A.D. 60-130), Polycarp (A.D. 69-155), and Irenaeus (A.D. 120-200) who validate such claims.

In case you are wondering why John was not included with this *"alphabet soup,"* it's because modern scholars believe the Gospel of John is not "historical" but only "theological." They throw him out any chance they get. That's why it's always, "The Synoptics...*and John*." John is a fairy-tale account according to the modern scholar. It's the Gospel that has gotten the most people saved, more people under conviction, and is used in witnessing all the time. No wonder *someone* doesn't like it.

In case you think I am being unreasonable and hard onEhrman, let me remind you that in his works he makes fun of the Lord and makes fun of people that *believe* in the Book. He tries to doctor this up by attempting to stay *neutral*, but you'd have to have a mind like his to buy it for a even a minute. *"Sometimes Christian apologists say there are only three options to who Jesus was: a liar, a lunatic or the Lord. But there could be a fourth option - legend."* This is Ehrman's logic. Well, if He was *"legend"* then He would be a liar, wouldn't he? It would mean He lied and the people who talked about him lied. Ehrman wrote an entire book[40] on the subject of a *"Historical Jesus"*: whether or not Jesus really existed and his conclusion in the book was that Jesus *did* exist; he just became a legend like Iron Man. That would mean He and His followers were *liars*, not that they created a "legend" out of a martyr. Given that we have papyri that date within decades of John's "original writings," who presents Jesus Christ as the **"Son of God"** in very clear terms, the idea that his followers, after years and years, have turned Him into a super-hero type legend is a bit of a stretch.

Ehrman compares having faith to a cult-like mentality such as Nazi Germany and states, *"there are few things more dangerous than inbred religious certainty."*[41] Are there?—I thought you believed in absolute *"truth."* Remember when you said, *"the search for truth takes you where the evidence leads you, even if, at first, you don't want to go there."*[42] Surly the

---

[40] Bart D. Ehrman *"Did Jesus Exist? The Historical Argument for Jesus of Nazareth,"* 2012

[41] Ehrman, *"God's Problem,"* 2008, page 260

[42] Ehrman, *"Forged,"* 2011, Introduction

evidence of א and B would be outstanding cases, no? What about the complete conjectural basis of your textbooks? For, they are based on the same type of textural criticism as Metzger and Hort, give or take a few points. Would truth be uncertainty or certainty? If anyone is "religious" it is Ehrman, with his blind and cloned approach.

To Ehrman, truth *evolves*; it evolves in accord with the thoughts of his peers and their views on the Book, which are based on *"conjecture" and guesswork.* There is no *absolute truth* anywhere on planet earth for him—but hang on, didn't you also say, *"Different* authors *have different points of view. You can't just say, 'I believe in the Bible'."* Why not? You say that you *don't* believe in it, so why can't people believe in what it says?

"People need to use their intelligence to evaluate what they find to be true and untrue in the Bible. This is how we need to live life generally. Everything we hear and see we need to evaluate—whether the inspiring writings of the Bible or the inspiring writings of Shakespeare, Dostoevsky, or George Eliot, of Ghandi, Desmond Tutu, or the Dalai Lama."[43] That's how it's done—the entryway to doubt. The Bible is no different than the work of George Eliot. You just read him say it. He takes a *neutral approach to the Book, just as his teachers did*: Hort, Metzger, Weiss, Wells, Birch, Lachmann, Griesbach, Nestle, Kenyon, Grant, et al. They produce **"after his kind."** That Book does not take a neutral approach on you, (Heb. 4:12-13) it is a *critic.* Let's continue.

Problem: "When Noah takes the animals on the ark, does he take seven pairs of all the 'clean' animals, as Genesis 7:2 states, or just two pairs, as Genesis 7:9-10 indicates?"[44]

---

[43] Ehrman,*"Jesus Interrupted,"* pages 281-282

[44] Ibid, page 10

Saving Private Ehrman

Answer: Let's address a concerning issue in his *reading approach*. Take a moment to examine verse 8, a verse *conveniently overlooked* by him. Do we discern a recurring pattern here, revealing how Ehrman and his associates can cause confusion and turmoil in seminary students?

Imagine going into a seminary with little to no Bible knowledge—you haven't read it through a few times, let alone once; you haven't the slightest idea as to what's actually *in* the Book and then you get a professor like Ehrman. Imagine this negative bias against the Book and pounding for 1-8 years by other faculty, staff, *and peers*. Some experience 4-8 years of it. Hearing: *"The utilization of this particular term in the King James translation can be deemed highly regrettable. The intended word choice ought to have been..."* and, *"It is essential to acknowledge that translations, by virtue of not being the original texts or asserting divine inspiration, lack inherent inspiration. Thus, it is imperative to approach them with a discerning mindset."* And, *"We are currently equipped with dependable translations that bear significant proximity to the original texts."* And again, *"We have reliable translations today which are close to the original,"* and then, *"In order to discern the author's intended meaning, it is imperative to rely on the original Greek text and engage in a careful analysis of the author's intent."* On and on...

In Genesis 7:8 we see some unclean and clean beasts which you were told about in verse 2 and 3. The **"two by two"** or "pairs" as Ehrman puts it, is talking about *the male and females in verse 8-9;* **"by sevens"** is if they are *clean beasts* or fowls of the air. If they are *unclean beasts*, they are only in pairs, as seen in verse two. At what point does Ehrman become an unreliable source?

Problem: "God tells Moses 'I appeared to Abraham, Isaac, and Jacob as God Almighty, but by my name The LORD' [=Yahweh] I did not make myself known to them' (Exodus 6:3). How does this square with what is found earlier, in Genesis, where God does make himself known to Abraham as The LORD: 'Then he [God] said to him [Abraham], I am The LORD [=Yahweh] who brought you from Ur of the Chaldeans' (Genesis 15:7)?"[45]

Answer: *"Yahweh"* is what pretentious people call Jehovah today. It's always been Jehovah in English. Yahweh is actually the name of a desert pagan god of the Canaanites. If you think I'm pulling your leg then look into it. In Hebrew, the name *"Jehovah"* appears as יהוה. It's what's known as the "Tetragrammaton."

Yahweh doesn't make much sense but *no one really knows its exact pronunciation* and it was done that way on purpose. In the Authorized Version it usually appears as **"LORD"** or **"JEHOVAH,"** and sometimes **"GOD."**

Its pronunciation is impossible based on the letters that make up the Tetragrammaton. In most Tanakh's you will see it as יְהוָה —if you were to literally try and pronounce it, it would sound like you were just breathing in and out while making strange sounds. The English **"JEHOVAH"** fills in the gaps, otherwise it would be something like, "Ye-h-v/w-h" or some variation thereof. Since there is no "J" sound in Hebrew, people like to think it's *"Yahweh,"* just like **"Jesus"** would be *"Yeshua"*; **"Joshua"** is another name for it in English. "Yeshua" has the same in-vogue-ness or imitation "veritas" today for Jesus' name as "Yahweh" does for Jehovah.

This problem we have here is a prime example of a King James text shedding light on the Hebrew. Yes, the English can do that. I have not seen anything to the contrary and am open to discussion. Show me one thing you can get from a Greek New Testament, any Greek New Testament, or a Hebrew O.T., that I can't find in a King James Bible. You

---

[45] Ibid

can't do it. But I can show you things that you *can't* find in "the" Hebrew *or* Greek.

Why is that? Ever wonder why expositors in *Christianity have essentially stopped pulling light out of bibles since, roughly around 1980?* These revelations, so to speak, are either from Larkin, Bullinger, Ruckman, Scofield, or their students. It *does not* come from White, Metzger, Aland, MacArthur, Evans, et al. Meanwhile, Ehrman is still stuck in his NRSV or *his own* translation abilities, just like most "biblical scholars" today. Nevertheless, We will be quick and swift with **"the sword of the Spirit"** (Eph. 6:17).

This "error," like a few of the previous ones, has been spotted by, or shown to a man who is so *far gone* that the only hope left is to pray. How does one get this far away from truth? Ehrman is trying to get at the idea that LORD means the same thing (Jehovah), so how could they not know His name or what it meant? The first thing of note is that *Moses* is writing all of this that happened in the past.

Let us look at *the English*: **"And I appeared unto Abraham, unto Isaac, and unto Jacob, by the name of God Almighty, but by my name JEHOVAH WAS I NOT KNOWN to them"** (Exod. 6:3) and **"And he said unto him, I am the LORD that brought thee out of Ur of the Chaldees, to give thee this land to inherit it"** (Gen. 15:7).

Do you notice anything interesting about these two verses? *In English*, one says **"JEHOVAH"** and one says **"LORD"** thus solving the "error" of the text. Where is the problem? It's not in my Book. It's an *improvement* on the Hebrew. It's really that simple. But let us go a little beyond that. Ehrman *didn't mention* Eve using the same word **"LORD"** in Genesis 4:1 when she bare Cain and right after she bare Abel, his twin brother. He didn't mention it because *he's stuck on the Hebrew*. He believes it's "closer to the originals" and he's only looking at the Tetragrammaton (see above), which *first appears* in Gen. 4:1 as **"LORD"** *not* attached to anything else such as **"God,"** as in "**LORD God.**"

If we apply *the English to be the standard* we get different results *and* a revelation at that, instead of a contradiction. We see it again, in Genesis 4:26 when Seth and others began **"to call upon the name of the LORD."** You will see it again in Genesis 5:29 when Lamech names Noah, his son.

The first time we see the word **"LORD"** used at all is in Genesis 2:4 and occurs in verses 5, 7, 8, 9, 15, 16, 18, 19, 21, 22 etc. This is not **"LORD"** by itself but **"LORD God."** The word **"LORD"** *appears in relation to man* and *the covenants of God to man* as you see in Genesis 2:15-17, when God gives His conditions for Adam staying in his paradise.

Nevertheless, some will want more of an explanation. Now to the good stuff, LORD or JEHOVAH means "the Eternal," "the Immutable One," "He who Was and Is and Is To Come," as you see in Genesis 21:33. The *full meaning of this name was not given until* Exodus 3:14, which states, **"And God said unto Moses, I AM THAT I AM: and he said, Thus shalt thou say unto the children of Israel, I AM hath sent me unto you."** Christ confirms this meaning by calling himself Jehovah in John 8:58 by saying **"I am."**

What Ehrman did not see was the reference that *confirms* all of this in Genesis 32:29, where Jacob *wants to know the name of God indicating that Abraham, Isaac, and Jacob never knew the revelation of* **"JEHOVAH"** *as His name*. You see, Moses was telling you, the reader, all-along *who* He was, but Abraham, Isaac, and Jacob did not have the full revelation of that Name yet.

Someone wasn't reading their Bible. Jacob never even got His name, **"And Jacob asked him, and said, Tell me, I pray thee, thy name. And he said, Wherefore is it that thou dost ask after my name? And he blessed him there"** (Gen. 32:29) but *Moses did*, **"And I appeared unto Abraham, unto Isaac, and unto Jacob, by the name of God Almighty, but by my name JEHOVAH was I not known to them"** (Exod. 6:3),

"And God said unto Moses, I AM THAT I AM: and he said, Thus shalt thou say unto the children of Israel, I AM hath sent me unto you" (Exod. 3:14).

This is also where Ehrman gets the idea that chapter one and two were written by different authors. LORD is used in chapter *two* but you don't see it in chapter *one*. So, what does the destructive critic do? "They *must* have been written by two different people since some of the words are different." I thought the *words* didn't matter? With that logic then chapter three must have had a different author as well, and chapter 4 and so on. Maybe chapter 15 had 4 writers. All conjecture, no proof, a rabbit put into a hat to trick you into giving up the *words* God spoke, and *who* He spoke them through.

Satan was never interested in attacking the "fundamentals of the faith" or even the belief of Jesus. He knows very well *who* Jesus is and so do his companions, **"Thou believest that there is one God; thou doest well: the devils also believe, and tremble"** (James 2:19; also see Mark 3:11, 5:7, 1:24; Luke 4:34, 41). *They believe in the Virgin Birth, the Son of God, the Resurrection, and the Trinity just like you do.* They have been attacking what God *said* since the beginning of man, **"Yea, hath God said."**

When Lucifer quotes Scripture, such as in Matthew 4:6, **"cast thyself down: for it is written, He shall give his angels charge concerning thee: and in their hands they shall bear thee up, least at any time thou dash thy foot against a stone,"** people don't ask what he quoted. The devil quotes Psalm 91:11-12 which reads, **"For he shall give his angels charge over thee, TO KEEP THEE IN ALL THY WAYS. They shall bear thee up in their hands, lest thou dash thy foot against a stone."**

Notice any *omission* there? The devil omits **"to keep thee in all thy ways."** Now, why would he do something like that? Everything the devil temps Jesus Christ with is yet future, he was offering it right then, right that moment. It couldn't possibly be *the same guiding force behind* the ESV,

NIV, NKJV, NEB, NET, NASV, NRSV, etc., could it? Maybe the offering *now,* of money, prestige, accreditation, admiration, etc...no, that's just silly. The devil would't do that. He wouldn't use "good godly men" who practice **"yea, hath God said!"** Well at least according to James White he wouldn't. The Bible is off limits to the **"wiles of the devil"** if you believe White and his friends. In Luke 4:4 the *omission* is, **"but by every word of God."** The excuse given for the omission is because it was already said in Matthew 4:4, so there is no need to repeat it...**"Yea, hath God said."**

Problem: "The fifth plague was pestilence that killed 'all of the livestock of the Egyptians' (Exodus 9:5). How is it, then, that a few days later the seventh plague, of hail, was to destroy all of the Egyptian livestock in the fields (Exodus 9:21-22)? What livestock?"[46]

Answer: By now you should be familiar with the modus operandi of "Sola Scriptura"—using Scripture to answer Scripture. The first thing to note is that there is no time period given between Exodus 9:5-22. Sometimes in the Bible 2,000 years can be separated by a comma, or a verse, as we have seen previously in Isaiah 61:1-2, but also in Genesis 3:15; Psalm 118:22-25; Luke 21:24; Isaiah 53:10; Jeremiah 23:5. The Book shows you how to read it. It's like reading any book by any author where there are rules and a flow to things that are *dictated by how the author writes* and uses tools in his writing, like how I use italics. By now you may have gathered that I use italics to *emphasize* something, but that *"isn't always the case."*

The typology of *Exodus* is the Second Advent of Jesus Christ. The typology of the *plagues* in Exodus 7-12 done unto Pharaoh and Egypt is something that will happen again, in

---

[46] Ibid

the Tribulation (Rev. 11:1-8). If we take the typology of the Tribulation which is seven years (Dan. 9:24-27), or half the time being 42 months (Dan. 12:1-4, 7, 13; Rev. 13:5, 11:2-3, 12:14) we have a workable timeline for the plagues in Exodus. As we go from Exodus 9:5-22 an entire year could have passed *besides* the day mentioned in 9:6. A cow for instance can be fully grown anywhere between 8 months to 3 years. Sheep? Six months. Horse? 5-8 years. Oxen? 4 years. So, some of them could have been killed again in Exodus 9:21-22.

Most commentators will make the plagues in Exodus one right after another, but in *type* and in applying common sense given our problem here, it just doesn't work. The next thing we notice is that 9:3 reads, **"upon thy cattle which is IN THE FIELD,"** indicating that they were *of age*, meaning being *used for work*. There were undoubtedly some growing up and maturing towards that point. **"All the cattle of Egypt"** in verse 6 that died weren't *literally all the cows*, the word **"cattle"** here is used in a general sense as in "horses, asses, camels, oxen, and sheep" (see Exod. 12:29 and 9:3). Sort of like how we would say "field animal" or "barn animal."

Furthermore, 9:21-22 is talking about those *not* **"left in the field."** Both man and cattle went into houses (Exod. 9:20), as in, the younger cattle that weren't killed in Exodus 9:6 which *had time to grow up* by Exodus 9:22. How do I know this? Because God commanded the firstborn of the cattle to be killed in Exodus 12:29 along with the firstborn children. That shows a distinction.

Remember that *this man thinks he can tell you what should and should not be in your Bible. He doesn't know what's in it to begin with, let alone enough knowledge to alter it.*

Ehrman also has some "philosophical" problems with God which is surprising he didn't talk about it here, where God *kills a lot of innocent firstborn children* in Egypt. God keeps things pretty balanced, if you noticed the amount of people that died here, it amounts to about 22,273 (Num. 3:43), *right down to the cattle* (Num. 3:44-45). The Levites replace the firstborn that were killed in Egypt (Exod. 13:12-15; Num. 3:12, 8:17, 11). **"A false balance is an abomination to the LORD"** (Prov. 11:1).

What about these *philosophical differences* such as Joshua 6? Ehrman asks: *"Are we really to think of God as someone who orders the wholesale massacre of an entire city?"* and *"I suppose it makes sense that God would not want bad influences on his people- but does he really think that murdering all the toddlers and infants is necessary to that end?...What is one to make of Psalm 137, one of the most beautiful Psalms,...but takes a vicious turn at the end, when he (the writer) plots his revenge on God's enemies: 'Happy shall they be who take your little ones, and dash them against the rock.' Knocking the brains out of Babylonian babies in retaliation for what their father- soldiers did? Is this in the Bible?"*[47]

These are good questions, and many struggle with them. I did before I was saved. "How could an 'all loving God' be so monstrous?," I would ask myself and usually just left it at that, and not look too much into it. I was happy believing God was a monster. It meant I didn't have to believe in "all of that craziness." I thought I had enough evidence to form my opinion.

The biggest challenge for any young Christian today is not to get pulled into the world. Youth preachers look like they just got out of a Doja Cat video sometimes: Air Force Ones, Jordan Dunk's, and the "coolest" fashion to grab a young minds attention by saying, *"Hey, we are like the world, look at us. We are cool."* Does this actually work? Regardless of your preachers sense of "style," the best time to get saved *is anytime*, Moses didn't really start his ministry until he was about 80 (Exod. 7:7).

Amongst these challenges are "philosophical" ones. Did Noah appreciate the world being drowned out? Do you

---

[47] Ibid, pages 10-11

think he enjoyed hearing thousands clamor for the rocks in hopes of avoiding the watery grave? Im sure there were some things he missed—He did become a drunk after the flood (Gen. 9:20-21). The grandest question is: do we deserve to still be here based on how we treat each other and how humanity generally lives? How does God view the human race as a whole? Imagine possessing omniscience and being omnipresent—having complete knowledge of everyone's deepest and most concealed desires and thoughts. Some of these innermost thoughts of the heart, if projected onto a screen, would likely repulse the average person and have many on their knees in horror. God, however, sees, comprehends, and scrutinizes the innermost depths of human hearts. What lies within your own heart? Do you possess the authority to sit in judgment of the Creator? By what right do you claim such privilege? Sure, it's good to be critical, but honestly you can't argue with: **"There is none righteous, no, not one."** These questions and observations can be challenging for a Christian at any age, but you have a resource: *the Bible.*

Chapter 9: The Righteous Atheist

"which are some things hard to be understood, which they that are unlearned and unstable wrest, as they do also the other scriptures, unto their own destruction."
— 2 Peter 3:16
"The entrance of thy words giveth light; it giveth understanding unto the simple."
— Psalm 119:130

PROBLEM: Psalms 137:9 was too harsh for God to write so He never wrote it.[1]

Answer: For the sake of argument, let us suppose that God did *not* write the Bible. In such a scenario, we must consider the reasons behind this notion. Does it not align with the rest of the Bible? Take, for instance, the case of Babylon, where God chose to employ them as a means to punish the Jews, only to later bring about their downfall through the rise of the Medes/Persians for punishing the Jews. And then, "in a twist of events," the Medes/Persians themselves were overthrown by the Alexandrian empire because the Medes overthrew Babylon, thus continuing the chain of conquests. Such historical complexities beg us to question the providential orchestrations at play—history is centered around the Jew.

---

[1] Ehrman, *"Jesus, Interrupted,"* pages 10-11

"**It is impossible but that offences will come: but woe unto him, through whom they come!**" (Luke 17:1). The Jew is the center. The verse we are dealing with (Psa. 137:9) has an "offense that must come." Who will do it? Until we get there, let's first hash out why **"the finger of God"** is on the passage or not on the passage.

What about Exodus all the way through Deuteronomy, where God tells the Israelites to **"utterly overthrow"** the people of the land that they are to inherit (Exod. 23:24), to *kill* witches (Exod. 22:18), *kill* adulterers (Levi. 20:10), *kill* disobedient and rebellious children (Deut. 21:18-21). God will **"laugh at the trial of the innocent"** (Job 9:23), and **"laugh"** at the powers of the kings of the world (Psa. 2:4). When it comes to inheriting the land they are told to **"destroy all the people"** (Exod. 24:27), to put the people **"into your hand"** (Exod. 23:31), to not **"make a covenant"** with them (Exod. 34:15). (Are we seeing where Muhammad got his "religion"?)

But *why? Why? Why?*

Why drive all these people off the land and cause war to break out in the process? For that, you have to ask *why* God would drown out *an entire world civilization of anywhere between one million and one billion-plus by a worldwide flood as talked about in Genesis.*

"And GOD SAW that the WICKEDNESS OF MAN was great in the earth, and that every imagination of the thoughts of his heart was only EVIL continually. And it repented the LORD that he had made man on the earth, and it grieved him at his heart. And the LORD said, I will destroy man whom I have created from the face of the earth; both man, and beast, and the creeping thing, and the fowls of the air; for it repenteth me that I have made them" (Gen. 6:5-7).

In relation to their quest for land, they invaded and seized territories inhabited by, no doubt, peaceful, admirable, and culturally rich peoples—Or were they? Same thing, **"Defile** not therefore the land which ye shall inhabit, wherein I dwell: for I the LORD dwell among the children of Israel" (Num. 35:34). **"(For all these abominations have the men of the land done, which were BEFORE you, and the land is defiled;) That the land spue not you out also, when ye defile it, AS it spued out the nations that were BEFORE you"** (Levi. 18:27-28).

The **"abominations"** that the nations who inhabited the land *before* Israel did are all mentioned in Leviticus chapter 18 dealing with sex. Here we are given the reason for getting the **"nations"** out of the land. What else can "defile the land"?—Murder (Num. 35:33-34). Israel inherited the land, but it was *conditioned* on working and keeping the Law: **"Therefore shall ye KEEP mine ordinance, that ye COMMIT NOT any one of these abominable customs, which were committed BEFORE you, and that ye defile not yourselves therein: I am the LORD your God"** (Levi 18:30).

"In that I command thee this day to love the LORD thy God, to WALK IN his ways, and to KEEP his COMMANDMENTS and his statutes and his judgments, that thou mayest live and multiply: and the LORD thy God shall bless thee in the land whither thou goest to possess it. BUT if thine heart turn away, so that thou wilt not hear, but shalt be drawn away, and worship other gods, and serve them; I denounce unto you this day, that ye shall surely perish, and that ye shall not prolong your days upon THE LAND, whither thou passest over Jordan to go to possess it" (Deut. 30:16-18). It's conditional and based on *works* of the Law.

Israel *did* turn to **"other gods,"** almost as soon as they had inherited the land. **"And yet they would not hearken unto their judges, but they went a whoring after OTHER GODS, and bowed themselves unto them: they turned quickly out of the way which their fathers WALKED IN, obeying the commandments of the LORD; but they did not so"** (Judg. 2:17).

That is only the children of the fathers who *originally* inherited the land, after Joshua died, **"And also all that generation were gathered unto their fathers: and there arose another generation after them, which knew not the LORD, nor yet the works which he had done for Israel. And the children of Israel DID EVIL in the sight of the LORD, and served Baalim"** (Judg. 2:10-11).

Man is having a really hard time following simple instructions, eh? This had been an ongoing issue, for in Joshua 24:23, Joshua is giving a speech to Israel and says something very telling; **"put away said he, the strange gods which ARE AMONG YOU."** Israel had idols right then, and were worshipping other gods *even then* after thousands had died in the wilderness from disobedience and *before* they are going into the land to inherit it.

God had brought them out of Egypt with signs and miracles, and wonders but that *is how we are*; we forget so quickly, just as they did. This also solves another "contradiction," of Judges 1:19. The LORD was with them, *but* did not help them win *entirely* since they *did not give their heart to the Lord. They had and worshiped idols among them,* **"That thou mayest love the LORD thy God, and that thou mayest obey his voice, and that thou mayest cleave unto him: for he is thy life, and the length of thy days: that thou mayest dwell in the land which the LORD sware unto thy fathers, to Abraham, to Isaac, and to Jacob, to give them"** (Deut. 30:20).

Man gets family and patriarchal leaders (Gen. 4-5) and he murders and becomes like disobedient children; man sets up government and he pushes God out of it and creates confusion (Gen. 10-11); man receives the Law and education in spiritual matters and he produces idolatry and self-worship (Exod. 20); man is given a king to rule over him with God to rule over the king and man ignores God's commands (1 Sam. 15); man is given the O.T. books of Scripture and then uses it to kill God's Son (Matt. 1-27);

given the Bible man then corrupts it to usher in another Dark Age (current). **"But we are all as an unclean thing, and all our righteousnesses are as filthy rags; and we all do fade as a leaf; and our iniquities, like the wind, have taken us away"** (Isa. 64:6).

Sodom and Gomorra were destroyed by "fire and brimstone," which is where we get the expression. What about all the children and innocents that were taken by the Lord on that day? What do we know about this place?

1. It is from the line of Ham (Gen. 10:19), as was Nimrod who built the Tower of Babel (Gen. 11), as were the Philistines, as were the inhabitants of Gaza, as was Egypt, the Canaanites, Hivites, Arkites, people originally of Nineveh (capital of Assyria), etc. None of these places are held in positive view within the Bible.

2. It is worth noting that Ham, the first individual recorded in the Bible to have engaged in an illicit act with his father Noah (Genesis 9:21-24), is likely associated with the practice of sodomy, particularly given the clues and contextual details surrounding the incident. Noah's awareness of **"what his son had done unto him"** indicates that he became aware of some impropriety upon awakening from his inebriated state. Interestingly, we observe a connection between drunkenness and nudity, as exemplified in Habakkuk 2:15, where the provision of alcohol precedes sexual encounters between men—where a man gives another man drink. Genesis 19:32 further illustrates the interplay between sex and alcohol through the narrative of Lot and his daughters, who resided in the city of Sodom. Their decision to intoxicate their father in order to preserve their lineage reveals the influence of cultural norms. Notably, the term "culture" derives from the root word "cult" and is defined as "the collective intellectual achievements shared within a society." It is important to recognize that culture can be

either good or bad; all that is necessary is the *shared beliefs* that shape the community.
3. According to the account in Genesis 19, Sodom and Gomorrah were plagued by a depraved population. Lot, encountering a group of angels (who look like men), attracts the attention of the townspeople. In a disturbing turn of events, some men from Sodom gather outside Lot's door, intent on engaging in a brutal act of rape—not merely as a sexual assault but as a submissive act towards the two angels in Lot's company (Genesis 19:1-7). Shockingly, instead of surrendering the angels, Lot offers his own daughters in their place, which raises unsettling questions about the prevalent norms of such a community (Genesis 19:8). One might wonder why no one else in the city intervened to prevent this mob of rapists from violently pounding on Lot's door.
4. We can look at the men's disinterest in pursuing Lot's two daughters in two possible ways. First, it could suggest that the daughters were considered unattractive or "not easy on the eyes"—homely. Alternatively, it implies that Sodom was a city predominantly inhabited by homosexuals who were not interested in engaging in sexual acts with virgin female flesh. This finds support in Genesis 19:31, where Lot's daughters express their concern that there is no man on earth available to them for procreation **"after the manner of ALL the earth."** This sentiment arises as they find themselves secluded in a cave, for Lot was hesitant to enter the city of Zoar due to witnessing *the same sins* prevalent in Sodom, which resulted in the complete destruction of the city. These scenarios suggest that either Lot's daughters had grown up in an environment surrounded by homosexuals who displayed no interest in them, or that they were simply unappealing in physical appearance. In either case, this observation reflects a society focused primarily on fleshly desires, lacking spiritual depth.

5. God destroyed Sodom and Gomorrah because **"the cry"** was **"great," "because their sin is very grievous"** (Gen. 18:20). In an attempt to save Lot's life, his brother Abraham engaged in a remarkable dialogue with the Almighty, as depicted in Genesis 18:23-33. It is an amazing view of the twenty-first Century man trying to bargain with God. Abraham's motive is to save his brother but if we look at it spiritually, and through the lens of Dr. Ehrman's problem, we get a very interesting take on the passage. Abraham starts with a plea to save the righteous out of the wicked, since God is going to take out the entire city in one-go. He starts with asking for 50 to be saved if they are righteous in verse 26, then 45, then 40, then 30, then 20, and finally 10. If there are *just 10 righteous in Sodom* then God will not destroy the city. Just 10, out of an entire city. God knew there wasn't even 10 so he dispatched two angels to check the place out and get Lot out of there since that was what Abraham *really* wanted (Gen 19:1). Well what about the kids you say? In 19:13 an angel is explaining the situation to Lot, **"because the cry of them is waxen great,"** who is **"them"**? They are not only the repenting of the people but also the *victims* of the city. Is it then possible then to conceive that many of these people prayed for the event to take place? Is it possible for people to be so beaten down and demoralized by others that they might wish death and the death of the persecutors with them? No doubt the children were taken straight up to Heaven since we are told in Romans 4:15 and 5:13, **"for where no law is, there is no transgression"** which see. There must be a **"knowledge between good and evil"** (Deut. 1:39; Gen. 2:9), for they are innocent until that time. **"Moreover your little ones, which ye said should be a prey, and your children, which in that day had no knowledge between good and evil, they shall go in thither, and unto them will I give it, and they shall**

possess it" (Deut. 1:39). There is a very clear case in which the children not having an understanding of good and evil and were not held accountable.

6. We have a similar case in Sodom as we did before the flood of Noah's day in relation to unrighteousness when God wiped a civilization off the face of earth.

7. If Sodom was *not* destroyed, what kind of an effect would this have had on the world of the O.T. saints? We see in 1 Samuel 15:3 where God commands Saul to **"utterly destroy"** the Amalekites because of what they did to Israel in Exodus 17. Saul does not (1 Sam. 15:9) utterly destroy them, he only destroyed what was **"vile and refuse."**. This is a lesson to man directly from God Himself worthy of heed in the dealings in history and human nature. What *you* may consider to be good may not in fact be good, and what *you* consider to be **"vile,"** may not in fact be vile. As the Lord said, "**Look not on his countenance, or on the height of his stature; because I have refused him: for the LORD seeth not as man seeth; for man looketh on the outward appearance, but the LORD looketh on the heart**" (1 Sam. 16:7). David had to deal with the Amalekites later in 1 Samuel 27.

8. Sodom and Gomorrah are likened **"spiritually"** to Egypt (Rev. 11:8). In Revelation 11:8 Jerusalem is called **"Sodom and Egypt."** They are likened to Sodom, because there will be a homosexual leading the nations and gathering them together to unite them. This would be the Antichrist. **"Neither shall he regard the God of his fathers, nor the desire of women, nor regard any god: for he shall magnify himself above all"** (Dan 11:37). Who is the **"he"** in the passage? He is a **"king"** (Dan. 11:36), who **"shall speak marvelous things against the God of gods," "he shall come in peaceably, and obtain the kingdom by flatteries"** (Dan. 11:21). He is **"a vile person"** who will **"place the abomination that maketh desolate"** in the sanctuary (Dan. 11:31). Jesus refers to

this in Matthew 24:15 where the context of that passage is that the person must **"endure"** (Matt. 24:13), to **"the end"** (Matt. 24:3) and to take **"heed that no man deceive you"** (Matt. 24:4). **"He"** is a prophet who will show **"great wonders"** and appear **"like a lamb"** (Rev. 13:11-13). **"He"** will show **"signs and lying wonders"** (2 Thess. 2:9). **"He"** will **"sitteth in the temple of God, shewing himself that he is God"** (2 Thess. 2:4). Many will mistake him to be God. Now what about "Egypt" that is mentioned with **"Sodom"** from Revelation 11:8? It is in type the Antichrist kingdom. Egypt, like Judah, has a **"sceptre"** (Gen. 49:10 Cf. Zech. 10:11), that one day will be **"broken"** (Isa. 14:5). Babylon, Egypt, and Assyria are all likened to Antichrist kingdoms and **"will be laid waste"** in the future (Nah. 3:7). Egypt has a ruler and its ruler is a type of the one working behind the Antichrist and is likened to a dragon: **"Thus saith the Lord GOD; Behold, I am against thee, Pharaoh king of Egypt, the GREAT DRAGON that lieth in the midst of his rivers"** (Ezek. 29:3) He is in the **"midst of the rivers"** because he is a **"serpent"** (Gen. 3:1), that is a water creature like Leviathan (Job 41)—it is satan himself (Rev. 12:9). Satan has a trinity which counterfeits God. His trinity consists of a *spirit* (the unclean spirit), the *father*, (the devil himself), and a *son* (the Antichrist). In Ezekiel 31:3 the **"Assyrian"** has been interchanged with **"Pharaoh's"** place as the Antichrist. The one moving the **"sceptre"** is still the same as it has always been. This is evident in Ezekiel 28:12 where God has a message for the king of Tyrus and is obviously not directed at the man, but what is and who working in the shadows *behind him*, for he *was not* **"in Eden"** nor was he an **"anointed chreub"** (Ezek. 28:13-17). We mustn't forget: **"For we wrestle not against flesh and blood, but against principalities, against powers, against the rulers of the darkness of this world, against spiritual wickedness in high places"** (Eph. 6:12).

We do things that go against God's judgments and statutes that can have ramifications for hundreds, even thousands of years. A most obvious and clear case being that of Adam and Eve eating the fruit (Gen. 3). After some time, Eve looked on the tree and **"saw it was good,"** and that it **"was pleasant,"** and that it could **"make one wise"** (Gen. 3:6). All of which are *positive*. You ever consider that? Every thing she considered was positive. She did not consider the possibility that if she did eat, trillions would die horrible deaths of starvation, cannibalism, old age, sickness, cancer, heart attack, war, famine, etc. In fact, the very first thing that **"old serpent"** said was **"yea"** (Gen. 3:1), then he questioned what God said. Fast forward to today in 2023, and look around the scene of Christianity. Give it a good hard look. Everybody is so focused on **"God is love"** (1 John 4:8), that people forget the other side of God.

"(For the LORD thy God is a jealous God among you) lest the anger of the LORD thy God be kindled against thee, and destroy thee from off the face of the earth" (Deut. 6:15).

"And it shall come to pass, that as the LORD rejoiced over you to do you good, and to multiply you; so the LORD will REJOICE OVER YOU TO DESTROY YOU, and to bring you to nought; and ye shall be plucked from off the land whither thou goest to possess it" (Deut. 28:63).

"For our God is a consuming fire" (Heb. 12:29).

"Set me as a seal upon thine heart, as a seal upon thine arm: for love is strong as death; jealousy is cruel as the grave: the coals thereof are coals of fire, which hath a most vehement flame" (Song of Sol. 8:6).

What people don't notice in John 3:16 is the fact that it's *past tense*, like a lot of John's Gospel. **"God so LOVED"** as in, the condition has been set at Calvary back in A.D. 33[2] for

---

[2] Some give different dates within a few years. You will never be short of different takes on chronology.

God's mercy to be on you in this age. You have to take the **"love"** *with* 2 Peter 3:10-12; Revelation 20:15; Malachi 4. The theme of the entire Book is God returning and *slaughtering* millions in the process, and taking his rightful Throne. You thought it was your salvation—no, that's the theme of *our* book; the pages of our own lives.

The **"fear of the Lord"** (Prov. 1:7) has been turned into a "reverential respect" as opposed to a down right shaking scared as in, **"the joints of his loins were loosed, and his knees smote one against another"** (Dan. 5:6), and **"trembling"** (Phil. 2:12), and down right **"terror"** (2 Cor. 5:11), like how you would treat the **"master"** (Mal. 1:6) of the universe who could put an end to it all just as quickly as He started it. *That doesn't get people in the doors*, instead what *does* is just talking about the "love," such as 1 Corinthians 13 in an ESV where **"charity"** has been interchanged with "love." Allowing a sodomite or a child molester to interpret *"love"* anyway they please. Love is just adult consent, right? Is that Biblical?—Turns out, it isn't.

What we have walked upon here and discovered is *the fall of modern Christianity rooted in "philosophical differences" with God Almighty*. The Bible gives you a hint about "philosophy" in Colossians 2:8. **"Except there come a falling away first"** (2 Thess. 2:3) God's plan will *not* reach fruition. He has told you what is going to happen. The question is, *how big is the fall*? How far away does Christianity have to fall for our Lord and Savior to return? The hallmark is found in 2 Timothy 4, **"For there will come a time when they will not endure sound doctrine."** We also see in chapter 3, **"ever learning and never able to come to the truth."** Sort of like… modern "Christian scholars" who will *eventually* be able to say **"thus saith the Lord GOD"** and tout the newest bible versions as being, "1,000's of hours of the *current, most up-to-date,* and *newest* Christian research." **"Sound doctrine"** would be God's *ability to preserve all his "w-o-r-d-s,"* not just a few or 70%, or even 98%, but *all, like He said He would*. The conversation has shifted from **"doctrine"** towards "love" and "teaching." This is not "love" dear reader, this is moist saliva dripping from the fangs of wolves, laying in wait with deep pockets.

Doctrine is the first thing listed in what **"scripture"** is profitable for in 2 Timothy 3:16. Paul averages about once per-page when mentioning **"doctrine"** in 1 and 2 Timothy. Does your pastor talk about doctrine? Does he teach **"sound doctrine"**? It has fell to the wayside along with Biblical literacy. New versions have changed it to *"teaching"* in many cases. Teaching *does not mean the same thing as doctrine.* Doctrine involves a set of teachings that contain **"traditions which ye have been taught"** from Paul and the Apostles—not the pope or the "Holy Mother Church" (2 Thess. 2:15 Cf. 1 Tim. 1:3, 10, 4:6, 16, 5:17, 6:1, 3). *"Teaching"* is the act of *presenting the doctrine,* as in 1 Timothy 4:11. It is not the doctrine itself, *which is found in the Bible.* For example, *how* else would you know that the Roman Catholic Church is wrong on about 99% of their *doctrines* (Rev. 2:14-15)? By **"study"** (2 Tim. 2:15). You have a Book in front of you to double check and see if someone is lying to you or not about what they are saying. "Doctrines" are statements of belief; "teachings" cover more area.

The Bible says **"call no man your father upon the earth"** (Matt. 23:9), the Catholic Church does. The Bible says there is **"one mediator between God and men, the man Christ Jesus"** (1 Tim. 2:5), the "Holy Mother Church" says other saints may intercede for you and Mary too to "help with your prayers." The Bible says, **"Thou shalt not make unto thee any graven image"** (Exod. 20:4), the Catholic Church says that you can have "aids in worship" such as statues of Mary and the saints. The Bible says Jesus **"offered one sacrifice for sins for ever"** (Heb. 10:12), the Catholic Church says no, we sacrifice Christ every Sunday at 11 o'clock in the form of a wafer via magic.

What you have today are many millions of Christians who are Biblically *illiterate*. How is it that more bibles (any version) are produced today, with *the most people ever* in history who are able to read, and the Bible being the number one selling Book in history, still to this day, yet today there are *fewer people who are Biblically literate*? It appears to be inversely correlated. How can you explain that? Did you know only 46% of professing Christian adult Americans can name the first book in the Bible?[3] It's *Genesis*! As in, "gene," "generate," "genealogy"... Only *11%* of people who own a Bible read the Bible *daily* and 19% read it *once a week!*[4] This is all while having the belief that the Bible is *"the word of God."* When a person believes something there is usually *action taken on that belief*. There appears to be a gap in what Christians profess and what they practice. A contributor to this gap, is no doubt the entry of bibles not representing what God said, but rather *close* to it—"reliable translations."

Yes, more people are turning to atheism, but there are *more* Christians today *than ever before* in history due to population size; but *less Biblical literacy*. According to pewresearch.org the majority of Christians are leaving and becoming atheist like Ehrman. People don't **"fear"** God anymore. They read the Bible and decide, *"well if a god can do all these things, and is willing to kill babies, then I don't want to worship and be involved with any god that does that kind of a thing."* Meanwhile, on Calvary everything had already taken place, the judgment and future demise of Satan (John 16:11; Eph. 2:2), the ability to enter into eternal rest if the **"gift"** is accepted (Rom 5:15-18), and if you missed that you even have *another* chance later to get it (but it will be a lot more difficult, Rev. 6-19).

How fitting for man to think he knows better. We crucified God in the flesh (1 Tim. 3:16; Mark 15:15-27), as he was

---

[3] Pew Research Center, *"U.S. Religious Knowledge Survey,"* 2010

[4] Center for Bible Engagement, *"The Power of the Bible"*

naked, sweating, groaning, and bleeding. We shot dice for God's clothes (Matt. 27:35), mocked Him, tempted Him (Matt. 27:42-43), offered him vinegar in place of water (Luke 23:36), we betrayed God as a friend (Luke 22:47-48), and jammed a spear in God's dead body to make sure he was really dead (John 19:34). *That is us.* That is what our fallen nature is like when we give into it: the **"old man."** It is no different than a bunch of drunk soldiers doing their duty and trying to get on with another routine crucifixion.

We are the ones who set up the death camps of Nazi Germany, where Jews were crammed into chambers and gassed in the thousands per day, taken to trenches and shot; babies thrown in on the top of the adult and adolescent bodies. That nature is as just as much *in you* than it is *in them*. It is fallen. We designed the iron maiden, the rack, crucifix, pear of anguish, and the thumbscrew in the Dark Ages and at Chelmno, Belzec, Sobibor, Treblinka, Majdanek, and Auschwitz we tried to exterminate, *in the most efficient way possible*, the entire Jewish race. We rape, slit each others throats, kill babies as they are still in the warm bath of their mothers womb, we gas people, mutilate human flesh, make people work in negative 40 degree Fahrenheit weather in Russia. But what does God have to do with all of this? *"He could have stopped it"* — yes, he could have, but He didn't. He even told you the Holocaust was going to happen in Deuteronomy 28. His kids were kicked out of the garden and now they are making a mess of things, but man still thinks he can do it just fine. **"Come before winter"** (2 Tim. 4:21).

The book of Job, the first book written for the Bible, deals with these very issues. In it you learn about what God *allows* to happen verses what He *directly causes* to happen. The will of God is for **"all men to be saved"** (1 Tim. 2:4) in this age. That's his *directive will*. Now, will that actually happen? Probably not, since men and women are free-agents and act accordingly. If God *forced* everyone to be saved then He wouldn't be much of a Father but a rather a tyrannical monster, exactly how most atheists today paint Him. John Calvin (A.D. 1509-1564) became utterly confused surrounding this topic. When he came to Romans 9 and Ephesians 1 he threw the baby out with the bathwater. Calvin made salvation only to those who were "elected" somewhere out in eternity, and they were *in Christ* within that eternity. That would inevitably mean that those in the Body of Christ would have to *fall out* (Gen. 3) and then somehow get *back in* the Body again by the death of Jesus Christ.

You may be wondering, how does someone *know* if they are actually "elect" or saved in Calvin's philosophical nightmare? *They don't know.* The only way to know is by "good works." If someone is *really* saved, then it will show in their life through *works*. This is called "Lordship Salvation" and is taught by MacArthur, Mathison, Crenshaw, etc. This of course, keeps you in salvation by works anyway you put it. Calvin also had people "predestined" for hell, otherwise called "reprobation" in Calvin's system. No matter what these individuals did, such as *believe on Jesus Christ the way the Bible tells you to*, it just isn't good enough. These people could believe, but *still* be destined for hell. In fact, according to John Girardeau reprobation is, *"foreordaining some human beings, for their sin, to destruction, in order to the glorification of God's retributive justice."*[5] So, what you just read was that all those of whom aren't "elect" will be glorifying God in hell by being in hell, since they can't choose to be there or not. Calvinism is a damnable heresy that sucks in the most well meaning of persons.

Palmer, of the NIV subscribes to Calvin's nightmare and got so lost in John 3 dealing with the New Birth that he assumed the New Birth wasn't a choice, similar to how a baby doesn't choose to be born by his mother. He made the fleshly birth the Spiritual Birth and the Spiritual Birth the

---

[5] John L. Girardeau, *"Calvinism and Evangelical Arminianism,"* 1984, pages 9-10

The Righteous Atheist 413

fleshy birth like Nicodemus did (John 3:4, 9). It is exactly the opposite of the very character of God, and an exact simile to Lucifer. *Why would God **"reason"** with a sinner if he cannot be saved* (Isa. 1:18-20)? Also, Paul knew where he was going for sure (2 Tim. 4:17-18) and so did many other Apostles. Of course, *Arminianism* wasn't fully correct either.

God allows Lucifer to do all sorts of things to Job, just not to kill him, that is the *directive will*, everything else is what you would call the *permissive will*, meaning God *allowed* it to happen but didn't necessarily like it. Another example is when Israel asks for a king (1 Sam. 8:5-7) when God doesn't want them to have a king yet (*directive will*). He lets them have a king (*permissive will*) so they get Saul—a man run by his ambitions. They wanted to be **"like all the nations,"** or in other words, like the *worlds system*, which is exactly what modern Christianity is doing today. Israel was not to be like them (Num. 23:9; Deut. 7:6, 14 etc.) and neither is the Church (2 Cor. 6:14-17; 1 John 2:15). God knew that Israel would one day succumb to the world, wanting to be like the others (Deut 17:14), so He asked them in the past to have the king of that day, in the future, *read a Book* (Deut. 17:18-20) to keep his head on straight. These were the *conditions*. The reward being **"that he may prolong his days in his kingdom"** (Deut. 17:20).

This is not true in the Church age. In the O.T. the righteous were rewarded in the here and now with many children, prosperity, and health, etc. It was a sign that you were in God's favor if you had a lot of money in the O.T. In the N.T. it has been *turned upside down* (1 Cor. 1:25-28). Paul died in prison and he was penniless. The "Prosperity Gospel" is complete and utter nonsense. All of the Apostles died horrible deaths for the exception of John who even himself was imprisoned for a time on Patmos. This is the true meaning of, **"It is easier for a camel to go through the eye of a needle, than for a rich man to enter into the kingdom of God"** (Mark 10:25). If a rich man, who has the favor of

God cannot get into Heaven, *then who can*? **"And they were astonished out of measure, saying among themselves, Who then can be saved?"** (Mark 10:26).

Back to Job. Why do good people suffer? Do bad people get what's coming to them? Why is everything so unfair at times? All questions presented and asked in the book of Job, written roughly around the time of Abraham, Jacob, and Esau. When Job's friends are having these lengthy moral discussions with him, but not once bring up the Law that was given to Moses from God to Israel. Why not? It's because there was no Law of Moses yet, it hadn't been given nor had it been written. Not only that, but the author of Job is **"Elihu,"** as seen in Job 32:2-6, 15-16.

The word **"Job"** itself means "one persecuted." Further, there is a **"Temanite"** in Job 2:11 who is a descendant of **"Teman"** a relative of Esau (Gen. 36:15). The book's date is around 1700 B.C. Written *before* Moses ever wrote Genesis, and probably preserved by Samuel and Solomon. The *sequence* of events in Genesis chapter 1 to around chapter 22 all take place before Job arrived on the scene. The **"Buzite"** in Job 32:2-6 is from **"Buz"** (Gen. 22:21). Further, the whole story takes place **"in the land of Uz"** (Job 1:1), named after **"Uz,"** Aram's son (Gen. 10:23) in the land of Edom (Lam. 4:21). This is the same place as **"Idumea"** in Isaiah 34:5; and Ezekiel 35:15 (Cf. Isa. 63:1).

In Hebrew **"Idumea"** is אֱדוֹם which is "Edom" (אֱדֹם). You don't need to go to the Hebrew for that, phonetically Idumea and Edom sound very similar and are referenced to the same place geographically in Scripture. Of course, scholars try and date the book between 700-400 B.C. which just won't work.

To hit home the point even further, the book of Job mentions the universal flood of Noah's day as if it was still very much on the minds of the people and the writer (Job 8:8, 21:12, 22:15, 16, 20:7-15, 31:33, 15:19). Some think that the sacrificing in Job was because of the Mosaic Law, but need I remind you that Abraham was tithing in Genesis 14:20

The Righteous Atheist

before any Law was in place, Noah was sacrificing, as were Cain and Abel. Noah, Cain, and Abel were also Gentiles— **"For when the Gentiles, which have not the law, do by nature the things contained in the law, these, having not the law, are a law unto themselves: Which shew the work of the law written in their hearts, their conscience also bearing witness"** (Rom. 2:14-15). Noah and Job were Gentiles, as was Abraham. There was no Jew around at this time until Abraham circumcises himself and Isaac, then Jacob shows up, who's name is **"Israel"** (Gen. 32:28), and then the twelve sons (twelve tribes) hence when God speaks to Abraham in your Bible, it's at *chapter twelve*—the number of Israel that comes from *his seed*.

Job was a man that **"escheweth evil,"** which means to shun away from; to turn away deliberately from evil. There was **"none like him in the earth,"** he must have been a very righteous individual (Job 1:7). He was **"perfect"** and **"upright"**—as **"perfect"** as a man could be. How then, could anyone accuse Job of being "self-righteous," but that is just what the issue was (Job 40:1-14). It takes a personal intervention and revelation from God *Himself* to solve it (Job 42:1-6). **"Gird up thy loins now like a man: I will demand of thee, and declare thou unto me. Wilt thou also disannul my judgment? wilt thou condemn me, THAT THOU mayest be righteous?"** (Job 40:7-8). This is in response to Job's words, as found in chapter 31, his self-righteous attitude, and saying things like: **"Oh that I knew where I might find him [God]! that I might come even to his seat! I would order my cause before him, and fill my mouth with arguments"** (Job 23:3-4 also see 27:6).

Sound familiar? How about every single *atheist* and *secretly or openly self-righteous person on the planet*. The atheist says, "oh, if I could just give God a good talking to, I'd really get some things across! If He could just appear and prove himself to ME!—I would tell him what a monster He really is! His book is garbage and it doesn't make any sense—it's all just fairy tales for adults!"

The self-righteous says, "Me?—What have I done? I have done *everything right* (like Job) and still I suffer and get no recognition!—it's everyone else…." Job sheds some light in 10:15, **"If I be wicked, woe unto me; and if I be righteous, yet will I not lift up my head. I am full of confusion; therefore see thou mine affliction"** That doesn't sound like clarity surrounding the human condition, but it's one of the clearest things ever written. The guy just said **"I am NOT wicked"** above in verse 7. If he is too prideful from doing good—it's bad; and if he's too wicked, then it's bad. How is a man supposed to win?

How about, **"Therefore I will not refrain my mouth; I will speak in the anguish of my spirit; I will complain in the bitterness of my soul"** (Job 7:11).

You see, Job started out great (see Job 2:10) but as time went on his friends started getting to him. Job doesn't realize that **"every man at his best state is altogether vanity"** (Psa. 39:5) until later, at the end of the book. That's in your most optimal and most proficient state of existence on earth. Even when he *tries* to be righteous, it's still hued with sin and immorality. Even his birth started him out on a bad foot—**"how can he be clean that is born of a woman?"** (Job 25:4).

What about the most righteous state? **"But we are all as an unclean thing, and ALL our righteousnesses are as filthy rags"** (Isa. 64:6). This is what modern Christianity hides from you, and this is what Ehrman didn't grasp at Princeton or after when having "philosophical issues." Ehrman, like many, supplanted himself as God.

How oft does the atheist say in his heart: **"Depart from us; for we desire not the knowledge of thy ways"** and likewise, **"What is the Almighty, that we should serve him? and what profit should we have, if we pray unto him?"** (Job 21:14-15). These were the very words said by those just before the flood of Noah's day—**"Which were cut down out

The Righteous Atheist

of time, whose foundation was overflown with a flood: Which said unto God, Depart from us" (Job 22:16-17).

The question that creates an atheist is exemplified in Job 21:7, **"Wherefore do the wicked live, become old, yea, are mighty in power?"** The well intentioned person looks around and sees hatred and suffering—they conclude that God must not care about all those well meaning people or that there is no God. What Job is asking is: "Why do bad people prosper and make out good—at the expense of good people?" "Why does the Wall Street banker who robs millions get away with it?" "How come Americans throw away food while there are those starving in third-world countries?" "How do celebrities and senators get away with so much but I am held to a different standard?" "Why do the rich abide by a different set of rules than the poor?" How did Pope Innocent III get away with launching crusades against the Albigenses? What about Pope John XII that murdered many and was caught sleeping with someone else's wife? How about Pope Pius XI who signed a concordant with Hitler?[6]

Job continues on after 21:7 in the following verses. **"Their houses are safe"** like Bill Gates' home and the Clintons being surrounded by cameras and security guards, like Hitler and his armed guards. **"Neither is the rod of God upon them."** Job continues on and shows you the **"rod of God"** in action, verses 13-18 refer to the flood. Those who aren't included have their **"day"** (see verse 30).

What about all those acts of love and good moral judgments, sacraments, mass attendance, Hail Marry's, and practitioners of the "Golden Rule"? **"Hast thou an arm like God?...Then will I also confess unto thee that thine own right hand can save thee"** (Job 40:9, 14). There is something the righteous atheist could hang over God, it's what Job is playing around with in 7:17 and 9:32-33. **"For he is not a**

---

[6] John Toland, *"Adolf Hitler,"* 1976, pages 678-679

man, AS I AM, that I should answer him, and we should come together in judgment. Neither is there any DAYSMAN betwixt us."

That something is that God **"is not a man"** and there was no one to *represent* and come in-between man and God in his horrid state—**"How then can man be JUSTIFIED with God"** (Job 25:4)? How could a man relate to God before He was a man?

Enter stage right: **"THE MAN"** Jesus Christ, **"Behold the Lamb of God, which taketh away the sin of the world"** (John 1:29). The MAN that **"learned he obedience by the things which he suffered"** (Heb. 5:8) and all you have to do is have faith, **"KNOWING that a man is NOT justified by the works of the law, but by the FAITH of Jesus Christ, even we have believed in Jesus Christ, that we might be JUSTIFIED BY the faith of Christ, and not by the works of the law: for by the works of the law shall no flesh be justified"** (Gal. 2:16, also see Rom. 10:1-4).

Jesus Christ comes *between* you and God, and represents you to God, **"there is one mediator"** (1 Tim. 2:5). **"We have an advocate with the Father"** (1 John 2:1) just like the **"daysman"** that Job was hoping for. How mad do you think God would be if you turned down that "gift"? **"He that believeth on the Son hath everlasting life: and he that believeth not the Son shall not see life; but the WRATH OF GOD abideth on him"** (John 3:36).

The book of Job hits the point home again when Elihu is responding to Job, **"Thinkest thou this to be right, that thou saidst, My righteousness is more than God's?"** (Job 35:2). *God's righteousness is defined as his* **"Son"** in Romans 3:21-26, 10:1-4; John 16:9. You can either trust on His Son or continue in your path to death (John 3:36; Rom. 6:23). Trust your own righteousness or trust His. All the chips are on the table, all in—what's it gonna be?

Job's lamentations resonate with the voices of contemporary atheists such as Dawkins, Dennett, Harris,

The Righteous Atheist

Hitchens, Roth, and Onfray, and even Ehrman himself. In the book of Job, we find Job expressing his anguish by saying, **"Oh that my grief were thoroughly weighed, and my calamity laid in the balances together!"** (Job 6:2). Here Job basically ignores everything Eliphaz said in the previous two chapters. What he is saying is "I'm not getting a good deal here—I'm not getting a square deal…I'm not getting the deal that *I deserve!*" He knows the accusations that his friends are bringing on are not correct concerning himself but Job still sees this punishment as unjust and uneven. Lawyers would say it like, "The scales of Lady Justice are out of balance, and not in our favor." This is the modern atheist looking around and not liking what he is seeing. He then comes to the conclusion: *there is no God.*

Then you have Dawkins' assertion about life: *"no design, no purpose, no evil and no good, nothing but blind, pitiless indifference."* **"Vanity of vanities, saith the Preacher, vanity of vanities; all is vanity"** (Ecc. 1:2). In one vain sentence Dawkins sums himself up and the modern atheist—there is nothing, there was nothing, but here we are, it's all just one big gray soup of animalistic *relativism*. Progress! Job's friends are accusing him of being immoral but in Dawkins' world there is no morality—it's all just *"blind, pitiless indifference."*

Job, as atheists do, will accuse God of sin, **"For the arrows of the Almighty are within me, the poison whereof drinketh up my spirit: the terrors of God do set themselves in array against ME"** (Job 6:4).

Job *just said* he didn't deserve any of this, yet God is giving it to him anyway; God must be wrong in His judgments. The atheist is plagued by God even when they don't believe. The atheist can not stand the *practical* answer to this (aside from the prophetic application), because he himself does the same thing and he does not want to relinquish his *imagined power* of his "mastership of his own soul," **"Whatsoever the LORD pleased, that did he in heaven, and in earth, in the seas, and all deep places"** (Psa.

135:6). The atheist can not stand it. He wants to *be like* the Father. The sad fact is, you are going to have to serve someone, then you die (Job 7:1).

In fact there have been many atheists who regretted their entire life's work as their hair turned gray. For instance, Jean-Paul Sartre was a 20th Century atheist philosopher. He famously wrote, *"Hell is other people."* Naturally he was a devoted Marxist and held Che Guevara in high regard. Later in life he is quoted with saying:

> *"I don't feel I am the product of chance, a speck of dust in the universe, but someone who was expected, prepared, prefigured. In short, a being that could be here thanks only to a Creator..."*[7]
>
> *"In these final philosophical reflections Sartre seems to repudiate much of his life's work and embrace the need for an objective morality"*[8]

At the end of the book of Job, God *restores everything plus some* to Job. Job in many places is a picture of a man in hell, but at the end of Job it pictures a man in Heaven after suffering in this earthly fallen-life. God is eternal (Isa. 57:15), and sees the big-picture when we cannot. We see what is here and now—we are but a **"worm"** (Job 25:6; Mark 9:44, 48, 49) in the dirt.

The image that some churches in modern America want to hide from you is *this* very image: *the suffering*. **"Take up the cross, and follow me"** (Mark 10:21). Today, it's about *self-acceptance* instead of *self-denial*. That isn't Bible but this is—**"let him deny himself"** (Luke 9:23). The fact is, that in the Bible God controls catastrophes and weather (Levi. 26:4; Nah. 1:3; Job 37:17; Isa. 29:6; Deut. 28:24; Exod. 9:18, etc.) is completely *avoided* by most modern preachers. I recall going

---

[7] Steven Wang, *"Satre's Faith,"* article on Bridges and Tangents, Feb. 21, 2010

[8] Ibid, impression by Wang during the interview.

to a church service one time when the opening statement by the pastor was how sad it was that *other pastors* in town were saying, *"God caused a town to flood."* The audience "awwwwed" in such a way that obviously spoke towards their opinion on Biblically-minded pastors; *"aww, those poor ignorant rednecks. They must not understand God's grace."* God *did* cause that town to flood. He also causes forest-fires, hurricanes, earthquakes, volcanoes, and tornadoes. It sounds harsh and no one wants to hear it—but that's Bible. That Book is against man; it does not paint man in a good light.

This self-titled *"bible believing"* church (oh yeah, man, they also *use* an NLT), as they so *claim*, did not read Jeremiah 5:12-13 which states that **"the word is not in them"** if they do such things. That is not my opinion—it's just Bible. Why do you think so many people *don't read it*? Listen, do you *really* want to hear **"I form the light, and create darkness: I make peace, AND CREATE EVIL: I the LORD do all these things"** (Isa. 45:7)? What is a modern preacher going to do *with that*? Nothing. He will avoid it like a leprous man and say, *"the God of the O.T. is not the same God as the one in the N.T"* just as Marcion did in the Second Century. Well, you have two god's now. What are you going to do with two gods? There aren't two god's, they are both the same, **"Jesus Christ the same yesterday, and to day, and for ever"** (Heb. 13:8), **"For there are three that bear record in heaven, the Father, the Word, and the Holy Ghost: and these three are one"** (1 John 5:7). Jesus came *first* as a **"Lamb,"** but He comes back as a roaring **"Lion"** (Rev. 5:5; Gen. 49:10), who will establish dominion on earth while sitting on the physical Throne of David (Joel 3:9-19; Jer. 25:15-38; Psa. 83:1-18; Psa. 2:4-12; Isa. 24; Rev. 19; Joel 2:1-11, etc.). **"Kiss the Son, lest he be angry, and ye perish."**

I have a friend who is saved, but has backslidden into what he calls a *"more rational approach, based on evidence."* Man, I know the kick. A passage that really bothers him is Deuteronomy 22:28-29. God has a man, who raped a woman pay for her in marriage. He couldn't get past it. He heard some YouTuber going on about it and he just never investigated the thing for himself—so much for "evidence" and a "rational approach." Well, is this *"moral"*? Is this something God would do? Let's read the passage and *think* about it, instead of having a gut based reaction without understanding.

First, the Bible holds a very negative view on rape in its varying degrees, as in the case of: Amnon and Tamar; Noah and Ham; Lot and his daughters; Judah and Tamar; Dinah and Shechem. It's also worth noting that this law in Deuteronomy 22 actually *helps* the woman. It's very counterintuitive, but in those days if a woman did not have the protection of a man, especially that of a husband to care and provide, she would not fair well. Today, a lot of women work and contribute to half the family income in some cases, so this law appears to be harmful and a head-scratcher at best. The law actually causes the victim of rape to be more secure within that time, like the marrying of many wives such as what Solomon did, this also allowed protection for those women. But, let's dig into it.

In the text we have a **"virgin"** who is not married being rapped by a man (verse 29). The next verse we see the punishment for being caught.

1.) The rapist has to pay **"fifty shekels of silver"** which is about *half a kilogram to a kilogram of silver.* The average Israelite from 1450-600 B.C. did not have half-a'-kilo of silver just hangin' around the homestead. This person would have to be in debt to the father of the woman he raped and/or work hard for it, or get it by some other means such as selling off his possessions (if he had any). The judges would decide if the man would be sold into slavery to pay the debt, pay by some other means, or possibly be put to death based on the consequences of the other rape cases in Deuteronomy 22:23-27. The idea here is that if this "cat" has a "fat bag lyin' aroun'" then he was "on his hustle" and "gettin' on his grind"—ya feel me? If he could pay it, he was well-to-do and could therefore support a woman and *possible* child on the way.

2.) These matters were brought before judges of Israel in smaller communities. With no TV, no iPhone's, and no Newsweek, nothing, people were always "all up-in" each others business. *Everyone* would know what the man did and therefore his reputation would be ruined; he would be watched by the father of the girl closely and the community. People are always watching and talking.

3.) If he could pay the debt, now that everyone is watching him and has taken close note that he is "the rapist," he then must marry the girl who he raped and he **"may not put her away all his days."** He is "locked in." The judges and the community will hold him to it. This is assuming he has made it this far.

4.) Since the man has raped the girl, there is a possible third party that the man is now responsible for by law. The man has to take care of the child too. Maybe it's twins or triplets.

5.) During this time the average woman was better off having someone around to protect her, or a male such as a father or husband. If they were not married, no husband, no engagement, no father, and no brother then oftentimes women were sold into slavery. In Israel's Law the slave was treated fairly (Exod. 21:7-11) but if the woman wound up in another nation, then it's another story.

6.) This is an *arranged marriage*. It is not how marriages are typically arranged such as separate families choosing who each will marry, but any arranged marriage is not a marriage that we think of as "good" in the United States where two people who are in love then get married and live happily ever after…or do they? The divorce rate for *arranged marriages* is 4% and the divorce rate in the States is *40-50%*. It is possible then, that the rapist and the girl, dare I say, fall in love at a later time?—Who knows, but if it was a Hollywood movie you'd probably watch it and cry by the end, don't even lie.

   7.) Just the opposite as above, the woman could make the rest of his days absolutely miserable as Tamar and Amnon's situation (2 Sam. 13:6-29).

   8.) It keeps sex a sacred act. In the Bible marriage is the union of man and woman, as opposed to the *ceremony* or *legal document* given to you by the state. Marriage in the Bible is not a legal document. If you are going to force yourself on a girl and disrespect that union, then you are going to marry her and take care of her for the rest of your life; with the rest of the town and people making sure you are holding up your end of the bargain. This is so counterintuitive to the way the west and Americans think; most having been raised on Television in the family living room and having gone through the women's "sexual liberation" (ironically coinciding with the invention of the birth-control pill) in the 1960's and 70's, and other masses of brainwashing media, it is a strange and foreign concept. *That's Bible*. It happens to be an *eastern* Book—it's Semitic. That Book is not like the world; *it's "Holy."*

   Having said all that, is Deuteronomy 22:28-29 really that unfair? The passages above it on rape give the woman the befit of the doubt as in verses 25-27—no one heard the woman yell due to the location but it is assumed that she *did*. Today a rapist gets his name on a registry and anywhere from 2 years to 10 years to life in prison (sometimes less) in the United States. If there is *a kid* involved and she decides to keep the kid, in this case the rapist would not be able to pay any child support, since he is in prison making hardly any money if any at all, leaving her to fend for herself and her child. Many rapists get off in five years (or less), court fines, name on a registry, criminal record, and probation. They can always move to another state if permitted. In the case of the woman having the child, the rapist will have to pay child support if the courts agreed upon child support payments, but *the rapist can turn around and sue the girl for child custody.* Welcome to America!—What "righteous law" we have!

Now that we have a little better understanding of the God *of the Bible*, we can then ask the atheist the same question by looking at their argument. Their argument, although rudimentary and circular at best, is as follows:

- Evil and suffering exist.
- If God were omnipotent then He would be able to prevent or stop these bad things.
- If God were all good, (God is love), he would be able to prevent them.
- If there were an omnipotent and all good God, evil and suffering would have no place in the world.
- Therefore, there is no God, if anything not a good God but rather an evil, maniacal, egomaniac at the head of the universe.

This argument is circular because it forces the atheist to believe in *absolute terms* which *is Bible:* "heaven" or "hell," "good" or "evil," "dark" or "light," "love" or "hate," "saved" or "lost," etc. The atheist does *not* believe in absolutes, he believes that morals are *societal norms accepted by the majority.* The accepted morals help the populace survive hence, *"there would be no normalization of killing because it would wipe out our species."* Well being gay doesn't advance or prolong our species, but it is culturally *accepted by the majority of people and often even pushed on young children in grade-school.*

The argument assumes that if God were omnipotent and all-good, He would prevent or stop evil and suffering. While this seems reasonable on the surface, it overlooks the possibility of God having reasons beyond our comprehension for allowing such things to occur. The existence of evil and suffering does not necessarily negate the existence of an all-powerful and all-good God. It is important to recognize the limits of human understanding (Isa. 55:8) when discussing matters of God's intentions and purposes. After all, you are dealing with an unchanging Being in a universe in which everything is in a constant flux. But we can learn about God's dealings with man and His revealed dispensations via the Bible. That's the *one* thing He left in order to get to know Him—*a Book*.

The atheist will say, *"there are nuances not found in your argument."* Then they will point out that *"atheists can have absolute standards."* Really? Like what? "Evidence-based science"? "Human rights"? "Cultural values"?

A great example of this is found in Sam Harris' book titled, *"Letter to a Christian Nation."* Most of it is your standard-line against the Bible and other parts of it are actually confusing Roman Catholicism with Biblical Christianity.

He states, *"Everything about human experience suggests that love is more conductive to happiness than hate is. This is an objective* [emphasis his] *claim..."* That sounds nice. Love is good...what about all those wars and fighting for resources and such?—He goes on, *"It is clearly possible to say that someone like Hitler was wrong in moral terms without reference to scripture."* Well now, he's brought "moral" reasons into the conversation and Scripture. What if someone else loves money and the other person loves being with family?—Creates a rift don't you think? Maybe some arguments? Someone else's *"happiness"* is getting in the way of another persons *"happiness."* He continues: *"our own search for happiness, therefore, provides a rational for self-sacrifice and self-denial."*[9] How might someone say Hitler was wrong in killing without an objective standard? Almost all of Germany's *"objective," "search for happiness"* was based on

---

[9] Sam Harris, *"Letter to a Christian Nation,"* 2008, page 24

killing a bunch of Jews and creating a perfect race via eugenics for "Das Vaterland!"

Ancient Greece accepted pedophilia,[10] while others such as Rome generally did not. Socrates himself was said to "partake" with young boys,[11] it is now "doctored up" by calling it *"pederasty"* in which the difference between *pedophilia* and *pederasty* is a few years of age.[12] Socrates had sex with young boys, but *so was everyone else in Greece, so it was "normal."* Is Pedophilia to be accepted? Evil is an *absolute* in which the atheist *can not define*. The beating up and killing of Jews in Nazi Germany was normal, does that make it *"good"*? What makes it *"evil"*? The 66,000,000 people murdered in an atheistic Russian regime was accepted for the *common good* of the state. Is that "good"? What about "corrective rape" in South Africa? Likewise, in the same place, gang-rape is considered "male bonding,"[13] is that "good"? It's *normal* amongst these groups mentioned and contributes to some of their *"happiness."* Without absolutes, there is no reference point in which to calibrate these issues.

Like atheists, modern Christian scholars have the same problem with having a *final authority*. In a debate between Greg Bahnsen and Edward Tabash, Tabash says, *"If the God of the bible actually exists, I want to sue him for negligence for being asleep at the wheel of the universe when my grandfather and uncle were gassed to death in Auschwitz."* Why sue him for negligence? What gave you the idea that killing was *"evil"*?

---

[10] Nicole Holmen, *"Examining Greek Pederastic Relationships,"* Inquiries Journal, Vol. 2 No. 02, 2010.

[11] Plato, *"Plato in Twelve Volumes,"* Vol. 8, Translated by W.R.M. Lamb, Plato, Charmides 155d, 1955

[12] *Authors Note*: one is a "man-boy" relationship while the other is "man-child." One is a "mental state being attracted to prepubescent children" and the other is between "adult and adolescent males." The only real difference between the two is that pederasty is strictly between males and the age range.

[13] *"Preventing Rape and Violence in South Africa,"* Medical Research Council, 2009

What would a country look like that was *not* founded on anything absolute but replaced with *relativism?* Everything is *"relative,"* you *"make your own truth,"* this is decay in guise of progress, it is decadence.

A woman today says, *"I have a right to abort my baby"* and also says, *"God is evil for murdering people and allowing the murder of people."* The woman cannot see her own hypocrisy, just as the modern atheist such as Ehrman thinks he is morally superior to the God of the Bible, although, he would never claim it *outright* and in the open.

A person can essentially be programmed by either **"the world"** (1 John 2:15) and it's system or from God. Without Him you are left to your own devices, and it never ends well for anyone. Solomon once wrote, **"no man knoweth either love or hatred by all that is before him"** (Ecc. 9:1). Meaning, you need some sort of standard in order to properly judge things. He also said, **"yea, also the heart of the sons of men is full of evil, and madness is in their heart while they live, and after that they go to the dead"** (Ecc. 9:3). Without a standard (a final authority), *anything goes* and is fair game: eugenics, mass genocide, sterilization, gas chambers, lies, murder, rape, and while you're at it *change the words of the Living God*, et al.

What makes these things evil? David once said, **"Through thy precepts I get understanding: therefore I HATE every false way"** (Psa. 119:104). Do you **"hate every false way"**? Why is it **"false"**?

The further man gets away from absolute truth and *it's rejection*, the closer he gets to relativism—**"Woe unto them that call evil good, and good evil"** (Isa. 5:20). The closer man gets to relativism, the closer he gets to playing God— He becomes God. **"I will be like the most high"** (Isa. 14:14).

The United States was founded under a King James Protestant Reformation Bible, and it was founded by men who were raised up on it like the **"milk"** (1 Peter 2:2) of their mothers breasts. The Constitution and Declaration were based on Christian principles set down before Jefferson began to write. The founding fathers were mostly deists and did not openly recognize Jesus Christ in any government document. It is a sad fact many "patriots" don't wish to face. One need not go any further than Jefferson's "personal bible." He mutilated the text so thoroughly to only teach the "philosophy" of Jesus Christ by (literally) cutting out everything he fancied untrue. They all believed in a God, but not personal salvation through a man named Jesus Christ. They didn't believe in the Person, Jesus Christ (not in their elder years at least).

Despite this, they were influenced by the majority of people, as all good politicians are; if they do not heed to public opinion then they don't have an office to be in. Public opinion at that time was heavily based on Christian ideals. They wanted to escape the clutches of Catholicism and saw their workings in the annals of history as a corrupt church-state setup, therefore, the the United States became the first country in the world to separate church and state powers; something Catholics and Islamists strongly disagree with to this day.

The only "Christian" killing going on at mass-scale was that of Pagan Rome merging with Christianity. By merging church and state, they had excuse to *kill* in the name of Jesus, not only "pagans" but Christians who followed after Biblical Christianity. This contradicted the "Holy Mother Church" and her teaching of the church being the "interpreter" of Scripture. The Bible reading and *believing* Protestants had one authority as opposed to two: *the Bible vs. The Roman Harlot's ideology.*

Anyone today who is a raping, wine-fed, murdering, Bible-rejecting, tradition-following, ecumenical church-state leader, is no *follower* of Jesus Christ no matter how much they *profess* it. That would be every-single pope since A.D. 325.

"Religion has caused more murder than atheism." As atheism sweeps the globe, it becomes evident that it, too, has a significant record of violence and bloodshed when it comes to instances of murder and killing. The high body count in the atheistic sphere and, admittedly, the "religious" sphere only exemplifies that there is an underlying reality of man that many do not wish to face. One group says, "we are fallen" and offers redemption and the other group says, "we are animals" and offers the comfort of bleak relativism. In the last century alone, no biblically-centered Christian movements have killed 6 million+ Jews, nor would they ever attempt it. Hitler and his right-hand men *claimed* Catholicism[14] but wanted to reinstate the old pagan ways of Germany (*"Rise and Fall of the Third Reich,"* page 240). There are 40-80 million dead under Mao who was as anti-religious, anti-bible, and as bigoted as one could get. There is the 66 million mentioned earlier under communist Russia, and 43 million of the 66 under pro-atheist Stalin of Russia. Then the 3.5 million in North Korea, which is an "official" atheist state regime.

> *"It is furthermore imperative to put the propaganda of atheism on solid ground. You won't achieve much with the weapons of Marx and materialism, as we have seen. Materialism and religion are two different planes and they don't coincide. If a fool speaks from the heavens and the sage from a factory--they won't understand one another. The sage needs to hit the fool with his stick, with his weapon."*[15]

---

[14] See John Toland's *"Adolf Hitler,"* 1976 and Norman H. Baynes, *"The Speeches of Adolf Hitler,"* April 1922-August 1939, Vol. I, 1942, pages 19-20

[15] *"Letter From Gorky to Stalin,"* Library of Congress Soviet Exhibit at University of Illinois Urbana-Champaign

China has had many anti-religious crusades, one famously being the invasion of Tibet and the slow taking over and control of the Tibetan form of Buddhism. The Dali Lama has been on the run since 1950 due to Tibet being held captive by Chinese invaders (still to this day) forcing the Dali Lama to play the role of politician to seek aid for his country. The people of Tibet are being persecuted and jailed for practicing their religion in a place they have occupied for over 2,000 years. "Re-education" camps or otherwise called "internment camps" were often filled with Buddhist monks and people of other faiths. Recently, in 2018, Chinese *government officials invaded the homes of Christians* who were having Christmas services.[16]

Did you know that populations that believe in hell actually *fair better*? So much for the anti-religious utopia.

> *"Across countries, the belief in a contingent afterlife is associated with greater economic productivity and less crime."* [17]

In examining the interplay between beliefs in a hellish realm and the dynamics of economic growth, a rather intriguing pattern appears to manifest itself. It seems that those individuals who maintain a conviction not solely in the concept of a Heaven but also in the existence of hell tend to witness a hastened pace in economic development. The prospect of eternal damnation and hell-fire for transgressions acts as a potent deterrent against immoral behaviors, motivating individuals to strive for ethical conduct and maintain a social fabric conducive to harmonious coexistence. Such a moral compass, firmly anchored in the belief of retributive consequences, gives rise to a more conscientious and disciplined approach towards

---

[16] *"Alarm Over China's Church Crackdown"* BBC, 18 Dec. 2018

[17] Joseph Henrich, *"The WEIRDest People In the World,"* 2020, page 147

personal and collective endeavors, which can positively impact economic growth—if you want bigger cities, stronger people, and faster growth then preaching on hell-fire and the collective belief in it is the way to go.

When people have *absolute standards to go by, people work together more efficiently.* I believe John Lennon's song called *"Imagine"* can now be rendered completely off-base and the musings of a deluded drug addict—"Imagine, all the people...living life in peace..." John Lennon was dead *wrong.* He was the same person that sang, *"Happiness is a warm gun."* He found happiness on December 8, 1980 on 1 West 72nd Street on the Upper West Side of Manhattan and it wasn't heroin.

Isn't it interesting that in America more and more people who are *professing* "Christians" believe that hell is *"metaphorical"?* Is there a correlation there? People also commit *less crime with a belief in hell.* No, it can't be! All those fire-and-brimstone old-time Baptist preachers were on to something. No! it can't be! Not them!—Anybody but THEM! Believing in *only heaven* "is associated with *more* murder."[18] Time to go get some plain-preachin'.

Given that we have already talked about the permissive will of God, God always has a way of evening things out. "You reap what you sow" (Gal. 6:7). He will allow bad things to happen but he will also turn calamity into good. Joseph told his brothers after they had left him to be enslaved by the Egyptians, **"But as for you, ye thought evil against me; but God meant it unto good, to bring to pass, as it is this day, to save much people alive"** (Gen. 50:20). Paul says this in Romans 8:28, the man who was whipped, beaten, and stoned on his journeys of spreading the Gospel, **"And we know that all things work together for good to them that love God, to them who are the called according to his purpose."** See, you tell that to someone in one of

---

[18] Ibid

Hitler's death camps or one of the more impoverished places in India or Africa, where children are pulling ten foot parasites out of their bodies—It becomes difficult to see.

Paul was faced either with death by lions gnawing on his bones or the guillotine. He took a stand so loud when given a hearing by Nero that even his friends that were with him backed out (2 Tim. 4:15-17). That's Paul for you. He was ready to go home. He chose the guillotine. Paul disobeyed God and was imprisoned for it. The Holy Spirit told him not to go to Jerusalem (Acts 21:10-14), but *he went anyway*. If he would have obeyed, he would have made it to Rome without a shipwreck (Acts 23:11, 27:23-26, 41-44). See, God accomplished what He needed all while Paul "reaped what he sowed" (Gal. 6:7). Think about that for a while.

Another example of this would be *how* you got your Bible. Many people died in the process of getting its contents to you in its now complete form. People take it for granted, but do you ever wonder who guarded and looked after those pages, specifically? How many hands they must have passed through, how many lives, and bloodshed they have witnessed. Just how, through the many centuries that Book you hold in your hands now came to *you*? The Book itself is a bloody Book from start to finish. The NIV, ESV and so on, do nothing but stomp on the work of such brazen men and women. All one needs to do is read *"Foxes Book of Martyrs"* to have a seriously meaningful understanding of Genesis 50:20 and Romans 8:28 with the *permissive will* of God.

Another example being the Roman Catholic church. They could have utterly wiped out Protestantism and the Reformation from forming during the Dark Ages thus the only available words would be that of modern bibles (since they are Catholic bibles), the landscape as we know it today would be very different—no Erasmus, no Wycliff, no Waldensians, no Martin Luther, no William Tyndale, no Huss, no Wesley, no Sunday, no Larkin, no Scofield, and a slew of other Christians who were either murdered or would have had their futures cut short due to the Catholic Church still ruling. Those who were murdered were murdered for believing what God *said* as opposed to the **"tradition of men."** Instead, the "Holy Mother's" imperialistic conquest was distracted by the Ottoman Empire in the 14th and 15th Centuries.

Speaking of "traditions of men," the Islamic crusades were all in *"self defense"* of course, since Muslims can't engage directly such as offensive moves...like *killing Jews today* is "self defense" in Israel. Smile, don't be close-minded (and so the hijab is now a symbol of feminine power in the United States but a symbol of oppression everywhere else—oh, don't be bigoted). The God of the Bible is one who works in history, He does not take a side-line approach.

The Quran is believed by Muslims to be *the literal, true, word of Allah*. Not all Muslims are "terrorists," but if you take the Quran literal, then undoubtedly it is *not* a "religion of peace" but one of political conquest, just as the Roman Catholic Church is. Sura 9:5 says, *"slay the idolaters wheresoever you find them, capture them, besiege them, and lie in wait for them at every place of ambush,"* all while trying to tell you that *"there is no coercion in religion"* (Sura 2:256). Some other English translations read *"compulsion"* in place of *"coercion."* Essentially, the saying is trying to rewrite all of Islamic history from A.D. 600 forward. They have been trying to rewrite history since Muhammad talked to the 600-winged angel.

For instance, the title-deed for land where "The Dome of the Rock" now stands is *to the Jews* and is written on paper in 2 Samuel 24. The Dome of the Rock is sacred to Muslims because it is supposedly where Muhammad ascended into Heaven. As he was doing so he left a footprint on a rock which is now there. Muslims are willing to kill over this rock but of course they aren't polytheistic or idol worshipers like the Catholics and their statues of Mary...no, who would consider such a thing! This is where Muhammad ascended into Heaven (by oral tradition) but his body is buried in Medina. Jesus Christ ascended into Heaven and His body has never been found.

The Dome of the Rock sits atop where Solomon's Temple was and the second Temple in the New Testament stood. It has been with the Jews since before 1,000 B.C. The Muslim shrine which is now there also has some of Muhammad's beard hairs—Muslims will kill over these beard hairs.

In any history, written by *anyone*, in respects to Islam, you will find an *Islamic political-state-religion* invading and *forcing* conversion or death. If not death, then slavery. Muhammad attempted to be another Moses, but fell short and failed utterly. Take the test of a **"prophet"** in Deuteronomy 18:19-22 and apply it to Muhammad. He just *didn't pass*. The "prophet like unto Moses" from Deuteronomy 18:18 is Jesus Christ, not Muhammad. He was a madman who deceived a lot of people.

Was man made from a "blood clot" (Sura 96:1-2) or "mud and clay" (Sura 15:26, 3:58, 30:20) or a "drop of semen" (Sura 16:4, 75:37)? There is more than one creator in Sura 23:14. Mohammed killed people, Jesus gave life. Mohammed claimed[19] Mary was raptured into heaven like Enoch and Elijah (the *"Assumption of Mary"*[20] is official dogma of the Roman Catholic Church; he would have come into contact with Catholic dogma around A.D. 600). **"Let no man deceive you"** (2 Thess. 2:3). Muhammad also gave out the law in which no man could have more than four wives...except for himself who had twelve.[21] This is a common move by cult leaders. They are always hyper-focused on sex, such as Jospeh Smith and the Mormon church enacting polygamy, or

---

[19] Martin Lings, *"Muhammad: His Life Based on the Earliest Sources,"* 2006

[20] The Catholic Assumption of Mary: This is not quite a "rapture" but is stated that Mary ascended into heaven and was ultimately "sinless." They will use Revelation 12 at times to prove it. The woman in Revelation 12 is Israel, not Mary or the Church.

[21] op cit. Lings. Author's Note: Some sources say 14 not including slaves and concubines.

the Bikram yoga instructor who took advantage of his status over his female followers. There is, of course, Charles Manson who used others vulnerabilities and the need to "belong" against them. Some of his followers thought that if he was willing to have sex with them then they must really "be someone special."

Here are some more simple observations on the cult of Muhammad:

Muhammad was not a Jew, Jesus and Moses *were* (Moses was from the tribe of Levi, Jesus was from Judah). Muhammad's prophecy was frankly, a joke compared to Jesus Christ and Moses (a coin toss is not prophecy). Moses and Jesus both volunteered to bear the sins of their people (Exod. 32:32 for Moses). Muhammad didn't know where he was going when he died (Sura 46:9), Jesus and Moses did (Deut. 31:14, 32:48-50; John 16; Matt. 26:12 etc.), Muhammad died and stayed dead, Jesus and Moses did not (Moses appears on the Mount of Transfiguration Matthew 17 and again in Revelation 11). God spoke *directly* to Moses but not to Muhammad, a 600 winged angel delivered the message to Muhammad according to the Hadith (Bukhari, Volume 4, Book 54). The Quran has angels bowing to Adam in Sura 18:50. No angel would bow *to a man* (see Heb. 2:7; Rev. 22:8-9, 19:10; Num 22:27), find me one case where an angel bows to a man—you wont be able to find it. According to the Quran (Surah 10:94), a Muslim *is to read* the O.T. and N.T., *to see if the Quran is true: that is the test of the Quran, that is all one has to do to see if it's true*. But alas, **"men loved darkness rather than light"** (John 3:19). Some would rather be blind, dumb, and stupid than accept truth.

The N.T. was complete by A.D. 95 and Muhammad had access to both the O.T. writings and the N.T. writings in which Muslims are to *ask about* (Sura 16:43). According to the Quran, Allah wrote both the O.T. and N.T. (Sura 5:47-48, 66, 68; 138; 4:136). There are *"seven heavens"* (Sura 41:12) as

opposed to three in 2 Corinthians 12:2, Genesis, Job, John, Acts, Matthew, Isaiah, and the Psalms:
1. The atmosphere where clouds are (Acts 1:9-10; Job 35:5)
2. Outer space (Psa. 19:1; Gen. 1:8; Psa. 148:4)
3. God's throne (Matt. 6:9; John 14:2; Psa. 148:1-2; Isa. 14:13-14)

There are many more issues found in the Quran (see the chapter called, *"The Witnessed"*). The God of the Bible has been able to translate His words into *many* languages, including Greek (O.T. quotations in the N.T. from the Hebrew), Latin, Syriac, Coptic, Gothic, German, English, etc., but the god of the Quran, *"Allah,"* can't even seem to do that much since the "revelation" of the Quran must be *read* in Arabic and *recited* in Arabic.

I mean, for goodness sake, the O.T. prophesies say the prophet/messiah *will be a Jew* (Gen. 49; Mic. 5; Isa. 53; Jer. 23; Deut. 18; Isa. 40; Mal. 3, etc.) not an Ishmaelite.

Why am I bringing this up? I am trying to get at the point that not all *"holy"* texts are "Holy," just as not all "holy men" (the pope) are what they seem. The Christianity of Catholicism is not the Christianity of the Bible and the god of Islam is *not the same God of Abraham, Isaac, and Jacob.* The majority of modern Christian scholars aren't the scholars of time past nor do they hold the same view of Scripture; **"For their rock is not as our Rock"** (Deut. 32:31).

Muslim scholars have a lot in common with Christian scholars today: Muslim scholars reinterpret the Quran to fit a modern or western society; Christian scholars do the same. Muslim scholars will alter the text (in the footnotes) by telling you the exact opposite of what the text actually says; Christian scholars do the same but will actually *alter the text.*

When it comes to the Bible from *"the God of Abraham, Isaac, and Jacob,"* it has proven the test of time and the test of prophecy. It is the only Book that can *read you* and your attitude when you pick it up. It is why so many "scholars" can't seem to read simple English (it "criticizes" them as they read it Heb. 4:12). It is also why some leave the faith and do not continue with the same earnestness as when they first began.

"**I know thy works, and thy labour, and thy patience, and how thou canst not bear them which are evil: and thou hast tried them which say they are apostles, and are not, and hast found them liars: And hast borne, and hast patience, and for my name's sake hast laboured, and hast not fainted. Nevertheless I have somewhat against thee, BECAUSE THOU HAST LEFT THY FIRST LOVE**" (Rev. 2:2-4).

That passage marks the beginning of the fall of Christian scholarship and the Church. Where it winds up, and where we are now is the state of *Laodicea*, "**of the Laodiceans...I know thy works, that thou art neither COLD NOR HOT: I would thou wert cold or hot....So then because thou art LUKEWARM, and neither cold nor hot, I will spue thee out of my mouth. Because thou sayest, I am rich, and increased with goods, and have need of nothing; and knowest not that thou art wretched, and miserable, and poor, and blind, and naked...and anoint thine eyes with eyesalve, that thou mayest see...** (Rev. 3:14-18). So much for the *"neutral approach"* to textural criticism of the New Testament. What you just read was in no way "neutral."

Back to our original question: so what about Psalms 137:9? The atheist cries for a "just God" but when God actually enacts judgment, they then cry for something else; like Cain in his punishment from God, "**my punishment is greater than I can bear**" (Gen. 4:13). No one likes punishment unless you are a masochist.

In Psalm 137:8 we have, "**O daughter of Babylon.**" The Psalm itself is *historically* referring to Israel's captivity by Nebuchadnezzar, who is likened to a "**dragon**" in Jeremiah 51:34 who is the "seed of the serpent" (Gen. 3:15) just as

Pharaoh was in Ezekiel 29:3. The serpent will have a physical seed (the Antichrist) just as God has one (Jesus Christ).

You see, the average Christian scholar will see the term **"dragon"** and change it because dragons aren't real, it must be a "jackal." The NIV shows you how adept they are by changing **"dragon"** to "great monster" in Ezekiel 29:3 which prevents you from getting the cross references so you can see the truth.

Babylon itself is referred to as a **"her"** in Jeremiah 51:45, and people are to be *"called out of her"* in Revelation 18:4. The **"dragon,"** making Nebuchadnezzar a type of the Antichrist, as well as the setting up of an **"image"** that he builds in Daniel 3:1. The dimensions of this image are 60 by 6, and the **"image"** being mentioned 6 times in Daniel 3:1-7, which in type, is a match-meet for Revelation 13:18 (666).

In Revelation we have Babylon in *mystery form*, **"MYSTERY BABYLON THE GREAT, THE MOTHER OF HARLOTS AND ABOMINATIONS OF THE EARTH"** (Rev. 17:5). Spiritual Babylon is a **"mother"** with children. In Psalm 137:7 we have a reference to **"Edom,"** Esau is Edom (Gen. 36:8). In Malachi we read, **"And I hated Esau, and laid his mountains and his heritage waste for the dragons of the wilderness"** (Mal. 1:3). Now, when did this happen? It hasn't happened yet, it is yet *future*. The Bible has an uncanny way of speaking in terms of things as already happened, because they are as good as done after they have been written. For example, in Joshua 1:13, 14, and 15 notice the *past tense* used towards something that is yet *future*, **"as he hath given you,"** **"have possessed it,"** and **"hath given."** They haven't possessed the land yet in Joshua chapter one, but they do later. Here is another, Psalms 22:16, **"They pierced my hands and my feet."** Why, it's past tense, but when it was written, it wasn't—it was yet future. That is a future prophecy on the crucifixion of Jesus Christ, which is now *past*. I'll give you another, Revelation 18:19. That is the fall of "Mystery Babylon" spoken *as if it had already happened*. It has not, *yet*. We read again in Isaiah 34:10, now talking in *future* tense, **"it shall lie waste."** This place in Isaiah 34 is Edom, just as we read in Malachi 1:3, (also see Obad. 15-18). **"For the day of the LORD is near...it shall be done unto thee: thy reward shall return upon thine own head," "there shall not be any remaining of the house of Esau,"** see verse 19 in Obadiah. **"In the day that thou stoniest on the other side, in the day that the strangers carried away captive his forces"** (Obad. 11 and see Ezek. 35:5, Mt. Seir is in Edom). We have this prophetic connection to Babylon and Edom. When Jerusalem was destroyed by Nebuchadnezzar, this act was not recorded in 2 Kings 25:1-21 or 2 Chronicles 36. Edom had a hand in it. The reference to Edom in Psalms 137:7 is *historical* for what they did in relation to Jerusalem in Obadiah 1-14, but *prophetical* for what is yet future.

We have Nineveh also connected to this prophecy, where the **"Assyrian"** is from (Ezek. 31:2-10; Cf. Isa. 14:11-19). In Nahum 3:1 it is likened to a **"bloody city,"** with **"whoredoms," "mistress," "harlot," "witchcrafts,"** and "selling nations," (Nah. 3:1-4). *Sound familiar?* **"With whom the kings of the earth have committed fornication, and the inhabitants of the earth have been made drunk with the wine of her fornication"** (Rev. 17:2). **"Babylon...that made all the earth drunken: the nations have drunken her wine"** (Jer. 51:7). In Isaiah 13, it's talking about Babylon (see Isa. 13:1), **"Behold the day of the LORD cometh, cruel both with wrath and fierce anger, to lay the land desolate: and he shall destroy the sinners thereof out of it"** (Isa. 13:9) which is when the Lord comes back (see Isa. 13:10 and Rev. 6:12-13).

Did you notice Isaiah 13:16? **"Their children also shall be dashed to pieces before their eyes; their houses shall be spoiled, and their wives ravished,"** again all of this is *historical* in relation to the Medes/Persia taking over Babylon (Isa. 13:17), but what about verse 19-22 in Isaiah 13? That has *not* happened yet. Here again we have *a blend of history with prophecy*. The ones doing the "dashing" in Psalms 137 would be the Medes and Persians **"drunken"** with the wine of spiritual Babylon, "that great whore," which will also happen again in the future except it won't be Persia.

One of the greatest types of this in modern times is Hitler as Antichrist, and Nazi Germany as the Antichrist-kingdom. Carl Jung once said,

> *"We do not know whether Hitler is going to found a new Islam. He is already on the way; he is like Mohammad. The emotion in Germany is Islamic; warlike and Islamic. They are all drunk with wild god. That can be the historic future."* [22]

These things must happen, **"but woe unto him, through whom they come"** Luke 17:1. In other words, if someone fits the *type*, **"woe unto him."** Ever wonder how such atrocities happen in the world, such as described in Solzhenitsyn's book, *"The Gulag Archipelago"* or how so many people could follow one man to their own destruction (Hitler), or how so many could take an experimental vaccine just because it was deemed "safe" by media conglomerates (SARS-CoV-2, Moderna, Pfizer, CNN, MSNBC, FOX, etc.)? Well, it shouldn't be *that hard* to get everyone to take a **"mark,"** such as one mentioned in Revelation 13:17. No, I don't believe that the Covid vaccines were the **"mark,"** but I do believe it was some sort of prototype that will happen again in the future, guided by forces that we simply cannot compete with on our own. He is **"the god of this world"** (2 Cor. 4:4), and many walk in his step, **"the prince of the power of the air, the spirit that now worketh in the children of disobedience"** (Eph. 2:2). If you're an **"axe"** God will use you as an axe just as the king of Assyria was historically used—**"Shall the axe boast itself against him that heweth**

---

[22] Carl G. Jung, *"The Symbolic Life: Miscellaneous Writings"*

therewith? or shall the saw magnify itself against him that shaketh it? as if the rod should shake itself against them that lift it up, or as if the staff should lift up itself, as if it were no wood" (Isa. 10:15).

To continue on with the answer here, what we have is a self-righteous atheist who thinks God Himself is going to pick babies up and slam them into walls. *By thinking that God approves of everything that happens creates an atheist.* He doesn't, He allows circumstances. Because He allows it, it is still God's will. There is nothing acting outside of the will of God. (That is something to wrap your mind around.) It just isn't His directive unless He states it. He has laid out consequences for actions in His Book, and how human of us to turn around and say, *"no, I don't like this, you are mean and unfair."* He did say, "if you mess with those Jews, I'll mess with you"—did that stop anyone?

The Adamic nature gets the best of everyone at one time or another. Ehrman and friends have trouble looking at the dark side of man, as most do, but find it *easy* to have "philosophical" disputes with God Almighty instead of having those disputes with man, who disregards God. I apologize if I burst the bubble of naiveté, but many nations throughout history have slaughtered children and babies during war and conquest. It is certainly nothing new and it wont be stopping anytime soon.

The Mongols opened the stomachs of pregnant women and slaughtered the baby right then and there. Imperial Japanese troops would toss babies into the air and run them through with their bayonets in the Nanking Massacre. The Japanese would also stab a pregnant woman in the stomach with no remorse whatsoever; some even laughed. They would put needles into the others eyes and have sons rape their mothers while taking pictures and laughing.[23] Nazis

---

[23] See *"The Rape of Nanking"* by Iris Chang

were throwing babies into pits of fire, and bashing them against walls. Babies have also been used as bait in Islamic wars in the middle-east. No one need tell you how horrible these events are.

The sad fact is—according to your Bible—these things *will* happen again. Not believing they will will not make a difference in the slightest degree; neither will "philosophical" disputes with the Lord. Whether or not you prescribe to a post-modern relative approach to truth or convince yourself that as an atheist you do have absolutes in which to rest, it will not hinder the stark reality presented in those pages between black covers. Much of the Book was written to mess a person up. Many do not believe that, but that's Bible—**"Whom shall he teach knowledge? and whom shall he make to understand doctrine? them that are weaned from the milk, and drawn from the breasts... But the WORD of the LORD was unto them precept upon precept, precept upon precept; line upon line, line upon line; here a little, and there a little; THAT THEY MIGHT GO, AND FALL BACKWARD, and BE broken, and SNARED, and taken"** (Isa. 28:9, 13).

That Book will test you. It looks back at you when you read it. It's a two-edged sword (Heb. 4:12) that swings both ways. You don't believe me? Still, even after that? How about—**"Therefore have I hewed them BY THE PROPHETS; I HAVE SLAIN THEM BY THE WORDS of MY mouth: and thy judgments are as the light that goeth forth"** (Hos. 6:5). People don't realize what that Book is—it will damn a person just as many times as it will save a person. The Lord will let you have it, any way you want it—**"So I gave them up unto their own hearts' lust: and they walked in their own counsels"** (Psa. 81:12, also see Rom. 1:24, 28 for Gentiles).

These "a priori" "philosophical" differences are the result of our rejection of God. You see, when you read enough history books you begin to see a pattern—human collapse brought on by hubris and decadence. The book that exemplifies this to the utmost is *the* Book, that's why no one wants to read it. It tells it like it is, in plain-English. Today man thinks that since he has made air-conditioning that he no longer needs God and sits in his air-conditioned home pondering up musings on how God should have done it differently. They are nothing more than a man who believes he can do it better than God Almighty—a child out in the frigid cold tundra wondering around for daddy. It's dark, **"come before winter."**

Chapter 10: Conclusion

"All the words of my mouth are in righteousness; there is nothing froward or perverse in them. They are all plain to him that understandeth" — Proverbs 8:8-9

THE Bible is a unique Book, so unique that your mentality and attitude as you read it is directly correlated with what you will get from it, or rather *be given*. The Book reads you, you don't read it. If you approach it with humility, and as a brother once said, *"like a child"* you will pull from it completely different sets of treasures than the person who is *destructively* reading it. The destructive critic says, *"well in the Greek...the originals probably read...and in the oldest and best it...'***firstborn'** *should actually read as...a better rendering would be"* and so on. When you come to the Book, it's the *closest* you will get to approaching God in the material world. People treat it as if its contents don't matter, or present themselves neutral (which is worse), all while *professing* that they do matter. Something isn't lining up correctly mentally there, all the circuits aren't firing, the candle isn't burning, two crayons short of a rainbow, etc.

The more a person reads the Book, the more the person becomes *separated* from society. You become a **"peculiar"** person (Exod. 19:5; Titus 2:14) a **"stranger"** in the world

(Levi. 25:23). You become a **"holy priesthood"** (1 Peter 2:5). It scares people because no one wants to be like that, really. No one wants to be the lone wolf, or feel alienated; no one likes to feel alone in the world. Jeremiah felt that way and he ended up leaving (Jer. 20). He put his Bible down and stopped witnessing. No one liked what he had to say because it was just plain *negativity*. Jeremiah wasn't going around saying *"Oh, dear people, God loves you and He wants to be with you so that He can share his graces upon you, let Him shower His gifts upon you and your family."* That ain't preachin', man.

Jeremiah was a street preacher who preached about *destruction, damnation, death, and hell*; so were the majority of the O.T. prophets. They named names and places. You can tell by someone's preaching if they actually read the Book or not, and what sort of mentality they have towards the Book. You can also tell by someone's *"teaching"* of the Book.

The earliest time in Christian history in which a "university" or "scholastic" approach was taken was the time of Origen and then later, his friends Jerome and Augustine. It birthed the Catholic Church, an enemy of the Scriptures, a contributor to "orthodox corruption." On the other side we have those who stayed *in* the Book and *believed* it; they didn't apply allegory, or make something symbolic when it wasn't called for. They weren't neutral towards the text and they had a *final authority*. This is the school of Antioch where the Christians were **"called Christians first."** These Scriptures, and their approach towards them, came back into being after the Dark Ages i.e., after the rule of the Roman Catholic Church.

This time involved revivals and new-Born Christians in astonishing numbers. The **"light"** (Psalm 119:105) had turned on. The school of Antioch was back in full swing and with it, the words of the Living God were published throughout the world. This doesn't end without a fight from *the adversary*, that **"old serpent."** The spirit of the **"serpent"** has been at work behind the Catholic Church since the days of her infancy, "Mystery Babylon the Great" will take her final form at a later date, but she needs a counterfeit bible to do it. Almost all modern versions (300+) are just Jesuit Rheims Dark Age texts brought back from the dead through the neutral approach of textual criticism and the resurgence of buried manuscripts such as ℵ and B presumed as being "closer to the original."

The textural critic does not have a final authority and is therefore a member of the modern day cult of *relativism* whose king over these members, these **"children of disobedience"** (Eph. 2:2) is the **"prince of the powers of the air."** Lucifer has **"ministers"** who are **"transformed as the ministers of righteousness"** (2 Cor. 11:15) that do his work. A man who acts *as* God is **"shewing himself that he is God"** (2 thess. 2:4), then he needs a bible *like* God's. Who is more susceptible to the **"wiles of the devil"** (Eph. 6:11) than a man working with the very words of God all while claiming *"neutrality"* on it?

"Prove all things" (1 Thess. 5:21)—prove it to yourself, don't take my word for it. I have provided ample sources within the footnotes to further a study on the subject; I've given names, dates, titles, and page numbers. **"Let no man deceive you"** (2 Thess. 2:3). More importantly, **"Let no man deceive himself"** (1 Cor. 3:18).

Universities are the breeding ground for the modern apostasy of the Church. Lucifer first tried to kill off those who believed the words of the living God (A.D. 33-325) by the use of violence en masse via the Roman state of nonbelievers; all those beautiful new-Born Christians, many of them remain unnamed, but what they did will not go unnoticed. That didn't work so he tried a different approach: a counterfeit church with its pontiff called "Holy Father" (A.D. 325-500) who developed his own book and counter authority. The church took the Scriptures and corrupted them, and hid them from the site of men—lights out. She also murdered those who were believers of Jesus Christ and believers of the words of Almighty God by the millions (A.D. 500-1500), she became **"drunken with the blood of the saints"** (Rev. 17:6). Those who believed that water baptism alone saves a person instead of the Blood of Jesus Christ and His finished work were damned. Satan had accomplished something…for a time.

Alas, the Reformation abated the old **"whore."** People were standing up everywhere to the "lady of the night." Those dark clouds abated. Those had seen her for what she really is, and had been vomited out of her mouth, she was naked and the world saw her for who she is. Those brave souls who stood against her went forth and witnessed, began schools, began revivals, shut down bars, and men were convicted of their sin (1500-1881). She quietly changed her appearance in the back alleyways of hell. Now, the old whore has risen again, she has deepened herself in the trenches of the intellectual elite, she has challenged the very words of the LORD God; she has announced a false means of gain; she has made comfortable the nesting places of demons the very hallways and classrooms of modern seminaries. The self professed Christian campuses, she has handed out her counterfeit bibles and the "learned men" have accepted them on high-flying hubris (1885-____). She loves pride, she loves those who are haughty in their whiles.

The seminaries and universities have now dispatched these "teachers" from rat and owl infested seminaries out, into local churches, where they question the words of the Living God and place their own authority above that of the LORD God. They control local churches by means of financing, prestige, and association. In turn, they deem those who *do* believe the words as members of *a cult*, as has happened to the Montanists, Donatists, Paulicians, Bogamiles, Cathari, Waldenses, and Anabaptists in their own day. History only repeats itself—people never learn. These, now titled, *"cult"* members are deemed dangerous, and

Conclusion

called "hell raisers" by those who recommend such trash as an RSV or ASV. They are bringing back the Dark Age text that extinguished the light that was meant for the world. I would rather be called a "hell raiser," or a "heretic" than sit back and let the black sheet of hell cover the world once again, as it has before. I am, then, a "hell raiser." I will raise as much hell as need be and I will not stop, no, I will not stop.

What it all boils down to at the end of the day is whether or not one *believes*, or doesn't believe, the *"w-o-r-d-s"* he is reading. What is *your* final authority? Is it an ESV?—then stand on it! Take the stand. A Christian is to **"WAR a good warfare"** (1 Tim. 1:18), to **"endure hardness, as a good SOLDIER of Jesus Christ"** (2 Tim. 2:3), and to **"FIGHT the good fight"** (1 Tim. 6:12). You are called to be a soldier for Christ Jesus.

There are a few possibilities on how you may take this information, as given in this work.

(1) You can *ignore* it and pretend as if it isn't happening.
(2) You can *accept* it and the information, after looking at the evidence and praying about it.
(3) You can *choose to side* with the Christian "scholars" who are bringing in the apostasy of the Body of Christ.
(4) You can *choose to side* with the evidence and fight the good fight by preserving and believing the words of God.

You see, people think that the "last days," as prophesied by Paul in 2 Timothy 3-4, is going to be brought on by "liberals" who aren't saved and therefore *outside* of the Body of Christ. This is *not* the case, as a "careful read" in the AV of the passages mentioned in 2 Timothy will "shed light" on the matter. The apostasy is from within.

There is a war going on, and it isn't against an enemy that you can see. He's the same enemy that questioned what God *said* in his *first interaction with a person* (Gen. 3). He's the same enemy that *alters the word of God for his own benefit* (Matt. 4:6;

Luke 4:10-11; cf. Psa. 91:11-12). He's the same enemy who's prime goal is *attacking* the word of God (Luke 8:11-12). He is the most subtle enemy you could imagine. The fact that our war is *NOT against flesh and blood* (Eph. 6), but with principalities and powers, a *spiritual* war, it makes it even more difficult than imaginable. It is inevitable that the Body of Christ will reach apostasy because it has been written, and if the Lord doesn't come back soon (I hope it's today), it will reach levels you never thought possible. Luckily, we have a weapon for our war—a **"SWORD"** (Eph. 6:17). *You enemy wishes to rid you of your defensive and offensive weapon,* rendering you as effective as using a beanbag, or a wilted noodle in the fight. *Wake Up!*

I ask you, dear reader, *which side are you on*?

I am on the losing side, no doubt, since the apostasy *is going to happen, regardless of what I do*. It may even be delayed for a time, or it may be hurried; depending on the enemies reactions and counter attacks.

"Yea, and all that will live godly in Christ Jesus shall suffer persecution" (2 Tim. 3:12).

"But and if ye suffer for righteousness' sake, happy are ye: and be not afraid of their terror, neither be troubled" (1 Peter 3:14).

"For whosoever will save his life shall lose it: and whosoever will lose his life for my sake shall find it" (Matt. 16:25).

"Look to yourselves, that we lose not those things which we have wrought, but that we receive a full reward" (2 John 1:8).

Wouldn't you rather go out fighting **"the good fight"**; or would you rather go out believing the pomp, and accepting the praise of people like Metzger, MacArthur, White, Liberty, Fuller, and company. Seminaries are pumping out thousands every year with the same atheistic and critical mindset as Metzger and White. Their forces are overwhelming at this point. The Lord needs soldiers. If any of this has offended you, *good*, it wasn't for you. The Lord needs soldiers. You can go back to teaching your Tuesday morning women's Bible study and gossip about the neighbors. The characters in this work *are* on the *winning* side—yes, you read that correctly; but they are on the winning side *only temporarily*. It's the side for "over-educated, under-intelligent ****** *********'s"— (John Gotti, mafioso boss of the Gambino crime family of New York [1990]).

Satan wins for a brief time, he gets his laughs by undermining the word of God by the very scholars who professed to dedicate their lives to upholding and honoring it. **"Woe unto you, scribes and Pharisees, hypocrites!"** (Matt. 23:14). Lucifer has his rule whilst the antichrist is on earth. The world is being primed for those conditions as you read this now. In the end, satan loses, as it has been written, and the saved in Christ rule forevermore with the Lord Jesus Christ into Eternity.

As the Church is called out, before that man of sin (the antichrist) is revealed (2 Thess. 2), how would you like to meet the Living God at the Judgment Seat of Christ? How would you fare? What if He asks you about His Book? What will you say? What works have you done for Him, and what works have you done serving your own flesh?

Having looked at the evidence on *"modern Christian scholarship,"* what are you going to do with it? What are you going to do, now knowing that Jesuits have infiltrated the most commonly used Greek text for modern translations?—now knowing that "textural criticism," at its core, is nothing but an acknowledgement of agnosticism, at best?—now that you know that seminaries consider "Scriptural Infallibility" to be "dangerous"?—that the majority of Christian preachers and professors mean lost pieces of paper when they say "Scripture," and then commence to correct the Bible with whims and superstitions?—now that you know that none of them actually believe there is a God breathed Book that is inspired anywhere on earth, thus defying what the

Scriptures *say* about the Scriptures? What are you going to do?

The Body of Christ is art war—with *itself.* It is a *Civil War* — a tidal wave gaining in speed and height since the days of Paul (2 Cor. 2:17), and now beginning to crest in the age of Laodicea (meaning: "rights of the people").

In one corner, the apostate scholars and in the other, the Bible believing crew.

Which one are you?

"Prepare to meet thy God."

Did any of these verses make an impression upon the reader:

"And the scripture, foreseeing that God would justify the heathen through faith, preached before the gospel unto Abraham, saying, In thee shall all nations be blessed." Galatians 3:8

"For the scripture saith unto Pharaoh, Even for this same purpose have I raised thee up, that I might shew my power in thee, and that my name might be declared throughout all the earth." Romans 9:17

"And thou shalt write upon the stones all the words of this law very plainly." Deuteronomy 27:8

"And thou shalt not go aside from any of the words which I command thee this day, to the right hand, or to the left, to go after other gods to serve them." Deuteronomy 28:14

"Keep therefore the words of this covenant, and do them, that ye may prosper in all that ye do." Deuteronomy 29:9

"I have said that I would keep thy words." Psalm 119:57

"The entrance of thy words giveth light; it giveth understanding unto the simple." Psalm 119:130

"Turn you at my reproof: behold, I will pour out my spirit unto you, I will make known my words unto you." Proverbs 1:23

"Every word of God is pure: he is a shield unto them that put their trust in him." Proverbs 30:5

"Add thou not unto his words, lest he reprove thee, and thou be found a liar." Proverbs 30:6

"Then the LORD put forth his hand, and touched my mouth. And the LORD said unto me, Behold, I have put my words in thy mouth." Jeremiah 1:9

"For the prophecy came not in old time by the will of man: but holy men of God spake as they were moved by the Holy Ghost." 2 Peter 1:21

"The words of the LORD are pure words: as silver tried in a furnace of earth, purified seven times. Thou shalt keep them, O LORD, thou shalt preserve them from this generation for ever." Psalm 12:6-7

"Neither have I gone back from the commandment of his lips; I have esteemed the words of his mouth more than my necessary food." Job 23:12

"But there is a spirit in man: and the inspiration of the Almighty giveth them understanding." Job 32:8

"And it shall be, when he sitteth upon the throne of his kingdom, that he shall write him a copy of this law in a book out of that which is before the priests the Levites:

And it shall be with him, and he shall read therein all the days of his life: that he may learn to fear the LORD his God, to keep all the words of this law and these statutes, to do them: That his heart be not lifted up above his brethren, and that he turn not aside from the commandment, to the right hand, or to the left: to the end that he may prolong his days in his kingdom, he, and his children, in the midst of Israel" Deuteronomy 17:18-20

"How sweet are thy words unto my taste! yea, sweeter than honey to my mouth!" Psalm 119:103

"Thy word is a lamp unto my feet, and a light unto my path." Psalm 119:105

"As for God, his way is perfect; the word of the LORD is tried: he is a buckler to all them that trust in him." 2 Samuel 22:31

"But if they had stood in my counsel, and had caused my people to hear my words, then they should have turned them from their evil way, and from the evil of their doings." Jeremiah 23:22

"For he whom God hath sent speaketh the words of God: for God giveth not the Spirit by measure unto him." John 3:34

"Sanctify them through thy truth: thy word is truth." John 17:17

"But I say, Have they not heard? Yes verily, their sound went into all the earth, and their words unto the ends of the world." Romans 10:18

"For the word of God is quick, and powerful, and sharper than any twoedged sword, piercing even to the dividing asunder of soul and spirit, and of the joints and marrow, and is a discerner of the thoughts and intents of the heart." Hebrews 4:12

"For we are not as many, which corrupt the word of God: but as of sincerity, but as of God, in the sight of God speak we in Christ." 2 Corinthians 2:17

"If a man love me, he will keep my words" John 14:23

"Wherewithal shall a young man cleanse his way? by taking heed thereto according to thy word." Psalm 119:9

"Thy word is true from the beginning" Psalm 119:160

"God is not a man, that he should lie" Numbers 23:19

"He that rejecteth me, and receiveth not my words, hath one that judgeth him: the word that I have spoken, the same shall judge him in the last day." John 12:48

"Hear the word of the LORD, ye that tremble at his word; Your brethren that hated you, that cast you out for my name's sake, said, Let the LORD be glorified: but he shall appear to your joy, and they shall be ashamed." Isaiah 66:5

"Be ye therefore very courageous to keep and to do all that is written in the book of the law of Moses, that ye turn not aside therefrom to the right hand or to the left" Joshua 23:6

"But I will shew thee that which is noted in the scripture of truth" Daniel 10:21

"That he might sanctify and cleanse it with the washing of water by the word" Ephesians 5:26

"for thou hast magnified thy word above all thy name." Psalm 138:2

"The counsel of the LORD standeth for ever, the thoughts of his heart to all generations." Psalm 33:11

"For the LORD is good; his mercy is everlasting; and his truth endureth to all generations." Psalm 100:5

"thy word is truth" John 17:17

"The works of his hands are verity and judgment; all his commandments are sure. They stand fast for ever and ever, and are done in truth and uprightness." Psalm 111:7-8

"I will delight myself in thy statutes: I will not forget thy word." Psalm 119:16

"For his merciful kindness is great toward us: and the truth of the LORD endureth for ever. Praise ye the LORD." Psalm 117:2

"For ever, O LORD, thy word is settled in heaven." Psalm 119:89

"Which made heaven, and earth, the sea, and all that therein is: which keepeth truth for ever" Psalm 146:6

"The lip of truth shall be established for ever: but a lying tongue is but for a moment." Proverbs 12:19

"I know that, whatsoever God doeth, it shall be for ever: nothing can be put to it, nor any thing taken from it: and God doeth it, that men should fear before him." Ecclesiastes 3:14

"Now go, write it before them in a table, and note it in a book, that it may be for the time to come for ever and ever" Isaiah 30:8

"The grass withereth, the flower fadeth: but the word of our God shall stand for ever." Isaiah 40:8

"Being born again, not of corruptible seed, but of incorruptible, by the word of God, which liveth and abideth for ever." 1 Peter 1:23

"As for me, this is my covenant with them, saith the LORD; My spirit that is upon thee, and my words which I have put in thy mouth, shall not depart out of thy mouth, nor out of the mouth of thy seed, nor out of the mouth of thy seed's seed, saith the LORD, from henceforth and for ever." Isaiah 59:21

"But the word of the Lord endureth for ever. And this is the word which by the gospel is preached unto you." 1 Peter 1:25

"It is the spirit that quickeneth; the flesh profiteth nothing: the words that I speak unto you, they are spirit, and they are life." John 6:63

"Which things also we speak, not in the words which man's wisdom teacheth, but which the Holy Ghost teacheth; comparing spiritual things with spiritual." 1 Corinthians 2:13

"And the LORD said unto Moses, Whosoever hath sinned against me, him will I blot out of my book." Exodus 32:33

"Go ye, enquire of the LORD for me, and for the people, and for all Judah, concerning the words of this book that is found: for great is the wrath of the LORD that is kindled against us, because our fathers have not hearkened unto the words of this book, to do according unto all that which is written concerning us." 2 Kings 22:13

"For I testify unto every man that heareth the words of the prophecy of this book, If any man shall add unto these things, God shall add unto him the plagues that are written in this book: And if any man shall take away from the words of the book of this prophecy, God shall take away his part out of the book of life, and out of the holy city, and from the things which are written in this book." Revelation 22:18-19

"And it came to pass, when Moses had made an end of writing the words of this law in a book, until they were finished" Deuteronomy 31:24

"Oh that my words were now written! oh that they were printed in a book!" Job 19:23

"Thus speaketh the LORD God of Israel, saying, Write thee all the words that I have spoken unto thee in a book." Jeremiah 30:2

"Then Baruch answered them, He pronounced all these words unto me with his mouth, and I wrote them with ink in the book." Jeremiah 36:18

"As it is written in the book of the words of Esaias the prophet" Luke 3:4

"And Joshua wrote these words in the book of the law of God, and took a great stone, and set it up there under an oak, that was by the sanctuary of the LORD." Joshua 24:26

"If thou wilt not observe to do all the words of this law that are written in this book, that thou mayest fear this glorious and fearful name, THE LORD THY GOD" Deuteronomy 28:58

"And in that day shall the deaf hear the words of the book, and the eyes of the blind shall see out of obscurity, and out of darkness." Isaiah 29:18

"The preacher sought to find out acceptable words: and that which was written was upright, even words of truth." Ecclesiastes 12:10

Appendix A

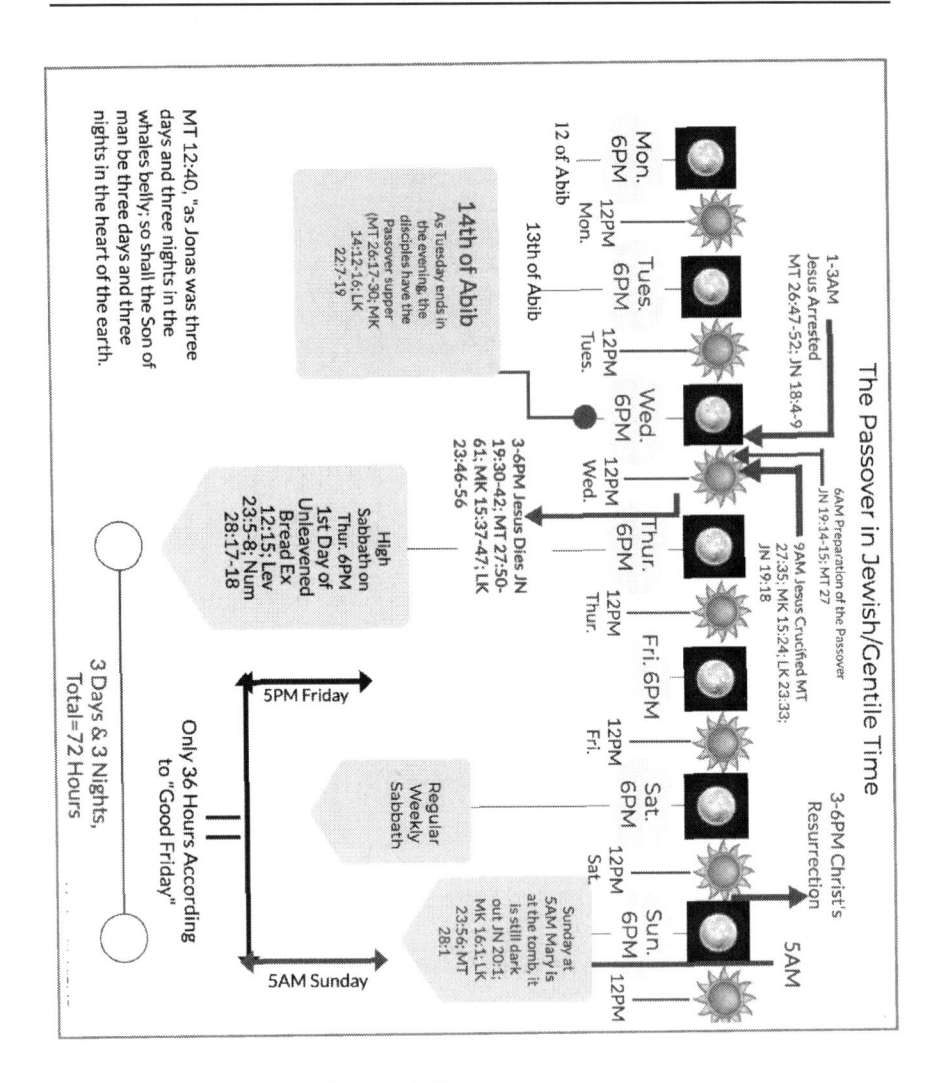

Figure 1: 3 Days & Three Nights

Appendix B

Figure 1:
1 Timothy 3:16 "God was manifest in the flesh"
The ESV does not maintain its claim of being in the same "stream" of English bibles (see pages 223-4 and chapter seven).

Luther's 1522	"Gott"
Tyndale's 1534	"God"
Coverdale's 1535	"God"
Matthew's 1537	"God"
The Great Bible 1539	"God"
Geneva 1560	"God"
Bishop's 1568	"God"
King James 1611	"God"
Revised Version 1881	"He"
ASV 1901	"He"
RSV 1952	"He"
NIV 1973	"He"
ESV 2016	"He"
CSB 2017	"He"

Figure 2:
Matthew 5:22 "without a cause"

Irenaeus A.D. 115-202	"Without a cause"
Taitian A.D. 140-180	"Without a cause"
Cyprian A.D. 200-258	"Without a cause"
Augustine A.D. 354-430	"Without a cause"
Luther's 1522	Omits "without a cause"
Tyndale's 1534	Omits "without a cause"
Coverdale's 1535	Omits "without a cause"
Matthew's 1537	"Without a cause"
The Great Bible 1539	Omits "without a cause" but includes "(vnaduysedly)" or in todays spelling: unadvisedly
Geneva 1560	Same as The Great Bible
Bishop's 1568	Same as The Great Bible
King James 1611	"Without a cause"
RV 1881	Omits "without a cause"
ASV 1901	Omits "without a cause"
RSV 1952	Omits "without a cause"
NIV 1973	Omits "without a cause"

Figure 3:
2 Timothy 2:15 "study"

Luther's 1522	"Diligently...dividing"
Tyndale's 1534	"Study...dividynge"
Coverdale's 1535	"Study...deuydynge"
Matthew's 1537	"Studye...dyuydynge"
The Great Bible 1539	"Study...distributynge"
Geneva 1560	"Studie...diuiding"
Bishop's 1568	"Studie...deuidyng"
King James 1611	"Study...dividing" (studie...diuiding)
RV 1881	"Give diligence...handling aright"
ASV 1901	Same as RV
RSV 1952	"Do your best...rightly handling"
NIV 1973	"Do your best...correctly handles"
ESV 2016	Same as the RSV
CSB 2017	"Be diligent...correctly teaching"

Figure 4:
Mark 6:16 "from the dead"

Luther's 1522	"From the dead"
Tyndale's 1534	"from deeth agayne"
Coverdale's 1535	"againe from the dead"
Matthew's 1537	"from death agayne"
The Great Bible 1539	"from deeth agayne"
Geneva 1560	"from the dead"
Bishop's 1568	"from deeth agayne"
King James 1611	"from the dead"
RV 1881	Omit
ASV 1901	Omit
RSV 1952	Omit
NIV 1973	"from the dead"
ESV 2016	Omit
CSB 2017	Omit

Further Example:
Matthew 1:25 "firstborn"

Luther's 1522	"first son"
Tyndale's 1534	"fyrst sonne"
Coverdale's 1535	"fyrst borne sonne"
Matthew's 1537	"fyrste sonne"
The Great Bible 1539	"fyrst begotten sonne"
Geneva 1560	"first borne sonne"
Bishop's 1568	"first borne sonne"
King James 1611	"firstborn son"
RV 1881	Omit
ASV 1901	Omit
RSV 1952	Omit
NIV 1973	Omit
ESV 2016	Omit
CSB 2017	Omit

Appendix C

Jesuit Douay Rheims Readings of 1582

Matthew 6:13: "And lead us not into temptation. But deliver us from evil. Amen."

Matthew 5:44: "But I say to you, love your enemies, do good to them that hate you: and pray for them that persecute and abuse you."

Luke 2:33: "And His father and mother were marvelling upon those things which were spoken concerning Him."

Luke 4:8: "And Jesus answering, said to him, It is written, Thou shalt adore the Lord thy God and Him only shalt thou serve."

Luke 11:2-4: "And He said to them, When you pray, say, Father, sanctified be Thy name. Thy kingdom come. Our daily bread give us this day. And forgive us our sins, for because ourselves also do forgive every one that is in debt to us, And lead us not into temptation."

Some further readings from the Rheims which are found *restored* in the ASV, NIV, ESV, CSB, NLT, NASV, NRSV, LSB, and so on, are:
Matthew 1:25, 20:22, 27:4
Mark 1:1-2, 6:11, 9:44-48, 13:14, 15:28
Luke 2:14, 4:41, 9:54
John 4:42, 9:35, 11:41, 17:12, 18:36
Acts 1:3, 2:30, 7:30, 9:5-6, 10:48, 13:42, 15:23, 16:7, 17:26, 23:9, 27:14, 28:29; Acts 1:3
Romans 1:18, 25, 5:1, 11:6, 13:9
1 Corinthians 10:28, 11:24, 15:47
Galatians 3:1, 5:4
Colossians 1:14
1 Timothy 6:20
2 Timothy 2:15
Titus 2:13
1 Peter 2:2, 4:14; Revelation 14:5, 22:14

Appendix D

Not even a month had gone by when The ESV committee went back on their decision to make the text "permanent."

> "In August 2016, we posted on our website that "the text of the ESV Bible will remain unchanged in all future editions printed and published by Crossway [notice the period here...that wasn't where the period was at first]." The goal behind this decision to make the text permanent was to stabilize the English Standard Version, serving its readership by establishing the ESV as a translation that could be used "for generations to come." We desired for there to be a stable and standard text that would serve the reading, memorizing, preaching, and liturgical needs of Christians worldwide from one generation to another. We have become convinced that this decision was a mistake."

The reason given:

> "...to allow for ongoing periodic updating of the text to reflect the realities of biblical scholarship such as textual discoveries or changes in English over time."

They end with:

> "We know that no Bible translation is perfect..."[1]

---

[1] https://www.crossway.org/articles/crossway-statement-on-the-esv-bible-text/ . The original post can be seen here: https://www.esv.org/about/pt-changes/

Faith & Works

THERE is always a *condition* attached to Israel and the O.T. Today, if one accepts Jesus Christ and His finished work on the cross, that *is the condition and place* in which God will show you mercy (John 1:12, 3:16, 5:24; Rom. 10), not based on works (Eph. 2:8-9; Rom. 11:6; Gal. 2:16; 1 Peter 1:5), **"For by grace are ye saved through faith; and that not of yourselves: it is the gift of God."** A Christian starts off with everything *done*, and he is already seated in Heaven with Christ (Eph. 2:6). This is not the same as the O.T., in which conditions based on works of the Law, or *doing* things were in place. You had to *work* your way to be in God's good graces. Today, you are in God's graces because you are part of his Son (1 Cor. 12:13-27), that is, if you have accepted Jesus Christ. You are freed from this Law: **"Christ hath REDEEMED us from the curse of the law, being made a curse FOR US: for it is written, Cursed is every one that hangeth on a tree"** (Gal. 3:13).

The land and the success of Israel in inhabiting it was based on *works of the Law*, as well as their salvation before the Sacrifice of Christ. If you don't believe this to be so then do you ever wonder why Abraham was across from hell, in a different place, in Luke 16:22-31? Abraham had the righteousness of God imputed to him, *like* Christians do (Gen. 15:6; Gal. 3:6), *but there was no blood spilt by Jesus Christ yet* (Heb. 9:15). Animal sacrifice was for the *remission of sins (forgiveness), not redemption (clearing)* (Heb. 9:15 Cf. 9:19-22). He was forgiven but not "cleared." The *"clearing"* (redemption) from sin had not happened yet (Exod. 34:7). Abraham's "justification" happened about 10 years *after* he believed God (James 2:20-24), and is *not* like a Christians Justification which happens *right after they believe on Jesus*

Christ (Rom. 4:5, 6:23, 10:13). Jesus Christ had not been **"begotten"** on a certain **"day"** yet (Heb. 1:5-6). That **"day"** was when He was brought into the world to do what was written of him, for His First Advent. The passage on Abraham and hell in Luke 16 was *not* a parable, as most would say it is. Do you ever wonder why Jesus went down there to "Abraham's Bosom" and hell after He died in 2 Peter 4:6 and *preached "the Gospel,"* or who Jesus brought *back up* with him in Ephesians 4:7-9? The man made a jailbreak of all the O.T. saints who were **"gathered unto his people"** (Gen. 49:33; Deut 32:50; Gen. 25:8, 25:17).

In Genesis 49 Jacob was **"gathered unto his people"** *before* he was buried with his relatives in 50:13, so It *cannot* mean that he was *buried* with kin in 49:33. What does it mean? It means Jacob and all the other O.T. saints went to a place that wasn't hell, but not Heaven since the sins of man had not been *"cleared"* yet (Exod. 34:7; Num. 14:18).

You'll notice a change in the book of James from the Pauline doctrine of Grace through Faith. You'll also notice a change in the book of Hebrews and Revelation. Not everything in the New Testament is written to a Christian in our time. For instance, take Matthew, it is part of the New Testament but everyone in it until chapter 27 is under the Law. Why?—Jesus hadn't been glorified yet. The Sermon on the Mount is beautiful and applicable for any Christian but doctrinally you run into some issues: no Christian is in danger of **"hell fire"** if he calls *anyone* a fool in any context (Matt. 5:22). No Christian will be in danger of a council for saying **"Raca."** Have you ever said that? No Christian has to **"endure unto the end"** to be saved (Heb. 3:14, 6, 4:11; Rev. 14:13; Matt. 24:13) because he is saved and held there until the end (see references on pages 101-102, 131).

This is why, in the Tribulation, a salvation based on the *Faith* of Jesus Christ and *works* is in place, since it's dealing with the National Restoration of Israel (Rev. 12:17, 14:12; James 2; Heb. 3:6, 14, 4:1, 11, 6:1-9, 12, 10:26, etc.). That Book is put together like a German watch, or better yet, the human body. In Revelation 14:6 you even have *"another gospel" being preached*, **"And I saw another angel fly in the midst of heaven, having the everlasting gospel to preach unto them that dwell on the earth,"** that *can't* be for you as a Christian, since we are not called *to wrath* (1 Thess 1:10, 5:9; Rom. 5:9). That time is, "the *wrath* of God," as seen in Revelation 14:10. Paul tells you that you are *not* to accept any other Gospel than the one that he gave you for our time—*even if it comes from an angel.* **"But though we, or an angel from heaven, preach any other gospel unto you than that which we have preached unto you, let him be accursed"** (Gal. 1:8, and also see verse 9). During the Tribulation, before the Second Coming of Christ, it will be *faith and works* again, as it was in the O.T.

Having said all of this, Paul still harps on good works. Did Jesus Christ die *so you could sin* or did He die to save you *from the consequences your sins?* Did He die *for* your sins or *because* of your sins? He died *because of your sins and to save you from the consequences of them.* **"For God so loved the world that he gave..."** So why would a person want to keep sinning given this understanding? Right after Paul's confirmation of the revelation given to him in Ephesians 2:8-9 he says: **"For we are his workmanship, CREATED IN CHRIST JESUS UNTO GOOD WORKS, which God hath before ORDAINED THAT WE SHOULD WALK IN THEM."** He goes on in many passages where he confirms his revelation by concluding with the importance of good works. After another instance of the Grace given to a sinner (Gal. 2:16) he says in verse 19, **"For I through the law am dead to the law, THAT I MIGHT LIVE UNTO GOD."** The **"liberty"** (Gal. 5:1, 13; 1 Peter 2:16; 1 Cor. 8:9; Rom. 8:21) given to the saved sinner is truly a **"gift"** (Rom. 5:16). If something were expected in return, then the gift would be nullified and deemed uncharitable (1 Cor. 13:1).

Notes

Printed in Great Britain
by Amazon

8d7cf26e-4fb3-409f-ad1d-79d60b8439f0R01